HOLLYWOOD ROYALTY:
A Family in Films
BY
Pat Silver-Lasky

Including over 400 letters from
Producer Jesse L. Lasky
to Screenwriter Jesse L. Lasky Jr.

HOLLYWOOD ROYALTY: A Family in Films by Pat Silver-Lasky

All rights reserved. Except for the use in a review, the reproduction or utilization of this work in any form or by an electronic, mechanical, or other means, now not known or hereafter invented, including xerography, photocopying and recording or use or sale on the internet or in any information storage and retrieval system is forbidden without the written permission of the author.

I have listed some of the films to be found on the internet at the time of writing. These may not be permanently available. It is worth a bit of research by the reader to search them out.

Published in the USA by:
BearManor Media
P O Box 71426
Albany, Georgia 31708
www.bearmanormedia.com

ISBN: 978-1-62933-184-3
BearManor Media, Albany, Georgia
Printed in the United States of America
Book design by Robbie Adkins, www.adkinsconsult.com
COVER design by Lisa Hayden Miller <enigmamelody@gmail.com>

OTHER BOOKS by Pat Silver-Lasky

2015 A STAR CALLED WORMWOOD: ISBN: 978-1-78510-586-9, OuroborusBooks.Biz

2013 THE OFFER: ISBN: 9781492759669, OuroborusBooks.Biz

2012 SCAMS SCHEMES SCUMBAGS: (with Peter Betts) ISBN: 9781478282037, OuroborusBooks.Biz

2010 RIDE THE TIGER: ISBN: 0-9544194-3-X, OuroborusBooks.Biz

2005 SCREENWRITING FOR THE 21ST CENTURY: ISBN:0-7134-8833-6, (B.T. Batsford, UK)

2006 (Republished by Ritchie Books, UK)

With Jesse L. Lasky Jr.

1978: LOVE SCENE, ISBN: 0-690-01412-9, T.Y. Crowell, USA Angus & Robertson UK

1977 MEN OF MYSTERY ISBN: 0-491-02460-6, W.H. Allen/Star U.K.

1977 DARK DIMENSIONS: ISBN::#0-89696-001-3, Everest House USA

1980 LOVE SCENE ISBN 0-207-95824-6 (paperback), Sphere Books UK

1981 THE OFFER: 0-385-15767-3, Doubleday, USA

1982 THE OFFER:0-425-05549-3, Berkley-Jove USA (paperback)

'The films are the greatest known mass media in the world.'
- Alfred Hitchcock
The Truffaut interview with Hitchcock

'The worst misfortune for an ordinary man is to have
an extraordinary father.'
- Austin O'Malley

*This book is dedicated to the memory
of father and son, a family in films.*

ACKNOWLEDGEMENTS

Special thanks go to the wonderfully knowledgeable film historian and preservationist, Kevin Brownlow—who in November 2010 received the first Governor's Award from AMPAS for his work in 'film preservation and wide and devoted chronicling of the cinematic parade'—for taking his precious time to screen some of Jesse L. Lasky's silent films for me, and to grace this book with his keen editorial historical eye.

I wish to thank Marc Wanamaker of Bison Archives, who has contributed many of the photos.

And Peter Betts for his infinite help and for supporting my persistence in finishing this book.

TABLE OF CONTENTS

ILLUSTRATIONS		vii
PREFACE		ix
SCENE ONE	1880 – 1920	1
SCENE TWO	1921 – 1924	23
SCENE THREE	1925 – 1929	72
SCENE FOUR	1930 – 1934	129
SCENE FIVE	1935 – 1939	168
SCENE SIX	1939 – 1943	210
SCENE SEVEN	1943 – 1949	302
SCENE EIGHT	1949 – 1959	348
FILMS OF JESSE L. LASKY		365
FILMS OF JESSE LASKY JR.		373
NAME INDEX		375
BIOGRAPHY		385

ILLUSTRATIONS

COVER. LASKY AND JESSE AT SANTA MONICA	Cover
FRONTISPIECE: LASKY AND JESSE AT THE BEACH HOUSE	Frontispiece
SCENE ONE: THE FEATURE PLAY COMPANY	1
BLANCHE AND LASKY IN VAUDEVILLE	2
THE NEWLYWEDS	6
LASKY, DEMILLE, GOLDFISH	9
THE JESSE L LASKY FEATURE PLAY COMPANY	12
LASKY'S FIRST LOOK AT THE STUDIO	13
THE PORTABLE GENERATOR	14
STARS OF THE SQUAW MAN	15
GERALDINE FARRAR	17
BLANCHE SWEET	19
DEMILLE'S FIRST SOLO FLIGHT WITH LASKY	21
SCENE TWO: PARAMOUNT FAMOUS LASKY CORPORATION, WEST COAST	23
FAMOUS PLAYERS-LASKY (LASKY, ZUKOR, GOLDFISH, DEMILLE, KAUFMAN)	24
THE LASKY HOME GUARD, JESSE FAR RIGHT	26
LASKY'S STUTZ BEARCAT	27
LASKY BY CARUSO	28
LASKY, WILLIAM S. HART, MARY PICKFORD, DEMILLE	29
RUDOLPH VALENTINO	35
LASKY ELINOR GLYN IN NEW YORK	36
THE MAN WHO HAD 'IT': MILTON SILLS	38
BESSIE IN HER NEW STUDIO	40
THE COVERED WAGON	51
JESSE, CHESTER WORTLEY, AND HORSE	53
DOUGLAS FAIRBANKS AND LASKY	56
RICARDO CORTEZ	60

FOUJITA'S DRAWING OF JESSE, AGE 17.................................65
HANDWRITTEN LETTER 68
SCENE THREE: THE PARAMOUNT GATE....................................72
PETER PAN AND THE RACCOON SKIN COAT................................74
OLD IRONSIDES 89
GLORIA SWANSON 94
CLARA BOW AND LASKY...101
NANCY CARROLL 110
SCENE FOUR: FREDERIC MARCH, GARY COOPER, MIRIAM HOPKINS....129
JESSE ON THE RIO BALSAS...134
MAURICE CHEVALIER, MARLENE DIETRICH, GARY COOPER..........143
RUTH CHATTERTON IN 'ONCE A LADY'..................................153
'ZOO IN BUDAPEST'...160
LASKY, SPENCER TRACY, COLEEN MOORE, WILLIAM K. HOWARD......163
JEAN HARLOW AND SEÑOR BELLO.......................................166
SCENE FIVE: PICKFORD-LASKY PRODUCTIONS............................168
POSTER: THE GAY DESPERADO 169
DOUGLAS FAIRBANKS JR..181
FONTAINE, LASKY, MARTINI 196
PRESIDENT ROOSEVELT, SERGEANT YORK, ETC...........................210
BILL, THE HAWK AND COOPER 214
BETTY, SERGEANT YORK, BESS 215
ROBERT ALDA...291
JESSE, LASKY, IRVING RAPPER 298
CAPTAIN HIVELY AND LIEUTENANT LASKY JR............................302
THE PLAQUE AT SUNSET AND VINE 348
THE STONE WHERE MOSES MIGHT HAVE PUT HIS FOOT 359
SWANSON PRESENTING THE MILESTONE AWARD TO LASKY, 1951.......361
LASKY VISITS DEMILLE WHILE JESSE WORKS ON THE SCRIPT..........362
THE AUTHOR AND JESSE AT 20TH CENTURY FOX 385

PREFACE

When the Jesse L. Lasky Feature Play Company produced the first full-length film in Hollywood in 1913, they planted eager roots in a tumbleweed California town that was to grow into the movie capital of the world. Dubbed by his film contemporaries 'The first gentleman of Hollywood', Jesse L. Lasky was to become the spokesman for the industry. Yet with his quiet demeanor and gold pince-nez delicately balanced on the bridge of his fulsome nose, he didn't seem to belong to the boisterous, earthy movie business that he'd helped to create. He was of pioneer stock, a second-generation Californian born in San Francisco in 1880. His roots stretched back to a grandfather who came across America in a covered wagon and a great-uncle who was a court musician to a Prussian king. Lasky began his show business career as a cornetist, and music was always close to his heart.

He had become a successful New York producer with a string of theatrical and vaudeville companies touring the length of America when he turned his talents to making films. From all over America, young men and women flooded into this newly created mecca called Hollywood, hoping to find fame and fortune. From Europe came a torrent of talent whose lack of proper English was no barrier to success in this silent industry.

As head of production, Lasky 'discovered' many talents in a seemingly endless stream, including Maurice Chevalier, Valentino, Ricardo Cortez, Nino Martini, Gary Cooper, Spencer Tracy, Clara Bow, and Joan Fontaine. Directors, writers, and designers of anything and everything; all were brought to his studio in an explosion of localized creativity. Lasky was to see the silent films he produced play an international role in changing the tastes, styles, and desires of millions of people across the barriers of language, bringing new visions, new thoughts, and ideas.

Lasky's adventurous private life was every bit as dynamic and challenging as those of the stars he fashioned. In 1927 he was the eighth wealthiest man in the movie capital,[1] but in a few short months he was forced out of the company, Paramount Pictures, which no longer bore his name. In the years that followed, he rose resilient as an independent, made and lost fortunes, and made them again. When his final credits rolled on January 13, 1958, Lasky had personally produced more than 1,000 films.

Some of the day-to-day history of Lasky's working and personal life from 1921 to 1949 was recorded in his letters to his eldest son, Jesse Jr. Early dispatches offered fatherly guidance. As Jesse Jr. grew older, Lasky shared his thoughts, and increasingly more of his studio problems with his son, exposing a private glimpse into the life style of the Lasky family through two world wars. But letters impart only a fleeting image of the people and the times—like the glance of a stranger through the

---

[1] Estimated by Variety at $20,000,000.

window of a passing train. Many of the personal stories concerning the family were related to me by Jesse Jr.; his mother, Bessie; his brother, Bill; and his sister, Betty.

This was indeed a family in films. Jesse Jr. became a top screen writer. Eight of his forty-eight screenplays were written for Lasky's ex-partner, Cecil B. DeMille, including *Samson and Delilah* and *The Ten Commandments* (an all-time top ten box office hit).

Like his father, Jesse was never daunted by obstacles. During the Second World War, he left Hollywood to serve as a first lieutenant, then captain in the American Signal Corps, where for three and a half years he wrote, produced, and was in charge of Army training films. He served under General MacArthur, heading a unit that filmed three U.S. landings in the South Pacific. Journals from his diary and letters offer a stunning record of a screenwriter/cum wartime film maker in the midst of battle.

Jesse's brother, William (Bill), was to become an assistant director and an animal trainer in the industry. His short film *The Boy and the Eagle* was an Academy Award nominee. His sister Betty, a Hollywood historian, wrote a definitive book on R.K.O.[2] His mother, Bessie, trying to stay away from the Hollywood scene, became a successful artist who, among her critical successes, painted all twenty-one of the historic California Missions, now housed in the L.A. County Art Museum's History Collection. Bessie served as hostess to the talented and famous people in their thirty-room Santa Monica beach house, now a hotel.

This book offers an intimate glimpse into this ingenious man's triumphs and failures—and a rambling ride with the family who traveled with him. Jesse Jr. wrote in his own autobiography, 'The past is an abandoned stage. Its players are dead. All that we've kept of it are echoes and images. Some perhaps worth saving.'[3]

(For clarity, I will refer to the father as Lasky and to the son as Jesse or Jess. Also, I shall not change spellings in the letters written by Lasky and others.)

---

2 *RKO The Biggest Little Major of Them All*, 1984 Prentice-Hall.
3 *Whatever Happened to Hollywood?* W.H Allen London, New York 1973

SCENE ONE
1880 – 1920

THE FEATURE PLAY COMPANY

BLANCHE AND LASKY IN VAUDEVILLE

Jesse L. Lasky's love affair with show business began with his first cornet lesson at the age of nine and progressed to *The Musical Laskys*, a stage act with his younger sister Blanche.

By the time he was 31, Jesse had given up performing and was successfully producing New York vaudeville shows and touring road companies. In 1911, his sister Blanche was working with him in the New York office of Jesse L. Lasky Productions.

By the late 19th century, many Americans had begun drifting to Paris, London, Venice, and Rome, bringing home a taste for wine, antiques, and art. As the twentieth century began, Lasky was regularly traveling to Europe in search of talent for his shows. The entrepreneur had an eye for the unusual, the beautiful, the exceptional, the extraordinary, and was developing his own tastes and understanding of the wider world of culture. He'd been deeply impressed by the extravagant cabarets and music halls dotting foreign capitals, staged in elaborately baroque buildings. In Paris, the Folies-Bergère offered ravishing reviews, music, dancing, and amazing feats of daring and spectacular costumes. Lasky was surprised to see that this bountiful attraction was served up along with delicious gourmet foods and wines. Nothing like it existed anywhere in America, so the impresario decided he was going to offer New York the greatest, most lavish and spectacular entertainment they would ever see or taste. He would advertise it as 'More Parisian than Paris!'

Back in New York shopping for the right theatre, he soon realized that there was no building large or grand enough to house such an extravaganza. He turned to his financial partner in the vaudeville circuit, Henry B. Harris, and together they raised the gigantic sum of $100,000 to build a shiny new theatre on 46th Street just off Broadway. Harris took care of the financial side; Lasky's job was to oversee the creative side: design and construction, hire the talent, and mount the colossal review.

In 1912 their newly-built Folies-Bergère Theatre boasted a champagne bar, a balcony promenade, an orchestra pit, and a wandering Gypsy Orchestra to serenade the diners. The theatre could also claim the first midnight performances in America. Of the two hundred artistes on the bill, many of them were to become future film stars, the sultrily curvaceous Mae West of 'Come up and see me some time' fame among them. One of the acts Lasky found in Berlin was The Pender Troupe—eight British acrobats on stilts, the youngest a ten year old kid named Archie Leach. Years later, when Lasky and Cary Grant were both working at RKO, the actor reminded the producer that his stepladder to success began on 46th Street climbing up to his stilts.

For the box office to break even, the review had to stay open with continuous performances from noon until dawn seven days a week. But on Sundays, stores and bars were not legally allowed to open and it was even illegal in New York to wear costumes on the stage on Sunday—so the theatre remained dark. At $2.50, the price of admission, including dinner, was fifty cents higher than the Ziegfeld Follies, considered the greatest musical variety show on Broadway. When the press doubted that the 'extravaganza warranted the extravagance' even with dinner thrown in, sales plummeted.

Lasky was an innovator, but sometimes one can think too far outside the box. He and Harris realized they were putting on the largest, most expensive flop on Broadway. Years later, the showman wrote in his autobiography,[4] 'I learned from experience that in show business it is never enough to be artistic. You have to be practical as well. Broadway is a lonely place when you're broke.'

Lasky believed there was something else you needed: a bit of good luck. But luck was certainly not with Henry B. Harris in London. Hearing the bad news, he hastened to return to New York on April 15, 1912. His ship was the Titanic.

Two dynamics flowed in the Lasky blood: the spirit of adventure, certainly, and his abiding love of music. He was to take full advantage of both in his vastly productive life. When he was a young boy, his father Ike moved from San Francisco to the small town of San Jose, fifty miles down the coast, where he opened The Boston Shoe Bazaar. Ike was soon part owner of the San Jose Baseball Club, president of the Athletic Association, organizer of the Bicycle Club, a devotee of walking contests, and the best fly fisherman in the county—enthusiasms he passed on to his son, along with a vociferous appetite for adventure. Ike's Boston Shoe Bazaar sounded

---
[4] *I Blow My Own Horn* by Jesse L. Lasky with Don Weldon (Doubleday & Co.1957).

up to the minute, but by the time his children were teenagers, Ike was in poor health and teetering on the brink of bankruptcy. Since Ike firmly believed that both his son and daughter had inherited musical talent, he always found that extra bit to pay for their music lessons. Grandfather Bernard passed on stories about his own father, who had been a musician in the court of a Prussian king. The young boy considered the stories just another of his grandfather's *babaminzas*.[5] This tale was true. Lasky's great-grandfather had been Béla Lasky, a composer and musician in the court of the Prussian House of Hohenzollern under Wilhelm II. Béla wrote operettas and his music was called, 'incomparably amusing, bizarre'. 'The Hot Heart' was his best-known dramatic chanson—and there was a special significance to the year 1848. There was a revolution in Prussia and Béla made his way to Vienna where he became part of the flourishing Jewish Viennese cabaret scene. Grandfather Bernard came to America and kept traveling west.

Since 1909, Lasky and his sister, Blanche, had been living in a rambling apartment in New York on 61st and Broadway ruled by their mother, Sarah. That summer the three took a short break at Long Lake in the Adirondacks. One afternoon they were enjoying a pleasant tea dance on the hotel terrace when the ebullient theatrical producer peered through his pince-nez at an ethereal young beauty seated nearby. She had dark auburn hair, gigantic brown eyes, and the sweet face and expression of an angel. Bessie Ginsberg, fresh out of the Boston Conservatory of Music where she was studying to be a concert pianist, was sitting with her mother and a would-be suitor, a Mr. Lewis from Gloversville, New York.

Lasky was immediately smitten by the girl's other-worldliness, a quality she retained in her seventies and eighties when I knew her and listened to her stories of the extraordinary life she had led. When their eyes met, Lasky excused himself from mother and sister, who watched with some surprise as he went over to ask the girl for a dance. With her mother's approval, Bessie rose and placed her hand into his for the first time. On the dance floor, he invited her to climb the mountain with him the following day. Her mother agreed to allow such a 'perilous' adventure, and by the end of their hike, Jesse had asked Bessie to marry him.

It seems to have been a 'take it or leave it' offer, because with his usual forthrightness, Lasky allowed the flustered young lady only until the following day to think it over and give him her answer. Bessie's mother, wondering what was the rush, wisely sent for her husband, who arrived on the next train, leaving poor Mr. Lewis to beat a mournful retreat to Gloversville when Bessie told him she was to be married—even before she told her mother or Lasky.

That day the two families lunched together, after which, Bessie's father took the vaudeville producer aside, eyeing him carefully. He was certainly well dressed, his suit tailor-made in London, his shoes of fine English leather, and he spoke like a gentleman. Mr. Ginsberg asked him why he wanted to marry his daughter on such short notice. We will never know Lasky's reply, but the reasons were apparently sat-

---

5 Tall stories for small children.

isfactory because Bessie's father not only agreed, but offered his future son-in-law, 'If you haven't done anything about the ring, I can be of some help to you. I am in the diamond business.' Presumably he got it for him wholesale.

Although both families were Jewish, Bessie's parents had sent her to be educated at a Catholic convent school. Being a second-generation Californian Jew with no particular religious training since not much was available in the West, Lasky's beliefs leaned towards secular humanism. Jesse Jr. later said of this, 'The Laskys were Jews by heritage rather than practice. Neither Bess nor Dad was religious in the church-going sense, perhaps because Dad's pioneer forbearers had found no synagogues when their 19th century covered wagon reached California. My maternal grandfather, who had fled Russia in the 1880s because of religious persecution, sent both his daughters to be educated at the Sacred Heart Convent in Boston. My mother did not actually convert, yet she always felt deeply and mystically inclined to Catholicism.'

Though they scarcely knew each other, Jesse and Bessie were married in Boston that December, 1909. Lasky's obsession with work had allowed just time for a 'getting to know you' honeymoon before he deposited his new wife into the large family abode with his mother at the Pasadena Apartments in New York, while he and sister Blanche sailed merrily off to Europe in search of talent for their vaudeville circuits.

Bessie felt like a guest in the house, and such was life for the next few years, with Sarah the dominating force demanding obedience. Because she didn't approve of her new daughter-in-law playing the piano (it was too noisy), Bessie's creative dreams of becoming a concert pianist transmogrified into the quieter endeavor of painting, and her creativity soon found a successful footing. When Bessie's first baby was born, Sarah took over his rearing, having decided that Bessie was far too young to know what she was doing. After some hints, Bessie was allowed to choose the baby's name: Jesse Louis Lasky Jr. To that radical choice, Sarah had no objection.

Blanche soon found herself being courted by one of Bessie's ex-suitors; his name was Sam Goldfish. He had been waiting in the wings for Bessie's hand when this show business producer upstaged him. Bessie had turned Sam down because she found him 'slightly uncouth', although he always had plenty of money to spend and dressed in custom made suits. Still, she invited him to her wedding and it was there that his eyes fell on the groom's attractive sister.

Sam was born Schmuel Gelbfisz in the Warsaw ghetto, possibly August 17, 1879 or 1882. When no more than a child, Schmuel was shipped to relatives in Birmingham, England. The British family supported him and helped him learn English—although he was never to have a refined command of the language. They also advised Anglicizing his name to Samuel Goldfish.

In 1898, Sam took the first boat aiming for America, but it stopped in Nova Scotia, Canada instead. Eventually, he arrived in Gloversville, New York, the hub of the United States glove-making industry, and somehow, even with his bad English, he got

THE NEWLYWEDS

a job as a salesman in a glove factory. By the time he met Blanche, through sheer drive and ambition Sam had become the number one glove salesman on the East Coast.

When he proposed to Blanche, the offer of marriage to a successful businessman was tempting, because she wanted to get out of show business. But married or no, her brother insisted he still needed Blanche working with him, so she stayed on.

Part of Sam's attraction to Blanche had been Jesse Lasky, because Sam secretly wanted to get into show business. When he moved into the rambling Lasky apartment, Sam began trying to interest his new brother-in-law in producing the sort of thirty-second films that were being shown in New York City's penny arcades. The first Kinetoscope Parlor[6] had opened in April, 1894 at 1155 Broadway where, for twenty-five cents a customer had access to five Kinetoscope machines and could view a film though each peep hole. True, some were as long as a minute, but Sam had done his homework and told Lasky, 'There are healthy profits being made.' It became a nagging theme song from Sam.

'It's just a peep show, Sam', Lasky told him flatly. 'I produce vaudeville.'

Since the early nineteenth century, vaudeville had generated a foothold in America, catering to a middle-class, mixed-gender audience. The Keith circuit was the largest, but Jesse L. Lasky Productions were extremely successful. In a typical night's entertainment, Lasky's vaudeville companies could offer a variety of acts: dancers, acrobats, singers, and actors. Short plays and scenes from perhaps Shakespeare or a hit play were staged with or without music. No one could foresee that vaudeville would come to an end in the early 1930s—and it would be the movies that would kill it.[7]

In France, back in 1895, the Lumiére brothers, Louis and Auguste, had patented a projector that turned viewing films from a mere peep hole view into a picture that moved across a screen—a screen that could be viewed by a roomful of people. That year, one and two-reelers (ten minutes a reel) were being made in New York by Vitagraph, Biograph, Edison, IMP, and in Philadelphia by the Lubin Manufacturing Company, and in Chicago by the Essanay and Selig companies, and a few others.

Sam was persistent. 'Moving pictures are going places', he insisted.

Lasky conceded there were possibilities. He had seen Edison's *The Great Train Robbery*, filmed on the east coast in 1903 by 'Broncho Billy' Anderson. It was twelve minutes long and considered the best of the bunch. 'But the best is not good enough, Sam', Lasky told his persistent brother-in-law. 'We call those pictures *chasers* because we use them to chase the audience out of the theatre before the next live vaudeville performance. Why, even Louis Lumiére himself has called the cinema an invention without a future.'

The argument continued for weeks until Lasky later recalled, facing Sam across his desk, 'I've been a showman all my life, Sam, and I'm definitely not interested in making one or two-reelers with a couple of comedians clowning about—or filming a train crash with no story involved. The actors can't talk. They can't sing! Story is everything. And you can't tell a story in two reels.'

Still Sam persisted. Determination had got him to be the company's top glove salesman, and he had a brother-in-law who was the country's top vaudeville pro-

---

6 *The Free Dictionary* by Farlex. forum.thefreedictionary.com.
7 Trav S.D., *No Applause-Just Throw Money: The Book That Made Vaudeville Famous*, 2005, Faber & Faber Kenrick, John. *A History of The Musical: Vaudeville*.

ducer. If he could only convince Lasky to make films, he was sure he could sell them a lot faster than gloves.

Lasky weighed the competition. What if Lumiére was wrong and Sam was right? There had to be something more to this new entertainment. Just recently he had made friends with a balding young actor/writer, Cecil Blount DeMille, whose older brother, William, was a famous Broadway playwright with five shows running on Broadway. Lasky wanted to hire William to write an operetta for vaudeville based on an idea he had, called 'California', but William was busy and their agent (also their mother) talked him into hiring Cecil instead.

DeMille knew Lasky's reputation for producing short musical plays in vaudeville: '... always well constructed, well cast, well mounted, well directed. There was a definite Lasky touch, a Lasky finish and polish about his productions that made them unique', DeMille later wrote. 'The world was new to him every morning. For Jesse, life was a sparkling road full of unknown curves, 'round any one of which might lie untold adventure.' It was an accurate assessment of Lasky's character.[8]

Lasky and DeMille successfully co-directed the operetta 'California' and the two men became great friends, sharing a spirit for challenge. Lasky confided that he had decided to produce a moving picture with Sam, asserting that he had seen what was on offer and if, with his experience, he couldn't produce a better picture, he shouldn't be in show business. Stories interested him more than the actors, he explained. One could always get actors. First, he'd need a story—like a stage play with a beginning, middle, and end, and a one-hour play would require at least six ten-minute reels of film stock.

The more they talked about it, the more it began to seem possible. His growing enthusiasm enlisted Cecil into the enterprise.

The newly formed Jesse L. Lasky Feature Play Company featured Lasky as president (in charge of creative talent and decisions), DeMille, director-general (to direct the movie), and Goldfish, general manager (to sell it). Now, all that Lasky had to do was to find the vehicle and a star name that could draw an audience.

Stopping by the theatrical Lamb's Club on 44th Street with Cecil, Lasky was greeted by Dustin Farnum, the current Broadway matinee idol. Since their film would be silent, they would need actors whose faces could convey emotions without words, and certainly the handsome Farnum would be a perfect choice. The producer proposed the idea to him of starring in a sixty-minute film, the subject not yet chosen, but it would be a play, preferably something current. The actor's glance settled on playwright Edwin Milton Royle sitting across the room, whose current Broadway hit, *The Squaw Man*, mixed the Wild West with Manhattan drawing rooms.

'You get Royle to sell you his play, and I'll join you', the actor announced.

A hit play and a star? How could they go wrong?

With some effort, Lasky acquired the rights from Royle, but it left him with little finance. He offered the actor one fourth of the new company in lieu of salary.

---

8 'Cecil B. DeMille by Charles Higham W.H.Allen 1974.

LASKY, DEMILLE, GOLDFISH

Farnum was tempted but not best pleased when told he would be traveling with two directors and a camera out to Flagstaff, Arizona where some one-reelers had already been shot, and where they could film this story with authentic outdoor backgrounds. For accepting such a daring expedition, the matinee idol refused the proffered shares and demanded $5,000 hard cash before he would set a well-shod foot on the train. Lasky could see that financing this project wasn't going to be easy, but Sam was resilient and certainly had a magic touch for raising the extra cash.

Five men headed west to Flagstaff: Farnum, his dresser Fred Kley, DeMille, Alfred Gandolfi, a cameraman, and Oscar Apfel, a director who had already shot some one-reelers and who had been hired not to direct, but to teach DeMille the intricacies of the camera. Lasky remained in his Broadway office to keep an eye on his current theatrical productions, with Blanche at his side. Sam, too, remained in New York to raise more money and sell the movie rights. He had quickly learned the ropes of how to book a film. It meant selling the states' rights to each specific territory. A small state got one print; a larger state got two. New England got four or five. A flat sum was paid for each print, and the buyer could re-run his nitrate copy until it went up in flames (which some frequently did). Sam was so good at selling that soon he had $60,000 worth of contracts for a motion picture that wasn't yet made, by a company that had never made one before. The partners were on their way.

Cecil had been gone for two weeks and Lasky and Goldfish hadn't heard from him. But the telegram that finally reached the worried producer's hand was not sent from Flagstaff. It read:

FLAGSTAFF NO GOOD FOR OUR PURPOSE. HAVE PROCEEDED TO CALIFORNIA. WANT AUTHORITY TO RENT BARN IN A PLACE CALLED HOLLYWOOD FOR $75 A MONTH. REGARDS TO SAM. CECIL.

Lasky tried to calm a furious Goldfish, who wanted to order the would-be filmmakers back to New York where he could keep a parsimonious eye on them. But finally, Sam agreed to let them stay, and two-thirds of the company wired back to the wandering one-third:

AUTHORIZE YOU TO RENT BARN BUT ON MONTH-TO-MONTH BASIS. DON'T MAKE ANY LONG COMMITMENT. REGARDS. JESSE AND SAM.

Lasky publicly asserted that the reason the filmmakers passed up Flagstaff was because the weather was bad and there would be no facilities for processing the film. I've read reports that they got back on the train because of a thunderstorm and/or that DeMille had heard that in California one-reelers were being made to take advantage of cheap labor and constant sunlight. The director noted in his biography that they left Flagstaff because the scenery was all wrong for the story. Jesse Jr. told me that according to his father, DeMille and the others proceeded to Hollywood because when they got off the train at Flagstaff, there was a cattlemen/sheep men range war going on. Bullets were flying and they wanted to shoot a film, not be shot at. Whichever account is true, when the would-be filmmakers disembarked for the second time, they found themselves in a tiny orange grove among pepper trees in a village called Hollywood. Here, they set up business in a barn with a camera and a crate full of stock footage and plenty of vitamin C growing around them.

The barn at Selma Avenue and Vine Street was hastily converted. Horse stalls were turned into dressing rooms, offices, and a projection room. A small wooden platform was built outside as an open stage. Shooting on *The Squaw Man* began on December 29th, 1913, and took eighteen days. Cecil installed an office for Lasky next to his, and when the producer finally arrived he found a sign identifying the barn as The Jesse L. Lasky Feature Play Company. His fingers may have been crossed, but Lasky had faith in Cecil. Sam, although he had been able to convince the states' rights buyers of the company's solidity, still did not have the courage to quit selling gloves.

Cecil's sartorial style consisted of wearing puttees and riding boots. It was no affectation, just sensible protection against rattlesnakes and cactus when scouting locations on horseback. A cap with visor worn backwards made it easier sighting into a camera and kept the heat off the back of one's neck; cameramen had been doing it since 1903. This theatrically macho image quickly identified who was the director on his set, and while DeMille may have been on a steep learning curve, he was already leaps ahead of Apfel. News traveled fast that a new company was filming in California. The Motion Picture Patents Company (MPPC), which had initially been formed by Thomas Edison and Biograph, sent spies out to see if the Lasky Company was using illegal cameras or infringing on any of Edison's patents.[9]

This Trust monopoly was protected by one of Edison's patents for which it charged a license fee of two dollars a week—which was bringing in $1 million a year. When a new indie filmmaker ignored paying, the Trust was not above hiring thugs to put the offender out of business by stealing the films, wrecking illegal cameras, or burning down a studio. During those early days, Cecil was actually shot at by 'outriders' from the Trust, and a gun on his hip became part of his regular attire.

Although Lasky's company had an approved camera, they were doing something else that worried the Patents Trust just slightly. They were shooting a six-reel movie. Several had been filmed on the east coast, but the status quo was one or two-reelers, and the monopoly was concerned that a film of such length might mean less screenings—or even drive people away.

It was outdoor work on sets with no ceilings, so shooting stopped when the sun went behind a cloud. The actors rushed back the minute the sun returned, which earned them the nickname of 'The Sun Worshippers'. As if lighting were not enough of a problem, cold weather caused tiny flashes of static electricity inside the cameras that could ruin the film. It was chilly when they began shooting *The Squaw Man* in December and January, and the actors had to avoid steamy breath when they mouthed their lines. By the following July in the California heat, the overdressed company would be filming *The Call of the North* [10] using salt for snow. Lasky chose that story because he had a soft spot for Alaska. As a youth, he'd joined the rush to Nome in search of gold. He didn't find gold and had supported himself by shooting ptarmigan to sell to the gold hunters and playing his cornet in the local bar, thereby feeding stomachs and souls. In those youthful days, he'd also gone to Honolulu with his cornet, where he became the first white leader of 'The Royal Hawaiian Band'.

Now, in Hollywood in early 1914, the momentous day arrived. DeMille and Apfel had finished editing and the film was finally in the can. Cecil planned a gala event and Lasky 'trained' out from New York for the screening of The Jesse L. Lasky Feature Play Company's first film. He arrived in time to have pictures taken, one of the new film producer in front of the two-ton Ford truck portable generator Cecil had rented. Lasky wrote in his biography, 'I guess it was the first picture ever taken of a movie mogul's arrival in Hollywood.' Lasky slept that night at Cecil's modest rented house in Cahuenga Canyon, but the howling coyotes kept him awake.

The next day was the screening for executives (that meant himself and DeMille) and the entire cast and crew. Everyone was present including the girl, Red Wing. DeMille had cast her in preference to a trained actress because he wanted a real 'In-

---

9 'Edison v. American Mutoscope & Biograph Co.', 151 F. 767, 81 C.C.A. 391 (3/5/ 1907).
10 A print of *The Call of the North* is in the George Eastman House Motion Picture Collection in Rochester, NY.

THE JESSE L. LASKY FEATURE PLAY COMPANY

dian' to play the part. The room was crowded. Everyone had 'dressed up' to show that this was no ordinary event. The lights in the makeshift projection room dimmed. The title began on the screen—and then disaster struck the first feature length film ever made in Hollywood.[11] The film started crawling up the screen until the picture finally disappeared over the top of the frame. They tried everything to correct the problem with no success. DeMille sent the audience home, while he, Apfel, and Lasky studied the situation. Had they been sabotaged by one of the MPPC men?

What then? The projector looked okay. The film stock looked okay. Sadly, they sent Sam a message that they were facing complete ruin. Lasky got on the next train back to New York in the morning, hoping to make enough money with his vaudeville business to pay off some of their debts. But resourceful Sam sent DeMille a reply. He'd discovered there was one man who knew everything about film stock, Sigmund 'Pop' Lubin of the Lubin Manufacturing Company, the best laboratory for optical equipment in the country. So Cecil hopped on the next train with the 'creeping' film and Lasky met him in Chicago. Together, they took the film to 'Pop' Lubin in Philadelphia.

'There's nothing wrong with your film. We'll fix it', Lubin told them. The answer was simple. The film stock Lasky had purchased in New York and sent west with Cecil,

---

[11] *Cecil B. DeMille Autobiography*, 1959, Prentice-Hall Inc.

was Eastman perforated positive stock, sprocketed at 64 holes to the foot, punched along one edge of the film stock. In California, to save money, he'd hand punched which spaced his sprocket holes at 65 holes to the foot, not realizing it would make a difference. Naturally they did not match up, and the film couldn't run on his projector, which was geared for 64 holes. DeMille was learning how to be a director, but he hadn't learned about sprocket holes. The Lubin technicians pasted a thin strip of film over the edge of the negative, covering the 65-inch holes, and re-perforated it to 64 holes. No problem. The filmmakers were able to take their baby to New York for an invitational screening. The date was February 17, 1914, the place, the Longacre Theatre, and the sour-faced states' rights men declared *The Squaw Man* a hit.

(You can possibly watch some of the original *The Squaw Man* on the Internet: https://www.youtube.com/watch?v=XDjT_T_s5DQ)

The film was released through William W. Hodkinson's distribution company, Paramount Pictures. But the founding fathers of an industry did not see it as a pioneering achievement or a turning point in screen history. What they saw was that the states' rights rentals organized by Goldfish were going to double their investment. The partners had no difficulty in agreeing. 'Let's make some more movies, quick!'

The day after *The Squaw Man*'s screening, another filmmaker working in New York, Adolph Zukor, sent his congratulations to Lasky. The two men hadn't met, but Lasky had visited Zukor's Penny Arcade with Sam, where the public spent ten million pennies in the first year it opened. Zukor had added to his stockpile of product

LASKY'S FIRST LOOK AT THE STUDIO

THE PORTABLE GENERATOR

by importing foreign made films, among them the French four-reeler, *Queen Elizabeth*, starring the celebrated French actress, Sarah Bernhardt, and the Dutch actor, Lou Tellegen. Zukor's Famous Players production company was partnered with theatrical producer Daniel Frohman. Their motto was *Famous Players in Famous Plays*. Their first feature, *The Prisoner of Zenda*, filmed in New York and starring Broadway actor, James K. Hackett, had been released on February 18, 1913. By May 1914, Zukor and Lasky had signed separate five-year agreements with the Paramount distributors. Lasky considered Zukor an inspirational force and was intent on meeting his rival.

After *The Squaw Man's* successful release in New York, Lasky returned to Hollywood to evaluate the studio and enlarge the facilities. He was quick to buy for The Lasky Company, the land surrounding the barn. They chopped down the orange and lemon groves in order to build several more outdoor stages. Now they could shoot three or four films at a time.

That first year the company produced twenty-one films, and during the process, Cecil B. DeMille altered the parameters of filmic artistry. Having mastered the fundamentals, he proved to be a groundbreaking director. Admittedly there was a lot of ground to break, experimenting with so many new techniques. As his shooting schedules stretched from three—to four—to eight weeks, so did the quality of his films. And so did the budgets.

Lasky's search for talent led him back to more Broadway actors. Broadway star Robert Edison did not frown on motion pictures and starred in *The Call of the North*. Edison's 'Walk of Fame' star is on the east side of the 1600 block on Vine Street.

One of Lasky's most interesting casting choices was a star of the Metropolitan Opera House, Geraldine Farrar, a lyric soprano with ample vocal skills and dramatic flair. She had starred at all the great opera houses around the world and had sung with Enrico Caruso, the greatest Italian operatic tenor. But recently she had been having some vocal problems and jumped at Lasky's offer to play the cigar-rolling siren in a silent version of *Carmen*. Although no longer at the height of her glamorous image, she hardly looked like an overripe female opera singer. Farrar was slim and graceful and had great dramatic flair and expression.

DeMille was impressed with her acting, and when the film came out, Goldfish was impressed that *Carmen* was breaking all records and was Jesse L. Lasky Feature Play Company's biggest moneymaker.[12] The distinguished opera singer's appearance in a silent film might have been called a publicity stunt, but her performance was electric.

Discussing it from a historical perspective, critic Richard Dyer wrote in the Boston Globe that 'Farrar has a real screen face that the camera loves—alluring, vital, and in every moment expressive. Her face tells the story, and you can't take your eyes

STARS OF *THE SQUAW MAN*

---

12 Nash, Elizabeth, *Always First Class: The Career of Geraldine Farrar*, University Press of America, 1981.

off her.' In short, she possessed star quality.[13] Dyer had coined an image one would hear many times about actors. *The camera loves her (him)*.

DeMille advised Farrar to cut her motion picture teeth on her next film, *Maria Rosa*, and she did. In it, her co-star was Lou Tellegen, the handsome Dutch actor who had created this same role on the stage and had starred with and toured opposite Sarah Bernhardt in the French four-reeler that Zukor had released. When *Maria Rosa* opened at the Strand, the *New York Times* said it was 'as good as, if not better than Carmen.' Seeing Farrar's twin successes, serious theatre performers and other opera stars were no longer reluctant to appear in the movies.

(*Carmen* has been shown on the Internet: [14]
https://www.youtube.com/watch?v=oDE0tyZso1g)

A few months after the film opened in New York, Farrar invited Lasky and Bessie to an intimate dinner party where she and Lou Tellegen announced their engagement. To keep his star happy, Lasky offered Tellegen more work at the studio as an actor and let him try his hand at directing.

Those were heady days. Farrar's films were bringing in money for the studio and DeMille knew how to spend it. With his growing taste for spectacle, he gave up all attempts to perform his duties as inspector general overseeing the entire studio output. He insisted his concentration must be on his own films. For *The Woman God Forgot* (about Cortez's conquest of Mexico in the 16th century), DeMille built a 200-foot high pyramid stretching 2 square miles. He also constructed a gigantic garden with a pool including several thousand rare waterfowl (enclosed in wire fencing to prevent the birds escaping). In the evolving DeMille style, the prince's nymph attendants arose splashing from the pool amid the flutter of birds. Filming the 'big attack' scene took 1,000 extras led by Farrar as Montezuma's daughter. DeMille directed all six pictures that Geraldine Farrar made for the studio. One of them was *Joan The Woman*, in which she played Joan of Arc. DeMille's attempt for authenticity was expensive. He was using solid-built sets instead of backdrops, and he had a suit of armor made to measure for his Joan. When they finally clamped it on the singer, she couldn't move. DeMille, who called her Gerry, described her as 'a sardine in a can', so a second suit was commissioned, not quite so form fitting.

Lasky wrote in his autobiography that 30 years later he was grateful for that suit when he was making *The Miracle of the Bells* with the Italian star (Alida) Valli. He discovered that suits of armor for women don't even exist in museums. Unable to find one, he called Cecil, whom he knew always kept unusual artifacts from his films. He still had it; so the suit that Valli wore in *Miracle of the Bells* was the same one worn by Geraldine Farrar in *Joan the Woman*.

---

13 Richard Dyer The Boston Globe, January 5, 1997.
14 You can often find access to many silent and early films on the internet.

GERALDINE FARRAR

Dustin Farnum was also being kept busy at the studio. He appeared in *The Virginian*, sorry indeed, that he had not accepted one quarter of the company in lieu of salary. That $5,000 would have been worth $2,000,000 in a few short years. Seeking to improve the quality of his company's product, Lasky brought to Hollywood the Broadway designer, Wilfred Buckland, who was famous for lighting the stage triumphs of the most famous stage producer, David Belasco. Buckland introduced interior lighting to DeMille's films, for which the director invested a princely sum on a black velvet backdrop to film his night scenes for the film version of his brother William's hit Broadway play, *The Warrens of Virginia*.

(You can watch *Joan the Woman* on the Internet: https://www.youtube.com/watch?v=zUNhZ-RqsOo)

With this costly velvet cloth blacking out sunlight, Cecil was able to film interior night scenes and light them with sun reflectors, making him the first director to vary light intensity in a scene. Another Buckland 'first' was building architectural settings, vastly expanding the visual limitations of the stage. No longer was sharpness of detail the criteria, Cecil was now able to create startling effects of highlight and shadow. The result was an unexpected explosion of fury from New York. Sam insisted that he couldn't sell a film if half the actors' faces were hidden in shadow. 'Why pay the going rate for an actor and then photograph only half of him?' he complained in a cable.

Cecil's response was, 'Tell him to sell it as Rembrandt lighting.' And Sam did.

Business was now booming with more filmmakers pouring into Hollywood—and more films required more talent and more scripts. Lasky employed three more directors for their lower budget films, and for an average cost of $5,000, the producer found he could buy the screen rights to books and plays directly from the writers. He made sure his company owned the rights to produce as many versions of a book or play as they could possibly want. DeMille filmed three versions of *The Squaw Man*, the second in 1918 starring Elliott Dexter and the third in 1931, which was shot with sound.

The flickers were becoming respectable. In 1915, the Lasky Company released 36 pictures. One of them, *The Cheat*, written by Hector Turnbull and Jeanie Macpherson (actress-turned-writer and DeMille's current amour) starred Sessue Hayakawa as the Japanese villain and was an instant success. For the 1918 reissue with Hayakawa, the villain's nationality was changed to Burmese to satisfy objections by the Japanese Association of Southern California. Years later, Hayakawa was to star in *Bridge on the River Kwai*, recapturing his nationality and theatrical villainy.

(*The Cheat* on the Internet: https://www.youtube.com/watch?v=-eExydVWC00)

Other feature-length films were being scheduled at four or five reels, but in the following year (1915) the filmmaker D. W. Griffith made his infamously racist twelve-reel epic about the Civil War. *The Birth of a Nation* made an estimated $30,000,000 at the box office. One of Griffith's stars not in that film, Blanche Sweet, earlier had given a stunning performance in *Judith of Bethulia*. When DeMille and Lasky found out that Griffith had no contractual hold over Sweet, they were quick to offer her a contract. She became one of the Lasky company's most important early stars, and that year she appeared in seven pictures.

Certain now that Hollywood was to be their permanent home, in 1914 Lasky sent for his extended family: Bessie, Jesse Jr., and mother, Sarah. Blanche had already come out to join Sam, now well out of selling gloves and firmly ensconced in Hollywood. Lasky temporarily housed the family at the Hollywood Hotel—the only hotel in town.

By the time he'd produced *The Squaw Man*, Lasky had been married to Bessie for nearly four years and was father of three-year old Jesse L. Lasky Jr. Bessie had seen more of Lasky's mother Sarah than she had of her husband, and found her marriage a mixed blessing. At last reunited with her husband, she saw a chance to escape the tyranny of a strict mother-in-law, and confidentially asked Cecil's help to find her a house too small to include relatives. The director-general graciously turned over his little cottage in Cahuenga Canyon to the couple and their son while he, wife Constance, and daughter Cecilia moved to a larger house nearby, so after five years of marriage, Bessie finally had her little family to herself.

BLANCHE SWEET

But another marriage was not moonlight and roses. In 1915, Blanche divorced Sam. Shocking though divorce was at the time, it came as no surprise to the family.

All had borne witness to Sam's volatile temper. Blanche and Sam had been married for five years and had a daughter, Ruth, when she hired a private detective to follow the gossip. It seemed Sam's growing appetite for eager young girls hoping to break into films was casting new meaning to the word 'couch'. Blanche sued and was granted a divorce, but contrary to all reason, Sam's response was to claim that Ruth was not his daughter. Outraged, Blanche changed her daughter's name to Lasky. it was a position Sam maintained and had no further contact with Ruth until late in his life, when he recanted.

Though Sam was now no longer a brother-in-law, it was business as usual at the Jesse L. Lasky Feature Play Company. But the producer was worried about his other partner. Just when things at the studio were booming, Cecil was thinking of quitting the movie business. He'd been learning to fly so he could join up as a pilot and get himself into the war raging in Europe. America did not enter World War I until April of 1917, by which time Cecil had been taking flying lessons for over a year. Lasky, who shared his spirit of derring-do on land, had never been in a plane and was impressed with Cecil's fearless attitude. Over several highballs, he told his partner, 'Cecil, we've been through a lot of adventures together, and I want to have my first plane ride when you make your first solo flight.'

It might have been the gin talking because Lasky forgot all about his promise until a few months later when Cecil called from the flying field on what is now Wilshire Boulevard, and commanded in his most imperious manner, 'Jesse, I'm ready to solo. Be here after lunch!'

Lasky lost his appetite, but he drove to the field in his new pearl grey Packard Special—which Cecil referred to as the 'Corona-Corona' because of its extra long cigar-like wheelbase. Actor/director Rex Ingram had designed it for the producer, copying a racing car belonging to a famous racer, Ralph de Palma. Lasky recalled, 'It could climb hills only by backing up them, but it looked great.'

The day was extremely windy and Lasky hoped it might be a good reason for Cecil to postpone the flight. But the director handed him a leather jacket, a helmet, and goggles, and assured him that it was much easier for a beginner to take off into a strong wind. Lasky climbed into the forward cockpit as instructed and gripped the sides in silent terror. DeMille took off smoothly, and just as they were sailing along with the wind roaring in Lasky's ears and he was beginning to relax, Cecil shouted something he couldn't hear. Then the motor cut out!

That year DeMille was 34, Lasky was 35, and all he could think of was how the headlines would handle their deaths. But Cecil had only been trying to warn his partner that he was about to execute some aerial acrobatics—which he did with a great display of virtuosity and eventually making a perfect landing. Lasky found his knees a trifle weak as he climbed out and handed back his goggles. He never admitted it to Cecil, but it was years before he could go up in a plane after that initiation.

DEMILLE'S FIRST SOLO FLIGHT WITH LASKY

On the East Coast, Adolph Zukor was regularly producing his own pictures, and whenever Lasky was in New York, the friendly rivals arranged to lunch. Lasky viewed his opponent with great respect. Zukor was small of stature but his competitor began to think of him as a titan when he expounded astute theories about the budding motion picture business. The two men came from very different backgrounds: Lasky, with grandfather Bernard who had crossed the plains in a covered wagon in 1848—and Adolph Zukor, who was born in Ricse, Hungary in 1873. Zukor had been orphaned at seven and sent to live with his uncle, Kalman Liebermann; a rabbi who hoped the young lad would follow his example. But Zukor had other worlds to conquer and made his way to America. At an early age he entered the fur trade and soon made sufficient money to turn his talents to more trendy exploits. In 1903 he bought his first nickelodeon, thereby propelling himself into the film/entertainment business. He soon became a partner and treasurer of Marcus Loew's mushrooming chain of movie theatres.

It was not long before more up-and-coming film producers were joining the westward stampede. Palpably aware that they were selling their pictures to the same states' rights men for distribution, Zukor and Lasky wisely concluded that rather than compete for distribution, they should team up to fight off the encroaching opposition, so in 1916 the two men merged companies to form Famous Players-Lasky Corporation. The newly formed corporation soon bought out the Paramount distribution company from Hodkinson, making them the largest motion picture company of the silent film era, now able to distribute their own films and control where and when they were booked into theatres.

Famous Players-Lasky Corporation was to go through a few company titles: Paramount Publix Corporation (Paramount Pictures and Publix Theaters) before eventually deciding on Paramount Pictures. Lasky's title appeared on the stationary variously as 'Vice President', 'First Vice President', or 'Office of Jesse L. Lasky, Vice President in charge of Production'. Adolph Zukor remained in New York as Vice President in charge of Distribution and Finance. Although Lasky was constantly traveling between the West Coast and New York, his main office was now in Hollywood in charge of the creative side of production, finding stories, directors, and actors who could capture the imagination of the public without the spoken word. As soon as the war was over he began traveling regularly to Europe again and got into the habit of writing letters home. But Jesse was still too young to be the recipient.

SCENE TWO
1921 – 1924

*PARAMOUNT FAMOUS LASKY CORPORATION
WEST COAST*

The amalgamation also brought Zukor's star, the winsome Mary Pickford, to Famous Players-Lasky Corporation. Lasky assigned former journalist and budding screenwriter Hector Turnbull to write an original screenplay for her, based on the lyric of a popular song, 'Less Than the Dust'.

The resulting film should have been swept under the carpet and a worried Lasky had to find a proper vehicle for Zukor's discovery—or ruin the new partnership.[15]

'I started my association with Zukor on a blunder that would be hard to top', Lasky ruefully wrote... 'but Sam managed to top it!' Goldfish, with his usual blunt manner, had walked into a meeting between Mary Pickford and Lasky, uninvited. He remarked, along with a few other choice sallies, that Lasky 'shouldn't let Zukor butt in on the picture'. Loyal to the man who had discovered and nurtured her with a fatherly hand, Mary reported the conversation to Zukor, who in turn gave Lasky an ultimatum: 'Either Goldfish goes or I do!'

Ex-brother-in-law or not, Lasky realized that there was only one way forward. He and Zukor bought Sam out for $900,000. Sam, who didn't seem too perturbed, retained his stock options in the company and may even have voiced one of his

FAMOUS PLAYERS-LASKY
(LASKY, ZUKOR, GOLDFISH, DEMILLE, KAUFMAN)

---

15 Zukor, Adolph, with Dale Kramer, *The Public is Never Wrong: The Autobiography of Adolph Zukor*, G.P. Putnam's Sons, 1953.

famous axioms: 'Gentlemen, include me out.' He was gaining a reputation for epigrammatic quips like 'Give me a couple of years, and I'll make that actress an overnight success', and 'A bachelor's life is no life for a single man'. A few years later, in 1921 when Sam was told that Lasky's second son would be named after William DeMille and be called Bill, Goldwyn snapped. 'Why would you name him Bill? Every Tom, Dick, and Harry is named Bill'

Sometimes life has a way of turning adversity into triumph. Providence threw Edgar Selwyn into Sam's path. Lasky had known the actor/writer/producer in New York. In 1915 Selwyn was starring in his own play on Broadway, *The Arab*. Lasky bought it and the star. Playing an Arab horseman in the theatre, Selwyn had no problem, the horse presumably being tethered somewhere off stage. But making movies separates horsemen from the saddle-sore, and to DeMille's disgust, he was forced to employ a stunt-double to ride for the actor—thereby creating another Hollywood 'first'.

It was that same Edgar Selwyn who went into business with Sam Goldfish, fresh from Famous Players-Lasky with the jingle of $900,000 in his pocket. In 1916, the two men joined names to form Goldwyn Pictures Corporation. (It has since been noted that the alternative 'Selfish Pictures' was not an option.) Feeling that if he couldn't name the company after himself, he should name himself after the company, Sam Goldwyn was born.

Riding high in his new 'mogul-ish' position, the press hinted that he was having simultaneous affairs with two top stars, Mabel Normand and Mae Murray. It would be ten years and many casting couches later that he would marry again, and it would be Lasky who would introduce him to Frances Howard, a stunning New York actress, then under contract to Famous Players-Lasky. Howard gave up acting, gave birth to Sam Goldwyn Jr., and was to play a supportive role in Sam's highly successful creative life.

With a production program of 104 features that year, Lasky was beginning to feel the weight of his schedule. He needed someone to take charge of assigning writers and directors to each film, so he brought in an expert on silent film construction to be in charge of this phase of production. For Frank Woods, Lasky created the title of supervisor. He assigned writer/producer Turnbull to be in charge of all the supervisors. One of them was Tom Geraghty.

Lasky said of the supervisors, 'For some time they didn't even get screen credit, but they were the first members of a profession, now represented by the Screen Producers Guild.' The term supervisor didn't last long. Soon 'Producer' was the title given to all who serve as a link between top management and individual productions. When eventually Sam Goldwyn became an independent producer, he needed no such link, being always in sole control. Other filmmakers soon followed suit.

The new prosperity afforded busy executives those little trinkets of the super-rich. Lasky bought himself a Stutz Bearcat sports car and made a bet with comedian

Mack Sennett that he could drive it across the continent in three weeks. He won the bet, but unfortunately, wrecked the car.

World War I intervened. On April 6, 1917, President Woodrow Wilson's policy of neutrality and the powerful peace sentiment in Congress was finally declining and the United States entered the war. Jesse, now seven, and young Bill Buckland found something useful to do in Hollywood. They marched in the Lasky Home Guard Band to raise money for the war effort.

It was Lasky's idea to take advantage of celebrities whose names were known in other fields. That year, Famous Players-Lasky, with a five-year record of no failures,

THE LASKY HOME GUARD, JESSE, FAR RIGHT

made several pictures with a famous female impersonator, Julian Eltinge, who could be outrageously glamorous in drag. Lasky daringly presented him at the opening as a man—daring, since he never appeared as that gender on stage. Magician Harry Houdini also appeared in several thrillers where he could show off his famous escapology. In one film, he was dumped in a river bound with shackles and locks. The audience saw him escape with no film editing tricks. Today's audiences probably wouldn't believe such stunts were not computer generated.

LASKY'S STUTZ BEARCAT

When Lasky heard that two rival producers, Joseph Schenck[16] and his partner Julius Steger were about to make a movie with the distinguished opera star, Enrico Caruso, known as 'The Voice of the Century', he wished he'd thought of it first, since he had had such phenomenal success with Geraldine Farrar. He called Schenck and offered him $40,000 to buy out their eight-week contract with the singer. Schenck handed over Caruso's contract, happy to make a profit without having to shoot a foot of film. With such an expensive outlay, Lasky decided that in eight weeks they could film two pictures and hastily assigned writers to come up with two original stories for the singer that would not include singing.

Hopes ran high for Caruso's first completed film until reports of the opening day's box office takings came in. For the producers, *My Cousin* in 1918 was another 'first'. Their first flop! They had to refund the rental money that had been paid by complaining exhibitors. *My Cousin* was withdrawn and Lasky immediately cancelled the second film, sadly acknowledging, 'The public was smarter than I was and realized they'd been cheated of Caruso's glorious voice.' Caruso, an excellent caricaturist, took the failure in stride and presented a cartoon portrait to Lasky.

The producer continued to commute between Hollywood and New York, business-lunching with Zukor in all the fashionable eateries: Delmonico's, Sherry's, the Astor, and the Ritz. Zukor's was the final word on all important financial moves and

---
16 Pronounced Skenck.

budgets. One vital decision they made together was to settle on the name of Paramount for the company because, as it had been the distributor, it was well known to the cinema-going public. Now they advertised their films with this slogan:

IF IT'S A PARAMOUNT PICTURE IT'S THE BEST SHOW IN TOWN.
But the company needed to expand and diversify. Lasky wanted to make some higher budget features. Zukor, in charge of finances, okayed a number of them to be set up under a subsidiary title, Artcraft Pictures.

LASKY BY CARUSO

Mary Pickford's films were now to be made for Artcraft Pictures. Up to now, she had been filming in New York. She was finally sent out to the West Coast, where Cecil directed her first two Hollywood films. But Lasky was quick to see that the dramatically theatrical 'DeMille touch' was not right for Mary's homespun 'America's sweetheart' image, so he assigned Marshall Neilan, a former actor turned highly successful director, to her next films. It was Neilan who directed some of

LASKY, WILLIAM S. HART, MARY PICKFORD, DEMILLE

Pickford's most popular pictures, including *Rebecca of Sunnybrook Farm*; films that suited her piquant charm.

(Rebecca of Sunnybrook Farm was shown on the Internet:https://www.youtube.com/watch?v=z7qCmBGPFYw)

The competing female star on the lot was the equally piquant Marguerite Clark. Friction soon built up between the two ladies as to which star was getting the choicest parts and the most money. Pickford was earning $10,000 a week and getting a 50% slice of profits when, thinking she could do better, she decided to set up her own company.

There was a budding 'Star' on the lot. Gloria May Josephine Svensson had come to California from Chicago in 1916 and appeared in Mack Sennett's Keystone Cops. In 1919, with her name changed to Gloria Swanson, Lasky signed her to Famous Players-Lasky, and under the directorial guidance of DeMille, whose dramatic style suited her down to a false eyelash, she became a silent star with *Don't Change Your Husband*. Her next film was based on one of Sir James Barrie's plays, *The Admirable Crichton*. Before its release, the publicity and sales departments objected to the title, assuming the American public would confuse it with 'admiral', and sea pictures weren't popular. Cecil came up with a title, saying, 'We'll call it *Male and Female*. I guess the sales department and the public will understand that!'

They did. But when Lasky screened it in London for author Barrie, who had the final say on its release in Great Britain, the producer was worried. 'Sir James', he stammered, '…it wasn't my idea, but you see, sir, our director, Cecil DeMille is a very determined and sometimes a difficult man and . . . well . . . he decided to call it *Male and Female*.'

There was a dead silence while Lasky waited for the heavens to fall. 'Sir Jame's hand shot out so quickly it gave me a start', Lasky later remembered. 'But instead of striking me, he grasped my hand and said, 'Capital! I wish I'd thought of it myself.'

Swanson was a great hit. With her sultry voice, her fame would continue on into the talkies. A few years later, when she demanded $1,000,000 to renew her contract and Zukor and the East Coast moneymen cried no, Lasky felt that it was a mistake the studio would regret. Hollywood was to learn that stars of her ilk were worth what they demanded.

The industry was growing fast. Hollywood now included Carl Laemmle's Universal Film Manufacturing Company and Triangle, who released the films of Mack Sennett, Thomas Ince, and the much-praised D. W. Griffith. Talent was being bartered, and soon the Lasky Company acquired Triangle's William S. Hart, Douglas Fairbanks, Charles Ray, and top writers Anita Loos and John Emerson.

In 1917 the company turned out fifty-two standard Paramount releases, eighteen Artcraft high budget films, and thirty-four Realarts films—another subsidiary with medium-priced budgets.

Lasky wrote in his autobiography, 'The output of pictures from the West Coast was stepped up so drastically that 'Jesse L. Lasky Presents' appeared at the top of the screen about five times as often as 'Adolph Zukor Presents'. I thought I detected a slightly reproachful look in the eyes of my luncheon companion. In the interests of better digestion, I suggested a change of policy, and from then on all our pictures, whether made in the East or on the West Coast, were 'presented' by Adolph Zukor and Jesse L. Lasky in tandem.'

The company's expansion was so volatile that Lasky couldn't churn out films fast enough. Sidney Kent, who had started as a writer, had taken over the selling job that Goldfish originally enjoyed and was screaming for product. Seeing growing competition in booking theatres, Zukor was busy buying up theatre chains. The corporation soon owned 2,000 houses and was establishing film exchanges overseas. Lasky was administrating the building and the design of showcase theatres and studios in London, Paris, and Berlin. They even had a studio in Poona near Bombay, where it was so hot that the film practically melted in the cameras—but it was to be the start of India's booming Bollywood industry.

In 1917, Jesse unwittingly began his Hollywood career as a visitor on DeMille's set for *Joan the Woman*, with Geraldine Farrar clanking about the location in sweltering armor, preparing to mount her mighty caparisoned steed and lead the victorious charge against the vile English. Bold French knights were poised in position behind her. Touring cars of visitors fringed the outer field a safe distance from the action. Some stood on open car seats; a few stood at the foot of the director's tower upon which the camera was mounted.

Imagine the scene: Seven-year-old Jesse stands with the Vice President in charge of Production and his mother, the beautiful Bessie.

'Camera! Action!' shouts the director, peering into the camera as the knights charge behind the ironclad Geraldine. Sand flies as hooves clatter heavily in the powdery earth. Horses thunder forward! Swords flash and people on the sidelines gasp. But have no fear, the noise will not be heard; it's a silent film.

In the dust that spirals through the action, a small boy dashes purposefully into the field to rescue a fallen wooden sword flashing highlights of silver paint. He scoops it up, grasping it to his chest and runs back to Mom.

'Hold the charge!' DeMille shouts. Horses are reined in. Actors hurry back to their places. All is chaos! But it's too late. Jesse has ruined the shot. This decided Lasky to keep his son away from the studio and to encourage the boy to seek an adventurous outdoor life.

Hollywood was expanding, and amidst developing studio rivalries, Sam Goldwyn heard that Lasky had fired Geraldine Farrar's new husband, Lou Tellegen, for being unable to complete his assignment as a director. Farrar had just finished her sixth film with DeMille, and before Lasky could find another project for her talents, Goldwyn offered the new husband-wife team a contract to star together. The pair too readily accepted and all Farrar's future films were made for Goldwyn Productions.

Sometimes life has a way of turning adversity into failure. The Farrar/Tellegen marriage was not to last, and Goldwyn's matinee idol came to a sad end. Having fallen asleep with a cigarette, Tellegen accidently set fire to himself, badly scarring his face. He was to spend years in surgery to no avail. Finally, his health failing and his career at an end, he committed suicide. But that was all in the future....

In 1919, a romance that had been developing between Blanche and Hector Turnbull culminated in their marriage. Sam saw this as an opportunity to stop paying his ex-wife $5,200 a year in alimony. The judge agreed to cut the alimony in half, decreeing that she was still due $2,600 in consideration of her financial loss by divorcing. She agreed not to make any further claims against him. But animosity ran high, and in the face of Sam having disowned his daughter, Hector Turnbull legally adopted Ruth.

In 1920 an airmail service began between New York and San Francisco. The first mail-carrying planes arrived in California on August 8th and would be of great service to Lasky not only for business, but for keeping in contact with his family, and in particular with ten-year old Jesse. When in his New York office, he never let a week go by in which he did not write to his son. The letters were generally dictated to his right-hand man and personal secretary, Randy Rogers, who typed, and on some occasions, even signed letters for the boss when he had to dash off to a meeting. This faithful amanuensis was to stay by Lasky's side throughout his entire career, and when the money ran out he stayed anyway, working for nothing until Lasky was back on track.

'The viewpoint of the businessman cannot be completely reconciled with that of the artist', Lasky noted with some concern. 'The East complains that costs are too high, shooting schedules too long, titles hard to exploit, stills unimaginative ...' Because the heavy new eastern banking interests under Zukor were edgy about the enormous sums spent on what they considered intangibles, the Hollywood studio was soon obliged to accept a cuckoo in their nest named Harris De Haven Connick, whose mandate was to keep production costs down.

In our world of e-mails, smart phones equipped with texting, Skype, Facebook, Twitter, and Instagram, it's hard to realize that it took hours to place a long-distance phone call and weeks for a letter to arrive. The first transcontinental phone call from the Hollywood studio to the New York office had to be arranged a day in advance with the telephone company. The event made the newspapers, and the press reported it as just another publicity stunt. That cinched it for Connick, who saw phone calls an unnecessary expense, and all further communications between east and west was restricted to telegrams. Connick also objected to the 'insidious practice of using too many words in those telegrams'. He decided that to save money, three specific words should be shaved off; for example, the word 'Regards' was wasted space so this friendly greeting was dutifully eliminated. But after a month of *regards*-less telegrams, hurt feelings ran so high it nearly wrecked the studio.

Connick's most damaging edict was that no story property should cost more than $10,000. Then along came Edith M. Hull's shocking, romantic novel, *The Sheik*, chronicling the provocative adventures of a ravishing girl swept off into the desert to be ravished by an Arab chieftain. Lasky brazenly ignored Connick's edict and paid the author what she demanded: $12,500 for the film rights. But when he realized that none of their male contract stars would be convincing playing a passionate desert lover, Lasky set the book aside and nearly forgot all about it. It was not until several months later when he covered the opening night of Metro's *The Four Horsemen of the Apocalypse* that Hull's book was to resurface in his mind.

Metro's picture was sumptuously produced at a cost that would have given Lasky's nemesis, Connick, a stroke. Metro had the picture of the year. The producer was deeply impressed, and in particular, by an unknown Italian actor who appeared as a tango-dancing gaucho from the Argentine. But Lasky assumed Metro must certainly be aware that they had developed one of the greatest box-office potentials of all time in this handsome, charismatic newcomer, and must certainly have him under contract.

Still, he couldn't dismiss the actor from his thoughts and jotted down his name on a pad on his desk. Still, he might have forgotten all about the man, when a few weeks later his secretary announced that a Mr. Rudolph Valentino was in his outer office. He walked into the office reeking with charisma. Lasky was more surprised when Valentino told him he was looking for a job.

It seemed that the actor had quarreled with director Rex Ingram and had created the impression of being difficult (not without some validity). To Lasky's surprise, Metro had not bothered to take an option on their actor's future services. (Those were not the days of high-powered agents who would have started a bidding war for Valentino.)

The actor told Lasky he had waited for exactly one month with no word from Metro and finally came to Lasky on his own.

Lasky was curious. 'Why choose me?'

'Because this is the biggest studio in town', was the actor's logical reply.

The Vice President did not let Valentino leave his office until he had signed him to a five year contract—and dictated an order to his secretary: they were immediately to search for suitable story material.

'But Mr. Lasky, you already have the best possible story for him!' his secretary reminded. Lasky had been debating about another actor for the part, James Kirkwood. But looking at the actor sitting across his desk, Lasky knew what he had to do. Of course—Valentino had to star in his $12,500 book purchase, *The Sheik*! He also recalled that they owned Vicente Blasco-Ibanez's bullfighting saga, *Blood and Sand*, a story smoldering with sexual innuendo, tailor-made for the bubbling animal magnetism that was Valentino's gift.

The screenplay was by Monte M. Katterjohn, who followed the novel as closely as possible. And although Lasky had him cut the 'rape scene' that would never have gotten past the censors, it was banned in Kansas City. The Corn Belt helped to make it a greater success elsewhere, and suddenly Valentino was the greatest star in the studio. The greatest star in Hollywood. The greatest star of silent films.

(You can possibly watch *The Sheik* on the Internet: https://ia700401.us.archive.org/28/items/TheSheik/TheSheik_512kb.mp4)

The actor married the beautiful costume designer/art director known professionally as Natacha Rambova. She was actually Winifred Hudnut, stepdaughter of Richard Hudnut, the multi-millionaire cosmetic manufacturer, and she was used to money and spending it. She was to design all his costumes and Valentino put all his business affairs in her hands. The studio found that if they wanted to see their star, they had to make an appointment with Natacha. On set, Valentino was aloof and did not make friends easily, but it hardly mattered to his career; his stardom was instantaneous.

Rambova hated her husband playing the sizzling Latin lover parts Lasky had cast him in and insisted Valentino play more 'classic' roles, starting with Booth Tarkington's 'Monsieur Beaucaire'. Totally against the image the studio had created for him, it was an 18th century drawing room drama that dressed him in white silk hose, powdered wig and lip rouge. It didn't go down well in Keokuk, Iowa in the 1920s. It wouldn't do any better now.

(*Monsieur Beaucaire* is possibly on the Internet: https://www.youtube.com/watch?v=hkQZ6GwVefA)

Valentino's career was all too brief. He died at the age of thirty-one of peritonitis after an operation. But because of the choice of films that his wife demanded, his luminosity was already on the wane. Had he lived until talking pictures, his career would surely have been over when the public heard him speak. His voice was high-pitched and didn't suit his steamy physical presence. Called 'the most perfect screen lover of all time', he inspired a fanatic female devotion that survived his death on August 23, 1926. 80,000 mourners, mostly women, caused a near riot at his New York memorial service. A funeral followed in California with the highlight of the event being a mysterious 'lady in black' who was never identified.

But that was still a few years away. There was plenty of excitement at the studio to keep the vice president busy. Years before he had ever dreamed of Hollywood, an exotic-looking British writer with flaming red hair, her lithe frame smothered in jewels and furs, created an international scandal with her novel *Three Weeks* which, in staid London was called 'too sensational' and was viciously attacked by the critics. Naturally it became an instant best seller.

Her name was Elinor Glyn and she could have graced the silver screen herself as a glamour queen. Her great-grandfather had been Sir Richard Willcocks, giving

RUDOLPH VALENTINO

her some small claim to British aristocracy, and her erotic, romantic novel was the hottest thing since *Lady Chatterley's Lover*. The Reliable Feature Film Company had filmed *Three Weeks* in the states in less than that. Not wishing them to steal a lead on Famous Player-Lasky, the producer invited Madame Glyn to come to Hollywood to write an original screenplay for his sexy, newest star, Gloria Swanson. He had even thought up a title: *The Great Moment*. All Madame Glyn had to do was dream up what that might be. She did—and duly set sail for America.

Lasky greeted the author upon her arrival on the Mauritania and threw a press reception for her at the plush New York apartment he had rented for her, after which he was to escort her to a photographer's studio. Madame Glyn swept up a leopard skin rug from the floor and marched out on Lasky's arm. Refusing the chauffeur driven limo, she insisted on walking down 5th Avenue, handing the leopard skin to Lasky to carry. It was an omen of things to come.

In Hollywood in 1921 with the script finally finished, Madame Glyn's contract gave her the choice of leading man. Her harried director, Sam Wood, running be-

LASKY, ELINOR GLYN, SWANSON IN NEW YORK

hind in his planning schedule, and with the hottest star at the studio, Gloria Swanson waiting to see who would be her co-star, Wood grumbled to Lasky that Glyn had turned down all the studio's male stars, complaining that they didn't have 'It'.

She had interviewed everyone, including extras, in search of this illusive quality that only she seemed able to identify. To everyone's relief, Glyn finally settled on established leading man Milton Sills, who had twenty Broadway productions under his belt before coming to Silents in 1914 in *The Pit*. Glyn informed Lasky that Sills had 'It' in a big way. Since the actor had previously been a professor of psychology and philosophy at the University of Chicago before taking up acting, perhaps his charisma was psychological. The 'It' word soon became the soubriquet for sex appeal, male or female.

Glyn's next screenplay was for Clara Bow and was simply called *It*. Bow was labeled for life the 'It' girl. Doggerel verse was tossed around about the seductive author: Would you like to sin With Elinor Glyn on a tiger skin? Or would you prefer to err with her on some other fur?[17] The screenplay was again by Monte M. Katterjohn, who had written *The Sheik*. When Glyn finally arrived in Hollywood, she was parked temporarily in the penthouse of the Ambassador Hotel. She informed Lasky that she was happy to remain there but insisted that the management install a kitchenette for her, since she liked to prepare her own meals. When she returned to London somewhat earlier than expected, Lasky happily took over the apartment and installed his mother Sarah in it, where she remained for life.

Lasky home life was expanding to fit their escalating station in life. The family of three was now living at 7209 Hillside Avenue, which was at LaBrea, a five-acre estate in an exclusive section called The Outpost off Highland Avenue. Among the staff of servants (twelve), vying between the new beach house and The Outpost, were Swedish born Gus Liljenwall and Jenny Hendrickson, a young Finnish girl. Gus was head gardener and chauffeur; Jenny was the upstairs maid. The two met at the house and married in 1922. Their son Robert[18] told me that when his mother had twins she named one Sophie and the other Bessie, after Mrs. Lasky who gave them an apartment above the garage. Lasky gave Gus the family limousine to drive his wife and the twins home from the hospital and added a case of scotch whisky in prohibition days. Jenny was befriended by Louella Parsons, who was always in search of gossip for her *Hearst* column. Jenny kept her ear out and was willing to spill a few beans for a healthy tip. She saw a lot of Valentino, who was the life of many of the parties at the Lasky home. With his wife at the studio it was quite a different story.

Lasky's passion for adventure was unabated. Whenever he was free to indulge his own extravagant sojourns into the wild, young Jesse would be taken on an exciting expedition down some canyon, up a mountain, along a river's rapids or some narrow

---

17 Glyn, Anthony, *Elinor Glyn: A Biography* (Hutchinson, London, 1955), p. 35.
18 Robert Liljenwall became a senior strategic marketing and branding consultancy while teaching at UCLA where he was named a Distinguished Instructor of the Year.

THE MAN WHO HAD 'IT': MILTON SILLS

cliffside trail trekking for weary miles on sore feet. When Jesse was only seven they would travel with cowboy guides into some wilderness. It was the beginning of an intense relationship between father and son A busy producer he was, but he deeply desired not to miss being part of the rearing of his eldest son. He took to writing Jesse from New York when the boy was about ten and brother William was one year old. By the time Jesse was eleven and had experienced a few of his father's expeditions, he received this letter. (Early letters were addressed quite formally and were of little consequence concerning studio matters. That would change.)

June 1, 1921
Master Jesse L. Lasky, Jr.
7209 Hillside Ave.,
Hollywood, California.
My dear Jesse:

I just received your typewritten letter and very funny drawing which made me laugh very much. I was so glad to get even one little letter from you. Soon after you receive this letter I will be getting ready to start for home and maybe I won't be glad to see you and mother and little Billy . . . you will have both the Geraghty boys to play with all summer. This will be good news to you and Bill (Buckland) because now the whole gang will be together again.

As soon as I get home we will have to begin to plan for another trip into the mountains. I think we will get the same guide we had last year and a flock of mules and go into some very wild country. You will be able to take your new rifle. Well, take good care of mother and keep your eyes on the squealer, brother Bill. Give my love to grandma, Uncle Hector, Aunty Blanche and big Bill. With much love,

Your loving Dad,
Jesse L. Lasky Sr.

He refers to the children of Thomas Geraghty, writer and a supervisor of the company, and the great art director and designer, Wilfred Buckland, whose son Bill was Jesse's best friend. The reckless adventurer finished his letter to his son with this promise (or threat?).

In the early days of writing to his son, Lasky often added Sr. to his full name with flamboyant formality. 'Uncle Hector' was Turnbull, the prolific writer/producer who was now married to Blanche. Wilfred Buckland was 'Big Bill'. Bessie had made a friend of Wilfred's wife, Veda Buckland, and had gone with her to visit a growing artists' colony up the coast in Carmel. It inspired her to take her painting so seriously that Lasky asked Wilfred to design a studio for her above the garage in their Hillside home.

From the outset, Bessie did not feel at home in the social side of Hollywood life and found any excuse to avoid much of it, cosseting herself away in her new studio painting or reading on her favorite subjects, philosophy and comparative religions, open to all inspirational ideas. While she was always the perfect hostess with servants to do the work, Lasky found he was forced to attend many public dinners, picture premieres, and theatrical first nights alone, and soon realized that he and Bessie were living in separate worlds. He wrote '... but if I had forced her to live in mine, I would have lost her, and that would have been a tragedy for me.'

By 1920 everything was coming up roses for the high stakes players in Hollywood. Any misdemeanors caused by the inhabitants (A little booze, a little sex, a little drugs) were hastily hidden. But in 1921 the soft underbelly of scandal was pierced by a Famous Players-Lasky comedian whose avoirdupois had earned him

BESSIE IN HER NEW STUDIO

the name of 'Fatty'. Roscoe Arbuckle was not only a top comedian, he was also a skilled comedy director. It was he who trained the great Buster Keaton to become the major comedy director of the day. Fatty's on-screen unsophisticated earthiness stretched to off-screen dubious hi-jinx with a taste for bootleg booze and accessible females. On Labor Day weekend, September 5, 1921, he spirited a gang of friends away from the prying eyes of Hollywood to far away San Francisco and threw a three-day party at the St. Francis Hotel.

'The Fatty Arbuckle case' was the first of four major Paramount related scandals in the course of a few short years. Since Lasky's job was to hire, nurture, and fire talent, and Zukor's job was to pick up the tab, the onus fell on the West Coast Vice President to see that everything was above board, and if it were not, to see that whatever it was was discreetly hushed up.

There was also the case of Olive Thomas, wife of matinee idol Jack Pickford (Mary's brother), who was a star in her own right. Olive apparently drank her husband's medicine thinking it was water and died. Any suggestion of suicide was kept out of the press, but one might wonder if she noticed a funny taste?

Arbuckle's case was particularly tragic. At his trial, his studio friends had been forbidden by a Zukor edict to give evidence or make any character defense for him for fear it would reflect on their own careers. Arbuckle's wife, who knew he was no saint, pleaded for his defense in court and was shot at as she emerged from the courthouse. It was Lasky's dubious duty to minimize the scandal factor, but despite studio efforts, William Randolph Hearst's nationwide newspaper sensationalized the story. Hearst bragged that the Arbuckle case 'sold more newspapers than any event since the sinking of the RMS Lusitania.'

Truth not the total criteria, it was established that on September 5, 1921 Arbuckle drove to San Francisco with a couple of men friends (Lowell Sherman and Fred Fischbach) and checked into three rooms at the St. Francis Hotel with a substantial quantity of bootleg booze and the intention to 'party'. Among the female guests was a minor actress Virginia Rappe, who was twenty-six. At the trial that followed, another guest, Bobby Rose, testified that Maude Delmont (otherwise known as Madam Black, purveyor of party girls) had brought Rappe. Testimony claimed that Rappe had recently had an abortion—one of several in the last few years. She was suffering from cystitis and stomach pains, worsened by the bootleg liquor. Apparently, Arbuckle, while alone with her in a bedroom, rubbed her belly with ice to ease her pain. Her screams brought the others. No one considered it an emergency, no doctor was called, and she was put to bed by the group. She wasn't taken to a hospital for two days, where she died of peritonitis. The cause: a ruptured bladder.

Madam Black, possibly seeing a chance for extortion, told the police Arbuckle had raped Rappe and the impact of his overweight body had caused her bladder to rupture. However, the doctors found no such evidence. Someone spread whispers about the inappropriate use of a Coca-Cola bottle. As West Coast head of the studio, a fraught Lasky tried to hush up the sordid event, to no avail.

Murder was now added to the charge. One month after the girl's death, Arbuckle wrote to his personal producer at Famous Players-Lasky, Joe Schenck, who naturally passed this letter on to Lasky to deal with:

Roscoe C. Arbuckle
640 West Adams Street
Los Angeles, California
Oct 1st 1921
My Dear Joe,

It seems I never write to you unless I am in trouble. But this is one time Joe I was not to blame and when something happens in a half an hour that will change a mans whole life its pretty tough especially when a person is absolutely innocent in deed word or thought of any wrong.

I can't go into details about this affair as it would take me a week to tell you about it and explain it to you in detail so you would understand it. However Joe I want to tell you now, and have always come clean with you. I have never lied to you or crossed you in one single act or statement since I have known you and I am telling you now that I am absolutely innocent of all the accusations you have heard against me. I simply tried to help someone in distress, the same as you or anyone else with human instincts would have done in the circumstance.

I want you to have explicit faith and confidence in me and tell Mr. Zukor to have the same. I have done no wrong, my heart is clean and my conscience is clear and when it is over I have got to come back and I will come back and make good.

I realize the position of Mr. Zukor and Mr. Lasky and I know what it means to them in more ways than one and their attitude during this affair has been wonderful and I want you to tell them that I appreciate it. I know what they have tied up in me at present and irrespective of whether we ever due business together again I will come out of this affair clean and vindicated so that they can realize on their tremendous investment.

I am not asking for sympathy or forgiveness, I have done no wrong but I do want you and the ones financially as well as personally interested that I am innocent, a victim of circumstance, the only one of prominence in the party and therefore I had to be the goat.

Tell Mr. Zukor before passing judgment to remember the Boston party. He knows what a shakedown is. Joe perhaps I need a bump to wake me up, but I think I got considerable more than was coming to me, needless to say the kind of a life I will lead from now on.

Best Regards, Roscoe

Arbuckle's first and second trials ended with a hung jury. Then on April 12th, the third jury began deliberations that only lasted six minutes. In that short time the jury wrote a statement of apology, which was unprecedented in American justice. Their verdict was unanimous. Not guilty.[19]

The jury foreman read the statement: 'Acquittal is not enough for Roscoe Arbuckle. We feel that a great injustice has been done him . . . there was not the slightest proof adduced to connect him in any way with the commission of a crime. He was manly throughout the case and told a straightforward story which we all believe. We wish him success and hope that the American people will take the judgment of fourteen men and women that Roscoe Arbuckle is entirely innocent and free from all blame.'

But somehow that unique apology from the jury did not help. The comedian's career was over—with three completed Arbuckle films not yet released. The final decision about releasing them was up to Zukor, not Lasky. Zukor was willing to take the hit and the films were shelved. Those three comedies, never shown, wiped out $1,000,000 and a good share of the company's profits for the year. As for Arbuckle, unable to appear on the screen, he was allowed to direct a few comedies under the pseudonym William Goodrich. Not until 1933 was he offered a chance to make a comeback, but it came too late. Arbuckle had a sudden heart attack and died.

As head of a studio, there were other 'human' problems for Lasky to deal with. The elegant, soft-spoken British director William Desmond Taylor (whose past had a shady tint) did not fare as well as Arbuckle. His murder on February 1, 1922 was highly publicized. Three women were suspects and nothing about them was 'the usual.' They were two movie stars and a mother: Mabel Normand, Mary Miles Minter, and Minter's mother. The case was never solved, but a lot of dirty monogrammed nightgowns were slung about. Were they embroidered with the initial 'M'—or was it 'MMM'? Answers were not forthcoming. William Desmond Taylor's murder was conveniently unsolved.

Then in 1923 on January 18th, one of Lasky's biggest stars, Wallace Reid, died of a drug overdose at the age of thirty. Lasky wrote: 'If anyone had asked me in the summer of 1921 to name the greatest individual assets Famous Players-Lasky had, Wallace Reid, Fatty Arbuckle, and William Desmond Taylor would certainly have been on the list. All of them would also have been high on a list of my favorite personal friend[s]. . . .'

To keep the industry's skirts clean in future, an edict emanated from the East Coast that sent a shudder through the studios. The U.S. Postmaster General under President Harding was offered a position in Hollywood with a threefold purpose: to prevent damaging propaganda, to impress on the industry the ethical responsibility

---

19   Edmonds, Andy (January 1991). *Frame-Up!: The Untold Story of Roscoe "Fatty" Arbuckle*. New York, NY: William Morrow & Company. ISBN 0-688-09129-6.

of its workers, and to prevent adverse government legislation. (With Zukor buying up cinema houses, there was also controversy about studio theatre-owning monopolies). It fell upon Lasky as the industry spokesman, to arrange an invitational dinner at the Ambassador Hotel to present 'General' Will Hays to 800 of the industry's leading executives. Hays had already cited Arbuckle as an example of the poor morals in Hollywood. The following day, 2,000 studio workers assembled at the Hollywood Bowl where again, Lasky introduced Hays and discussed the plan to institute a code governing film subject matter. It was to be controlled by the newly formed Hays Office. Morality clauses were injected into all future contracts, and under Lasky's guidance, Will H. Hays became head of the new Motion Pictures Producers and Distributors Association (MPPDA), Hollywood's own self-censor board.

Too young at twelve to follow the sordid tales in the press, Jesse was trying his hand at poetry and writing a few stories—an endeavor that was strongly encouraged by both parents. Jesse now had a little brother, Bill, and a new sister, Bessie, born on October 11, 1922. Two new babies meant a series of governesses, something Jesse had not been subjected to.

Father wrote to son:

Nov. 8, 1922:

…Yesterday I wrote mother and complained because I hadn't a letter from you and I am sorry now that I complained, because when I got to the office this morning I found your Halloween letter … It is the best letter I think that you have ever written. We are going to publish the part of your letter about your adventures on Halloween night in Paramount Pep. Won't that be fine? It will be the first time, I guess, anything you have written has been published in a magazine … We are going to have a fine time when I get home. The first thing we are going to do is to plan to build the Outpost … I am glad you sleep on the porch with mother. Please take good care of her and keep your eye on Bill. …

From 1914 until well into the 1920s, Hollywood continued expanding. The handful of wooden bungalows tucked among the straggling orchards and pepper trees had been superseded by the stately mansions and Spanish haciendas of the moguls and stars. The simple wooden and stucco dwellings of the technicians, actors, extras, and various merchants who catered for them all, spread from Hollywood east, and south into downtown Los Angeles.

By 1917 the town was overcrowded and there were not enough places to house the actors pouring into Hollywood. Lasky and Sam decided to do something about it. They built a highly desirable fifty-four-unit apartment complex, the first multi-story building in Hollywood. It was Moorish in design and thoroughly modern inside. The Hillview Apartments at 6531 Hollywood Boulevard soon became home to stars like Mae Busch and Evelyn Brent,[20] who moved in and stayed. The building included a large lobby, a writing room, a ladies only room, garbage incinerators, automatic elevators, and a useful rehearsal space in the basement. The ground level also housed a speakeasy. According to director Douglas Carlton, 'Everybody that was anybody in the silent movie days lived there.'

In the 1920s, the Outpost Estates in the Hollywood Hills was the first luxury residential neighborhood. Many of the original houses around Outpost Drive have been preserved. General Harrison Grey Otis, owner of *The Los Angeles Times*, built a clubhouse there called The Outpost. It boasted one of the largest neon signs in the world, which at last count, still lies buried somewhere beneath the weeds. Lasky was interested in developing the surrounding area.

With scandals swept under the carpet, the early Hollywood film colony generally entertained at home, keeping private lives as private as possible. There were few places to go: the Montmartre in Hollywood and the Ship Café on the beach pier where one could look forward to a teacup full of prohibition booze. The unsophisticated convent girl Bessie (who now preferred to be called the more fashionable Bess) with babies under the watchful eye of a governess and nursemaid, was soaking up culture, occasionally traveling to Europe with Lasky and playing hostess to the glamorous newcomers he was importing from Europe.

In silent days, of course it didn't matter how squeaky your voice, or unintelligible your accent, it was all about how you looked. Alla Nazimova, Nita Naldi, the vampish Pola Negri, Percy Marmont (the British star of *Lord Jim* in 1925) all were exotic newcomers, and young Jesse was 'dragged away from his lead soldiers' to meet them all at the house parties. To him, Douglas Fairbanks and Antonio Moreno were heroes. But seeing Charlie Chaplin in street dress was a gigantic disappointment, and when Western star, William S. Hart, who taught him a 'quick draw', autographed a picture to him: 'To little Jesse…' he hid it away, mortified.

By the 1920s, Famous Players-Lasky was building deluxe movie palaces in England and France under the supervision of Al Kaufman, Zukor's brother-in-law. Lasky traveled to Europe regularly to check on their progress. A leading French architect specializing in 'moderne' design was hired to create them, but when it came to picking a location for the Islington Studio in London, they accidentally chose a spot where heavy fog regularly settled when the rest of London was in sunshine. The inexplicable miasma that wafted through their sets adding an unintentional 'artistic' soft focus to many shots. Actresses' skirts flared because of huge fans attempting to keep the fog at bay. In director George Fitzmaurice's[3] *Three Live Ghosts* in 1922, the haze certainly added a ghostly effect. The $15 a week prop man on that and other films was a young Alfred Hitchcock.

---

20 This information was recently confirmed in *Evelyn Brent: The Life and Films of Hollywood's Lady Crook*, by Lynn Kear pub: July 30, 2009 pub: by Lynn Kear & James King.

No matter what problems he faced at the studio or personal pleasures he indulged in, Lasky was never too busy for that weekly letter to Jesse, and seeing to it that he had everything the son of a mega-rich producer could possibly desire. Sports were high on Lasky's list and dueling (as seen in Douglas Fairbank's films) had aroused Jesse's interest in fencing, so the proper equipment was duly sent. Lasky wrote in 1923:

Dear Jesse,

...By this time I guess you have your fencing shirt and I bet your fencing has improved...I guess you are pretty busy with your piano lessons, French lessons, and school. I hope you are catching up on your arithmetic....

P.S. Give Miss Mortonson our best regards. I hope you are helping her take care of Bill.

Miss Mortonson was the latest governess, and 'taking care' of little brothers can have many interpretations. Big brothers can sometime find their siblings an annoyance that must be dealt with. Jesse and young Bill Buckland spent their days playing with lead soldiers on a magnificent miniature battlefield with trees, hillocks, and houses that Bill's father, scenic artist Wilfred, had built for them at the studio and moved to a trestle table in Jesse's large playroom.

Jesse later noted, 'There was however, a real enemy.' Brother Billy, at the age of three would charge into the room like a relentless juggernaut, and with one plump arm, could sweep away an entire battlefield. Since the children were not allowed to lock doors, the three-year-old could not be barred from the playroom. Finally, the two friends decided that something must be done to end Billy's interference. On his next visit, they seized the child's arms and legs and dragged him screaming to the window.

'Each holding an ankle, we dangled brother Bill above the rose garden two stories below', Jesse recalled with wickedly unabashed glee. They hauled the screaming child back in, released him, and made him promise never to lay one destructive finger on their soldiers ever again. When Bessie and the governess rushed in, they found Billy sobbing on the playroom floor, unable to tell what had happened because he hadn't learned to talk well enough to explain. But in Bill's autobiography he recalled the incident, which not surprisingly, left him with a permanent fear of heights.

The culprits thought their enemy vanquished until one day Billy reappeared in the playroom. The older boys were just about to attack him when from beneath his jacket the cheerful three-year-old produced a lively writhing snake, so big he could hardly get his chubby fists around it. Jesse and Bill Buckland could only watch in terror as the toddler, waving the reptile at his torturers, proceeded to knock down three detachments on their battlefield with his wriggling snake.

Billy had found a weapon, a hobby, and a career. All his life he would be devoted to animals—including reptiles, bugs, birds, and insects—and would delight in keeping as loveable pets, creatures that would make his brother's skin crawl.

Lasky had gone on several enthusiastic expeditions with the famous Western author Zane Grey, who traveled with his own band of cowboys. With the help of Grey, the producer purchased a few snakes for Billy along with the entire writings of the author for the studio. He received a letter from Grey in Long Key, Florida complaining about how Grey's books were being filmed and entreating Lasky to personally oversee the filming of his works. From New York, Lasky wrote to his eldest son.

March 3, 1923
Dear Jesse,

...You know Zane Grey is a famous author who writes outdoor books. He is also a wonderful hunter, fisherman and explorer. Some time ago he was on a bear hunt and captured two little bear cubs which he named Teddy and Topsy. He is making me a present of the bear cubs, and we will build a bear pit at The Outpost just like the one in Central Park, and you can have the bears for pets. Isn't that great?

I am enclosing Mr. Grey's letter which you can read. The last paragraph tells about the bears. give it to me when I get home.

Lasky had marked the last paragraph, intent on taking advantage of Grey's offer.

FLORIDA EAST COAST HOTEL CO.
Flagler System
LONG KEY FISHING CAMP
L. P. SCHUTT. Manager
LONG KEY, FLA.,
February 13, 1923
Mr. Jesse Lasky,
Hollywood, Calif.

Dear Mr. Lasky:

You may recall that some years ago Hays Hunter made a picture out of my book 'Border Legion', and starred Blanche Bates. It was a failure. If I remember I got a few thousand dollars on sale of book, and retained five percent interest in profits.

Now Hunter is going to reissue the picture. I tried to buy back the book, but he wouldn't sell it. He made me an offer for my five percent interest.

I don't like this reissue possibility. But I cannot help it. Frankly, however, I can't see that it would cause us any harm, if they ever do.

The magnificence and richness and reality of my pictures as will appear under the Lasky title will create what my audience has always clamored for. Your 'Covered Wagon' picture makes all these westerns pale into insignificance, and it is so because of the strong and beautiful action against the natural outdoor background. If all my books that have been filmed could be reproduced this way it would be as if they had never been filmed at all.

I like very much the way Mr. Hubbard is starting on *To the Last Man*. It will make a great picture. I will be home last of March or early in April, and want to help all I can. You know, I suppose, that I intend to go to the Tonto Basin of Arizona with the company, and start them right with my men, horses, locations, etc. We had better not begin work down there until early May, as we have to go up high on the Rim, and there will be some snow left, and probably scant grass for the horses.

Why cannot you go down there with us for a few days? I will promise you a shot at a wild turkey gobbler - and a bear chase -and, by the way, I am going to make you a present of my bear cubs Teddy and Topsy, You will have some fun taking care of them. But they would fit in well at your studio.

With. best regards, I am
Faithfully,
(signed) Zane Grey

Zane Grey's letter referred to Lasky's film of *The Covered Wagon*. In a vote conducted by editors and critics of *Film Daily*, of the ten best motion pictures of 1923, *The Covered Wagon* had ranked number one. It was a great personal triumph for the producer and it might never have happened if his New York secretary, Jean Cohen, had not given him a copy of Emerson Hough's novel to read on the train, where he did most of his reading. When he changed trains in Chicago from the Twentieth Century to the Santa Fe, he had three uninterrupted days to plan projects. As the train chugged and puffed through the Kansas prairies, New Mexico, and Arizona, the story of the pioneers who had crossed those plains to reach California came to life for Lasky.

Gazing out of his train window, he realized he was looking at the same vista his grandfather had seen in 1848 from his unwieldy Conestoga wagon and he 'became a child at my grandfather's knee' remembering the stories he had been told. He knew *The Covered Wagon* was a movie that had to be made—and he had to be the person to make it. As Lasky turned the pages, he visualized it in filmic terms: four hundred wagons crossing the Platt River—a buffalo hunt, a prairie fire—and Indians attacking the circled wagon train. This was a drama of America's beginnings as a nation that stretched from coast to coast.

Lasky put the book into the normal channels for development of a new picture, turning it over to his chief supervisors, B. P. Schulberg and Hector Turnbull, whose job it was to return a schedule with proposed cast, director, and budget estimates. He was to make whatever changes he felt appropriate and send it on to Zukor for approval and/or comments from the New York execs and sales department. The revised schedule would then go back to Schulberg and Turnbull to be put into production.

But when Lasky saw the proposals, he was disturbed to see whom his supervisors had selected as director. True, George Melford could bring in a picture on budget, but Lasky distrusted his taste, based on the fact that the man wore a large elk's tooth dangling from his watch chain. He was more alarmed to see Mary Miles Minter assigned as Molly Wingate, the hardy pioneer heroine. He considered Minter of 'the brittle china-doll school of acting' and felt a Rolls Royce would have suited her better than a Conestoga wagon.

'I'm shelving the picture', he told his two executives.

Schulberg was delighted, until he heard Lasky's further plans. 'But I'm not taking it off the list permanently, Ben. This movie is going to be the greatest show we've ever made. But not the way it's set up now.'

Schulberg was staggered and reminded Lasky that he'd already assigned the director. 'Send him to me', the producer told him.

Lasky quickly talked Melford out of the assignment, promising him instead the next drawing-room drama. He also persuaded the delicate Miss Minter out of the lead with an offer of a showcase role swathed in Paris gowns. Then he sent for a young character actor who had already directed some 28 films for them. Furthermore, James Cruze was said to have real 'Indian' blood.

Cruze read the book overnight and his enthusiasm was explosive. His Danish parents had traveled to Utah in a covered wagon. He knew the territory well—had ridden horseback over much of it. He even knew where to find the buffalo. For the role of Will Banyon, Cruze suggested a matinee idol who was on the skids, J. Warren Kerrigan, and Lois Wilson, a young lady, as yet untried in an important role, for Molly Wingate.

But even with 'less expensive' actors, filming and locations were going to run high. Fingers crossed, Lasky sent the revised budget to Zukor and the estimating department in New York. A puzzled Zukor telephoned to tell him he must have made a typographical error. 'You've missed a decimal point, Mr. Lasky!' *The Covered Wagon* was now scheduled at a budget of $500,000—ten times the original budget.

'No, Mr. Zukor', Lasky assured him. 'The figures are correct.'

There was a ponderous silence.

'But Mr. Lasky, don't you realize? The Western is dead!'

'Mr. Zukor', Lasky told him quietly, '*they* don't understand—but you will. This picture is more than just a Western. Why, it's—it's an epic!'

'An epic?' Zukor queried. It was a word with which he was unfamiliar.

'E-P-I-C', Lasky replied and waited for the familiar Zukor pause—which was followed by a calm-voiced reply.

'An epic, eh? Well, that's different. You go ahead and I'll take care of the sales department.' Lasky was aware that had Zukor not been in the driver's seat the picture would never have been made.

Their chief location would be in Snake Valley, Nevada. The prop department began combing the countryside for wagons, which were bought or rented and transformed into covered wagons. They hired oxen and horses and an entire buffalo herd. The principals in the company including J. Warren Kerrigan, Lois Wilson, Ernest Torrence, and Alan Hale. There was a crew of 127 and 750 Native Americans working for eight weeks in a 500 tent camp for the first location. They moved on to Antelope Island in the Great Salt Lake for the buffalo hunt.

When he saw the first rough-cut screening, Lasky was dissatisfied with the ending and ordered a rewrite. This meant reassembling the entire company and rebuilding the wagon train in Sonora, California for some snow scenes. *The Covered Wagon's* final budget was an astounding $782,000.

It was advertised in 1923 as: THE COVERED WAGON - AN EPIC!

The term became lingua franca for the most expansive, expensive of Hollywood's future films, and this movie repaid its investment from the first two theatres that screened it to become one of the biggest money-makers of the silent period.

The leading drama critic and a serious playwright of the day, Robert Sherwood called it, 'The one great American epic that the screen has produced.' It lifted James Cruze to the ranks of screen immortals. And the Western hadn't even met John Wayne yet.

(*The Covered Wagon* on the internet http://fan.tcm.com/video/james-cruze-the-covered-wagon-1923-early-scenes)

There was trouble brewing in Paramount. That same year Cecil had begun preparations for his own epic, the black and white silent version of *The Ten Commandments*, and with his usual attention to detail, he'd purchased two magnificent coal black, perfectly matched horses to draw the Pharaoh's chariot. The pair had cost a hefty $2,500. Since the East Coast had set the film's budget at $700,000, Zukor expected the West Coast Vice President to rein in the director. It would have been easier to rein in DeMille's horses.

When Lasky tried to persuade his friend to curtail spending in the face of Zukor's mounting alarm, Cecil blasted him with, 'What do you want me to do? Stop now and release my film as 'The Five Commandments'?'

DeMille wired Zukor that as evidence of his own faith in the picture, he would waive any guarantee other than his regular weekly salary. He assured Zukor that it was going to be the biggest picture ever made. Zukor gave him a cautious go-ahead, but when the mounting costs reached $1,000,000, the moneymen decided that DeMille's extravagance was ruining the company. 'Horses for courses', it was not.

THE COVERED WAGON

The director, whose ego had inflated exponentially with every success, rashly faced Zukor with an offer to buy back his picture and film it as an independent for the $1,000,000—although, he wasn't actually sure he could raise such a sum.

Because he was absolutely certain Cecil could not raise the money, Zukor accepted his offer. But Cecil had one powerful card to play. The Italian banker A. P. Giannini, founder of Bank of America, had become an enthusiastic supporter of the director's work and was prepared to back DeMille all the way. It was the start of a profitable lifetime's business relationship between the two men.

Cecil's budget eventually reached $1,475,836.93, but the picture grossed $4,168,798.38 which, under the terms of DeMille's contract meant that his share was as large as, or even larger than Paramount's.

Lasky was aware that the DeMille battle between East and West Coast would have to be resolved, but for the moment believing the axiom that more business is done on the golf course than in the boardroom, he had hired a pro who often traveled with him to improve his game. Despite his complex life, he had begun writing regularly to his eldest son and hoping to interest his son in the game, noting in a letter . . . 'I played golf Sunday and made a score of 111. I did the second nine holes in 51, which is a record for me and I won four dollars. . . .' His words fell on deaf ears. Jesse was never to enjoy competitive games with his father. He had become a stamp collector and had bought an antique weapon, both of which got him interested in history—and research—and he continued to be a collector all his life.

For the moment a lot had been happening to young Jesse. On a summer visit to Europe with his mother he had contracted a mild case of polio and was unable to walk for several months. To pass the time in bed and encouraged by Bess, he began writing verse. Lasky hired a Doctor Rideau who prescribed physiotherapy and exercise, not poetry. Convinced that a horse would be the best thing for his son when he could finally take a few steps, Lasky hired a cowboy-cum-bodyguard whom he had met on several expeditions with Zane Grey. Chester Wortley was to become Jesse's constant companion for several years. Lasky sent Jesse and Chester Wortley to the Paramount ranch (recently purchased for outdoor filming) where Jesse was to learn to ride—with the idea that it would strengthen his legs. It did.

A year after Bill was born, Bess gave birth to a daughter whom they named Bessie. But since mother Bessie was now called Bess, it was decided to give the girl a more modern name and she was officially Betty from then on. The truth was that the three Lasky children were seeing even less of either parent. While Lasky and Bess were in New York, her younger sister, Louise, often stayed in California with the children and the current governess Miss Mortonson, and of course, the staff of twelve servants.

Lasky always kept his son informed about his mother's growing success with her painting. When he was older, he would keep the young man up to date about studio matters:

JESSE, CHESTER WORTLEY AND HORSE

November 13, 1923
Dear Jesse,

...I guess you were surprised, to get my wire that mother's picture had been accepted, to be hung at the National Academy. She is simply delighted and we should be very proud of her. I am going with her on Saturday, which is the day they call 'varnishing day', when all the artists whose works have been accepted gather to criticize the pictures...We thought it was a fine idea for you to fix up the interior of the Beach House with your weapons and turn it into a sort of hunting lodge. Chester and you can do anything you want with the house....

Lasky's first beach house was a small bungalow located at 409 Palisades Beach Blvd, Santa Monica. As Paramount expanded, the bungalow was replaced with the Santa Monica beach house at 609 Ocean Front which, through the next few years kept growing until it had twelve, then twenty rooms and a dozen servants. Lasky kept a chauffeur and huge Locomobile and a Rolls-Royce town car in New York and a sleek, pearl-gray Packard Special racing car, a maroon Rolls-Royce roadster with cozy rumble seat for two and a huge Fiat with Bosch Magneto gold-plated fixtures and rosewood dashboard, all garaged either at the beach house or the town house in Hollywood.

From then on, there was no time when the Laskys did not have houseguests at the beach. As a youth, Jesse remembered the free-flow of famous writers: Fannie Hurst, Rebecca West, Virginia Woolf, Louis Bromfield, and British writer G.B. Stern, who carried a walking stick that she told Jesse had belonged to Lord Byron. He remembered her having wild arguments in the swimming pool with Joseph Hergesheimer, the American novelist who had just sold one of his books to Lasky. Not known for good looks, Lasky described Hergesheimer as 'one tooth and a pencil'; a sharp contrast to the handsome F. Scott Fitzgerald, the alcoholic voice of the jazz age. The beach house was like a hotel with celebrities constantly streaming through it. Today, it is a real hotel.

Years later, brother Bill recalled life at the beach house and the parties. 'Many times, Betty and I were actually removed from the house to the Miramar Hotel in Santa Monica, where we shared a guest bungalow for a night or a week with Mademoiselle Branche (their new French governess). I remember feeling unwanted during these times. However, on most occasions we did remain at home in the isolation of the children's wing ... people would stay over from the parties, and the multi-colored guest rooms were always ready for them. I remember Mother telling an amusing story. After certain parties, she would see the same familiar faces day in and day out at breakfast. She didn't know most of the people. One day she whispered to Dad, 'That little semi-bald fellow with the pink cheeks down at the end of the table—he looks important. Is he a friend of yours?'

'No', Dad answered. 'I thought he was a friend of yours.'

'No', she responded. 'I never saw him before in my life.'

Bess didn't want to leave New York where she was now studying with several well-known painters, so Lasky bought a huge apartment for his wife to furnish with antiques acquired on her increasingly frequent solo trips to Europe. The two smaller children and governess, Miss Mortonson, were brought to New York to be with her. Jesse, now separated from the entire family and learning self-reliance, was rattling around the huge beach house and still regaining his health at the Paramount ranch with Chester. His father wrote:

November 13, 1923
Dear Jesse,

... Miss Mortonson has a double carriage for Billy and Bessie (*her name not yet changed to Betty*) and they certainly look cute going down Fifth Avenue. Everybody thinks they are twins they look so much alike when they are wrapped up in the carriage ... I am anxious to hear about your first horseback ride with Chester ... Hope everything is going well with you at school, and.

that you are keeping up the treatment with Rideau. We all send love to you and kindest regards to Chester.

Lasky needn't have worried. At thirteen, Jesse was becoming an excellent horseman. But unknown to his father, that year was the only time that Jesse was to appear in a film. Douglas Fairbanks was shooting *The Thief of Bagdad* at United Artists Studio on Santa Monica Boulevard and film extras were being paid five dollars a day. Jesse had seen a flintlock pistol in a junk shop that he coveted, but it was priced at thirty dollars. Although arithmetic was never his strong point, he figured if he could work as an extra for six days, that the pistol could be his. Extras in those early days were a motley crew and his father would definitely not have approved of such rag-tag employment, so it would have to be kept secret.

Jesse joined the long queue of would-be extras, and a sorry lot they were. To his delight, he was picked by the assistant director and bustled off to the makeup and costume tent. Dark body-makeup and a turbaned costume changed him into an Arab boy. Carefully avoiding a man who offered to teach him to swallow fire, he made it through the first day un-scorched. On the second day, he was singled out by the director, Raoul Walsh, to lead a camel across the stage for one of Fairbank's big action scenes. The floor was so shiny and spotless that between shots, anyone on set wore felt over-slippers. Jesse and his camel were to provide background 'atmosphere'. The assistant director warned, 'Hey you! kid! Don't let that camel crap on the set!' So with his eyes on both ends of the animal, Jesse led the ungainly creature around like a reluctant dragon.

Douglas Fairbanks was noted for doing his own stunts. He was to make a difficult escape from the bad guys across a row of gigantic jars running the length of the stage. Each jar had been spring-loaded to catapult Fairbanks to the next jar. Walsh's assistant shouted 'Camera!' and as Fairbanks executed his series of perfect leaps, the camel executed a series of imperfect droppings.

Walsh turned his wrath on the camel boy. Fairbanks, who suddenly recognized Jesse beneath the brown makeup began to roar with laughter. He announced that since his own son, Doug Jr., was at that moment starring in Lasky's film, *Stephen Steps Out,* Jesse Jr. deserved better than playing nursemaid to a camel in his picture. Walsh saw the chance for publicity, and photographers were signaled over. Photos of Jesse and Fairbanks were sped to the Bulldog Edition of the Los Angeles Examiner. Headlines read: DOUGLAS FAIRBANKS JR. WORKS FOR LASKY. LASKY JR. WORKS FOR FAIRBANKS.

Reading this news next day in his office, Lasky was not amused. He called Hector Turnbull to put the lid on the story and Hector promptly squelched the press. But it was to have repercussions for Jesse. Both his parents were heading for Washington D.C., and not returning home as planned, having bigger fish to fry, as his letter to Jesse explained:

DOUGLAS FAIRBANKS AND LASKY

November 20, 1923
Dear Jesse,

…We are going to Washington to see Mother's picture the opening day of the Corcoran Gallery, and they are arranging for us to meet President Coolidge at the White House … It looks now as if it will be impossible for us to leave New York for Hollywood until December 26th, the day after Christmas. In that event you and Chester will have to make some plans to spend your vacation as you would enjoy it most, and I will arrange for your Christmas presents to be in Hollywood by Christmas eve, you may be sure … I am afraid, old fellow, on account of your school, you won't be able to go with us … I will be more disappointed than you are.…

'To go with us' meant on a river trip that young Jesse would not have been disappointed to miss. He was fast learning what these adventures entailed, and feared that his father, with his usual gung ho attitude, would take too many risks with both their lives. The intrepid explorer was happily now wealthy enough to indulge in any daredevil whim he chose. Once, he allowed himself to be lowered on lassoes by his trusted cowboys, making him the first (and possibly only) man ever to descend by rope 309 feet down the arch of the Rainbow Natural Bridge in Utah. These 278 feet of salmon-red Navajo sandstone arch over Bridge Canyon are located some twelve miles northwest of Navajo Mountain in the deep canyon country of southern Utah. A dirt road goes part of the way. There is no connecting road and one has to hike the rest of the way.

Lasky also made three expeditions down the Colorado River when it was still uncharted territory. On one ocean-going expedition, he landed on the island of Tiburón off the coast of Mexico and barely got out alive with young Jesse, who was on most all of the madcap adventures, whole-heartedly not by choice, although he never voiced his disinclination. The last thing he wanted his father or himself to think him, was a wimp.

Lasky was the first white man to lead an expedition down the Rio de la Balsas in lower Mexico, all the way to the sea. For this risky experience, he had 'rapid water' boats specially built and transported hundreds of miles by trucks, to be shouldered the rest of the way by his team of cowboys. On trips to high lakes in the Sierra Mountains, canoes were carried by mule-back. But for the moment, his plans had changed and by the 3rd of December the news was:

December 3, 1923
Dear Jesse,

   ... we thought it would be a good plan for you and Chester to go to Albuquerque and return on the train with us. You will get on the California Limited, at Albuquerque on Christmas morning at 10.30 o'clock ... We will have a fine Christmas on the train—lots of surprises for everybody ... By getting home on the 26th I feel sure I can plan to start the river trip so that we leave Hollywood Sunday, December 30th, and have decided that you, Jesse, can make the trip with us, even if you have to miss a couple of days school....

Jesse carefully hid his anxiety concerning the river trip and put on an eager face. But train rides were a different matter. On the steam trains that shunted the Hollywood moguls back and forth between their playgrounds in New York and Hollywood, they traveled in style, often adding their own private railway carriages. Lasky and Bess changed trains from New York in Chicago, and picking up the California Limited, stopped over at the Harvey House Station Hotel in Albuquerque to meet his son. So Jesse was to see his family at Christmas after all, and that Christmas morning turned out to be a memorable day in Jesse's more than ordinary youth.

As the train sped them to California, Lasky rolled back the door to a private carriage and admitted his son to a spectacular sight. Not visions of sugarplums, but to Jesse, it was a train-ride to Heaven. Lasky had bought an entire collection of antique weapons at an auction, including a silver engraved Colt revolver that had once belonged to Wild Bill Hickok. These treasures were carefully displayed on the walls of the carriage. As the train puffed its way through a snowy landscape, the dumbstruck boy gingerly ran a finger over each pistol until, at Lasky's encouragement, he carefully took one down from its mount. The few flintlocks he had already acquired on trips to an antique store with Uncle Hector were soon to make room at the beach house for this plunder. They were treasured by Jesse and hung on some wall wherever he lived until the day he went off to war in the South Pacific, shortly after Pearl Harbor.

February 12, 1924
Dear Jesse,

...I think Mother wrote you about our trip on the Mississippi River, and how the guide pointed out the old wood burning stern-wheel river steamer which we used in Magnolia, the picture you saw with us at Uncle Hector's the night before we left. We found the South very interesting and the next time we cross the country together I am going to see that you get a chance to visit New Orleans.

The film he refers to as *Magnolia* was based on a play by Booth Tarkington. The name was changed before the 1924 release to *The Fighting Coward*. The director was James Cruze of *The Covered Wagon* fame. It starred Mary Astor, Noah Beery, and Ernest Torrence. Richard Arlen, who was to become a star, appeared in an uncredited minor role.

At home in New York, where Bess was spending much more time, Dody was the new nursemaid for the young ones—and there was another dangerous expedition that Jesse could look forward to. Since Lasky's attention was on making movies, not on world affairs, he was not to know that this lifestyle was about to come to an abrupt end.

When he was in Hollywood, Jesse was spending much of his time on his own at the Highland house with Chester, and with tutors because he had managed to get expelled from one of the only two private schools in town. To his chagrin after being barred the first, he was sent to the other, The Hollywood School for Girls. This would have been totally mortifying except that a few other boys were students there already—Doug Fairbanks Jr., Joel McCrea, Noah Beery Jr., and Jesse's best friend, Bill Buckland. William DeMille's daughters, Margaret and Agnes (who would become a famous choreographer) were there too, and Cecil's daughter, Cecilia and Jesse's cousin, Ruth (Goldwyn/Lasky).

With Bessie by his side, Lasky often spent a few days at his partner's great estate outside of New York, which he notes to Jesse.

February 25, 1924
Dear Jesse

...We went out to Mr. Zukor's farm. The ground was covered with hard snow and we got out some bobsleds and had a fine time sliding down the hills of the golf course. I must say that winter here is very nice and winter sports are a lot of fun. Mother and I miss you very much and we will be very glad to get home.

I was talking to Douglas Fairbanks yesterday and we are going to see his picture in a couple of weeks. I wonder if I will be able to find you in it....

They did find Jesse in the movie, leading his camel. And many years later (1979) when Jesse and I went to the Victoria and Albert Museum in London, England to see an early film exhibition mounted by Kevin Brownlow, the film historian and preservationist, he featured among other treasures of Hollywood's past, a small movie screen about a foot wide, running on a loop showing Fairbank's jar-jumping sequence from *The Thief of Bagdad*. As Fairbanks leaped down the row of jars, behind him, to our amazement, there was young Jesse leading his camel across the stage. Kevin had been completely unaware that the camel boy was Jesse and scarcely believed it. (Recently, I saw a screening of the film on television and that scene was missing. I wondered if Kevin had clipped the only copy?

March 10, 1924
Dear Jesse,

...We saw Griffith's new picture which is called 'America' last night, and I want you to see it as soon as it comes to Los Angeles. It shows all the stirring incidents leading up to the Revolution and fight for American independence, and one of several historic characters is that of Washington. It shows Paul Revere's ride which is thrilling and the best thing in the picture...Just found an Indian-head penny in my pocket and will put it in this letter....

The producer was now having 'temperamental star' problems with Rudolph Valentino who, counseled by his wife, Natacha Rambova, had refused to make any of the pictures offered him for several years, until finally Paramount was forced to terminate his contract. But those early films had been so successful that Lasky was determined to find another smoldering Latin lover.

One night in 1924, he and Bess were dining at the Cocoanut Grove, amused by an amateur dance contest. Bess pointed out that the dancer with the number 19 on his back had the attention of all the females in the room and easily won first prize. Lasky agreed the fellow was certainly handsome with a steamy Latin smolder about him. Assuming that any handsome man in town was an actor, he invited him to the studio the next day.

RICARDO CORTEZ

His name was Jack Crane, he was an actor, and he was waiting for the producer when he arrived. As Lasky led him into his private office, he noted the eyes of every woman in the business office were on him.

After a fruitful interview, Lasky explained to Crane, 'We've lost Valentino, and we'd like to replace him. You're the right type, but Jack Crane is no name for a Latin lover. We'd have to change it.'

'I don't care what you call me', Jack Crane smiled, 'if only you call me.' He'd already changed it from Jacob Krantz.

'Help yourself to a cigar', Lasky offered, pointing to a box of Ricardo cigars. His glance paused on the label. 'And you may as well help yourself to a name. Ricardo will do as well as any.' Lasky mentally combed the alphabet for a surname and came up with Cortez.

Given the Cinderella treatment, Ricardo Cortez became a minor star in the 20s. But neither he nor anyone else could ever replace Valentino. The producer was first to admit, 'That throne remained forever empty.' For the moment, Lasky found a minor domestic problem to solve. Jesse was still a boy with an ordinary boy's interests when on one hot summer day he and his pal, Bill Buckland, were hard at work building a couple of coasters at 7209 Hillside Avenue. They intended to race down steep La Brea Avenue to pepper-tree-lined Hollywood Boulevard. Their endeavors were interrupted by the arrival of Lasky with a command: Douglas Fairbank's son, Doug Jr. would be coming to visit them the following morning and Jesse and Bill Buckland were to invite him to be one of their gang.

Tight-lipped, the boys sneaked a look at each other and frowned. Doug Jr. was a year older than Jesse and intimidating. He was an actor. They were outclassed.

'What's the problem?' Lasky demanded.

Jesse knew his father would expect an important reason so he explained how he and Bill had been working all summer on the coasters and that the very next day they were going to have their first race. Naturally, as much as they would like to play with Doug, with all his acting and everything he wouldn't have time to build a coaster, would he? So naturally his father could see why Doug shouldn't come that day. Maybe some other day.

Lasky considered the matter for a moment. He might have been talking to one of his supervisors about casting a star. 'I'll pass on the coaster problem to Doug's father', he said judiciously. 'But you can both rest assured, tomorrow Doug Jr. will be joining you.'

The next day, the two craftsmen dragged their coasters to the top of La Brea with a hasty look around. No sign of Doug. They were about to launch themselves down the slope when a sputtering cough! cough! cough! came chugging up the hill. To their horror, it was a coaster, but not as Jesse and Bill knew one. This was more like a small automobile with an actual gas engine, and behind the wheel sat young Doug Jr., a friendly smile touching his already dashing features. It was the unlikely start of a beautiful friendship.

Summer was drawing to an end and it was almost time for Jesse to go back to The Hollywood School for Girls. The good part was he didn't have to. The bad part was, he was to be banished to a 'safe' boarding school as far away from show biz as possible with no chance of being cast in another film—with or without a camel. He was being sent to Blair Academy, an expensive preparatory school for boys in New Jersey, not too far from New York, where he would be looked after with some discipline, not by a cowboy and servants. The film executive now owned a large apartment in New York at 910 5th Avenue, and Pierce, the East Coast chauffeur, who sometimes also served as West Coast chauffeur, was always available to pick up Jesse and take him into New York for special events. Bess was spending most of her time in New York, and Bill and Betty had governesses and quarters of their own in the vast apartment.

The following week when Jesse tearfully opened his suitcase to pack, he discovered that it contained a flintlock pistol he had wanted to buy, a present from his much-loved Uncle Hector. Jesse always credited Blanche's writer-husband with starting him on his long and hectic writing career.

Both parents accompanied him to Blair Academy. Jesse, now in his teens, was beginning to hate being called 'Junior' and asked if they might just call him Jess. A letter followed the next day and the letters became a lifetime habit. In these early letters, I have chosen only highlights.

May 14th, 1924
My dear Jess,

You will notice I left the 'e' off your name. Well, old fellow, it was pretty tough leaving you at school, and Mother cried a little when our car drove away, but I watched you and I thought you behaved like the real good sport you are.

It seems to me that Blair Academy is a fine school, and I like the looks of the boys very much. I think your roommate Bill Champ is going to be all right and Joe Swarts is a fine boy. By the time you receive this letter you will know which one you like best.

I got up bright and early this morning and went right to the sporting goods store and ordered you a peach of a racket - 13 ounces in weight, and also had the racket put in a press and got a canvass case for it; also three new fast tennis balls. I have had the racket, press and canvas initialed so you won't lose them ... we are going to take Joseph and you with us and spend Saturday night and Sunday in the mountains at a summer resort nearby, and Pierce will take Joseph and you back to school on Sunday....

Lasky even had one of his writers who had been to a boarding school write to Jesse on how to get ahead. It is not certain whether Jesse took his advice. Lasky dictated this to his assistant, Randy Rogers.

May 19, 1924
Dear Jess,

... We will arrive next Saturday by motor and will come right to West Hall, so please be watching for us. As soon as the ball game is over, we will arrange for Joseph and you to go with us up in the mountains, to the Inn at Buck Hill Falls. We will have a nice weekend there, and get you back to school Sunday night....

Jesse was always encouraged to bring along a school friend. His father was delighted to entertain them. Like a general mapping every detail for his troops—obsessive at home as well as at the studio, Lasky always had staff who could carry out the minutiae. Bess was regularly traveling with him to Europe now, where Lasky checked on the European offices and sought new writing and acting talent. The letters flowed. Chester was always available in the West and more trips were being planned!

June 3, 1924
Dear Jess,

... Chester and Grandma Lasky will meet you at Pasadena. Chester and you will spend the night at the Beach House and the next day you can go with Chester to the ranch ... and everything is arranged for the Colorado trip....

Ten days later, Lasky wrote his son from Paramount Studio, France c/o Chester Wortley Esq., Brown, Kern County, California.

June 13, 1924
Dear Jesse

... Yesterday a friend of mine gave me several old swords and an old pistol to add to your collection ... you and Chester can meet me on my arrival in Hollywood. I suppose it will be necessary for you both to go ahead of me about a week to the starting place on the Colorado ... address me:
Ste. Ane. Fcse. des Films Paramount,
63 Avenue des Champs Elysees, PARIS.

Your loving, Dad

As Lasky became rich beyond his wildest imaginings, Bess was aware that he had strayed into the arms of at least one of the beautiful actresses who walked though his door. She considered divorce and confronted her husband. He did not deny dipping into the fleshpots, but pleaded she must stay for the sake of his position and the security it brought them both. And of course, for the children. He added that as long as they were discreet and maintained a strong family front, he had no objection to Bess having relationships of her own. She thought about it for a while and decided to accept the proposition. They mutually decided on separate bedrooms in all their homes.

In the 1920's, French and British liners transported their famous passengers in opulence, offering sumptuous suites, ornate lounges, elaborate dining rooms and, when sailing to Europe, the Laskys generally traveled in a two-bedroom suite with a private terrace. When the children were with them, they took adjacent quarters for their eldest son. The nanny shared a suite with the two small children.

In 1924 Lasky returned from France and Bess stayed in Paris beginning to design her own life. Searching for meaning in her high-octane world, Bess moved through a series of close relationships and discreet affairs that would include writer John Monk Saunders (author and screenwriter of *Wings*), the great violinist Jascha Heifetz, and sculptor Boris Lovet-Lorski.

Her eldest son later wrote, 'We were all rude invaders at Bess' personal court of musicians and poets, who drank pink champagne at her feet and complained about the vulgarity of the film business that made it all possible.' In her later years she spoke openly to Jesse and me about her lovers, telling us how John had written her poems and in Paris, Heifetz had scattered his bed with red rose petals when he took her to his hotel suite.

Bess had made friends in Paris among the artist colony. That year (before I was born) she met my aunt, a Rhodes Scholar studying painting in Paris. Rose Silver[21] was to become a lifelong friend, which I was not to discover until after Jesse and I were engaged. Bess often brought home drawings by artists she'd met who were, or would become famous in the not too distant future: Picasso, Pissarro, Dufy, Monet. On one trip to Paris, when Jesse was seventeen, she met the famous Japanese artist, Tsuguharu Foujita, who drew this portrait. Jesse was to get used to being alone in California for the summers with Chester. Lasky wrote from New York:

July 23, 1924
Dear Jesse

    ...you know of course that Mother remained in Paris to study her painting ...I will leave New York on August 2nd and will arrive in Hollywood on the 6th, and if you could meet me at the station it would be great. Having Chester with you will make it easy for us to arrange for the Colorado trip, and then after a few days you can go back to the ranch with Chester if you wish....

On October 4th Jesse was back at Blair and Lasky and was pleased to hear that his son had bought a football uniform and was playing guard on the blue team of West Hall. Jesse lost no time in sending members of the family photos of himself in his new togs. One, addressed to his sister Betty, assured her he would always be her friend. And he was.

---

21 Rose Silver (known also as Lisa Rhana) became a well known New York painter of ballet stars, who also designed many New Yorker covers.

FOUJITA'S DRAWING OF JESSE, AGE 17

For Jesse, being away from Hollywood illuminated his hometown with a new perspective. He was trying his hand at writing stories and had learned that his roommates and fellow students were thrilled to discover that his father could get them autographed pictures of some of the stars. He was suddenly in demand and Lasky was quick to oblige—but still in organizing mode.

October 8, 1924
Dear Jesse,

...I will keep the pictures of our motion picture stars to give you to take back with you, and Miss Cohen and I are hoping you have finished your story so she can read it on Saturday....

But Jesse's career as a purveyor of film-star photos was to be short-lived.

October 23, 1924

...I have decided to send you one more envelope of pictures, but they will be all, as I do not like the idea of your selling them. Mother will send you a box of fudge...I had to make a speech yesterday at our Convention, and talked for two hours and thirty minutes. How's that for a record for a long talk? Mother rides in the Park nearly every day now....

One can only wonder what Lasky found to talk about for so long. He counseled Jesse to write to uncles and aunts and arranged for his allowance of $3.00 to be sent to him regularly every Saturday.

October 29, 1924

...I received your letter with the press notices of the football game and I was glad to see your name in the line-up...When you come in we are going to take you to see Harold L's[22] picture *Hot Water*. It is the funniest picture I have ever seen and you will split your sides laughing at it. There will also be a football game which we will take you to see, so don't let anything prevent your coming and we will send Pierce for you...I am glad you are working on your story and you ought to surely have it finished by a week from Saturday, so you can bring it with you.

Lasky had his suits made in London's Savile Row on his frequent trips to England. He acquired pearl-grey spats and carried a blond Malacca cane with his initials on the gold top. With pince-nez clasped securely to his nose, he cut an impressive figure. He had hired a private athletic trainer who traveled with him, as well as the golf pro and an apparently sinister looking (according to Jesse) physiotherapist named Von Heim, who applied sadistic rubdowns to Lasky's expanding frame. 'Von is my hair shirt', he told his concerned son.

---

22 Harold Lloyd.

November 7, 1924
Dear Jesse,

...This is the first chance I have had to dictate a letter to you, as you know I was ill in bed a couple of days after you left... I think we will take you to the New York Hippodrome Thanksgiving night and to one of the big football games in the afternoon, probably the Army and Navy game... We received your report on your studies... Please try and get at least, 70.

Of next month's report card he notes:

...I just received your report for November and want you to know how pleased I am with it... You got 80% or better in every one of your studies. Your highest mark was 90% in History.

At least Jesse's history marks ranked high. Most of his adult life he was swamped with research for one historical project after another for the screen, from biblical epics like *The Ten Commandments* and *Samson and Delilah* to tales of the sea: *John Paul Jones* and *Reap the Wild Wind*, and those Canadian tamers of the wild in *Northwest Mounted Police*, and so many others. Years later, when Jesse was chief writer on one of the larger-scale movies for DeMille, he assured the director that the scene his boss was angrily waving about was historically correct in every detail. DeMille turned a beady eye on his young writer demanding loudly, 'Jesse, do you want me to be historically correct and boring? Use your imagination and give me some drama! DRAMA!'

For the moment, Lasky, bouncing back and forth between New York and Hollywood, this time without Randy to type for him, wrote in long hand over four pages.

Dec 5th 1924
The California Limited Santa Fe en route Thursday
Dear Jess,

... Well here I am, the second day out, en route to dear old Hollywood. It is snowing, a regular blizzard outside... I hope you do go in for wrestling. My trainer can give you some points on wrestling. North of 36 turned out to be a wonderful picture. You must see it, it is as grand as The Covered Wagon. If you ask Mr. Salisbury he will show it to you at the office... I am hoping you make the Honor-role.

North of 36 was a silent Western starring Noah Beery and Jack Holt, but was by no means as Lasky had suggested, as 'grand as *The Covered Wagon*'. However, it was one of Paramount's top hits that year and was significant in film history because the LH7 ranch held the largest herd of pure longhorns in the world, and the film is not only a drama based on Emerson Hough's novel but it is a document of the last real cattle drive in history.

The ranch and herd scenes had been planned to film at the Blakely and LH7 ranches west of Houston, but director Irvin Willat (who had replaced James Cruze) was so impressed with the location and the people, that he shot most of the film there. The film also boasts some early special effects. The crossing of the Red River was actually shot with cattle crossing a pond.

The next letter is of particular interest, Zane Grey being the most important Western writer of the period, and this incident being another animal drive—it is a rare piece of American history Lasky was trying to film and record.

Here is a photo of the original 4th page of the letter.

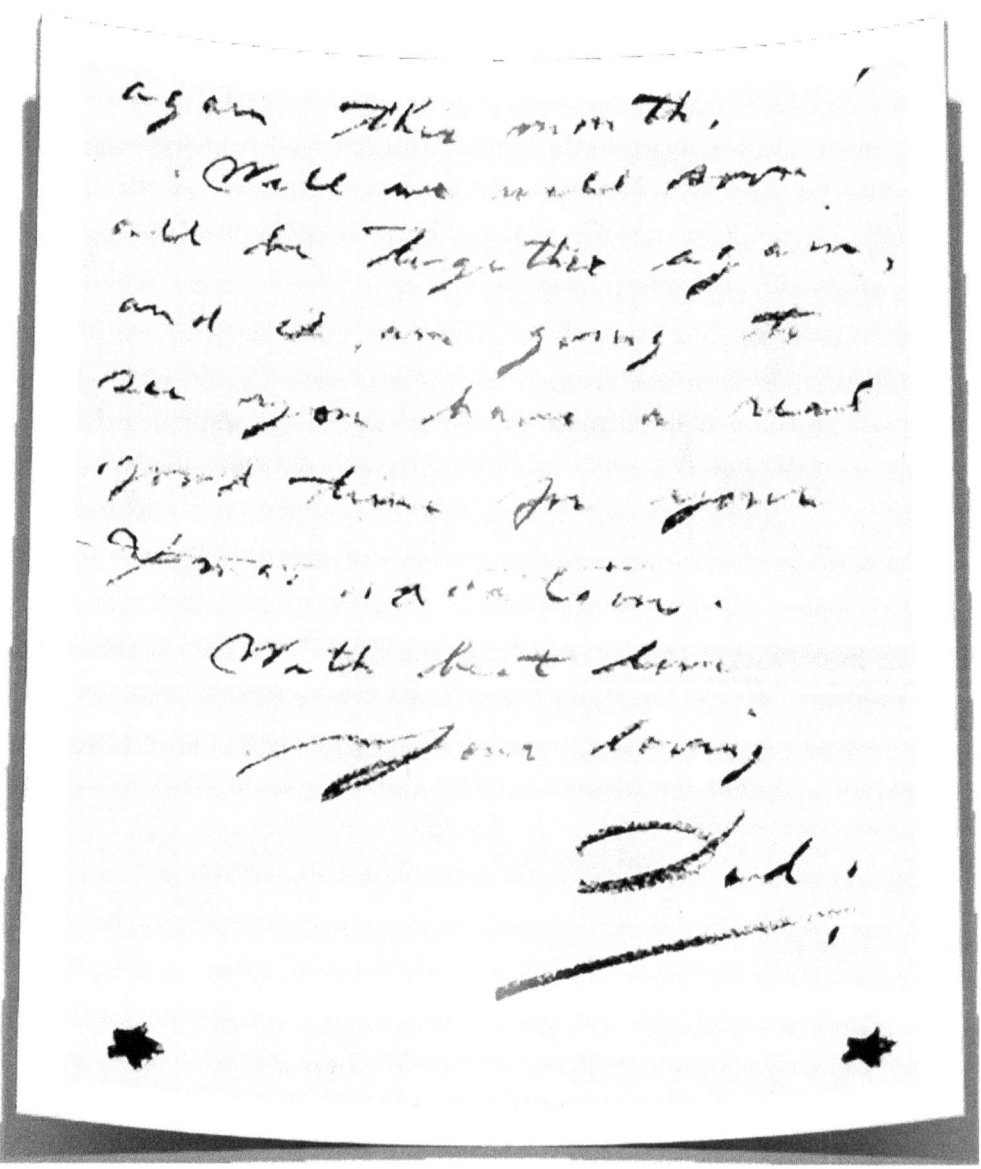

HANDWRITTEN LETTER

December 8, 1924
Dear Jess,

...To my surprise, I got the enclosed wire when I was on the train and so got out at Flagstaff and had five minutes' talk with Zane Grey and Chester. They were both about to start for the Colorado River with an outfit of ours from the studio, to take pictures of a drive of wild deer. It seems the feed in the Buckskin Mountains has been exhausted on account of the lack of rain and the forest rangers are going to drive the deer across the Colorado into the Mountains in Arizona where there is more feed.

It is the first time in history that they have attempted to round up wild deer, and they expect there will be nine or ten thousand in this drive. We are sending six cameramen to take pictures of the drive, and Zane Grey is writing a story around it which we will produce as a big picture called *The Deer Drive*...

Flagstaff, Arizona may not have become the home of the film industry possibly because of a sheep and cattle war, but those sheep and cattle ranchers continued encroaching into the pine forests of the rim, reducing the range of the burgeoning wild deer herds. By 1924 there was virtually nothing edible for the deer within eight feet of the ground. The formerly sleek, fat animals were reduced to staggering, starving zombies, and the game refuge had become an embarrassment to the government.

Zane Grey was a partner in this deer drive enterprise with Paramount Pictures who, at Lasky's instigation, were financing it for the exclusive film and story rights. Flagstaff resident George McCormick proposed to herd five to eight-thousand deer from the North Rim, down the Nankoweap and Horsethief Trails, swim them across the river, and bring them out on the Tanner Trail to the south side where the forests were healthy. Nearly one hundred Navajos and Paiutes were paid two dollars per day to herd the deer using shouts and cowbells. In addition, some fifty mounted cowboys were to ride herd.

On the North Rim, McCormick built a large V-shaped fence covered in miles of burlap to funnel the deer down into the Nankoweap trailhead. He readied his troops in the Kaibab Forest to drive the estimated ten-thousand to one-hundred-thousand mule deer towards Point Imperial.

Meanwhile, Zane Grey drove north with a crew (including his Japanese chef and his tailor) and established an elaborate base camp. 'I saw thousands of deer, most of which ran in small bands', wrote Grey. 'The ringing of bells, the yelling of the Indians did not seem to frighten them, but the approach of riders on horseback, trying to herd them, brought swift flight.'

Grey Hat Charlie, a Navajo Indian, when asked if the Indians ordinarily drove the deer, replied, 'Yes, drive deer, drive lots and lots of deer.' But when asked where the deer were driven, he swung his hand around and made a whistling sound, indicating every direction under the sun.

Summarizing the Great Kaibab Deer Drive, District Forester R. H. Rutledge called it, 'the most interesting failure I have witnessed'. Grey eventually wrote a book about it, *The Deer Stalker*. But it was one film of a Zane Grey book that was never made.

Bess was again in New York, not exactly tied to household duties, and Lasky wrote to arrange for his son and wife to be at the depot in New York when he got in from Hollywood—and for Jesse to be sure to:

December 12, 1924

... start training with Chris as soon as you reach New York. Enclosed is a letter which I just received from Chester, so you can see that he will be ready for you next summer.

Chris was Lasky's athletic trainer. Still concerned about his son's general fitness since his recovery from polio (although he had recovered completely), he wasn't going to let up on physical training. Home life was running smoothly but the storm clouds in New York were about to rain on DeMille's parade.

From the inception of the merger with Famous Players, DeMille had demanded his own separate unit. His contract allowed him to keep a small production staff on his payroll between pictures, and a handful of actors under personal contract. The terms of his deal also gave him 50% of the profits on his films, which had as mentioned, equaled Paramount's on his silent, *The Ten Commandments*. Zukor had been resentful of his director's imperious attitude, and in a curious way, his success. So on December 2nd, in a demand to downsize DeMille's financial power, Zukor asked Lasky to open discussions with the director about readjusting his contract to include specific restrictions. Sidney Kent, Zukor's right hand, wired Cecil from New York:

December 18, 1924
Dear Cecil,

IT IS NOT YOUR ADVANCE WE OBJECT TO AS MUCH AS THE ADDED EXPENSE CAUSED BY YOUR SEPARATE UNIT FROM WHICH WE FEEL WE GET NO RETURN COMMENSURATE WITH THE EXPENSE IT COSTS US. MR. ZUKOR FEELS THAT THIS MUST BE TAKEN OFF OUR BACKS....

Cecil had arrived in New York, planning to take his extended family—his wife and mistresses Jeanie Macpherson and Julia Faye along with their mothers and some of his staff—on a trip to Europe to begin work on *The Sorrows of Satan*. But Cecil's entourage did not sail. Instead, the company partners met for a showdown.

Sidney Kent, speaking for the company, told him, 'Cecil, you have never been one of us.'

Those words cut deeply into Cecil's soul. Always confident of his own potential, he made it clear that he would submit to no interference with his unit from Zukor. He was quite prepared to produce his pictures independently and he gave Zukor notice.

Cecil began the year of 1925 out of a job. If he had expected Lasky to intercede on his behalf, his friend remained silent at the parting of the second of the original partners. Lasky had not intervened because he knew that since *The Ten Commandments*, DeMille had found a strong supporter in the Bank of America's Mr. Giannini. He also knew that at this point in his career, DeMille would be much happier, and no doubt more successful, as an independent.

On January 10, 1925, DeMille set up his own production company. Now, only Lasky remained at Paramount of the original partnership—and he wondered when his turn would come.

SCENE THREE
1925 – 1929

THE PARAMOUNT GATE

January 12, 1925
Dear Jesse,

...I also arranged so that you get your dancing lessons during your March vacation...Next Saturday, I have to go south to Atlanta, Georgia. We are having a Convention of all our theatre managers down there and I have to make the usual speech...When you come home, be sure and bring your skates....

Although Lasky made time for such school matters, the producer was now deeply involved in filming the book *Peter Pan* by Sir James Barrie. The decision had been made to film it in the New York Astoria Studio that Lasky had built. The sales department was uneasy about the film's title, since Americans were not familiar with the book, but Sir James wisely refused to allow it to be changed. Years later, Jesse noted, 'The assumption of rural naiveté frequently stunted the mental growth of film production.'

For a change, the studio needed to find a girl without sex appeal (flat-chested enough to play an androgynous boy/sprite). Two girls were perfect: Mary Brian was in Hollywood in 1923 after winning a beauty contest, and Betty Bronson was in New York. Lasky could not decide between the two. As Sam Goldwyn might have said, he 'solved the solution'. Betty Bronson won the part of Peter Pan and Mary Brian played Wendy—which resulted in long-term contracts for both girls with Paramount. (Mary would later prove herself equal to the challenge of talkies—as the frontier heroine in her first all-talking movie, *The Virginian*, in 1929.)

Betty Bronson stirred Jesse's fifteen-year-old heart when he saw photos of her in costume. The following year when he met her in his father's office, he was smitten. As the juvenile blades at Blair Academy were allowed to take young ladies to tea dances, with his father's permission Jesse courageously asked his dream girl for his first ever date. She was a few years older but he was the boss' son. She accepted. He sent her gardenias along with a bit of his poetry. For such a momentous occasion, his father provided him with the trappings of a young man-about-town: his first tuxedo, a raccoon skin coat, and a derby. It was Prohibition, and although he didn't yet drink alcohol, Jesse felt an older and sophisticated actress like Betty Bronson would expect him to carry a hip flask. No problem. He slipped into his father's room where he knew there was a drawer full of silver flasks filled with bootleg hooch.

But on second thought—suppose his father saw the bulge, stopped him and took away the flask? Better safe than sorry, he slipped a second flask into his raccoon skin pocket and slapped on his derby. He had just about made it through the front door when his father appeared to wish him farewell. Seeing what he perceived as a suspiciously guilty expression on his son's suspiciously guilty face, he paused for a word.

'Jess, you're going out with a very fine young lady and probably an important future Lasky star. I would be sorry to think that you might under any circumstances

PETER PAN AND THE RACCOON-SKIN COAT

violate the laws of our country and carry a flask.' He held out a hand. 'If you have a flask, I would like to have it.'

Jesse handed one flask to his father, who patted his son's furry shoulder. Honor being satisfied, Jesse hurried out to his father's waiting Locomobile with Pierce at the wheel.

When Jesse offered the other flask to his date, the young star was shocked. He later remembered, '... An uncomplicated eighteen-year-old, she thought she had fallen into the hands of a degenerate sixteen-year-old.'

She refused to taste the stuff, and when he later gulped some down to prove how degenerate he really was, he became ill and had to send her home in a taxi. But all was not lost just yet. His father wrote the mortified Lothario.

January 26, 1925
Dear Jesse,

...Before Betty Bronson left for California she came in to say goodbye and asked for you and then left you her photograph, which we are sending to you by parcel post.... I just got back from the South and Mother is back from Atlantic City. We left Bill and Miss Mortonson in Atlantic City as the little fellow wasn't feeling very well and we hoped he would gain some weight there. However, Miss Mortonson and Bill will be back on Saturday also, so we will all be together once more... Monday morning we are sending you three big Ruben sandwiches and some cakes, so be on the lookout for them... Mother is going to Atlantic City today to visit Billy and Dody and is taking little Betty and Helinor with her....

I am still exercising every morning,
Is Zat So!
Is Zat So!
Is Zat So!

Best love,
Your loving Dad

Lasky flaunted teenage jargon to keep up with his son. Jesse was left with memories of his date with Betty Bronson and an autographed photo to console him, but he had a plan. On his next visit to his dad's office, he snatched a stack of Bronson's photos from the publicity department. Carefully copying her signature when he got back to school, he sold 'signed copies' for 50 cents each. There is no record of what he did with his riches.

February 14, 1925
Dear Jesse,

...I am just leaving for Palm Beach and Cuba and expect to have a fine vacation. I am to visit Morro Castle in Cuba. That is where they bottled up the Spanish fleet in the Spanish-American War ... I will drop you a line from Cuba and I wish you would write me a letter to Cuba. Enclosed is an envelope stamped and addressed so all you have to do is put your letter in it. ...

March 2 1925
Dear Jess,

...Well, here I am, back in New York again after a wonderful trip to Havana, First I want to congratulate you on making the honor roll with 84%. That is doing splendidly and I cannot tell you how pleased it made me when I heard the news. I was also surprised and pleased to learn that you had been made president of your class. ...

March 14 1925.
Dear Jesse,

...We are so glad Thursday is near. This is the longest time you have been away....I have some dandy pictures to show you, one in particular 'THE AIR MAIL' with Douglas Fairbanks Jr., which I know you will like. You will be thrilled by 'THE THUNDERING HERD.' ...

The Air Mail, filmed the year before, was Doug Jr.'s second film for Famous Players-Lasky. The cast included Billie Dove and Mary Brian. While Jesse was busy at school trying to meet with his father's approval, Doug Jr. played in two more films for Lasky. *The American Venus* and *Wild Horse Mesa*.

The Thundering Herd was another Zane Grey story with the studio's *regular* Western actors Jack Holt, Lois Wilson, Noah Beery—and an unknown Gary Cooper in an uncredited bit part. On a lowly budget, it was shot in the Malibu hills at the Paramount Ranch (Lasky Mesa, West Hills).

April 13, 1925
Dear Jesse,

...Thursday, Dody, Robina and the babies leave for the Coast. They will stay at the Santa Monica House. Saturday morning at 1:00 a.m. Mother sails on the 'Olympic' and the following Monday I leave for Hollywood ... Please write Mother a last letter from you before she sails. I will be away less than four weeks and Robert, Helena and the cook will remain at the apartment until my return. Auntie Blanche and Uncle Hector will arrive in New York on May 4 and will immediately get in touch with you. ...

Leaving her little children in the care of governesses on her trips to Europe, Bessie, with a curator's zeal, continued to fill the apartment and the two California homes with antiques. The New York apartment took up the whole tenth floor of 910 Fifth Avenue, at Seventy-Second Street. Lasky was paying $36,000 a year rental and had the dividing walls knocked out between two ten-room apartments, giving them twenty rooms. The Metropolitan Museum appraised her collection of antique furniture at $200,000 ($1,000,000 plus today) and when the Depression finally hit, she tried to sell some of it, but not many buyers with money could be found.

Lasky also spent another quarter of a million dollars enlarging their new beach house to twenty rooms and ten baths, with a sun-deck gymnasium, a convertible solarium-theatre and two swimming pools, one of fresh seawater pumped in. He had sold the original weekend seafront bungalow to William Randolph Hearst, who acquired the adjoining beach frontage and built a fabulous mansion for Marion Davies, which is also now a hotel.

Lasky had bought this beach house from Mrs. Langford Stack, mother of actor Robert Stack, then only six years old. (Robert was later to play the part of John Paul Jones in the picture of the same name, written by Jesse.)

Lasky noted, 'Each of the children had a suite: bedroom, study, and bath. By mutual understanding each member of the family was deemed an individual, entitled to pursue one's own interests in one's own way. Bessie had her artist's studio, as she has had in every home we have lived in since she started to paint, and if she felt like holing up in it for days at a time, there were enough servants so the rest of us could manage until her creative mood spent itself and she rejoined us.'

With servants east and west, and both parents living unhindered lives, the two younger children continued to make do with nannies and governesses, and Jesse, in boarding school, was extremely self-reliant. Bess wrote to him only occasionally and Jesse cherished her infrequent letters. Yet despite the high-powered life he was leading, Lasky never allowed a week to go by without his letter to his son.

April 18, 1925
Dear Jesse,

   ...Yesterday afternoon, the babies with Dody and Robina left for Hollywood, and last night mother sailed on the Olympic, so I am like you now, all alone!

   ...Mother received your last letter in time before she sailed and she was awfully pleased with it. I think it is the nicest letter you ever wrote us...Here is a bit of news—mother is going to have a special hanging all by herself, of eighteen paintings in a New York gallery next winter—isn't that wonderful? Last night we had the opening of our new picture made in France called *Madame Sans Gene* which brings in the life of Napoleon and many of the famous marshals of his army are in the picture. It is a picture which you will be very much interested in and one which I want you to see at the first opportunity.

Pierce will keep sending you your weekly sandwiches while I am away and as soon as I get back on May 16th, I want to arrange for you to come over and spend the weekend with me – just you and I together, a couple of bachelors. We will go to a show and have a good time . . . I will try and get in touch with Chester and Ken and make preliminary preparations for our next trip. Freeman, the explorer, is getting me in touch with a wonderful trip on the Big Bend of the Columbia River in British Columbia—a marvelous canoe trip which he wrote up in his book called 'Down the Columbia' It is very wild country, big game, some fish and not too difficult rapids . . . when I tell you all the particulars, you will be wild about it.

'Wild' was not the first emotion that sprang to Jesse's mind.

April 20, 1925
Dear Jesse,

. . . Enclosed you will find a gold coin which Joseph Hergesheimer[23] brought you from Mexico. I think they call the coin an Azteca. Anyway you can look it up and find out what its history is and what it is worth, I think it is a rare coin.

I am just leaving for California where I will arrive Friday. Be sure and write me a letter addressed to the studio. I had a radiogram from Mother and she is getting along fine on the 'Olympic'. I don't think she was seasick. . . .

May 6, 1925
Dear Jesse,

. . . Chester told me he would rather have you with him all summer than make another trip with Zane Grey, and I told him you are going to put in the entire summer with him. The four of us will make our big trip together, and I am also going to plan a little trip on which we can take Mother, as she has never camped out with Chester and Ken. Chester brought you and myself, as well as Mother, some things from Mexico. I have not seen them yet, but it was nice of him to think of us all. They are two wonderful boys.

. . . I am glad you were on the winning team in the debate, also very glad you are improving in tennis. I have had to do a lot of dancing lately, and every time I dance I think of you and your new steps.

I have one or two new ones to show you myself. . . .

---

23 A prominent American writer of the early 20th century known for his novels of decadent life amongst the wealthy.

At Blair, debating was something that Jesse found he excelled in. Like his father, he was to become an impromptu and much in demand after-dinner speaker, and tennis was to become his sport for life.

May 28, 1925
Dear Jess,

…I received a cable from mother from Southampton, just as her steamer sailed, and she will be here on Wednesday as I understand it takes seven days for this steamer to cross.…

June 2, 1925
Dear Jesse,

…I will have an interesting experience tomorrow. I have a pass from Washington, which will permit me to go out on the revenue cutter that will meet mother's steamer, The Homeric, in quarantine where the doctors go aboard before the ship comes up the bay. I know it will be an interesting trip going down the bay in the tug with the newspapermen and you can imagine mother's surprise when she sees me climb up the ladder and go on board.

…What do you think of the plan of mother and me motoring down Monday morning and meeting you at Blair at noon? We can have a picnic lunch on our way back along the road…had a nice letter from Dody and she says Bill and little Bessie have gained over two pounds each. She also writes that Chester called at the Beach House.…

As usual, the younger children were seeing little of their parents and it was to take its toll.

June 4, 1925
Dear Jesse,

…Well, I just got back from the steamer and mother is here safe and well. She tells me she wrote you a long letter which was mailed from the steamer this morning, so you ought to have it as soon as you receive this. Mother has her hair bobbed, and it looks great…Mother joins me in sending best love.

Your pal and Dad

September 19, 1925
Dear Jesse:

Today is your birthday and mother and I have just sent you a wire…The night I left Blair I didn't reach town until 9.30. I suppose by this time you are all settled. Which room did you get? …You are lucky to have such a nice boy to room with you ... Little Billie and Bessie (Betty) are fine and we all send our best love.

September 25, 1925

... First, I want to congratulate you on the fact that you are president of the Ball and of the Literary Society and Treasurer of the Sunday School Class. Pretty soon you will be holding as many offices as I am.

... I also ran 'The Vanishing American' for Arthur Brisbane, editor of the New York American, and Courtland Smith and they thought it a marvelous picture... Have you heard from Betty (Bronson) yet? I suppose it is too soon.

Mr. Brisbane made mother a present last night of a new fangled golf practice outfit which permits you to drive a golf ball with all your strength in your drawing room. It really is a great little apparatus and I am sure will help anyone who wants to practice driving ... We had a great piece of luck and found a way of arranging the new apartment so that you will have a very fine room and bath right next to mother's room....

Jesse carried on a brief correspondence with Betty Bronson, to the envy of the 'Blairites' who had to make do with the phony autographs Jesse had added to her pictures.

September 30, 1925
Dear Jesse,

... Well, I was looking over the first edition of the Blair Breeze, which you will remember I subscribed to, and imagine my surprise when I saw the article about you with the heading 'Lasky—President'. I am wondering if you saw the article as you never mentioned it in any of your letters ... Enclosed is part of a letter from Courtland Smith's son. I thought it would amuse you to see how he expresses himself. His letter reminds me of the kind of letters you used to write me when you were younger ... I am glad you are getting along well on the mandolin and I am certainly looking forward to hearing you play it....

October 3, 1925

... I just received the second edition of the Blair Breeze and I notice an article about you which says you were elected President of the Congress Society. I think that is splendid, particularly as through the Congress Society you will have an opportunity of doing a lot of speaking. Just what is the Congress Society?

Lasky was so proud of his son that he announced it to his general manager, Walter Wanger, who felt obliged to write to young Jesse personally. (Wanger later became a highly successful producer.) Lasky hastened to advise his son:

October 9, 1925
Dear Jesse,

...When you write Mr. Wanger, I think it is best that you head your letter 'Dear Mr. Wanger'. That is really the correct way to address men much older than yourself and usually, if you know them very well, they will ask you to call them by their first name.

...We sent a print of 'The Pony Express' to President Coolidge. He ran it at the White House and thought it was a wonderful picture, so the other day he was booked to go to Omaha to speak to the American Legion who are having a Convention there. I sent word through our man in Washington that we would be glad to put on a baggage car and furnish the President motion picture entertainment during this trip. He accepted our offer and we showed him 'The Vanishing American' and he and Mrs. Coolidge sent word yesterday that they thought it was the finest picture they had ever seen....

The Pony Express was not a Zane Grey story. It was directed by James Cruze and starred Lasky's cigar-band discovery, Ricardo Cortez. *The Vanishing American*, a pro-Navajo story was from a Zane Grey novel and starred Richard Dix and Lois Wilson, big names of the moment. Both Lasky and Zukor were listed as 'Presenters'. The company continued churning out medium and low-budget Westerns along with their more expensive roadshows, which were launched with two-a-day screenings at higher prices and usually ran two weeks or more in a cinema before moving on.

October 13, 1925
Dear Jesse,

...Sunday, was little Betty's birthday. She was three years old. That reminds me! Have you had any word from Betty Bronson?...Mother and the little ones join me in sending you much love....

P.S. Mother says be sure and bring your Mandolin.

Jesse's first romance seemed to be fading into his memory faster than in his father's.

October 22nd, 1925
Dear Jesse,

...They have about finished painting and plastering the apartment and it looks like we will be moving in next week...the babies are getting along splendidly with their new nurse....

Neither parent had time for children now, and it was another new nurse for the little ones to get used to. Years later, Jesse wrote of his mother: I couldn't understand why she wished to pack our New York apartment with more and more shipments of spindly chairs and chests of drawers that popped marquetry flowers in the steam heat of New York like a boxer spitting out teeth. Dad agreed, but he wasn't home enough to complain too bitterly. Bess had become far too elegant for Grandpa, too. Her aging Russian-born father would always enter by the servant's entrance, much to her annoyance, and sip tea in the kitchen with the butler. He felt more at home there than among what he called 'bric-a-break'. But in 1925 all Jesse wanted to do was come home and see his parents.

October 26, 1925
Dear Jesse,

... I agree with you we ought to be able to arrange for you to come home once more before Thanksgiving. However, I will be in Chicago on November 7th and although mother would love to have you for that weekend, November 14th would be better for me as I would then be home ... so let's plan on your coming home November 14th, unless it should interfere with an important game or something else that I do not know about. ...

Jesse had to remain lonesome for his family. At the studio, Lasky had a new find to excite him. In 1925, Merian C. Cooper and Ernest B. Schoedsack shot an amazing documentary called *Grass*. It followed the journey through Persia (Iran) of the nomadic Bakhtiari tribe traveling barefoot, herding their livestock, sometime as many as 50,000 animals, up snow-covered mountain passes to fight their way across raging torrents and vertical cliffs heading for the grazing lands on the other side before their animals starved.

Schoedsack was an ace newsreel cameraman, and Cooper was an intrepid flyer. They shot their film for $12,000. Lasky saw it and arranged for it to be distributed by Famous Players-Lasky. It was a huge success and ran at the Criterion in New York for many months. Lasky hastily put the filmmakers under contract and sent them to northern Siam (Thailand) to film a picture featuring an elephant stampede, marauding tigers, and any other wildlife action they could encounter.

On this assignment, Cooper and Schoedsack were given a budget of $60,000, which they exceeded by $10,000. When they returned, it was some time before they finally appeared in Lasky's office, sputtering apologies for their overspend. They handed him a check for $10,000. It was raising this sum that had delayed them.

Lasky was stunned. He had ordered the accounting department to supply the pair with funds as needed. They hadn't understood that they were working on an unlimited expense account. Lasky tore up the check and congratulated them on their brilliant work, which was to be called *Chang*, certainly one of the most successful travel films ever made. Eventually, the team shared in the profits.

(To see a clip of *Chang* on the internet, go to: http://www.tcm.com/mediaroom/video/375612/Chang-Movie-Clip-Such-A-Man-IsKru.html)

Next, the producer decided to try a new technique that had been brought to him. Cooper and Schoedsack spent the following year shooting fantastic footage in the Sudan and Portuguese East Africa for a proposed film, *The Four Feathers*. They brought back reels of jungle footage, amazing shots of wild baboons and stampeding hippos that were blended into matching footage on sets filmed at the studio with the Paramount stars.

This was another cinematic first for Lasky. Actors were suddenly able to be seen in authentic foreign settings and never leave the studio. It was the beginning of a process that soon developed into the technique of rear projection: blue and eventually green screen. *The Four Feathers* release in 1929 would be a great success with Richard Arlen, Fay Wray (who would eventually become a pawn in the paw of *King Kong*), Clive Brook, William Powell (soon to star in *The Thin Man*), and the leeringly jowly Noah Beery.

Lasky was back on the East Coast and wrote to his son:

November 2, 1925
Dear Jesse,

   ...Betty (Bronson) is expected here in about two weeks as she is going to work in a picture called 'DANCING MOTHERS' at the Long Island Studio and the picture starts about November 16th.

   ...It is true what you read in the papers about our liquor being stolen. It was shipped to New York in a freight car with the furniture and after the furniture was unloaded, some masked men entered the car and held up a railroad detective and one of the express men who were watching it, and carted it all away in a big truck. Although we have had detectives and the police out looking for it, we haven't even got a clue so far, so I guess it is all gone. Mother also lost four barrels of household goods but the latter were insured....

Prohibition was still on and yet Lasky had the police looking for his missing booze. The thieves certainly knew just what they were looking for and had no interest in Bess' antiques.

November 10, 1925
Dear Jess,

   ...While in Chicago, I called on the famous comedian, Eddie Cantor, the star of one of Ziegfeld's musical plays called 'KID BOOTS'. He asked me if anybody played the ukulele, and when I told him you were strumming on something with strings, he autographed it, inscribing it to you and I brought it home with me, and it is now in your room. Your gun case is now up, and on your next trip you will enjoy putting your guns in place....

November 18, 1925

...Well, mother's exhibition opened yesterday at four o'clock and it was a really big success. The gallery was crowded all day with very distinguished people of all professions and they all pronounced mother's work very fine and I guess from now on we will hear a lot of Bessie Lasky, the American painter. You certainly would have been proud if you could have been present to hear the fine things that very critical people said about mother's work.

We were glad to receive your letter and to hear that you have increased your list of correspondents and that you have one more candidate for the Prom....

November 28, 1925

...Well, here am I, settled in Hollywood! Had a nice, restful trip...The Lasky Studio is going to play the Fox studio, and I certainly wish you could be here to follow us around, the same as you did when we played the Metro-Goldwyn outfit. I will let you know how the tournament comes out.

...I hope you heard from the book publisher, Mr. Putnam. Do begin to outline your story so that you can get seriously to work on it. You might be able to do a little work on it during Christmas vacation. The more I think of your writing the story the better I like the idea....

In 1926, Jesse, at sixteen, had sent a collection of his poetry to publishers Boni & Liveright in New York, who, with no encouragement from his father, published his first book of poems, *Songs from the Heart of a Boy*. It sold so well that they gave it a second printing the following year. Noting the success of Jesse's first book, George Putnam asked for, and published his second book of verse, *Listening to Silence* in the same year.

Putnam's name would perhaps be forgotten today except for what happened a few years later. In 1928, Putnam met the great flying ace, Amelia Earhart. In 1935, he asked her to fly the Atlantic and follow the trip with a book for his firm. She became the first person to fly solo across the Pacific from Honolulu to Oakland, California. Lasky described her as 'A shy, gentle, uncommunicative person who frequently dropped in wearing her customary breeches.' She became a great personal friend of Bess's and eventually married Putnam.

Eleven years later, the Putnams told the Laskys of Earhart's secret plans. Nearing a fortieth birthday, she wanted to be the first woman to fly around the world. Bess was annoyed and asked Putnam why he was letting her make such a potentially dangerous flight. 'She has had glory enough', Bess declared.

'Letting me?' Amelia laughed. 'It's his idea. But I'll do it to please him.' That was not entirely true, and she added, 'I have a feeling that there is just about one more good flight left in my system, and I hope this trip is it.'

'It will be her last trip', the publisher assured them.

Unfortunately, it was. On June 1, 1937, Earhart and her navigator, Fred Noonan, took off from Miami on the 29,000-mile journey and were never seen again. But for the moment, tragedy in the Putnam household was far in the future. Lasky was concerned for his son's poetic progress and offered advice, instructions, and assistance, as usual. The boy's career as a writer had begun.

January 8, 1926
Dear Jesse

. . . Enclosed herewith are your contracts and a letter from Mr. Putnam. You are to sign both contracts on the last page where it is marked with a cross in pencil. One of the contracts you may keep, and the other mail to Mr. Putnam. To make it easier for you, I am enclosing a stamped envelope, properly addressed and you simply have to put one of the contracts in the envelope and mail it.

If you wish, you can send the second copy of the contract to Miss Cohen and she will keep it here in the safe for you. If you want to do this, I am enclosing another addressed stamped envelope so that you will have no trouble in mailing the second copy.

I certainly want to congratulate you on getting a contract for a book. It is more than I expected and I know it will inspire you to write a great story when the time comes. . . .

Lasky also sent a letter to Jesse's school:

January 7, 1926
Miss Bingham,
Secretary to the Headmaster, Blair Academy,
Blairstown, New Jersey.
My dear Miss Bingham:

Might I trouble you to send me the following information with reference to my son, Jesse Lasky Jr. I should like to know in what courses he is now enrolled - what textbooks are used and roughly the subject matter of each course. I should also like to know if you are able to estimate what position my son would be in with respect to each particular course at the end of the current school year; that is, how far he will progress in the text books which you name if he does not finish them by that time.

If you have a catalogue which would show these courses descriptively, I should thank you to send me a copy.

I trust this is not putting you to too much trouble, but I am very anxious to keep in closer touch with my son's progress.

Very sincerely yours,
Jesse L. Lasky

The book Lasky was encouraging Jesse to write was not poetry, but about their dangerously adventurous summer expedition the previous year.

January 13, 1926
Dear Jesse,

...I am glad you signed the contract and are already working on the book. The more I think about the book, the more I am convinced that you ought to make the first chapter 'From Needles to Yuma', then follow with the chapter on 'Kite to Lees Ferry'. I will explain my reasons when I see you, but this won't prevent you from working on the chapter...The other day a Colonel and a Major from the Regular Army came up to the office with some orderlies and some cameramen and I duly took the oath of office and received my commission as Major in the Officers Reserve of the Signal Corps...Mr. Putnam brought Art Young, the bow and arrow man up to meet me and Mr. Young shot a blunt arrow through a board to demonstrate his skill. Afterwards, I showed them two of our trips - Needles to Yuma and the Tiburon reels... we all swore to make the African hunting trip some summer....

Mr. Putnam sent you a book on hunting with the bow and arrow, which I am forwarding to you under separate cover....

Lasky had chartered a yacht for the trip to Tiburon in Baja, California, which was more accessible from the sea. It was supposed to be a hunting adventure for Jesse, who had been equipped with rifle and bow and arrows. Tiburon was a barely explored territory, and as the small group set up camp on shore, they were attacked by a wild tribe, believed to be cannibals. Grabbing all they could carry, they just made it back to the yacht, followed by a stream of arrows. Lasky had filmed footage of the trip, but not, perhaps, of the chase back to safety.

Bess, who rarely saw much of young Jesse, but suspecting unsavory trends in his teenage character since his earlier attempt to seduce Betty Bronson with a hip flask, decreed that he was to spend his spring vacation in Europe with his father, who was going to visit all of the company's film exchanges. But it appeared that 'with his father' was misleading.

It had been arranged that Randy Rogers (Lasky's personal assistant and a flamboyant character in his own right) was to accompany Jesse as his companion. But it was not as Bess or Jesse had imagined. When Lasky left Paris for Prague, Randy and Jesse arrived in Paris. When Lasky reached Vienna, the pair followed to Prague—and so on, through Czechoslovakia. Randy had been instructed to keep his schedule one country behind Lasky until they would eventually meet up in Berlin, where they were to travel home together.

All was going according to plan until somebody made a mistake in bookings and Randy and Jesse arrived at the famous Donaplota Hotel in Budapest to find that Lasky was still in residence—although not in his suite. Randy left a hasty note of explanation in Lasky's box and swiftly whisked his young charge off to dinner and a movie. When they returned to the hotel that night, Randy saw with slight alarm that Lasky had not picked up his message. He hurried his charge to bed.

But Jesse was awakened at dawn by gypsy music drifting up from the main street below. He crawled out of bed and peered down to see four open carriages carrying an orchestra of musicians in brightly colored costumes. Marching ahead of the carriages and leading a band of men in rumpled tuxedos were gypsy singers and striking young Hungarian actresses in sparkling gowns and feather boas drinking champagne from silver goblets. The axis around which they all pranced was Jesse's father.

'Come away from the window, Jess. He might see you.' Randy's voice behind him offered wise advice. 'I don't think he'd appreciate knowing that you know.'

In the early morning, they dressed hastily and checked out of the hotel, retrieving the note Randy had left and any hint that they had ever been there. They were unaware of what followed.

Just as Lasky was about to crawl into bed, Adolph Zukor arrived at his suite. Like a scene in one of Paramount's comedies, Lasky pretended that he was actually just getting up. Zukor was pleased; he liked to see an executive rise early.

A word about Randolph Rogers—his nickname was not far off the mark, according to Jesse. Randy, he was called, and 'randy' he was. He wore a thin, pointed moustache, pomaded black hair, and no young actress entered Lasky's outer office without sending Randy's adrenaline into overdrive. He was a direct descendant of Judge Cotton Mather, who in 1692 in Old Salem, burned many a female witch. The ladies Randy came into contact with were more likely to set him on fire.

Back in California, Lasky was already planning his son's next adventure.

April 15, 1926
Dear Jesse,

...Had a good talk with Chester and we are trying to work out a trip which would take us to Alaska for some real big game hunting and fishing. We may charter our own boat and sail from Seattle as we can get to the place we have in mind on what they call the inside passage, and if we get rough weather there are endless islands and harbors where we can camp. We plan to make the trip consume the month of August. However, I am to meet the man who knows all about the country on Sunday and then I will let you know more about it.

We have not settled on a summer house here yet. Just now it looks like we might take Will Rogers' house, which has a swimming pool and polo field in the back of the Beverly Hills Hotel . . . Remember me to Norma, the Fifth Avenue debutante. It sounds like the title of a motion picture. Wasn't it wonderful, Mother being hung in the Paris Salon? There is no doubt in the world but she is a truly talented artist and some day will be known as a great American painter. . . .

The Alaskan adventure was not to be. Jesse came home that summer, and so the letters stopped for the time being.

Always on the hunt for the next Valentino or Swanson, Lasky never forgot the advice of his first partner, Henry B. Harris, during his theatrical days with the Folies-Bergère: 'Don't turn anyone away without a hearing.' And only once did this open mind and door policy backfire. He was looking for a girl with a perfect figure to play the sculpture's model in the proposed film *The Naked Truth*, when a showbiz mother appeared with her teenage daughter and announced, 'Mr. Lasky, your search is over. My daughter has a perfect body.' She turned to her daughter. 'Show Mr. Lasky, dear.' With that, the sweet young thing untied one bow and dropped every stitch.

The girl didn't get the job, but in another case, the open-door policy worked out quite differently. In 1926, a week before Lasky's film *Old Ironsides* was to open, an inventor named Lorenzo Del Riccio who couldn't get past the door of other Paramount executives, came knocking on Lasky's door. The producer told him he could have just five minutes. Those five minutes were to revolutionize the entire film industry a quarter of a century later.

Always pioneering and searching for any inventions or ideas that might improve motion pictures, Lasky had suggested earlier that year that Paramount start an executive training program for bright young men. They did, at Long Island with men chosen from five different universities. Del Riccio was a graduate of Brown University. Each of these trainees was to make a mark in his own way. Monty Woolley became a famous actor, Frank Tuttle, a famous director; one of them became an Ambassador to France. But in 1926, Del Riccio was out of a job when the training program was dropped. He came to the producer with an invention because he knew Lasky had started the program and was a man of ideas.

Del Riccio brought him a supplementary projector lens that could enlarge a screen image to vast proportions. Lasky sent him to the Rivoli Theatre where he arranged for a test of the new lens. He chose a sequence from his soon to be released roadshow film about the frigate Constitution, known as Old Ironsides. In Great Britain, the film was called *Sons of the Sea* because the Brits didn't understand the nickname which had been inspired by a cannon ball having bounced off the frigate's hull. James Cruze directed, with an all-star cast.

Old Ironsides was the most celebrated naval vessel in American history and had already been immortalized in Oliver Wendell Holmes' poem. The fact that Congress had at that moment authorized the ship's reconstruction for a patriotic cruise to inspire school children gave the film a certain marketing value.

When Lasky arrived for the lens demonstration, he noted that Del Riccio had abandoned the normal-sized silver screen (much smaller than today's). The inventor had chosen instead the reverse side of a painted backdrop that filled the entire proscenium arch. The demonstration began with a sequence from *Old Ironsides* projected in normal size—until the moment when the mighty ship came sailing toward the audience, to the rescue of a merchantman seized by Tripoli pirates. Then the picture suddenly exploded to four times its size—and the frigate seemed to be sailing right into Lasky's lap!

'I never felt such a dramatic impact from anything in a full lifetime of show-business!' Lasky exclaimed and immediately coined a name for it: MAGNASCOPE. He authorized the necessary budget to re-cut the silent picture to project the sea battle sequences through this great new lens upon a large silver screen to match. When the ship came charging towards the first-night audience in the Magnascope sequence, the projectionist's cue sheet instructed him to increase the film speed to twenty-six frames per second. The theater orchestra stepped up the tempo and volume, and the first-nighters rose to their feet and cheered! The following day, *The*

OLD IRONSIDES

New York Times also created a first: They ran the review of the picture on the front page. It was a triumph.

Although the company installed the lens in many of their theatres, few put it to use because business was booming and nobody needed gimmicks. Nevertheless, the wide-screen was used in *Wings* and on several other films at the time: *Chang*, *The Last Waltz*, and Walter Wanger's *Stagecoach*. Paramount offered del Riccio $100 a year during the life of his patent for each theatrical installation of the lens, but the inventor, acting on the advice of his lawyer, sold it outright to Paramount for $25,000. Years later, Del Riccio told Lasky that had his lawyer not advised him to accept the studio's cash offer, he would have collected $2,380,000 in royalties.

After the opening of *Old Ironsides*, Lasky put del Riccio on the payroll and set up a research lab for him at the Long Island studio. The inventor was given a free hand to work on anything that would improve motion pictures. This was possibly the only motion picture research lab ever put into operation, and fourteen useful devices came out of it in the years from 1926 to 1929. Much to Lasky's disappointment, the lab was finally abandoned by the East Coast moneymen. Del Riccio's influence on the modern-day picture business, while tremendous, is little known or understood.

But for all its first-class factors and critical success, *Old Ironsides* was a costly flop at the box office, and for such matters, the East Coast moneymen had a long memory. Lasky turned his thoughts to sixteen-year-old Jesse, now the proud owner of Eddie Cantor's banjo, who was asking permission to take banjo lessons. He'd been accepted at the Junior School of Princeton, Hun School, and his father was quick to approve anything to keep him occupied.

October 18, 1926

… I believe Mother has written you that the banjo lessons are O.K. I bet what you have in mind is to make the Glee Club when you get into Princeton.

… I will break the news to Mr. Putnam that Boni and Liveright are publishing your poems. Incidentally I will see him Wednesday as I am giving a luncheon to Emil Jannings[24] who arrived today from Germany, and have invited Mr. Putnam who will be one of about one hundred guests we are having for this occasion … I do think that you should make every effort to enter Princeton in two years, if it is humanly possible. …

Encouraged by the fact that at fifteen, his poem about Thomas Edison[25] had been published in the *New York Herald Tribune* and he'd been paid ten dollars (which is about the same fee one gets for poetry some eighty years later), Jesse's taste for poetry had sprouted into two published books of verse. He quickly began a third.

---

24 German actor, to become the first Oscar recipient, honored with the Academy Award for Best Actor in 1929.
25 One of the most prolific inventors in history, holding 1,093 U.S. patents and world wide, including the phonograph, a long-lasting electric light bulb and the tin foil phonograph.

A few years earlier when he had asked his father if he could have a typewriter, Lasky sent him an old one from the studio. But Jesse found a name scratched on it and for months refused to touch it, insisting it was haunted. The name was William Desmond Taylor, the actor-director who had been murdered on February 1, 1922. Jesse's desire to write finally overcame his fear of a ghostly presence and that first book of poetry, *Songs from the Heart of a Boy* had been typed on the haunted typewriter.

Jesse had sent his first book of verse to Thomas Edison for Christmas the year before, having met him with his father. He carefully preserved the reply in which he was proud to have been addressed as 'Mr. Lasky'.

```
December 24. 1926.
Mr. Jesse L. Lasky, Jr.
910 Fifth Avenue,
New York City.

Dear Mr. Lasky:
   Until I received a copy of your book of poems that you kindly
sent me, I did not know that there was a poet in your family. But,
come to think of it, your father is far from lacking in imagination,
so there is nothing strange in inherited imagination running to the
side of poetry.
   Let me thank you for sending me a copy of your book, and with the
greetings
   of the season,
   I remain

       Yours very truly,
       Thos A Edison.
```

January 19, 1927
January 22, !927
Dear Jesse,

   ...a great many people have mentioned to me that they have read your book and everyone speaks of it in the most favorable terms, some of your admirers being really enthusiastic about the quality of your poems. Douglas Fairbanks was especially enthusiastic about them....

Lasky was impressed to discover that his son was also writing love letters for his more reserved schoolmates for $3 a letter. No doubt Jesse got the idea after reading

Edmond Rostand's play *Cyrano de Bergerac*, in which the hero writes such billet-doux for his innocent rival.

In the following letter Lasky makes the first mention of DeMille's ranch in the Malibu Hills, where years later, when Jesse became DeMille's chief writer, he was to spend many an exotic weekend at Paradise.

January 25, 1927
Dear Jesse,

    ... I had a wonderful week-end at Mr. DeMille's 'Paradise' Ranch, and got up at six o'clock in the morning to motor down to meet Mother who arrived Sunday morning on a perfectly beautiful sunny day ... You seem to be having a tough time of it at school; with being quarantined and having a cold, I suppose you are feeling very low ... Has the quarantine been lifted yet? ...

Jesse seemed to get himself in trouble with school authorities from time to time, but he was making a small name for himself in other areas.

January 31, 1927
Dear Jesse,

    ...I am simply amazed at the number of people out here who have read your book. Everywhere I go someone comments on it ... 'Old Ironsides' had the most brilliant opening imaginable at Grauman's Egyptian Theatre last Friday night. Mother and I had as guests for dinner and at the opening Douglas and Mary (Fairbanks), Frank and Bertha Case, Will Hays, Carl Van Vechten the author of 'The Tattooed Countess' and 'Nigger Heaven', and also Grandma. Mr. Van Vechten saw a picture of you on Mother's dresser when he entered our living room at the Ambassador and immediately asked if that was my son, the poet. When I answered in the affirmative he immediately commented at great length, on the quality of the poetry which he thought showed real promise ... The other night we previewed at a small theatre our new picture 'The Rough Riders' which is finished. It looks to me like it is going to be the most popular of all the big pictures. It is really a wonderful human document, with marvelous comedy and tense drama, and a really fine love story; in fact, the picture has everything to make it a very popular success. ...

The Rough Riders was the story of Teddy Roosevelt's adventures with the First United States Volunteer Cavalry in Cuba during the Spanish-American War of 1898, before he became president. It was directed by Victor Fleming, a particularly rough-riding director. The producer's son was riding a bit roughshod at Blair and he marked his next letter:

Personal Correspondence
February 7, 1927
Dear Jess,

...I am not finding fault, but I would like to know what you did to get a 60 in conduct, I trust you haven't tried to burn down the school or burn up the campus....

On the other hand, Lasky continued to be surprised at the interest in Jesse's books of verse as press comments appeared, both favorable and adverse.

March 3rd, 1927

...I have been hearing some fine things about your book. Enclosed are two press clippings to add to your collection. I think the criticism rather ridiculous but it is well to get used to criticisms as that is the lot of anyone who chooses a career that invites criticism. (No more than a celebrity expects)...Keep up the good work....

March 4th, 1927

...Enclosed is a press clipping that just came in which I think is one of the best you have received thus far...George Gershwin was in our party last night and commented enthusiastically on your book which he had read....

March 7th, 1927

...In case you did not see the Sunday Times, I am enclosing a copy of the advertisement that appeared in the book review supplement. We are looking forward to next week when you will be home for your vacation...Mr. Herbert Rothschild, a prominent lawyer in San Francisco, had seen the advertisement of your book and ordered several of your books from his book dealer, two of which he is sending on for you to autograph....

Jesse was now formally paying court to local debs, who would all be picked up by Pierce and taken to dinners and theatres with the family. The latest young lady was Grace.

March 11th 1927
Dear Jesse,

...I go to Boston on Wednesday night so as to be there to speak at Harvard University Thursday morning. I may not be home in time for dinner Thursday but Mother will be home and will dine with you and Grace, as I understand you have asked her for dinner, and I will get in about 9.30 o'clock.

We are having a showing of a very special picture with the orchestra at the Criterion Theatre at 11.30 Thursday evening, so instead of going to a café we will probably go to the Criterion....

The film that Lasky referred to here is the documentary, *Chang*. New cinemas (still called theatres in America) were being built to accommodate large audiences and deserve a mention. In New York, the Roxy Theatre, opened on March 11, 1927 by Samuel Roxy Rothafel, was a 6,214-seat house at 153 West 50th Street at 7th Avenue. The opening night film was *The Love of Sunya*, produced by and starring Gloria Swanson with her new backer/lover, Joseph Kennedy (father of Jack, Bobby, Edward, etc.) The Roxy (later overshadowed by the opening of Radio City Music Hall in the Rockefeller Center in 1932) was demolished in 1960 and Swanson posed on October 14, 1960 in the midst of the ruins.

Broadway's first Criterion Theatre, originally the Lyric, had opened in 1895. In 1920, Paramount-Famous Players-Lasky, which also ran the Rialto and Rivoli, took over the Criterion and made it a reserved-seat showcase for its most important releases, including *Beau Geste*, *The Covered Wagon*, and DeMille's box office triumph, the silent *The Ten Commandments*. With the opening of the flagship Paramount Theatre in Times Square in 1926, the Criterion also began showing films from other distributors. Music was provided by a Wurlitzer organ, capable of sounding like a full orchestra. The Criterion survived the arrival of 'talkies' and was in operation almost to the time of its demolition in 1935.

In downtown Los Angeles, an 1,800-seat theatre located at Seventh and Grand opened as The Kinema in 1917, and was later renamed The Criterion, and still later,

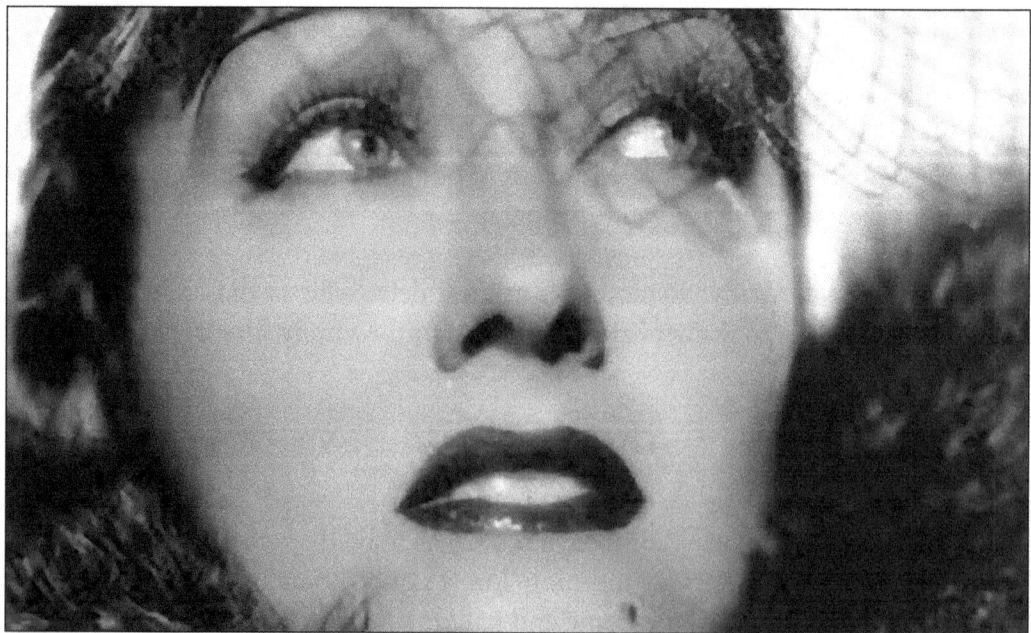

GLORIA SWANSON

The Fox Criterion in New York. In March of 1927, Lasky expanded his east coast offices in the Paramount Building and spent the train time between coasts.

Not a father to come home to a quiet dinner with the family, when he saw Jesse it was always to plan some spectacular adventure or to see a ball game, a film, a theater, or a rodeo. Life was lived on a high note and Jesse was learning to keep up with it.

The decade younger Billy and Betty found other excitements. Bess had been bitten by a dog when she was a child and her fear of them was sufficient to rule that the little children could not have a dog. Nobody seemed to want a cat. But ever since Billy had learned the power of snakes, he had been collecting them and a series of other creepy-crawlies. Betty, unafraid, shared in the fun of Billy's pets. Lasky described coming home one night to their New York apartment to hear his children's voices arguing.

'It's my turn!' Betty complained shrilly.

'No, it isn't! Let go!' Billy demanded.

He found the youngsters pulling on opposite ends of a six-foot boa constrictor, fighting over whose turn it was to feed the creature. Billy won because he was holding the feeding end. Lasky noted that another time, investigating a box in the hallway Bessie thought had been delivered for her, she was nipped on the finger by a baby alligator. There was also an owl and later kangaroo rats, giant moths, and falcons. But since each family member had a private bathroom, sitting room, and bedroom, Bill was allowed to keep his menagerie of serpents, frogs etc. in his bathroom. He was to turn this love of creatures great and small into a life's work.

While Jesse was learning self-reliance, Billy and Betty were still being reared by servants, traveling on their own with governess and nanny, scarcely seeing either parent. It was particularly hard on Betty.

April 5th, 1927
Dear Jesse

... Billy and Betty, Dody and the nurse arrived Sunday from Augusta. They report a fine time and look very well, however, little Betty is still showing the nervous condition which causes her to blink her eyes and the doctor has advised absolute rest and quiet for her for a couple of weeks, therefore, on Wednesday we are sending Dody and Betty to Atlantic City. This is a curious case inasmuch as the doctor says her physical condition is fine but she is suffering from what in an older person would be a nervous breakdown, due probably to pushing her too hard at school. A few weeks' rest will cure her but she won't be permitted to go to school anymore this season. Billy is back at school and getting along fine ... Mother and I are seriously considering sailing for Europe for four weeks, possibly about the 4th of June, but this is all very uncertain. If you are not able to obtain a leave of absence later on for a weekend at home, when the weather is warmer, Mother and I will run over to Princeton....

Bess had left the infant Jesse to his grandmother, with whom he always had a special attachment. As he grew older, his mother treated him like a friend and confidant, but she never bonded with the two younger children until they grew up. Lasky made up for not being a hands-on father by organizing great trips with Jesse. There were fewer with Bill because by the time his younger son was old enough for adventures the money was scarce. However, he always wrote to all his children. Now that Jesse was older and "a published author" he began talking about studio business in his letters.

April 11, 1927
(New York)
Dear Jess,

...Cecil DeMille is in town. I am lunching with him tomorrow and we are of course looking forward to the opening of his big picture 'The King of Kings' which we will attend.

April 12, 1927

...If you are permitted to have the weekend in town, Randy will call for you and as we will be at Westchester he will bring you to us there. You may notify Grace I have a front table for the formal dinner dance and I am sure it will be a delightful evening; you can take Grace home after the dance and then you can return to Westchester. Sunday morning we might squeeze in eighteen holes of golf and maybe a half hour of horseback riding.

...Mother is awfully keen about the idea of our all doing the Westchester dance Saturday night together and is praying for your success in making the week-end....

April 19, 1927

...Mother has taken a hold of my new offices and has refurnished them and I just can't wait for you to see them. They are the last word in good taste and I know you will admire them very much... Randy will come to meet you as usual... Give my love to Grace when you write to her.

April 21, 1927

...I am very glad you are taking up tennis again because it is great exercise for you. By the way, speaking of tennis, I have been running into Bill Tilden, American Tennis Champion, a lot lately. He is a very nice chap and we have a standing invitation to occupy his box the next time we happen to be where he is engaged in a match play.

Frank Case just sent me the most beautiful set of registered matched golf clubs... I am going to take you to Spaldings and see if I can get a set of these clubs to fit you.... P.S. If you have a copy of your story of our camping trips, will you kindly send it to Mr. Rogers.

April 26, 1927

...a charming letter from Mr. Bell expressing his appreciation of your fine efforts...The fact that you ranked first in your class with the general average of 77 is a real triumph, and nothing less. I really am pleased beyond words and I know Mother will be too...On account of my leaving for Chicago for our Convention on May 5th, Mother has decided to leave with me taking the children, Dody, John, etc. and closing the apartment. This means we will not be here for the weekend which you looked forward to gaining, starting May 6th....

Changing weekends was not allowed by the school and Jesse was to get used to coming into New York on his own and staying in a hotel alone if the apartment was closed. Nevertheless, Lasky wanted his son to be properly dressed on all occasions.

May 4, 1927
Dear Jesse,

...At the time you receive this we will be on our way to California...As the apartment will be closed, we have sent your tuxedo outfit to my office so that if you need it for the few days it will be here before we go west after school closes, it will be available. I am surely going to come over to school and pick you up or bring you back to New York on the last day of school....

Back in California, Lasky had been occupied with some heady headaches, about to make one of the finest films of his career, *Wings*. In New York, the producer had been introduced by George Putnam to John Monk Saunders, a young man with movie star looks. But Saunders had no desire to be an actor. A graduate of the University of Washington in Seattle and a Rhodes Scholar, he'd been studying at Oxford where he had acquired a posh English accent. He had also been a pilot in World War I, and Putnam, who had published his book *Wings*, suggested to Lasky that it would make a great film. Coming from Putnam, Lasky listened with more interest than he usually gave to people who brought him ideas for his next big hit.

The story followed the adventures of a young man who was 'born to fly'. In pitching the story to the producer, Saunders described the first shot: the youth lying on his back in a field watching an eagle flying through the bright afternoon sky—resonating his own desire to fly. The book's narrative tracked the flyer through every phase of his aerial experiences: ground school, training overseas, and finally into the airborne battles of World War I.

Nobody had yet filmed a story of planes and their pilots. Lasky realized the dramatic potential and macho glamour and could see *Wings* being his next big roadshow film. He also realized it would be one of the company's most lavish money eaters, with aerial battles leaving costly destruction on the ground. Obviously, he'd have to get the budget past the East Coast accountants.

Always ready to stand behind his creative intuition, with no hesitation he hired Saunders to adapt his novel for the silent screen and to remain as technical advisor during the proposed filming. To stir the novice's incentive, he offered him a percentage of the profits, even though Saunders had no screenwriting experience and knew nothing about filmmaking. Judiciously, the producer decided not to bring his 'discovery' to the coast immediately, knowing there was always suspicion and resentment of anyone new invading the close-knit Hollywood scene. Counting on the fact that the studio regulars toasted 'boy wonders' who had strong executive backing, he had his writer wait in New York until they could go west together and he could personally introduce Saunder's project with the proper sales pitch. He was confidant Saunders would prove himself.

Both his two chief supervisors, Ben Schulberg and Hector Turnbull were excited by the idea of shooting a story with airplanes. Schulberg suggested as a director, Billy Wellman, because he had been a pilot in the famous Lafayette Flying Corps in World War I. Wellman had actually been through much of the action that would be depicted. Although the director had recently been fired from MGM, in 1926 he directed *You Never Know Women* for Lasky's company, about the Chauve-Souris,[26] starring Clive Brook and Florence Vidor and had been extremely well received.

The thought of entrusting the most colossal venture the studio had ever undertaken to a $200-a-week director with no Hollywood hits (when top directors were now paid up to $1,500 a week) worried Lasky just slightly; but he was willing to risk it. Never above 'a bit of bribery to fan the flame of creative inspiration', Lasky put the project into the youthful director's hands with the promise that if he liked his work, he'd personally give him anything within reason. What would he want? Wellman, eyes glowing, suggested he'd quite like an automobile.

Although his hard sell had won the approval of the West Coast team, back east there were rumblings about the project. Returning to New York, Lasky made a personal pitch to Zukor. Couldn't he imagine leather-clad knights soaring the skies on winged horses? Helmeted, goggled heroes, white silk scarves twisted tightly around anxious throats, fighting aerial duels to the death? Devil-may-care American flyers battling Von Richthofen's Flying Circus far above the muddy misery of foot soldiers struggling in bloody combat below.

And Lasky had one thrilling addition. Although dialogue was not yet possible, he was determined to introduce the thunderous roar of the planes and the rat-a-tat-tat of the machine guns—creating an illusion of reality never before seen in the American cinema. Although the French had experimented with projected sound in 1900, nothing had come of it.

---

26 La Chauve-Souris was the name of a French touring <u>revue</u> during the early 1900s.

It was a fascinating idea perhaps, but the budget was outrageous, screamed the eastern moneymen. And how would the public follow specks in the sky that they could barely see? How could they tell the good guys from the bad guys—with all the actors wearing goggles? Whatever was Lasky thinking—wanting to put sound effects into a silent film? Did he not realize that some exhibitors protested that 'noise' in movies would shock the audience?

Fortunately, Zukor took Lasky's side because he trusted his partner's creative instincts, and the others were silenced. So *Wings* was launched with an untried writer, an unknown director, and in the lead roles, budding actor Buddy Rogers, established star Richard Arlen, and 'It' girl Clara Bow. Since America was not fighting any wars in 1927, the U.S. Army was extremely cooperative, wishing the film to represent military aviation in a positive light. It was a chance for the public to better understand why America's Air Force was vital in the St. Mihiel Drive in World War I, one of the first U.S. solo offensives extending from the Swiss border to the sea, in which U.S. Army fliers brought down 261 German planes—one-seventh of Germany's total flying power.

The government gave the studio permission to use Kelly Air Field in San Antonio, Texas, where the major sequence would be shot; preparations were meticulous. The entire French village/cum battlefield and trenches down to the last shell holes were recreated in Texas. Washington provided tanks, artillery, an entire infantry division and enough engineers and technical advisors to guarantee that nothing could possibly go wrong.

Wellman and his company arrived to begin shooting. But days passed, costs mounted, and not a foot of film was being shot. The East Coast men began asking, 'Why…?' They were not best pleased to learn that Wellman refused to start filming when the weather was beautiful and the sky clear blue. There was talk of taking him off the picture and replacing him with a more reasonable director. But Wellman's argument made sense to the producer: Airplanes in a cloudless sky would look like flies on a bed sheet. Lasky was adamant. The execs would have to be patient and trust the director.

For 30 days Wellman waited for clouds while he shot anything but the sky. Fortunately, the 31st day brought a photogenic cumulus cloudscape and Wellman, who had hired the best stunt fliers in America, started the cameras grinding. He even chanced his own safety, flying in the camera plane for many of the sweeping aerial shots of the recreated French village.

Because of the delay, time was now limited. They had only two more days left of shooting in Texas for what was to be the first aerial battle scene ever filmed. The 'action' was to destroy the village in one great battle with plenty of air power. Because of cost, it could only be shot and destroyed once. Top Army brass and indeed, the whole town of San Antonio, had been invited to watch the filming and to attend a celebration banquet afterwards.

Lasky's train arrived just in time for him to be whisked out to the field and up the hundred-foot tower that had been built for Wellman, his first assistant and several of the cameramen. It was a remarkable sight looking down. Several thousand extras in uniform were positioned in the fake French village, ready for the charge. The entire battlefield area had been mined with special explosives and assistant directors were scattered out of sight below, ready to set off the explosions. Cameras were hidden in key spots to film this once-in-a-lifetime recreated battle in close, medium, and master shots. The aerial camera was already circling the location. In those pre-cell phone days, Wellman had arranged a signal to his troops and warned them with some excitement. 'When I wave this red flag, we'll make $60,000 go up in smoke. Remember, men—there can only be one take!'

From beyond the camera lines, most of San Antonio had turned out to watch, including the mayor and his thirteen-year-old daughter. Lasky and Wellman invited the two to come onto the tower and up they climbed and Wellman hurried back down to oversee last minute details. The mayor was given a canvasback seat and they waited. The day was hot. The young girl grew restless. Then she spotted a friend in the crowd and shouted down at her.

'Yoo-hoo', she called. 'Yoo-hoo!' Her voice was drowned out by the breeze, so she grabbed up the piece of red material lying on the Wellman's chair and waved it frantically. 'Yoo-hoo, Mildred!' she shouted.

It was the red-flagged signal that all on the field below were waiting for. Assistant directors dutifully took their cues, and in every corner of that Texas field the battle was set into ear-splitting motion.

Tanks rolled forward through thunderous explosions.

Sheets of smoke and raging fires burst out everywhere.

Through shooting flames, the houses crumbled.

Falling bodies littered the field and over it all, the planes swooped and dove!

On and on, to its bitter and tragic destruction, every dollar of the budget went up in smoke—and not one camera was grinding. Not surprisingly, the celebration banquet was a flop.

Lasky made a ball-breaking executive decision. The battlefield would be rebuilt and destroyed one more time. It sent the budget soaring and the New York executives into convulsions. $2,000,000 spent on a movie which the East Coast considered already had too many speculative factors: an untried theme, a novice screenwriter, a novice director, and a handful of novice young leading men.

Wings was the last of the silent spectaculars, and it was the first movie to win an Academy Award for Best Production. It advanced the career of its leading actors, Buddy Rogers, Richard Arlen, and Clara Bow. It also discovered one who became more famous than all the rest—a tall, lanky cowboy from Montana, who had only taken the bit part because he needed employment at that moment. But the sales department noted that this gangling young man in only two minutes of screen time had made a deep impression on exhibitors—and on the audience.

CLARA BOW AND LASKY

Lasky called Gary Cooper into his office and signed him to a five-year contract. In 1928 he put Cooper in The *Legion of the Condemned* with Fay Wray, which Wellman also directed, using some of the outtakes and surplus footage left over from *Wings*. It was a beginning for the actor, but Lasky credited two pictures that followed for making a star of Cooper: *The Virginian*, featuring Walter Huston and directed by Victor Fleming, and *Seven Days' Leave* from a James Barrie story, *The Old Lady Shows Her Medals*. It was an association between the actor and the producer that would last a lifetime, and their greatest film together lay in wait for the far future. It would make Lasky a very rich man. For the moment.

Years later, when Gary Cooper was to play opposite star Helen Hayes in *A Farewell to Arms*, he was terrified of working with an actress considered to be the greatest on the Broadway stage. 'How can they expect me to play in a picture with someone like that?' he fretted. 'I can't act.'

Hayes, too, was unaccountably nervous about the assignment. 'When I act I'm pretending', she confessed. 'He'll show me up. He feels what he is doing. It was and still is the difference between an actor who can play many characters losing self to become the character, and a star who projects his own personality into the role, never losing self.'

A long letter to Jesse followed the film's opening:

May 23rd, 1927
Dear Jesse,

I returned on Saturday from San Antonio where I went to see the opening of 'Wings'…I had a very interesting experience in San Antonio which I will save to tell you all about (referring to the above incident of filming). I certainly became well acquainted with the Generals of the good old U.S. Army, to say nothing of the Governor of Texas and Secretary of War Davis.

Here's some good news. I just purchased the forty feet of land next to the Beach House so we are going to make some wonderful improvements at the beach. It is just marvelous at Santa Monica and you will love it this summer. Walter (Wanger) has been staying with us and we box every morning, also train with my new trainer who I like very much, and of course swim twice a day. The babies have their ponies and are developing into regular riders and will also be able to swim by the time you arrive.

Just saw Chester, and I arranged for you and I to run up for a couple of days fishing on the South Fork, shortly after we arrive. Chester and Ken have some marvelous plans for a trip which we will discuss while we are camping on the stream. You and I will start West about June 13th … and will stop at The Ambassador as the apartment will be closed. Randy is coming with me, of course.

Just received your report showing you ranked third, which is perfectly satisfactory, I notice you got 59 in French, which is the only thing anybody could criticize in this excellent report, so please work a little harder on your 'parlez-vous'.

Doug Fairbanks and Mary Pickford … are moving into a house four doors below us on the Beach, the other side of the Mayers (Louis B.); in fact, everyone is moving down to the beach and we are going to have a wonderful colony this summer … Randy is turning over your poems to Mr. Hanline in person this afternoon and we will probably have some kind of word next week on what is going to happen to them....

October 27, 1927

...I am leaving for Chicago tomorrow where we have a convention...I am dining on Sunday with Vice President Dawes and on Sunday night attending the opening of 'Wings' there, so my sojourn in Chicago will be interesting particularly on account of the Convention itself....

Studio executives who were still remembering the unprofitable reception of *Old Ironsides*, were drawing up lists of editing changes that each thought should be made to *Wings* and each had a different suggestion: Cutting a particular scene entirely—keeping it, but moving it to a different place—tightening a sequence with a snip here and a snip there. It was and is common practice that after sneak previews many films feel the shears of the editor. With pressure mounting for the world premiere, Lasky sent one of his most able supervisors, Lucien Hubbard, to be installed in a dressing room of the Criterion Theatre with cans of film, splicers, and shears, along with the long and conflicting list of cuts and rearrangements recommended by the various East Coast executives. As the audience entered in tuxedos and long gowns and took their seats, Hubbard was busy re-cutting the film, managing to stay one reel ahead of the projectionist.

Whatever Hubbard did or didn't choose to do worked, because one of the last great non-speaking films (the last being *Modern Times* in 1936) resounded with the roar of planes and the rat-a-tat-tat of machine gun fire, provided by Roy Pomeroy's RCA Photophone sound track, which ran double-headed with the picture. To all concerned, it was a tremendous success, and for such a major screening, music was provided by an orchestra. Further screenings would be accompanied by the magic of the wondrous Wurlitzer. *Wings* is said to have been a major influence on Martin Scorsese and on Robert Redford. Wellman later received an Oscar for writing one of Hollywood's favorite films, *A Star is Born*. (The film has been recently restored and DVDs are available on the Internet.)

November 3rd
Dear Jesse,

...hope you received your derby and fur coat...I am rooting for cold weather so you will have an excuse to wear them....

Lasky was commuting between his offices in Hollywood and New York so constantly, he said he felt like a transient, adding '...The only office I had that gave me a feeling of permanence and security for more than a few hours was a drawing room on the California Limited.'

After changing from the Santa Fe in Chicago to the Twentieth Century on the final three-day stretch, there was plenty of time to dictate long letters to Randy Rogers, who normally traveled with him. Lasky was still quite surprised at the success his son continued to have with his poetry. Putnam had vied for and was going to publish the third book.

November 21, 1927
Dear Jesse,

...We are of course delighted that Putnam is publishing your new volume and I am hoping you can do some work on it with his Editor during the Thanksgiving vacation. I understand they will be ready to work with you when you come to town... Until Wednesday, Best love from all....

December 1st, 1927

...Had lunch with Geo. Putnam yesterday and he mentioned that he had just signed your contract, so everything seems well in that direction... The other evening we saw the results of the pictures we took at White Sulphur on the Movietone and it certainly was interesting to see and hear yourself on the screen. I thought we were all pretty terrible excepting little Billy and Betty who were of course unconcerned and therefore quite natural....

The chauffeur, Pierce, was gone, and Frederick was the new chauffeur in New York. Life for the Laskys meant theatres, glamorous friends, elegant restaurants, Rolls-Royces, sports cars, horses, and spectacular holidays. With no end in sight to the money rolling in, Bess had learned to spend, spend, spend: Paris dresses and serious jewelry. She had the second largest string of pearls in America and servants for every home. She was totally in charge of her own life with no limit on anything she wished. Enduringly beautiful, she had admirers; men with whom she shared ideas and interests and who had more time for her than her busy husband. Family life to her meant independence, respect, freedom. It also meant freedom from childcare.

In this laissez-faire relationship, husband and wife were to become better friends than they had ever been lovers. When the family got together for holidays and birthdays, Lasky always added a touch of showmanship that included entertainments and activities for the little children whose friends were always included. Costume parties were the rage, and the younger Laskys never lacked invitations, as did their parents, especially during the Christmas holidays.

December 14, 1927
Dear Jesse,

...I am sending Frederick in the Rolls and Randy will arrange for him to pick up Grace and he will meet you at the Nassau Inn at twelve o'clock.

Enclosed is a letter to Eaves Costume Company. You can stop there on your way home and try on the costumes. We haven't made any plans yet for Friday night but if we are free we will have tickets for a show

That Christmas had been especially exciting for Jesse. He was able to get back to California and finagled a job writing silent film titles at the studio. And his father began to write more about happenings in his film world and less about Jesse's grades.

Jan 15, 1928
Dear Jesse,

... we had many interesting things happen after you left, the most interesting of which was the opening of 'Wings' at the Biltmore Theatre last Sunday night. Walter (Wanger) and I gave a party in a private room at the Biltmore Hotel to about twenty-six people including Will Hays, Mr. and Mrs. Cecil DeMille, Joe Schenck, the Thalbergs the Goldwyns, John Saunders and Fay Wray, Jules Furthman and Mary Brian, the Schulbergs and others. We had an orchestra and a wonderful dinner and we all walked into the Biltmore Theatre in a body. The picture had the benefit of a very fine orchestral interpretation of the score plus perfect sound effects and a very big screen for the Magnascope scenes, all of which contributed to the greatest motion picture opening Los Angeles ever saw. The public laughed, applauded and were thrilled as no other picture, including 'The Big Parade' and 'Ben Hur', had ever touched them before.

After you left, Julian Johnson told me he was very much pleased with the ability you showed in your title work and that some of the titles were being used and were very good. I am happy to say that your modesty as well as your ability created a nice impression about the studio.

We spent a very interesting evening at Doug Fairbanks house and during the course of the evening he commented on how much he enjoyed your (3rd) book and said he was going to write you a letter about it. Cecil DeMille also made the same comment and the same promise i.e. to write you about your book ... Harold Lloyd gave a barbecue and a day of golf at his new home where he has a nine-hole golf course. Douglas Fairbanks and I were invited and we had a great day playing golf and mixing with all the great professionals ... I forgot to tell you I gave Zane Grey a dinner which you would have enjoyed as the evening was devoted to discussing fishing and outdoor sports and future trips. Little Billy had a talk with Zane Grey and strange to say took a great fancy to him and has been talking about catching fish ever since. Our moose hide coats arrived and they look great and will be very practical to wear on our next outing.

I am working on a scheme that is terribly interesting and I know will intrigue you. I am taking east a man who has invented the slow motion camera. He has just improved his camera so he can do extraordinary things in slow motion. I am planning to send him to the Olympic games at the Hague, Holland this summer and we are going to make a feature picture about five reels, during the course of which, apart from showing all the world celebrities present at the games, we will show all the different champions in slow motion so that athletes all over the world can study the form of the champions who win the numerous events. This will certainly make a great picture for school and college men who are interested in athletics, as they will have an opportunity to study the form in slow motion of the various masters in the different athletic games.

I'll bet you would like to go over as assistant and title writer to my man - but there is too much else to do this summer. I also organized successfully the South Sea expedition which you know something about, and I am sure that is going to produce another 'Chang'.

Our new Rolls is finished and it will meet me at the depot on arrival with a new temporary chauffeur....

Their California chauffeur had suggested that Lasky should really, for economy's sake, replace his huge Fiat—the car with the gold-plated fittings. Therefore, for economy's sake, Lasky had taken the opportunity on his last trip to London to pay a visit to Rolls-Royce's showroom, where his eyes were drawn to a sparkling royal blue Prince of Wales model. Once focused, he seemed unable to direct his glance elsewhere.

The salesman observing the gentleman in striped trousers, grey spats, and carrying a blond Malacca walking stick with initialed gold knob, hastily informed him that only one other car like it existed, which had been made for the Royal of the same name. The customer was peering with such interest through his pince-nez that the salesman cleared his throat and added, 'That would be the Prince of Wales, sir.'

'These cars are actually only made to order', he explained. However, this particular blue explosion of metallic power had been ordered by a maharajah who had been killed in a tiger hunt. Details were not given; but for that reason the car was now for sale.

Seeing that he was slightly late for lunch with his friend Gilbert Miller, the British theatrical producer, Lasky lost no time in signing the order and arranging for its delivery to New York. His letter to Jess continued:

Jan 15, 1928 (continued)

...No doubt by the time you receive this letter you will hear from me by phone. I want to plan for you to spend one weekend with me while I am in New York.

I spent a weekend with Cecil at Paradise and we had wonderful talks on religion which did me a lot of good. He gave me a copy of a book called Daily Unity Word, a monthly publication, which includes one page to be read each day before one starts on his days work, the book has done me a lot of good and I want you to adopt the same habit and read a page every day ... Mother gave me a very interesting book which I have just finished. The Prophet by Kalil Gibran[27], which I believe you recommended to her. it is a marvelous bit of writing and I enjoyed it enormously....

January 24, 1928

...Let me know what time your train arrives and I will send the new car for you at Pennsylvania Station and in order that you can identify the car, I will send Lawrence along with the chauffeur. I understand you will be in before lunchtime so it will be a good idea if you come right up to the office. We can have a chat and then lunch together. I will get seats for a good show Saturday night and we will dine at some restaurant where there is dancing.

Had a talk with Mother on the 'phone; she is painting this week with Mr. Silva and of course is very lonesome...

P.S., Be sure and bring my studs. I brought your tuxedo with me....

February 14, 1928

...We had a preview of 'Abie's Irish Rose' the other night and it is truly a wonderful picture and I am sure will be a very successful roadshow....

Lasky didn't tell his son the truth about *Abie's Irish Rose*. The stage play held the record to date for the worst critical notices and the longest stage run in history, a total of 2,327 performances—until the deep South play, *Tobacco Road*, got worse notices and an even longer run. Nearly every studio had been bidding for the film rights. In order to get them, Lasky bid the highest price the company had ever offered for a book or play: $500,000 plus 50% of the profits.

The subject matter—the love of a Jewish boy and an Irish girl touched upon the sensitive issue of religious prejudice. Like *Uncle Tom's Cabin* with a racial prejudice theme, it was an important social document. It starred Buddy Rogers and Nancy Carroll, who were now both box office names—but the film was a serious flop.

Lasky regretted that another studio hadn't outbid him, but since the play had been running on Broadway for five and a half years and had six road companies, he concluded that there wasn't anyone left who hadn't already seen it—and it was not something anyone in their right mind would see twice, even from stage to film. The play closed Oct. 22, 1927. His letter continued:

---

27 Kahlil Gibran.

February 14, 1928

...I think Mother wrote you about the plans for the new Beach House. They are simply wonderful and your quarters and my quarters are going to be ideal. For instance, you will have a big sitting room next to your bedroom with a balcony in front of both rooms looking into the garden and we are also providing a room for the Harvard tutor if it should seem wise to have him live at our house. In fact we will have about five or six guest rooms. We also have an outdoor porch downstairs for dancing which will be one of the features of the house. You certainly can look forward to an interesting summer...Sunday night George Putnam brought over a famous old sourdough Alaskan, Scotty Allen, a northern character who is world famous, and he told us stories of Alaska until the wee small hours of the morning and I just wish you could have been present; it was a fascinating experience....

February 22, 1928

...We have been making some good pictures. Last night we previewed (Wallace) Beery and (Raymond) Hatton in 'Partners in Crime' at Glendale and it is a comedy knockout.

Plans for the beach house have been completed... Facing the ocean and in front of the veranda of the new house will be a tiled dancing floor large enough to accommodate forty couples. We will have some lovely parties next summer as the new quarters are built for entertainment....

A letter to Jesse from Randy followed. Now that Jesse was older, Randy liked to play the part of a pal.

March 3, 1928
Dear Patriot:

...Seen on the Boulevard: Josephine Dunn riding closely beside Charlie Chaplin in his Rolls Royce Roadster, and looking very charming...Passers-by looking in the Hollywood Bookstore window at Jesse L. Lasky Jr.'s 'Listening to Silence' and passing on in silence. And many extras out of work.

Enclosed is a copy of the Paramount Official Daily Bulletin which will give you an idea of present production work.

Hope to hear from you soon again. Keep up your good work!

The Magnificent Randy

And Lasky wrote:

March 8, 1928
Dear Jess,

>...I believe Mother sent you a book called *The Bridge of San Luis Rey*. I am reading it. It is a remarkable work and all the boys around the studio are discussing it. Let me know what you think of it. About a year ago we bought the picture rights to *From the Double Eagle to the Red Flag*. I carried the two volumes across the Continent on a couple of my trips but so far the length of this novel has always caused me to put off reading it. I did, however, have a careful and quite long synopsis prepared so that I know the skeleton or bones of the story. I shall be interested in discussing this book with you as we are going to make a picture of it some day and you can imagine it is going to be an extraordinarily difficult job to adapt such a story covering so many episodes and events....

On the 17th of March, Jesse got a letter from his book editor concerning his third book of poems:

> ...if you would care to drop in sometime when you are in town and have lunch with me. I should like to discuss what further impetus we may be able to give your book as well as any other matters that may come up....

There was more news from Lasky.

March 19, 1928
Dear Jesse,

>...I am planning to show 'Abie's Irish Rose', which is a wonderful picture, to the Paramount organization the Saturday night I arrive, at the Criterion Theatre, right after the performance of 'Wings' is over. If you can get away comfortably from school, we could spend a very enjoyable evening going to a show first and the private viewing of the picture afterwards....

Baby-faced Nancy Carroll was Paramount's hottest star, and Lasky had discovered her. Red hair cut in a fashionable bob, with etched 'cupid-bow' lips, she had started in musical theatre on Broadway at fourteen. A hunger to get into films brought her west. Lasky spotted her in a play and signed her. In 1927 she made her debut at Paramount in *Ladies Must Dress*. With her musical training and excellent stage voice, she easily bridged the transition into sound.

Equally successful at flaming flappers, zany comedy, or sympathetic heroines, Carroll appeared in seven movies in 1928. She was paired in three films with Buddy Rogers. Their next film, *Abie's Irish Rose*, turned out to be a financial disaster for the studio, which the studio could not blame on the stars. Carroll followed it with *The Shopworn Angel*, her first (partial) 'talkie'.

Lasky was aware of his eldest son's abiding interest in history and writing. He hired tutors to insure that Jesse would be able to pass the entrance exams, if not for Harvard, then for Princeton.

NANCY CARROLL

March 30, 1928
En route to New York:
Dear Jess,

...I left everything fine in Hollywood...saw (Ernst) Lubitsch's picture which he directed, with (Emil) Jannings, called *The Patriot*. It is a story of the mad Czar, Paul I of Russia, and is a most marvelous production. I feel sure we have another big road-show hit in this picture. It is a type of story you will love and nothing less than a marvelous historical document of the period... Mother and I have received an invitation from Vice President Dawes and Mrs. Dawes to attend the Vice President's official State dinner to his Cabinet and the Diplomatic Corps. This is such an important function that I did not want to miss it....

April 19, 1928

...We are now devoting ourselves to engaging the right tutor for the summer, and even during the summer you will have a weekly meeting with Mr. Kates to chat over your progress...I am sending you, under separate cover, a photograph of Vice President Dawes which I think, on account of the autograph, you will prize and value highly. Take care of the photograph and we will have it framed when we get to the Coast. Incidentally, I will arrange so that we will spend an afternoon at his home near Chicago when we are enroute to the Coast this summer....

May 5, 1928

...Mother came down for the showing of 'Wings'. I spoke from the stage but it was such a big auditorium - about 6,000 people - that I could not make them hear very well...Practically the Ambassadors of every country were present and the Army and Navy Departments and most of the leading Government officials.

I had lunch again at the Senate, this time in a different room with four of the leading United States Senators, and Vice President Dawes joined us after lunch. We sat in the visitors' private gallery and watched the Senate in session, which was very interesting. I also had an hour with Secretary of the Navy Wilbur in his office at the Navy Department. I met some of the leading Admirals of the Fleet. You would have been fascinated by the things Secretary Wilbur showed me. He dug up the original log of the 'Constitution' and showed me many old weapons and trophies of the Navy. If I ever get you to Washington again, I promise you a thrilling experience in the Navy Department.

I talked for three hours on our new productions at the Washington Convention and the whole organization was unanimous in pronouncing our new program the greatest we ever had. This, of course, made me feel very good ... We showed the new (George) Bancroft picture 'The Dragnet' at the Convention and it is an absolute sensation. It will probably be a bigger success than 'Underworld'. We also showed. Lubitsch's 'Patriot' which is a marvelous picture you certainly must not miss ... Keep up the hard work. I know it is a strain but remember there is no such word as 'fail' in our lexicon. ...

Years later, when Jesse wrote the film *John Paul Jones*, he became acquainted with a few admirals himself, in particular, Admiral Chester W. Nimitz.

The Dragnet was Paramount Famous-Lasky's hit of the moment. Directed by Josef von Sternberg, the crime drama starred George Bancroft as 'Two Gun' Nolan, and dapper William Powell as Frank Trent, and Leslie Fenton as a character called Shakespeare. There had been four writers on the project; one Herman J. Mankiewicz, who later worked with Orson Welles on the script for *Citizen Kane*.

Underworld was also a von Sternberg film. It starred Bancroft as 'Bull' Weed and the fine British actor, Clive Brook played the suavely spruce 'Rolls Royce' Wensel. We cringe today at the names of these characters, but in Silents, with only visual clues, it quickly identified a character's 'character'. These two films under the personal supervision of Lasky were highly successful.

Sound was now a very loud whisper—and not just for sound effects like the pop! pop! pop! of machine gun fire. Stars, like Emil Jannings, with thick accents would soon be finished in American films and would return to Europe or switch to directing.

A few short years earlier Lasky had written, 'The idea of sound in pictures wasn't new in 1926. It had been kicking around for over thirty years. We saw no reason to think it would catch on at this late date. It was *The Jazz Singer* in which Al Jolson sang his rafter-shaking "Mammy" and spoke a few lines of dialogue that is generally credited with turning the tide the following year.' Soon the studios were advertising their newest releases with lines like:

ONE REEL OF DIALOGUE - PLUS NANCY CARROLL SINGS!
MOST OF THE PICTURE IN SOUND!
TALKING ALL THE WAY THROUGH!

And one MGM billboard declared:

GARBO TALKS!

For the moment, Lasky was back in California, sensing that perhaps eighteen-year-old Jesse would soon follow him into the business. He would, but not as a producer.

May 12, 1928
Dear Jesse,

... Of course I am terribly busy and now we have the new problem of adapting ourselves to the coming of the sound movies.

We have already built a soundproof stage and are putting in very elaborate equipment and machinery for synchronizing sound. This summer you will enjoy watching the production of the first sound pictures, and incidentally you will be familiarizing yourself with this new and momentous change in the Industry from its very inception ... By the way, I have been corresponding with President Hibben at Princeton, also the Dean, regarding our making a picture with Buddy Rogers, using the Princeton Campus and buildings as background. Mary Brian is the leading girl in the cast and Randy will let you know where they are stopping in Princeton and you can look them up if you have the time....

May 21, 1928

Enroute to Chicago ... Not knowing whether I will see you before we sail on the 'Leviathan' Friday at midnight, I am dictating this letter on the train to be mailed to you from Chicago. I do not know whether you wrote to me ... Mother advised me over the 'phone that you spent a fine week-end together and that she contemplated going to Princeton the week-end ahead of my arrival. Whether or not she did, I have not heard ... (if) the tutor had been engaged and would arrive in Los Angeles on July 1st ... Even his name is inspiring—Benjamin Franklin Jones ... we are sending the Governess and the children to California to await our arrival there ... We are sailing from France on the Ile de France as you will notice by the schedule, on June 20th, which will bring us to New York just about the time School closes.

As the apartment will be closed on account of John and Edla (servants) going to California the first of June to open up the Beach House, when you arrive in New York which may be a day or two ahead of our arrival, go direct to The Ambassador. If you wire or write Henry Salsbury, he will make reservations for your room and bath in advance and will also take you to the steamer to meet us ... Along about May 29th or 30th, Frank Tuttle, directing Buddy Rogers and Mary Brian in a college picture, will be in Princeton. Thanks to my acquaintance with President Hibben, we were able to obtain permission to photograph the Princeton campus and buildings. Frank Tuttle says he knows you. It will be nice if you will look him up and say 'hello', also Buddy Rogers and Mary Brian.

A letter from Jesse's publisher complimented him on his poetry. Years later it would be Jesse's poetry that encouraged DeMille to hire him as a screenwriter. Jesse was to co-write eight DeMille films.

May 29, 1928
Jesse Lasky, Jr., Esq.

The Hun School,
Princeton, N.J.
Dear Mr. Lasky:

...I have read the new verses with pleasure and like them. I think 'Colorings' is the best. It seems the most original in construction with its fifth line in each stanza as well as the smoothest in melody. It seems to me that it represents quite a distinct step forward in your use of the rhymed and metrical forms. I have turned over your verses to our Mrs. Barbour in the Putnam Syndicate who is analyzing them for possible magazine sale.

I hope when you get a chance you will drop in to see me, and I shall introduce you to her. I think she might be able to help you materially in placing such things as your verse, articles, stories, etc. I am still very enthusiastic about your idea of doing some sketches about Hollywood. You might possibly wish to keep them anonymous, but you certainly should have some wonderful first hand material.

I am going ahead on the folder which is to be mailed out to a list of one thousand names, giving some dignified advertising to *Listening to Silence*. Mr. Rogers says that he is going to collect whatever reviews and comments you have when he sees you this coming Sunday. Whatever you can furnish along this line will help enormously.

I am looking forward to seeing you sometime after your school is over. I appreciate that before then you will probably be in the throes of such bugbears as examinations, etc.

With best wishes,
Sincerely yours,
Winfield Shiras
WS/S

The poem Winfield Shiras mentioned is 'Colorings', which appeared in Jesse's book, *Singing in Thunder*.

COLORINGS

I used to watch the purple dusk
As it set into purple seas
I used to see the purple gulls
Swing in the evening breeze
And in the hills were purple trees

I used to carve in rocks of pink
And paint the sunset flower
I used to give my thoughts a link

> Of the sunset's golden power
> And build my dreams a tower
>
> I used to weave the threads of blue
> Into a rope of sky
> And all the world looked on, none knew
> That the weaver was only I
> And the blue was my own sky.

Jesse passed his exams and graduated, but to his father's surprise, he had other ideas which didn't include Harvard or Princeton. The young man decided that he would like to go to the University of Dijon in France. Feeling that this could quickly bring his son's French up to conversation level, his parents agreed to the plan if he would travel and share an apartment with his Uncle Art, Bess' younger brother, who wanted to study music in France. The letters began again from New York when Jesse and Art arrived in France.

October 5, 1928
Dear Jesse,

...the most important thing is that Billy was entered in the second grade at the Ethical Culture School and it seems to be just the school for him, and I mean to keep him there year after year, without changing, so that he will get a good foundation for his future studies and college career. We just have word that they are going to accept Betty at the same school in the first grade and she will start on Monday... By the time you receive this, you will undoubtedly have started your routine of studies and established contacts with your tutors in Dijon. I hope also you will be established in your apartment. Margaret (Miller)[28] will hand you your fencing equipment and the other things you wired for from the boat, and she will tell you the latest news as we are dining with her at the Colony restaurant tonight and seeing her off at the boat.

Give my kindest regards to Art and tell him how anxious I am to get his own impressions of all your experiences to date. I know it will console you, as it does me, that you will be seeing Mother in less than three months....

When Jesse and his Uncle Art arrived in Paris to learn French the 'proper way', they were greeted by Mel Shauer, head of Paramount's foreign department office in Paris, who promptly notified the boss.

October 9, 1928
Dear Mr. Lasky

---

28 Wife of Gilbert Miller, theatrical producer.

... The travelers reported a fine crossing and looked very well. It was a great pleasure for me to have the three 'Dijonnais' for 'Dejeuner' at my home that evening. That is not really correct French because they came to dinner and Dejeuner is not Dinner. Anyway they were there and we enjoyed it immensely ... Jesse seemed completely thrilled. I feel certain that during the coming year his experiences will be wonderful for him. When you write him, please assure him that we shall be happy to be of any service....

Mel. A. Shauer

Delighted though he was, Lasky placed the ball firmly back in Jesse's court. He wrote from New York.

October 23, 1928
Dear Jesse,

    ... Of course I am enthusiastic over your having entered the Universite de Dijon. In a way the laugh is on you as you left America to escape a University and now find yourself enrolled in one just the same, however, the circumstances are quite different and I am entirely convinced now that you were right in formulating your own plans for your education and in fighting so valiantly to carry them out.

    On the other hand, I take a considerable measure of pride in the fact that your Mother and Dad proved themselves up-to-date parents and broadminded enough to listen and try to understand your viewpoints. Now the results you accomplish this Winter and Spring will tell whether or not we were all right. I am sure the answer will be in your favor and I know and trust you will make the most of your opportunities.

    You were right to buy the Peugeot car and you used good judgment in taking up your quarters at the Grand Hotel de la Cloche for the time being but I do hope eventually you will find more suitable and comfortable quarters. I suppose your next letter will tell me that you have started your fencing and painting, and Art his music. Mother, of course, is fascinated by your description of the antique shops and the possibilities for painting around Dijon and I know is looking forward eagerly to visiting you, although we are not sure of the date....

    Curiously enough, since you arrived in France, I have had a great deal of contact with French people. To begin with, Maurice Chevalier arrived last week and we gave him a dinner at the Ritz Hotel to which we invited three hundred guests, including the Consul General of France, French Officers from battleships in port and other distinguished French people. I was the Toastmaster and introduced the various speakers including one or two gentlemen who made their speeches in French because they could not speak a word of English.

After the dinner we had invited about five hundred more people - stars and artists from the theatre; the entire Press; leaders in Society and in other Arts, and the whole affair was one of the most brilliant ever held at the Ritz. Mother and I left the Ritz Hotel at four o'clock in the morning. In fact, Mother made such a hit with the French Consul General and some of the Officers from one of the French battleships that she is attending a tea dance tomorrow on board the French battleship Duquesne which is anchored in the Hudson, as a guest of the Captain and the Consul General. She is taking some other ladies with her and I hope she writes you about the affair which will be very interesting ... I forgot to tell you that Maurice Chevalier sang several songs at the dinner and was a big hit, and I am now being applauded for my sagacity in having brought him to this country....

Lasky had more serious problems on his mind. Over at Warner Brothers back in 1926, young Nathan Levinson had been working on sound recording with Sam Warner, and although there was no dialogue, he helped bring the first sound to motion pictures in *Don Juan*, starring the theatrical great, John Barrymore. It had been the first feature-length film with synchronized sound effects and a musical soundtrack. Lasky's film, *Wings* was released the following year. The same year Levinson worked on *The Jazz Singer*, in which Al Jolson stunned the world by ad-libbing a few words of dialogue and singing *Mammy*. In 1929 Levinson received a Special Award for Sound Recording at the first Academy Award ceremony. During his career, he was to receive twenty-four nominations, one Award, one Honorary Award, and two Scientific/Technical Awards.

In the years to come, three of those films would be for Jesse L. Lasky. In 1941 there was *Sergeant York;* In 1944, *The Adventures of Mark Twain;* and in 1945, *Rhapsody In Blue;* some of the most important films in Lasky's career in which he could indulge his love for music which had yet to come into its own with sound. By 1928, Lasky was well aware where the future must lead. It was a momentous time in film history.

October 31, 1928
Dear Jesse,

...You will be surprised to learn we are making such progress with sound pictures, I mean all-dialogue pictures, that today I am issuing instructions to make no more silent pictures beyond those that are now in work. When you return next summer, you won't know the motion picture industry, as we will be making nothing but dialogue pictures, dramas, musical comedies, operettas, etc. Last night we dined with Fannie Hurst[29] and her husband and went to

---
29 Fannie Hurst highly popular American novelist during the post-World War I era.

an opening. Miss Hurst asked to be remembered to you . . . I am busier than ever and will not be able to return to California until just before Christmas. It now looks almost certain that Mother will have to postpone her departure to join you in France . . . You will now take your Christmas holidays without consideration of Mother but I still recommend St. Moritz and Margaret will undoubtedly be sure to show you the ropes.

    I imagine by this time you have decided to continue indefinitely in your hotel rooms and I don't see how you are going to do better. . .I realize it would be utterly impossible for you to study Latin with any success until you master French, and there again I think you displayed good judgment . . . Next week is Election and by the time this reaches you it will all be over and I hope Hoover will be our next President which seems likely to be the case. . . .

Hoover did become President—and Jesse, now eighteen, had managed to find an American girlfriend in Paris.

November 17, 1928
Dear Jesse,

    First, and I imagine most important to you I want you to know that I read your letter to Mother the one that told us all about Berthe Fisher, and your trip to Paris, etc. She must be a charming girl and of course I am happy to know that you were fortunate in knowing and caring for someone who has the nice qualities that you describe. . . .

    I realize I have not written you in nearly two weeks but we have had a convention of our salesmen from all over the country, including men from England and France, and on top of that some terrific preparation for the opening of 'Interference' at the Criterion last night, which, by the way, was a triumph—our first all-talking picture - and I dare say I have never been as busy as I have been the last two weeks. . . .

Although *Interference* was not a particularly distinguished film, it starred William Powell and was significant, as it was J. Roy Pomeroy's first directorial assignment. Pomeroy, who was one of the early film men to design special effects and miniaturization for sets and background shots, had opened the Red Sea for DeMille's first version of *The Ten Commandments* and had been given his own space at the studio: The Pomeroy Department. He had been sent east to learn the secrets of recording sound from Western Electric and RCA. On his return, suitably enlightened, he demanded a raise from $250 to $2,500 a week and insisted on directing the first talkie himself. Because of his imperious manner, *Interference* was soon known on the lot as *No Interference*. Lasky's letter continued:

November 17, 1928

...Last night Billy and Betty with great pride showed me your letter to them and I had to read it out loud although it had already been read by Miss Goodal[30] and Mother before I arrived home. The fact that you wrote them made a profound impression on their little minds, and Billy enjoyed the stamps you sent him and asks for more.

We are not going to Hollywood for Christmas but instead are going to Nassau, Bahama Islands, and will probably take Jean Limur[31] with us... I cannot tell you how we miss you particularly when we plan trips like the one mentioned above ... we console ourselves with the fact that you will have a polish and education which you never would have gained if you had remained tied to the apron strings of your parents. Please remember me to Berthe Fisher, and I do hope you arrange for Mother and I to meet her when she returns to New York. I will try and not be too fascinating and will subdue my charming personality as much as possible so as not to become an actual rival, which I still insist could easily be the case if I were not such a square-shooter; all of which is another way of saying, I am as good a man as you are. 'Gunga Din'... I send you both my best love.

Hardly tied to any apron strings and left out of the Nassau trip, Jesse and Art asked permission to spend their holiday on a trip to the Holy Land, Jerusalem, and Egypt.

November 28, 1928
Dear Jesse and Art,

...I would consider such a trip as an integral part of your education, just as pertinent as anything else that you are doing, and of course I am quite ready to finance it in whatever style you determine to travel although I judge by Art's letter you are going to follow the same general plan as your trip to Mexico, and go in old clothes and get away from the beaten path of the tourists, which sounds not alone adventurous but sensible if your object is to increase your knowledge of these countries and the manners and customs of the people...

Mother's exhibition is a great success... George Putnam was asking for you today and tells me he is going to write you a few lines. He is very enthusiastic over the fact that you are writing a book and I think looks forward to being its publisher... I was the Guest of Honor at the Dutch Treat Club yesterday. This Club is composed of newspaper editors, magazine editors, distinguished authors, etc. I made a forty-minute speech and they tell me it went over great.... Saturday night we are attending a dinner to Amelia

---

30 The newest governess.
31 The writer, Jean Limur.

Earhart, the famous aviatrix, which is being tendered her by George Putnam, so you see life is about as usual here....

December 3, 1928

...you will see that I have decided to make my Christmas present to you both the trip to the Holy Land in good style, and I hope you will be pleased. Last night I was an end-man in a minstrel show at the Authors' League of America. There was an audience of over one thousand, and they told me that my talk was the best and funniest in the show. Even Mother, who is my severest critic said she laughed continuously ... I took the children out for a long hike in the Park yesterday afternoon and then took them to Mother's exhibition and Bill certainly seemed to enjoy her pictures. He is getting to be a very intelligent little fellow....

Jan 3. 1929

...You will be amazed when you return this summer to find the progress we have made in our talking pictures. We are turning out all talking pictures that are simply wonderful and, of course, our studios are being rebuilt and the whole industry is being changed over from silence to sound ... Not to be outdone by your literary endeavors, I have just signed a contract with Colliers Weekly for a serialization of a story of my life which I am to write in collaboration with one of their special writers and which is later to be reproduced and published in book form by Putnam's. Colliers Weekly is paying me $7,500 for the serial rights to my story and as George Putnam is managing the business end of it and is going to help edit it, I am arranging for him to share in this sum. It is going to be a big job but the writer, Mr. Davenport, will leave with me on the train for California and we will be able to do most of this intensive work enroute to Hollywood.

January 10, 1929

...Just think, we are now producing musical comedies and on February 1st we are even starting to produce 'The Cocoanuts' starring the Four Marx Brothers ... It will interest you to know that 'The Patriot' was chosen as the best picture of 1928 by the dramatic critics and motion pictures critics of the United States....

Ernst Lubitsch produced, directed, and edited the silent *The Patriot*, which starred Emil Jannings as Czar Paul I. Lasky and Zukor are listed as presenters. Unfortunately, the film is lost today, but a few tiny excerpts exist. Seeing this clip now, one realizes how much ham was being served to audiences of silents.

(You may still be able to see a clip from the 1928 film *The Patriot*: https://www.youtube.com/watch?v=JrdCaqpbc70)

January 29, 1929
Dear Jesse,

. . . Regarding my efforts and collaboration on my autobiography, I don't think my collaborator has the feeling and qualities to do the work justice. Seriously, what do you think of this idea, that starting this summer you undertake the work yourself under some such title as 'The Story of my Dad' by Jesse L. Lasky Jr. We could go away for a week and take Billy on his first outing trip and thus kill two birds with one stone. We could give Billy his first lessons in woodcraft and I would tell you the story of my life in detail, you making copious notes and then develop the story in your own style, also as my story is in demand and would be published serially in Colliers and also in book form, you would earn a good sum of money. If you like this idea, let me know and I will try and slide out of my contract with Davenport, who is now devoting some time to working up the notes I gave him, but I could arrange so he would turn over his notes to you.

Two days after my arrival in Hollywood, a new $400,000 building which we had just completed in the studio and which was to be devoted to four soundproof stages and other equipment necessary to the perfect production of talking motion pictures, was entirely destroyed by a most spectacular fire. You can imagine my emotions when, about 6.30 o'clock while I was having a conference in my office, Randy came in and calmly notified me that the sound stages were on fire. By the time we got out to the building, it was blazing, the Fire Department had arrived and finally four alarms were turned in, and the fire was not entirely under control until midnight. While this building was covered by insurance, it will set us back somewhat in our work, but we are already rebuilding the stages and they will be completed by the middle of May. . . .

I note that you want to get into the studio work for a while this summer and I see no reason why you should not do so. Our great problem now is good dialogue writers on the all-talking pictures. I am going to talk to you this summer about taking a course in the Drama sometime during the next three years of your further education. If there is such a course in connection with Oxford or Cambridge, England, I would heartily recommend your going after it. In your literary career you are surely going to want to write a play now and then, and such a course would be very valuable for many reasons. Incidentally, it would be an ideal training for anyone who ever means to dabble in talking motion pictures. . . .

Rebuilding the sound stages was going to take four months, and a worried Lasky knew that shooting schedules meant turning out a steady stream of talkies immediately. The noise of rebuilding slowed the work. A few nights after the inferno, the studio manager, Sam Jaffe, stayed late when everyone had gone home, brooding in one of the burned-out stages. The next night, with an air of mystery he refused to explain, he dragged Lasky into the deserted studio to see the devastation by moonlight. It was not a pretty sight, yet Jaffe had an odd gleam in his eye and a smile on his face. 'Listen!' he whispered expectantly. 'What do you hear?'

Lasky strained for a sound in the silence. He seriously wondered whether the shock of the disaster had affected the studio manager's sanity. Jaffe's brother-in-law, Ben Schulberg, had told him that since the disaster, Sam had been depressed and losing sleep.

'Sam, what the devil are you talking about? I don't heard a sound', Lasky exclaimed.

'That's just it!' Jaffe cried triumphantly. 'At night you don't need sound-proofed walls. You can work in the ordinary stages. Everything is dead quiet! No noises to penetrate the building and spoil the takes.'

So for the next three months, while the din of rebuilding proceeded on schedule during the day, all shooting commenced at 9 p.m. with blankets hung on walls to cushion echo vibration. At least a dozen pictures were shot at night.

February 12, 1929
Dear Jesse,

   ...Mr. Schulberg has been absent from the studio for two weeks and I have been doing much of his work in addition to my usual duties so that I am passing through an extraordinarily busy period. However, the talking pictures, while they have added to our problems, have also added a definite new interest to the work. I know you will be fascinated this summer when you come to realize the possibilities of talking pictures.

   To illustrate, we are going to do Galsworthy's 'Escape', a most delightful English play and every line will be Galsworthy as originally written by him. I point this out because it indicates the trend that pictures can and no doubt will take. Fine plays with fine dialogue, and well acted by capable players, are bound to advance the screen to new and greater heights. Some day you will want to write and supervise a talking picture in which every line of speech will be your own and which, whether it succeeds or fails, you at least will know will be a true expression of your own artistic soul...my outer office is teeming with directors, writers, supervisors, actresses and while the male contingent can well be kept waiting, the pretty actresses are another matter. You, my romantic son, will understand....

February 20, 1929

...Mother is leaving today for New York and plans to sail early in April... so that within a few weeks after you receive this letter she will be on her way to join you. She has had a nice time here and would have stayed longer but we did not want to leave the children in New York alone too long. I am returning to New York on March 4th.

I was amused and happy to receive your cable agreeing to undertake the biography. I imagine you are more intrigued by the possibilities of the large remuneration than by the importance of the material, anyway the opportunity is open to you if you are still of the same frame of mind when we meet.

I shall be anxious to receive your letter telling about your week-end in London. I hope you secured a wardrobe at my tailors because you will need it when Mother joins you....

March 7, 1929

...I had a very busy time in Hollywood as you may have surmised from my brief letters, but accomplished a lot of good, and I left well satisfied with affairs at the studio. You know our Long Island studios are open now and running full speed ahead and turning out some fine pictures.

I just had a wire that the Marx Brothers in 'The Cocoanuts', in which Oscar Shaw and Mary Eaton also appear, is a perfectly wonderful picture. Practically eighty percent of our pictures now are all-talking, with sound and music, and songs as well, and the product we are making at Long Island is entirely devoted to sound, no silent pictures whatever....

The four Marx brothers, Groucho, Harpo, Chico, and Zeppo (originally five, including Gummo) began their film career at Paramount in 1929 with the advent of talkies. *The Cocoanuts* was based on their Broadway appearance in their stage play. Masters of mime in vaudeville, they had made one silent short, *Humor Risk*, in 1921, which according to Groucho, was so bad it 'previewed once and died the death.' Presumably, it is lost forever (unless a reader knows of a copy tucked away somewhere).

The story was set during the Florida land boom of the early '20s. It co-starred the indomitable Margaret Dumont with a chest like a pouter pigeon, who was to remain a feature of their antics. Humor could now be engendered from dialogue, not only visual capers. The film presented the brothers running a hotel and the audience was offered such Groucho observations as: 'Hello? Yes? Ice water in 318? Is that so? Where'd you get it? Oh, you want some? Get some onions, that'll make your eyes water.' And 'Sorry gentlemen, but we seem to have no vacancies. We have plenty of rooms though!' And, 'I'm gonna put extra blankets, free, in all your rooms, and there'll be no cover charge.'

(Here is a clip from the 1928 film of *The Cocoanuts*
https://www.youtube.com/watch?v=-Dgj8_iYr90)

Both *The Cocoanuts* and *Animal Crackers*, which quickly followed in 1930, were based on their previous stage productions written by George S. Kaufman and were adapted for the screen by Morrie Ryskind. Zukor, Lasky, and Walter Wanger all served as executive producers.

In *Animal Crackers*, Groucho played an African explorer. It included a good deal of singing, dancing, and such gems as Groucho to three women: 'What do you say the three of us get married? You girls have everything; you're short and tall, and slim and stout, and blonde and brunette. And that's just the kind of girl I crave!' And puns like, 'While shooting elephants in Africa, I found the tusks very difficult to remove. But in Alabama, the Tuscaloosa...'

Thanks to talkies, the Marx Brothers were on their way to becoming the period's greatest film comedy team, rivaled only by the treasured Laurel and Hardy. *Monkey Business* in 1931 was a screen original. *Horse Feathers* in 1932 was their most popular film to date, and the brothers were featured on the coveted cover of *Time Magazine*.

In 1935, the Marx Brothers left Paramount because of disagreements over 'creative decisions and financial issues' and joined Irving Thalberg at MGM. Groucho always considered that the two movies he made there, *A Night at the Opera* and *A Day at the Races*, which were not adapted from stage presentations and had well-constructed story plots, were their best films. Lasky's letter continued:

March 7, 1929 (cont'd)

Irving Thalberg is on the train with me and he just advised me that he bought the sixty feet of the Jim Stack property adjoining our Beach House, so he ought to make a nice neighbor. I know you like Mrs. Thalberg (Norma Shearer).

The Sunday before I left Hollywood, I went down to the Beach House for the first time and walked all through it, including your quarters. It made me both sad and glad; sad, because it was empty and full of memories but glad because I realize the good times we can look forward to this summer....

March 16, 1929

...Mother and I finally decided the best thing to do would be for Mother to come direct to Paris and spend about three weeks with you and Art, during which she would devote most of her days to painting, and particularly to getting certain instruction in her work which she thinks she needs. We are therefore reserving accommodations for Mother and Louise[32] on the S/S Paris, sailing April 6th, and I suggest that you and Art meet her at Havre ... I am

---

32 Bessie's sister Louise Ginsberg Gordon.

arranging to sail on April 27th and Frank Case may come with me, in which event we will go to London to do some shopping, particularly some wardrobe from Leslie and Roberts, and then fly over to Paris, and we will leave Paris immediately after my arrival for a trip through Italy and Spain or wherever you want to go, and plan to sail for New York from some Mediterranean port so as to arrive home about June 1st . . . and then make that place a starting point for a motor tour. I will use two motor cars, one for Mother's maid and the baggage and the other for ourselves . . . I will see Gilbert Miller when he arrives next week and he will tell me whatever he can about you. I am looking forward to seeing 'Journey's End' which you know we own. Gilbert is producing it for the Frohman Company which is owned by our Company. I wish you had written me your opinion of this play and the chances for its success in America.

We were so happy to learn of the interesting time you had in London, and I am simply dying to see your London wardrobe . . . I can see you and I walking down the Rue de Rivoli like a couple of London Johnnies out to give the French girls a treat. Seriously, we are very lonesome, and it will be a happy day when I grip that good right hand of yours.

Things are fine here. The new nurse for the babies is so wonderful that we can leave them with her without worrying . . . I am enclosing, a program of the Ziegfeld 'Midnight Frolic' which will interest you. I loaned Maurice Chevalier to Flo Ziegfeld and he is a sensation on the Midnight Roof. I promise to give you a party on the Ziegfeld Roof the night after we all arrive, and you can notify Bert. . . .

Earlier that year, when Lasky had first seen Chevalier starring in a revue at the Casino de Paris, tilting his straw hat with a cocky air, he was aware that the singer wowed the heavily American audience with his devastating blue-eyed magnetism and seductive voice. Lasky felt the Frenchman could have the same appeal in Paris, Texas. Impulsively, he went backstage and asked him if he'd like to go to Hollywood and become a Paramount star.

'Would I meet Doug and Mary?' the singer asked with the infectious smile that thoroughly captivated his audiences.

When Lasky told Al Kaufman, who managed the Paramount Theatre in Paris, that he needed the legal department to prepare an immediate contract for his great discovery, Kaufman warned, 'Chevalier's been around for years. All the American producers have looked him over. Irving Thalberg and Louis Mayer saw him two months ago.'

Lasky had a serious moment of doubt. If Chevalier was such a prize, why hadn't someone signed him up already? Could his star-making radar have crossed wires? But he remembered MGM's lack of interest in Valentino, and seeing the Frenchman again, the producer was certain his instincts were right and he signed him to a five-year contract with options, starting at $1,500 a week.

When the New York office reminded him that foreign accents were toxic at the box office, Lasky started immediately on a huge press onslaught and organized a gala reception-banquet for his new star in the Crystal Room at the Ritz-Carlton the night after his arrival. New York's most distinguished celebs attended, including the French Consul and the French Ambassador from Washington. Chevalier captured the audience with his first song and held them spellbound through encore after encore. Even Zukor and Kent were impressed.

The great impresario, Flo Ziegfeld had also attended the banquet. The next day he phoned Lasky begging him to borrow Chevalier for his 'Midnight Frolic' on the New Amsterdam Roof.

Lasky hid his delight and told him that as a special favor he would postpone Chevalier's first picture long enough to let him appear on the Roof for six weeks if Ziegfeld paid the studio $5,000 a week. He later noted, 'Ziegfeld's gratitude was touching.'

The truth was that it would be at least six weeks before they could hope to start shooting on Chevalier's first Hollywood talking film, *Innocents of Paris*, and they had to pay his salary from the day he landed. Instead of losing $1500 a week the studio made $3500 profit—and they would have gladly paid Ziegfeld $5,000 a week for the huge publicity build-up of his appearing on the Roof.

March 26, 1929
Dear Jesse,

... By the way, here is something that will amuse you. Now that the talking pictures have come in, we are making a great many tests of different actresses at our Long Island Studio, and once a week they bring them over for me to pass on them and advise who should be engaged, etc. Imagine my amusement when following each other in succession, I saw a very excellent test of Grace Durkin, speaking lines very well indeed; her sister, an attractive little girl, followed by Evelyn Hoey, whom we are thinking of engaging and sending to our California Stock Company ... no matter which way I turn, I cannot get away from your conquests, but I will say this for your taste, they are all very nice and very pretty girls, and you will never be ashamed of having known any of them....

March 27, 1929

... I am having ten copies of 'Listening to Silence' forwarded to you from Putnams so that you won't have to wait for Mother to bring them over.

While Mother was reading your letter to me at breakfast, little Betty was sitting next to me busily writing in a copy book. Betty must have listened to the letter (you will remember you referred to your book, that it was getting along and would soon be finished), because she chirped up—'I am writing a story, it isn't finished yet but I want to read it to you'—and sure enough, she read us a little story about a dog who said 'bow-wow', etc., and we roared with laughter. One author in the family is enough and I earnestly hope Betty won't follow your example and try and rival you as an author....[33]

In 1929 Nancy Carroll filmed *Close Harmony*, Paramount's first all-talkie hit (in which Jean Harlow had an uncredited walk-on). She was nominated for an Oscar the following year for *The Devil's Holiday*. The studio claimed Carroll received more fan mail than any star of the day. Lasky wrote his son who was once again alone in California, with family news:

September 22, 1929
Dear Jesse,

...Betty is in the third grade and Billy in the fourth, and apparently holding their own...I like the atmosphere of the Long Island Studio very much. You feel you can breathe there without giving offence, and everybody is full of enthusiasm, and the place has an air of success about it that cannot be denied. Jimmy Cowan is a fine executive, and Hector (Turnbull) has become the very sunshine of the studio...I can't imagine a more delightful place for you to work in than Long Island, and I think by all means you ought to decide to come east with Walter (Wanger) and go right to it. New York really peps one up, and I feel by this time it is probably just what you need...by all means write Mother occasionally, addressing her letters to the George V ...We are now engaged in producing musical comedies and operettas and every once in a while I engage composers, librettists and lyric writers and send them to the Coast and to our Long Island Studio. Every time I talk lyrics now, I think of your enthusiasm when you started to collaborate with Martin Broones who, by the way, is working for Metro in Hollywood. I wouldn't be surprised if you should want to try your hand at some lyrics this summer....

But trouble was brewing in paradise. The first hints of the Depression had been seeping west to the high and mighty studios, who didn't really think it would affect them. They were wrong, but Lasky was still minimizing his own plight to his son.

November 1, 1929
Dear Jesse,

...We passed through a very trying week here. The stock market, after a series of bad breaks, went into an actual panic, the most serious in the history

---

33 In 1989 Betty Lasky wrote, 'RKO The Biggest Little Major Of Them All'.

of the country. Many people were wiped out, and everybody had cause to worry. Fortunately my affairs were in fine shape at the time, and I had no difficulty in weathering the storm, and now things are about normal again, so that the only net result to my personal fortune is a slight shrinkage in paper profits.

... The other day I had a most interesting experience. I had made a contract with Douglas Burden, an explorer and young millionaire, to release a picture which he agreed to make in the Canadian Northwest, on the life of the Indians before the white men came. After a year making this picture, he has returned, and the picture is simply wonderful ... It is more than an animal and Indian picture, as it has a poetic charm and beauty, and a simple but very human little story that is intriguing beyond words.

In spite of the stock market excitement, our plans for the West hold good, providing Mother has not changed her mind, as my main object in whatever we do is to please her and to make her happy. I am on the track of a piece of property near Bel-Air that sounds very interesting....

SCENE FOUR
1930 - 1934

FREDERIC MARCH, GARY COOPER, MIRIAM HOPKINS

In Great Britain, the conservatives were in power for most of the decade; there was mass unemployment, general poverty, and discontent. In America, although the Depression was rumbling Wall Street and fear had driven many New Yorkers to bungee jump from office windows without a rope, the Hollywood film people thought they were immune, believing that depressed Americans would now need entertainment more than ever.

During his summer break from University in Dijon, Jesse had traveled in Morocco and Palestine with Art and Bess, unaware that the axe was about to fall on the Laskys' gilded existence. He returned from Europe to share one last daring exploration with his father. For the moment, the world was still Lasky's oyster and life was for living to the fullest. Seemingly endless riches allowed him to travel like a fabled potentate, and his fame and power as the creative head of Paramount meant that without being asked, for this latest exploit the Mexican government sent the Army for his personal protection and even turned back a train for him.

He had begun to think of himself as invincible, indomitable. With dauntless courage, he saw every day as requiring a personal challenge. Jesse, who never sought out these adventures, could be as dauntless as his father when confronting danger, but was aware of the line between courage and folly. I include this fascinating letter to Bess of this particular exploration down the Rio Balsas. It was the end of an era, and was to be Lasky's last great trip with Jesse.

Father and son had arrived with Chester, Ken, and Hector and Randy at Guerrero, Mexico, (Randy only came to see them off). Lasky dictated this letter to Randy for Bess:

January 6, 1930
Monday Evening—Six o'clock.
at Puente sur Rio Balsas, Estado Guerrero, Mexico,
 (On the Eve of our Greatest Adventure)
My dear Bessie:

Imagine, if you can, a promontory 500 ft. high; a very primitive little Mexican Inn topping it, and the Balsas River flowing down below; across the river thatched Mexican huts; a scattering of banana and palm trees and cactus; a native girl in a bright seraph (serape) finishing her day's washing at the river's side; a pack-train of burros just approaching the river's edge; natives of every description scattered here and there in the foreground wearing colorful sombreros, mostly of straw; chickens, pigs and dogs spotting the scene with color, and directly behind me, as I sit on this promontory dictating this letter to Randy, our Victrola playing a gorgeous romantic Mexican record . . . Now, again imagine a trail leading from the edge of our promontory down to the river, and a score of picturesque Mexicans and Indians carrying our equipment to the boats—round duffle bags; cameras, boxes, guns; a box of apples, a box of oranges; some native pineapples and bananas; a Mexican in an attractive Jorongo (Serape), which is sort of a cape through which he puts his head, colored like a leopard skin, with a huge sombrero surmounting a red bandana which conceals his sleek black hair, struggling under the burden of a case of cognac which we have just tested at supper - four natives following him each with a case of wonderful Mexican beer, also just tested at supper—and down at the water's edge my canoe gracefully floating, looking very inconspicuous compared to the four great boats, 20 feet long and 5 feet wide, which only an hour ago were completed by the boat builders and are now being loaded by the Mexicans—and you have still another picture of our last night in Balsas... on our Conquest of Mexico, from the morning we left Mexico City. We departed from the city early in three automobiles, and a truck loaded with our baggage, and passing through the outskirts of the city, we saw many scenes of natives at picturesque market places, and the narrow streets, drove into a tropical valley and passed through a very primitive town named Cuernavaca (Cuernavaca, Morelos), which has been the home recently of Ambassador Morrow, and the scene of the courtship of Lindbergh and Miss Morrow.

We noticed as we left this town for the next five hours of our journey, that at intervals of a mile soldiers were stationed at the roadside in squads of two and three, fully armed, prepared for any emergency. This rather surprised me, and only at the end of our journey did Col. Fontes inform me that the soldiers were there because the Government officials were very anxious that nothing should happen to their distinguished visitor and guests which might cause a shadow on the stability of the Government. Col. Fontes advised me that when I refused to accept an escort of soldiers offered by Secretary Padilla, at the suggestion of the Minister of War, that they determined to see that we were protected whether we wanted it or not, and actually ordered the placing of the soldiers along our route.

About two o'clock in the afternoon, we arrived at a town called Taxco, and found that Col. Fontes had wired the night before to have a typical Mexican dinner prepared for us in the private home of a Mexican friend... which nestles a couple of thousand feet high on the side of a precipitous plateau. It was Sunday, always a gala day in Mexico, and the market place—the plaza of the town, was simply swarming with Mexicans and Indians in gala costumes, making the scene beyond description; and the square was covered with puestos (booths) where fruit, flowers, toys, hats, and miscellaneous small articles could be bought, and at the risk of missing our lunch, we left our automobiles long enough to stroll around the square... We finally tore ourselves away from the scene and entered a cathedral built early in the 17th century by a Frenchman who had become rich through opening up silver mines in the section, and wanted to make a gift to the town. The carvings and decorations of the cathedral were designed and built in Spain and actually shipped to Mexico through the Port of Acapulco, and carried by mule pack over the mountains ... After leaving the cathedral, we climbed a very narrow street, and entered a typical Mexican home, where a real feast or banquet awaited us. When the lunch ended, we returned to the cars, as we had to make a railroad train that left a little town at the end of the automobile road, at five o'clock ... we came upon a sight which caused us to put on the brakes abruptly. Immediately on our right was a large circle, a typical bull-fight arena but very primitive, and the entire circle covering an acre or more of ground was surrounded by Mexicans in gala attire, watching other Mexicans going through a rodeo, bull-dogging steers, etc. At intervals, when the scene became exciting, a primitive brass band struck up a tune, and the Mexicans laughed and shouted their approval. At least one hundred gorgeous buckaroos were seated on horses riding around the arena...In the midst of this exciting adventure, Chester warned us we would miss the train unless we rushed to the automobiles, so with a feeling of real regret, we...raced towards the town where we were to catch our train. Sure enough what might have been expected, happened, for when we arrived at the little railroad station and inquired if the train had arrived, the natives laughed and stated, 'Train gone, another train mañana.'

This meant that we would have to remain in the little town until five o'clock the next evening, but Col. Fontes who has not failed us in any emergency thus far, and who having been a Director-General of the Railroads of Mexico, seemed able to meet every situation, calmly went to the little telegraph office and in a few moments came back and advised us that he had telegraphed the railroad dispatcher in Mexico City, and that the dispatcher would notify the Balsas stationmaster, sixty miles away, to immediately have the train returned to our station and pick us up and take us to our destination - Balsas on the Rio Balsas ... (at) ten pm, when the little train consisting of an engine and one day coach arrived from Balsas, and the conductor informed us he was ready to take on his distinguished passengers. A young Lieutenant in a white uniform was presented to us, and through an interpreter, advised us that the Governor of the district, when hearing of our plight, ordered an escort of soldiers to protect us on our night ride to Balsas – as you must understand the country through which we were passing has never been entirely settled and safe. The train rumbled along about twenty-five miles an hour, over the roughest single track I have ever encountered, and along towards midnight, the lights in the car went out and could not be induced to give illumination again; so sitting in utter darkness, the soldiers at one end of the car we passed through what seemed most mysterious country and arrived at Balsas.

In a moment the car was surrounded by natives, but they were quickly dominated by our two men, the *Kaftanish* brothers, both wearing pistols prominently displayed in their holsters, who took charge of matters with real military authority. At this point I should explain that the Kaftanish brothers had been sent by Chester from Mexico City, and on better acquaintance, we think they are two of the most valuable members of our party. They have built four seaworthy boats that could not be improved upon, and have worked day and night directing a score of natives in order that the boats should be ready for our arrival.

It was great meeting Ken again, and we were soon escorted up the five hundred foot hill I described in the beginning of this letter, into a primitive and not very inspiring inn. We were assigned to cots in the halls and in the so-called bedrooms, each cot being covered by a single sheet and nothing else, but before retiring, the Chinaman who runs the place, conjured up a splendid supper, and at 1.30 am, we retired to the cots, and were advised to carefully turn our beds over and inspect them to be sure that no scorpions were crawling around, as only the night before one of the Mexicans had been bitten by a scorpion...And now I am back to the beginning of this letter, just sitting on the promontory ... The light is just fading, or rather the light of twilight is turning from gray to pink with a tinge of salmon red—the sunset that you know so well in California.

In order to get away from the snorers of the night before and the possibility of scorpions for bed-fellows, we are going to sleep in the boats tonight which we propose to anchor in the middle of the river. They are long enough for two cots to be laid end on end and we will sleep there, not alone for the cool of the river, but to guard our outfit, which is now all assembled for an early start at daybreak tomorrow ... Jesse joins me in sending best love to you and the babies. I will wire you just before we get into our boats in the morning. The date of that wire will be January 7th. After that we will be out of communication for a period somewhere between two and three weeks, but please don't worry, as you will hear from us by wire from Acapulco on the Pacific Coast, and if you could see the wonderful boats and the fine crew of twelve men, experienced and capable, that make up our party, you certainly would realize that we are prepared to cope with anything that may lie ahead of us. The boats have air-tanks and are non-sinkable. We carry life preservers and ropes and at the stern of each boat we have a man with plenty of previous experience in river work.

We are getting some wonderful pictures, and we are now sure that we will pass through a couple of hundred miles of country that no white man has ever seen.

Goodnight, my dear wife —
Your loving husband.

But all was not going as well as Lasky had indicated to his wife, or that Randy knew. Further down the Rio Balsas several days into the expedition, while the others were lunching and resting and without a word to anyone, Lasky decided to shoot the awesome length of rapids ahead on his own.

Startled at seeing his father climbing into a canoe alone, Jesse shouted for him to wait and ran down to the riverbank. But he was too late. By now, several others had turned to watch and some to run to the water's edge.

Gripping the paddles, Lasky pushed the canoe out into the water. Before he could gain command of the craft, the current precipitated him forward. He paddled with impressive strength, fighting for control as he was swept into the eye of the rushing surge. The canoe twisted and spun around, submitting to the powerfully uncontrollable churning of flashing, racing water.

Running to keep abreast of his father's careening craft, Jesse saw it smash into a rock and shoot out of the water. It upended, then overturned, spilling Lasky into a churning explosion of water. And then he was gone, disappearing beneath the swirling undertow.

Jesse threw himself into the river, frantically swimming for the spot where his father had vanished. Further down stream he saw his father's head pop up, struggling for air as he tried to swim free of the sucking pull of water. With all the might of his youthful arms, Jesse swam into the flow, hauled along by the force of current, fighting against its speed. Amazingly he reached his father and grabbed hold of him,

JESSE ON THE RIO BALSAS

somehow pulling him free of the swirling maelstrom. Lasky regained his breath and clinging together, they managed to reach the shore. By now, several of the Mexican guides were at the river's edge to pull them out.

That afternoon a father's gratitude could find no words—and a son's anger at what he considered his father's irresponsible derring-do, went unexpressed. It was not the only time that Jesse would jump into water to save his father. The second time would be even more of a surprise.

From Acapulco, on the Pacific Coast, the crew of twelve men who made up the party all arrived safely. Home again, father and son were once more separated. Jesse returned to the University of Dijon, and Lasky could brag to his friends about their adventure, still living in the exalted climate of privilege.

February 4, 1930
Dear Jesse,

…Doug goes about telling everybody with much glee and enthusiasm that I do the things that he is supposed to do and that I am more like Douglas Fairbanks than he is himself. He made me promise to go up to his place next week and tell him the whole yarn, and I know we will have a lot of fun … I have been asked to entertain the son of Prime Minister Ramsay MacDonald, who arrived here Sunday, and who has put himself more or less in my hands for the week. He is a fine young chap, an English architect, and is making his first visit to Hollywood. I gave him a luncheon in the studio yesterday, and tonight I am taking him to the Fights downtown, etc…

March 5, 1930
On Board Santa Fe 'Chief'
(to Jesse in Dijon)

…Just think, I will have been away from New York over two months; you can imagine, therefore, how I am looking forward to getting home and being with Mother and Billy and Betty … I left things very fine in California; the Studio has never functioned so well. Just before my departure, I gave a banquet to Mr. Zukor and had present fifty of the leading executives of the studio. I presided as toastmaster, and the result was highly gratifying.…

By this time, you are aware of our future plans. We are trying to sub-lease the new apartment (in New York), and will purchase a home this summer somewhere in Beverly Hills … You understand, of course, we will continue to visit New York at intervals, but instead of living in an apartment, we will stay at the Savoy-Plaza, or some equally good and new hotel. Our Paramount stock has been going up steadily, so I now feel we can afford a really fine estate, and I know you will enjoy joining with Mother and me in selecting and planning the place.…

While in Hollywood, I attended Cecilia DeMille's wedding. She married a man about thirty-eight-years old . . . By the way, I succeeded in getting Carroll (Case) a job as Second Assistant Director to Eddie Goulding in our studio. I don't think Carroll knows that I secured the job for him, and as he did not call on me, I have not seen him since his arrival in California . . . Incidentally we have been turning out some fine pictures. 'The Vagabond King' has opened, and is a great success. Dennis King is in London, doing 'The Three Musketeers' for Ziegfeld. We will have him back next summer . . . I wish you would call on Bob Kane . . . Kane is producing some short subjects which we are distributing, and will experiment in a minor way making French pictures out of our American subjects. He is a very nice fellow, and you would enjoy meeting him and visiting his little studio which is near Paris . . . I succeeded in having Joe Schenck and Sam Goldwyn buy the 120 feet of beach property next to us, so this summer we will have Schenck and the Goldwyns as neighbors.

The coming of sound has brought a wonderful colony to Hollywood, and I attended some lovely parties. Musicians like Oscar Straus and Frimil (Friml); opera singers like Lawrence Tibbett and Mary Lewis - celebrities of all kinds tumble over one another, but it is becoming to be a real art and intellectual center. . . .

Bess, not to be left out, had compiled her own poetry and was offering it for publication. Lasky was afraid it might be a 'vanity' offering and took steps.

March 15, 1930
(En Route to Palm Beach)

. . . Not wanting Mother to make a mistake regarding the publishing of her book, I determined to get an expert criticism, and to learn if her material was good enough to publish. At this time it happened that by arrangement with Horace Liveright, I was engaging Maurice Hanline to go to the Coast as a literary advisor, editor, dialogue writer, etc. It was therefore quite easy for me to ask him confidentially to read Mother's poems which, by the way, have increased in number since your departure, and give me a frank and honest opinion as to their value. To my surprise and gratification, Hanline stated they were really excellent, and offered to help edit them. . . . Hanline paid you a nice compliment last night, inasmuch as he feels that someday you are going to be a brilliant writer. . . .

Our company is going to build a very fine long-run presentation theatre on the site of our original Vine Street studio. It will be a big, attractive theatre to compete with Grauman's Chinese Theatre, and the company, as a compliment to me, and because of the fact that it was on this site that I founded the original Lasky Company—without my knowledge, decided to name it 'The Lasky Theatre'.

Well, seeing that I have not heard from you direct . . . I think I have written you as much as you deserve; however, no hard feelings - how could there ever be between us, when I remember your expression as you dove into the Balsas and risked your life to save mine. Maybe it is just that, and other incidents between us that make me long for a direct word from you. How many times Mother and I have said—'If only Jesse could be with us in this private car.' We have a new Victrola, with marvelous new records, and every luxury imaginable and a gorgeous suite of rooms awaits us at the Breakers Hotel, Palm Beach, facing the ocean, where we will bathe all day.

March 23, 1930
On board our Private Car

. . . We are en route home from Palm Beach after what Mother calls the most delightful week she has ever spent. What a time you would have had if you could have been with us. Mother, who always claims she doesn't care for society people, was taken up by the Palm Beach smart set, and had the time of her young life. We attended teas, luncheons, dinners, and functions at exclusive Palm Beach Clubs, and made a lot of new friends. . .While at Palm Beach, Mother and Randy, who by the way stayed with us throughout the trip and lived on our private car in the utmost luxury, picked up two of the cutest little dogs imaginable —Esquimo Spitz dogs —and we have them with us on the train as a surprise birthday present for Billy . . . On Saturday, we are letting him celebrate his birthday, and he has invited about 25 school friends and I am providing a magician and a Punch and Judy show, and it is going to be a very nice children's party indeed. . . .

Bess, who now would admit a dog to her house, added a rare note to this letter by hand:

Hello, Jesse,

The best is yet to come when we sit over our camp fire at George V and you hear of the tropical week at Palm Beach . . . You can never know the feast of soul that I had drinking in the tropics the balmy soft velvety air the splendor of the sun and the warm beautiful tropical waters to say nothing of the many famous people that we had heard about, to visit them in their palatial homes, where everything is of the utmost extravagance, in the most perfect taste. Yesterday's tea, for instance was given at Stotsbury's son's house—a multi-millionaire who collected a Moorish palace brought it over and planted it in his jungle where he has monkeys and every tropical plant and tree imaginable.

One side of his house is completely Moorish windows opening on Lake Worth and it has the feeling of a houseboat. He lives in this dream place and enjoys life to the fullest. They had a hundred people with tables in the garden, where a soft orchestra played and colored boys dressed in costume, danced. It was all so unreal and filled with magic that I sat on a low divan facing the lake talking to a young, very interesting writer and he agreed that we were in a dream and would wake up suddenly to find it completely gone. Well, I woke up this a.m. and it has all vanished, but I shall always keep the memory of perfumed gardenias, swaying palm trees, and the warmest of radiant sunny days—more later.

Love, Bess

In the heart of Beverly Hills today you can drive down Lasky Drive off Wilshire Boulevard. In the 1920's, before the Beverly Hilton Hotel was built, there used to be a racetrack in that spot of barren, flat ground. Lasky was a stockholder and director of the track and loved to race around it in one of his custom-built sports cars, throttle out, in competition only with himself. When that bit of Beverly Hills was eventually subdivided, one of the streets was named after him. There is also a Lasky Ranch near Universal City, a Lasky sandwich (chicken and ham), and a Lasky cocktail (Bourbon, soda, lemon slice on the rocks). Where today the National Broadcasting Company stands, Adolph Zukor had plans for an extravagant Lasky Theatre in honor of his partner. It was never built because of the Depression. Bess was right; they were living in a dream world and it was about to vaporize.

Lasky was negotiating for the film rights to Theodore Dreiser's classic novel, *An American Tragedy*. His old friend, publisher Horace Liveright, was acting as Dreiser's agent. Over lunch with the author at the Ritz, they discussed the project. When they got to the coffee, Lasky made his offer: $90,000.

A firm-lipped Liveright, quietly but forcefully responded, 'Mr. Dreiser won't accept that.'

Dreiser's face turned crimson, his eyes bulged, and exploding a mouthful of expletives, he called Liveright a liar and threw his coffee in the publisher's face. Shock, embarrassment, and leave-taking followed.

Feathers were smoothed and eventually Lasky purchased the novel at his price. *An American Tragedy* nearly turned out to be one.

On April 30th, Jesse was in Budapest staying at the Ritz when he received a long letter from his father's first assistant, Albert A. Kaufman.

April 30, 1930

...This is to notify you that we are engaging you as the Production Department's representative in Spain. You are to proceed to Barcelona where you will be under the direction, and subject to the orders of our Mr. Messari, until further notice. You will receive compensation at the rate of $50.00 per week, and all expenses when you travel for the corporation. Your compensation will start on the date you arrive in Barcelona, and we will expect you to report to Mr. Messari not later than May 11th, 1930.

You understand, of course, that the principal object of your trip to Spain at this time is to perfect your Spanish, and nothing described herein should be allowed to interfere with this object of our stationing you in Barcelona. We would like a letter from you every two weeks, briefly reporting on anything that might be interesting to the Production Department, as follows: Acquaint yourself with the leading Spanish artists—principal leading men and leading women—and musical comedy leading people. You are to collect photographs and briefly describe anyone you discover who, in your opinion, would be successful in Spanish pictures made either in Hollywood, New York or Paris, and, of very great importance, you are to try to discover Spanish artists who speak English well enough to play in English-speaking productions, which later can be copied in the Spanish language.

In order to develop an immediate means of securing and engaging the very best Spanish types to enter motion pictures, we have requested our Mr. Messari to organize a school...we charge you with the definite responsibility of seeing that no artiste is put into the school who, when trained, would not be a good type for leading or important character roles in Spanish pictures to be made in Hollywood, New York or Paris...We would like you to form, during your stay in Spain, a definite opinion as to the future possibilities of Spanish talking pictures made by our corporation, for the Spanish market, as far as you are able to observe it....

With my kind regards, I am
Yours sincerely
Albert A Kaufman
Assistant to First Vice President

P.S. You will kindly send your reports every two weeks, to the following executives: Robert Kane, Paramount Cinestudio Continental S.A. Paris, Jesse L. Lasky, Paramount Building, New York City, Walter Wanger, B.P.Schulberg, Lasky Studio, Hollywood, California. A.A.Kaufman, Geoffrey Shurlock. ..Any other information of interest need only be sent to Mr. Kane, Mr. Shurlock and Mr. Wanger. Photographs with descriptions of players should he mailed to Mr. Kane, Mr. Wanger and Mr. Shurlock.

Jesse was dropped right into it and apparently managed to deal with the task successfully, which gave him the opportunity of meeting interesting, talented people on the way. His father visited him in Paris with Bess and Art, then sailed back to New

York alone. He wrote from the ship, instructing Bess in New York to travel with Bill and Betty to California and closed with:

May 11, 1930
Dear Bessie,

...I am just counting the days until we are all together in Hollywood, and I am very glad that we are having Jesse come over the middle of July. I am beginning to miss you very much, as you can see by the tone of this letter.

My love to Art, and Boris (Lovet Lorski, the sculptor) if he is still with you.

With oceans of love,
Your devoted husband

Filming *An American Tragedy* was Lasky's next main project, and he was trying to decide on a director important enough to take on such a venture when he met Sergei Mikhailovich Eisenstein in Paris. The famous Soviet Russian director had made film history in 1925 with his artistic triumph, *Battleship Potemkin*, followed triumphantly by *October: Ten Days That Shook the World* in 1928. Lasky hurriedly signed Eisenstein for his first directorial job in Hollywood for the princely sum of $100,000, agitating East Coast feathers more than slightly.

Filming those historical Russian epics, Eisenstein had developed the art of montage. Now ensconced at Paramount with more money than he had ever seen, the wild-haired Russian studied Hollywood film techniques and confidently—and slowly—wrote an adaptation of Theodore Dreiser's massive two-volume novel.

Lasky still had time to keep his eldest son informed. He wrote from the Overland Limited between Chicago and San Francisco, and with a touch of false bravura, added:

May 19, 1930
Dear Jesse,

... Without any preparation, other than an hour's conference on the train to Atlantic City, I found myself presiding at the first session of our Convention, but I mastered the situation with my usual eloquence, and they told me I made a great speech and up to my very high standard - h'um, h'um, h'um??
I punctuated my speech with two brilliant interruptions. First I introduced Eisenstein, who gave a fine talk and made an immediate hit with the delegates; and later, I introduced Mrs. Schoedsack, who just arrived from Sumatra where the Schoedsacks have been making a wonderful picture for us for nearly a year. She told the story of the picture and it made a great impression. We all feel it is going to be a knock-out....

At that moment, David O. Selznick,[34] having taken over B. P. Schulberg's position at the studio, issued one of his many memos to come, this one to Schulberg, who had been elevated to a more senior position at Paramount.

October 8, 1930
Selznick to Schulberg

I have just finished reading the Eisenstein adaptation of An American Tragedy. It was for me a memorable experience; the most moving script I have ever read. It was so effective, that it was positively torturing. When I had finished it, I was so depressed that I wanted to reach for the bourbon bottle. As entertainment I don't think it has one chance in a hundred....

Selznick goes on to say that if the studio wants to make the film as a glorious experiment and purely for the advancement of art, he doesn't think it's the business of the company, and suggests that they have ... the courage not to make the picture, but to take whatever rap is coming to us for not supporting Eisenstein the artist— with a million or more of the stockholder's cash...

October 8, 1930
Selznick to Schulberg (cont'd)

Let's not put more money than we have into any one picture ... that will appeal to our vanity through the critical acclaim ... but cannot offer anything but a most miserable two hours to millions of happy-minded young Americans.

Readily agreeing with Selznick that Eisenstein's concept was far too expensive for anybody ever to film anywhere, Zukor's East Coast financial decision-makers overrode Lasky and reassigned the project to someone they considered more trustworthy. They chose Josef von Sternberg.

In von Sternberg's hands, the film stayed on budget, but it was an American box office flop. Lasky felt it was because the film did not have a happy ending; and although he considered von Sternberg a genius with a camera, he thought that the director was twenty years ahead of his time, which is not necessarily a good thing.

Stuck with what to do with his 'genius', Lasky handed Eisenstein a project called *Sutter's Gold*. But when the accounting department read Eisenstein's proposal, they saw red, not gold, calculating his concept would be 'an unwarranted, reckless extravagance, completely out of all range of reality', for a start.

Regretfully, Lasky was forced to let the Russian go. Yet he couldn't help wondering what those films would have been like had he been allowed to make them.

---

34 *Memo From David O. Selznick*, Rudy Behlmer, Viking Press, 1972

Perhaps he shouldn't have wondered, because Eisenstein didn't head straight back to Mother Russia. Having found new financial backers who were enchanted to have bought a genius, Eisenstein went off to Mexico on a three-month location to make his own epic.

After two years of shooting and still with an unfinished film, the backers called a halt and confiscated the footage. The genius returned to his homeland where Stalin eventually allowed him to film a biopic on the 13th century, *Alexander Nevsky*. The story echoed a warning against the rising forces of Nazi Germany. To insure the project was going to be successful, the first General Secretary of the Communist Party of the Soviet Union's Central Committee installed minders in the form of a co-scenarist and an assistant director to see that the completed script was filmed on time and on budget. Prokofiev composed the music, and not surprisingly, the film won the Order of Lenin and the Stalin Prize.

Meanwhile, von Sternberg had been on a leave of absence from Paramount. Back in Germany he had directed *The Blue Angel* with Emil Jannings. While there, he wrote incessant letters to Lasky, allowing him to bring a young actress he had discovered to America and Paramount. Lasky sent Sidney Kent to Germany to take a look.

'SHE'S SENSATIONAL. SIGN HER UP' was Kent's telegraphed response. Without even seeing a photo of her, Lasky did just that.

For the next two years, von Sternberg directed all of Marlene Dietrich's films at Paramount. With Gary Cooper as her leading man, her first picture, *Morocco*, was a hit. *Shanghai Express* topped it. She was screen magic and stayed that way well into her later years. When close-ups showed too many lines, she reinvented herself with a brilliant stage career; and when age finally caught up, she hid herself away in New York, and subsequently in a Paris apartment where she would allow no one to see her but her daughter.

Jesse returned from Europe in July and the flow of letters stopped. On his twentieth birthday he was home alone at the beach house. Bess was off to Europe once more and Lasky was in New York where the babies and governesses were ensconced. His father sent Jesse a check for the occasion.

September 19 1930
Dear Jesse,

...Our heartiest congratulations on your Birthday! How does it feel to be out of your teens? Enclosed is my birthday present which I trust will be acceptable. Because Mother is so tied up trying to get ready to sail next Tuesday, I told her that you would accept this present as coming from the both of us....

Things are simply booming here, and it is really inspiring to work in New York again. I know you are going to love working here, and I hope it won't be long before you are on your way. Walter (Wanger) told me over the 'phone that you spend a lot of time at his house, which pleased us very much. Business is very good again, and I was never so busy as I am at this moment....

MAURICE CHEVALIER, MARLENE DIETRICH, AND GARY COOPER

October 30, 1930
New York:
Dear Jesse,

...Both Hector and Jimmy Cowan have asked when you are coming...
When Walter looks at 'Laughter', I hope he will show it to you. I think it is one of the most refreshing and best produced pictures I have seen in many months, and I believe will be successful at the box-office. 'The Royal Family' which is just being completed at Long Island also looks very good, and they have a very interesting schedule ahead of them....

Laughter, a romantic comedy starring Nancy Carroll and Frederic March proved to be a great success for Paramount and Douglas Z. Doty (story and screenplay) was nominated for an Oscar.

The Royal Family, the high camp tribulations of a Broadway theatrical family irreverently based on the famous theatrical family of the Barrymores[35] from a hit play by Edna Ferber and George S. Kaufman, again starred Frederic March, this time opposite Ina Claire, a star of Broadway and London's West End, whose special talent for sophisticated high comedy caused critic John Mason Brown to call her 'the ablest comedienne our theatre knows.'

So as not to confuse an American audience or infuriate a British one, the movie appears to have been called *The Royal Family of Broadway*, and Frederic March was nominated for Best Actor, but the little gold man eluded him. Not until 1932 in *Dr. Jekyll and Mr. Hyde*, did he receive the accolade when Lasky was no longer at Paramount, and Adolf Zukor was listed as the producer.

But a film March was to make for Lasky fourteen years later in 1944 would be a triumph for them both when he played the title role in *The Adventures of Mark Twain*. Curiously, it brought them no Oscars. Not until 1947 did March win again for *The Best Years of Our Lives*.

October 3, 1930 continues:

...Mother arrived safely in Paris and cables me she is thinking of going with Art and Louise to Egypt and sailing up the Nile. It now seems very unlikely that I can go abroad, and I have so cabled them...Betty's birthday is October 11th. I am giving her a theatre party, and she will have a little dinner party at home after the matinee...Billy got a bad case of poison ivy through exploring the woods of Westchester last Saturday and Sunday. He was laid up with a swollen face for two days, but he is now back at school. They are fine kids and seem happy and contented...As you say, the stock

---

35 *New Your Post* (Dec.13, 1932) John, Ethel, and Lionel Barrymore.

market is behaving badly, but there is nothing to be said about this except we are hoping for better times . . . Tell Walter I am now convinced, judging by the dramatization and reception of 'Bad Girl' last night, that a picture can be made of this subject. There are several other good picture possibilities among the current new plays. . . .

Historically, film companies have felt safer adapting stage plays or books to the screen rather than creating originals. Early on, marketing doctrine dictated that if a property was already established, some percentage of the public would be aware of the title, might even have read or seen it, and might therefore go see the film. However, the truer a novel or stage play is to its original form, the more work it requires to transmogrify into a movie.

To become a film, a play needs to open up the action and the visuals, and since the advent of talkies, in most cases the writer needs to tighten the dialogue because theatre audiences come to hear the words, the thoughts, the ideas, whereas movie audiences come to see the action. A movie must widen the visual vistas of a play beyond the proscenium arch. A book might spend a chapter with a character dipping a Madelaine into a cup of tea. The writer must find other places for his characters to inhabit. Get them outdoors. Find logical locations where they would exist. Breathe 'fresh air' into the story. Television brought in the use of original material, although certainly a percent of content is still based on books.

At the moment, Paramount was having differences with Warner Brothers. When Jesse finally arrived in New York, his father was back in California handling this crisis.

Referring to female Hollywood reporters as 'Chatter-Chippies', *Time Magazine* highlighted the war between Paramount and the Warners. At a time when Paramount was feeling particularly hit by the Depression (more than Lasky was willing to admit to his son), Harry Warner had lured three major stars away from Paramount, offering William Powell and Ruth Chatterton huge financial incentives, and topping the coup by capturing top money-maker Kay Francis. In the court battle that resulted, Warner Brothers won, but with caveats: they would have to allow Paramount to call upon Kay Franci's services when appropriate.

Through this dispute, Lasky remained personally friendly with the brothers. He was soon to be grateful for that friendship. Meanwhile, he was still enjoying a life of ease on his old stomping grounds.

January 26, 1931
Dear Jesse,

. . . We are awfully busy here, and the battle with the Warner Brothers has only added to our problems. I just returned with Cecil DeMille from a marvelous week-end in Paradise, and I am happy to advise you that I feel quite myself again ... I made a grand speech at the Academy the other night - several hundred of the motion picture industry attended, including Cecil and William DeMille, and everybody said it was really a wonderful talk. It certainly got a tremendous round of applause, and the usual number of laughs.

I attended the opening with Grandma of 'Trader Horn', and it is the most thrilling picture I have ever seen ... Metro was two years making it, as they had to remake it several times, and spent over a million dollars on it, and while you can find plenty of faults with the story they try to tell, the animal stuff is so wonderful that any reasonable spectator will forget everything else ... I know you will think often of me as you watch the Trader Horn expedition going down an African River.

I am going to several openings this week, including Charlie Chaplin's picture. Things at the studio are about as usual. There is an awful lot to be done here - more than I could possibly hope to accomplish in the limited time I will be here....

MGM's film, *Trader Horn*, shot in Africa, was the first 'authentic location' non-documentary talkie. It told the adventures of real-life trader and adventurer, 'Trader' Horn. Nominated for the Academy Award for Best Picture in 1931, Lasky regretted Paramount had not made it. He was lucky they hadn't. Edwina Booth, the female lead, contracted sleeping sickness in the jungle, which ended her career. She sued the producers. Several others also became ill, but not Harry Carey, the star, nor Duncan Renaldo (later to become a cult figure as, and in, *The Cisco Kid*).

Jesse was now working in the New York studio, having been given a job at Paramount on the production end of *Any One Man*. He felt like he was wasting his time when he wanted to be writing. His dad was in pacifying mode.

February 6, 1931
Dear Jesse,

...Well, be patient a short time longer. I will be home by the end of the month, and then we will have a good talk and definitely map out your future plans. In the meantime you may feel sure I will not be an 'obstructionist', and any reasonable plan that looks good to you, will undoubtedly meet with my approval....

Lasky's approval was soon to be of little importance. There were rumblings and frightened whisperings over ginned tea cups as plunging stocks crashed against the palatial gates of the five major players: Paramount, Loew's/MGM, Warner Bros., Fox, and RKO. The three minors, Columbia, Universal, and United Artists had less to lose; but when less is all you've got, losing matters. Blame had to be apportioned as stocks fell, and the question was, whose heads should fall? Lasky's letter continued:

February 6, 1931

...I understand there is more than the usual criticism and gossip about the West Coast. Some of it is justified, but much of it is unfair, and without the parties to the gossip weighing or understanding the facts in the case. If you are seriously concerned about what you hear, I am going to suggest that you sit down with me when I return, and let me show you the facts and relation of the two studios, the company's policy concerning them, and other matters which the gossipers are not in a position to know about, but which will impress you when you know them.

In this connection I particularly wish that you would not carry stories to Mother, especially when they are about criticisms of the West Coast or my policies. While I don't give a tinker's damn about this kind of talk, I know who inspires it, where it comes from, and have lived through many years of similar situations. I have always made it a rule never to worry Mother or let her know much about the politics, intrigue and the disagreeable side of our business. She is too loyal to me, and too sensitive anyway, to have her mind disturbed by things which she cannot prevent or help, and while you, being a man and actively in the business, cannot escape these things, most certainly between us we can prevent Mother from being upset unnecessarily. Unfortunately, I imagine, most of the talk comes from Blanche and Hec (Hector), and they certainly mean well, but when I get back I am going to ask them to refrain in the future from burdening Mother in these matters.

We are making a mighty struggle out here to improve the product, and one or two grand pictures are in the offing, particularly 'City Streets' which is going to pretty nearly make a star of Sylvia Sidney, and place (Rouben) Mamoulian in the class of the very big directors.

Another surefire box-office success full of charm and human interest, and amazing comedy, is 'Skippy'. Little Robert Coogan's performance as 'Snooky' (Sooky) is going to prove a sensation. He is just like his brother Jackie Coogan was at the age of six, when he was discovered in Chaplin's picture 'The Kid', which you may or may not remember....

In the film-noir *City Streets*, Sylvia Sidney, as Lasky had predicted, was to become a star whose long career led her eventually into television. The shooting gallery showman was played by Gary Cooper. An uncredited extra in the picture was Paulette Goddard, who years later was to become a DeMille star opposite Cooper in *Reap the Wild Wind*—which would be written by Jesse.

Bad times had fallen on Lasky's favorite expedition guide and mentor of Jesse's youth. Lasky's letter continues:

February 6, 1931

...I don't think I told you that I saw Chester Wortley over a week ago, and had a nice visit with him in his little house at Glendale, and a long talk with Ken. I gave them a little financial assistance, also loaned Chester a small projection machine and some silent pictures, and have done what I can to make his lot a little easier. While the doctors have practically pronounced his case as hopeless, he is still putting up a good fight, and as he can walk around the house, he is not as uncomfortable as you might think. His is painfully thin, and has been told that he has cancer of the stomach and knows that his case is supposed to be incurable, but I had him talking and laughing, and I know my visit helped him a lot. He is depending now on Christian Science, and it is funny, but I feel in my heart if he only had enough Faith, that might help him, as it has others, after the doctors have failed. I have asked Cecil DeMille to call on him, and Cecil will talk to him along religious and human lines, and I know his visit will be helpful.

I am taking Mother and Edgar Selwyn to the opening of 'Cimmarron' tonight, and after the show, a crowd of golfers 'The Divot Diggers' are going to Agua Caliente on a special train. I am looking forward to a good time; two days of golf; two nights of gambling; some good liquor - but not too much....

Although Lasky remained eternally optimistic, the movie business could no longer avoid the truth. The Depression had finally reached Hollywood. Letters and telegrams flowed from Lasky back in New York to Jesse, now in Hollywood. First, a cable to Jesse.

September 21, 1931

STOCK MARKET SITUATION SERIOUS BUT FEEL CAN WEATHER THE STORM WORK HARD AND BE ECONOMICAL MUCH LOVE FROM ALL DAD

September 25, 1931
Dear Jess,

... arrived in New York just in time, as the stock, as you know, dropped to a dangerously low level, and I had to take a hold of my affairs to protect my interests. I think I have everything in pretty good shape, and if the market does not go any lower, things should be all right. Of course everyone here is much more pessimistic, and there is much more evidence of the general depression than is visible in Los Angeles. People talk of nothing else, and everyone is suffering from financial losses, so New York is none too cheerful.

The house is running smoothly, and the children have been fortunate in having their nature teacher, Miss Lunt, to take them on excursions every day.

Yesterday Billy found a live snake, which he is keeping in the bathroom, and today he is over in Staten Island hunting for a turtle to bring home. We are thinking of making the nature teacher, Miss Lunt, their governess, as she is not going to be at the Ethical Culture School this season....

We are building quite a big Editorial Board or Story Department at the Home Office, and I can see a very good opportunity for you, if it should ever seem wise or necessary to come East....

Randy added a more worried opinion. It was followed by the first hints of Lasky's personal financial disaster.

September 30, 1931
Dear Jesse,

'... Our heads are spinning as the market is simply withering away. What Price Happiness!'
Randy

Lasky finally wrote his son the truth. Jesse had taken the small job at the Hollywood studio as a lowly assistant on a film called *Any One Man*.

October 5, 1931
Dear Jesse,

...It is two weeks today since I arrived in New York but it seems more like one year ... I found my personal affairs were seriously affected. So along with all the other business problems, I had to take immediate hold ... What I am telling you is entirely confidential, and must not be made known to anyone. The fact is that Harry Warner, President of Warner Brothers, turned out to be a real friend indeed, and I have accepted some temporary financial assistance from him. Also, I availed myself, in a small way, of Mr. English's influence at certain banks.

The first thing that I had to protect was a block of 20,000 shares of Paramount stock...margined down to a low figure, but there was imminent danger of the stock going much lower...and I would be called on for margin. I had enough available cash to protect the stock down to about 7½ but after studying the matter, I determined to take it out of the Broker's hands so it could not be dumped overboard in case of a crisis, and with Harry Warner's help, this has been accomplished and the stock is now where it cannot be sold and will be returned to me intact after times get better and the price of the stock improves...My next problem is to do something about the buildings which have used up so much money, and Mr. Stern is now working on that situation....

I am happy to advise you that my affairs are now in such shape that no matter how the market goes, I cannot go bankrupt, or broke, as it were; also, my contract with the company is a very binding one and has three years to run, and I am trying to adjust my affairs by reducing all expenditures so that I can live within my salary. This will hardly be possible while we have the expensive apartment in New York, but as soon as we can get rid of the apartment, it will be a much simpler matter to live within my salary... There is still no chance of renting the apartment but we are holding down our expenses pretty well....

Everyone coming here from the Coast tells me you have a fine job. Keep up your spirits - you can only do the best you can... We are dining with the Turnbulls tonight, and seeing Charles Laughton in his new play. I am trying to engage him to go to Hollywood for one picture. He is a great character actor. I have had marvelous reports on the new Chevalier picture, in fact, the Great Maurice himself was in today, and said it was 'magnifies'....

October 19, 1931

...You are very wise to live at the Beach House because it costs me nothing and saves you rental expense at least, and Andrew (a servant) has to be paid anyway. It must seem more like home than any other place you could have found... Business seems to be picking up in the theatres, particularly when the product is good, and our pictures seem to be coming through better. The Gary Cooper-Claudette Colbert picture 'His Woman', just finished at Long Island, looks very good. The Cheat needed a lot of retakes, but when finished may also come through, although George Abbott's direction was absolutely without heart or feeling.

I was surprised a week ago to receive word from Mr. Schulberg that he wanted to abandon making 'Any One Man', feeling the picture would not be box-office and that the cast was weak and would not help it. After analyzing the situation very carefully here, I called him on the telephone and told him that it must be made. We needed the picture, and as we had invested so much money in it I thought it was a good gamble, and I have a hunch by the time it is finished we will be glad we made it... treat this all as confidential.

Mannie Cohen seems to have won Ben's (Schulberg) confidence, and judging by his letters and telephone calls, he is accomplishing some good. He is certainly a hard working little executive, and when he learns more about the production end, will be very valuable indeed.[36]

Mother has been working hard reorganizing the household, changing servants, etc., but the last few days she is quite her old self again. Yesterday was a lovely day so we had a picnic up in the woods in back of Salsbury's place. We cooked chops and hot dogs in true California style, and we all

---

36 Lasky was to have reason to change his mind about Mannie Cohen.

enjoyed it enormously. We then took a long walk through the woods and the Fall colorings were just too beautiful. I played golf Saturday at Lakeville and broke a hundred.

As far as my affairs are concerned, everything depends on Paramount stock... We are still trying to rent our apartment, and if we can do this, we will move to a hotel until we can come to California... By the way, don't miss seeing Edgar Selwyn's picture *The Sin of Madelon Claudet*. It is the best tear-jerker produced in some time... I am hoping that the retakes on the (Ruth) Chatterton picture will make that one okay. Everything depends on the product, and if we can only get some real hits like 'Monkey Business' (Marx Bros.), Paramount stock will soar. The latter picture is just cleaning up ... I was quite delighted to learn that you have a story in the Bulletin and I shall look it up and read it with pleasure. If it isn't purchased by our studio, you might be able to land it at some other studio. If you want a good agent, I recommend John Flinn....

October 30, 1931

...This is probably the busiest period I have passed through in many years ...The business in the theatres is not what it should be, by any means, but we are still hopeful that when we get real winter weather, the theatre business will pick up... This kind of weather, which has been prevalent throughout the country, is bad for business. We are hopeful that our stock will not go any lower and a little later on should start slowly on an upward trend.

I have seen as much as I could of Grandma (who was visiting N.Y.) and she certainly spoke awfully well of you. She will be returning in a few days, as she does not want to cause any extra expense. I have also cut her allowance, poor dear, but she is more than willing to do her part, just the same as you are.

We were very much stimulated by receiving "High Man's Folly' and 'Touchdown'—both great pictures—and 'Touchdown', I am sure, will be a big box-office success. I am sorry I cannot give you any encouraging report about 'Once A Lady'. The first half of the picture seemed to drag and proved very talky. The latter half was better, but we don't anticipate this will be much of a box-office success. Chatterton's clothes and accent were both criticized, but it has not been released yet, so we shall see.....I am in close touch with Mannie Cohen and Schulberg, and Mannie seems to be doing great work. Mr. Zukor is going to visit the Coast for a couple of weeks. He leaves here on November 6th.... The Long Island Studio is plugging away. 'The Cheat' will be a fair picture and 'His Woman', with Colbert and Cooper will be quite good.

Coming from the New York theatre, Ruth Chatterton was an asset. In silents, she was characteristically cast as a 'highborn lady of culture and poise'. Having a trained theatre voice, Lasky was certain her talents would double in value with sound, and in 1928 he put her under contract to Paramount. But having nothing for her at the moment, Lasky loaned her to MGM, who starred her in *Madame X*, for which she was nominated for an Academy Award for Best Actress.

The following year, back at Paramount she co-starred with Frederic March in *Sarah and Son*, portraying an impoverished housewife who rises to fame and fortune as an opera singer; a sophisticated woman, unafraid of freely exploring love and sex. *Sarah and Son*, directed by one of the few women directors, Dorothy Arzner, was presented by both Adolf Zukor and Jesse L. Lasky. The film was another critical and financial success, and Chatterton received a second Academy Award nomination. That year, in a poll conducted by the West Coast film exhibitors, Chatterton was voted the second female star of the year, the first being Norma Shearer.[37]

But with the release of *Once a Lady*, directed by the famous stage director Guthrie McClintic, and featuring two British stars, Ivor Novello and Jill Esmond, Lasky was stunned when the studio's salesman complained, 'No more accents. The public don't like accents!' The two British accents combined with Chatterton's well-modulated, cultivated voice and impeccable diction clearly didn't go down well with an American Mid-west audience in the 1930s, who thought she was 'puttin' on airs with them English fellers'. The film was a flop and studio executives blamed it on Chatterton. Lasky considered her an asset and was looking for the right subject, but later admitted to accidentally dropping her from his roster because he forgot when her option was due. He said, 'She was stolen from under my nose.'

October 30, 1931

Later:

The stock hit 15 1/4 today. You may wonder why this sudden rise. By the time this reaches you, the news may be out but if it has not been announced, I will tell you confidentially what is going on. We are taking in a very strong man, Mr. John Hertz of Chicago, as Chairman of our Finance Committee, and putting on our Board of Directors, Albert Lasker and Wm. Wrigley. This will mean a much stronger Management and a very much more powerful financial support for the company. As it becomes known that these powerful interests are allying themselves with Paramount, it will create a new buying interest in the stock, and I would not be surprised if the stock continued to advance slowly through the buying support that it will get from the friends and allies of the men named above. This means a great deal to my personal fortune, so we should keep our fingers crossed and hope. Please treat this in the strictest confidence until the story comes out in the newspapers, which may happen about the time this letter reaches you. . . .

---

37 Married to producer Irving Thalberg, won the Academy Award for *The Divorcee*.

RUTH CHATTERTON in ONCE A LADY

He had faint praise for his son's developing story telling.

November 5, 1931
Dear Jesse,

...I read your story in the Bulletin and liked it pretty well. The difficulty lies in the fact that we would not want to do a prize fight picture because women do not care for them, and the record of prize fight pictures in our theatres is not very good. Also, while the story was interesting enough, it somehow lacked importance, and arrived at its happy ending without much struggle; in other words, I think it needs one more big situation before it is brought to a conclusion. In spite of this criticism...Universal or Columbia would be more likely to make this type of picture....

Lasky's evaluation of Jesse's story showed his own keen story sense. He pinpointed the basic difference between a screenplay and a novel. For the latter, character development is more important than plot line and action. Jesse hadn't developed his 'Act Two', in which a counterpoint event can introduce another conflict, building tension to the denouement in *Act Three*. The would-be screenwriter was soon to learn that in films, conflict breeds action, breeds excitement, breeds drama. Action doesn't necessarily mean car chases. It can be mental conflict and human problems to resolve.

For the moment, this was not his number one problem. Things were changing at the studio, and not all for the best. Jesse was holding down his small job on the film *Any One Man*, when his father wrote from New York with holiday matters in mind.

December 5, 1931

...I will not be leaving for California until some considerable time after January. This date will be decided after Messrs. Zukor and Mannie Cohen return from Hollywood, therefore, we should definitely arrange for your Christmas vacation in New York...The reason I am not sure when you should leave is because I do not know when your unit will be finished with 'Any One Man', and I suppose you won't want to leave until that picture has been previewed or, at least, roughly assembled...Things are about the same here, except the latest slump in the stock market has caused us all a little extra worry, but one hears so much of other people's troubles in New York that you actually begin to forget your own. Mother is in good spirits, and some very interesting developments have arisen ...she is working on a proposition which might establish her as a commercial artist, and through which she might make some money on her own account. As a consequence, she is full of pep and enthusiasm, and I am happy to say does not worry too much about the Depression.

The children are fine ... Billy plays constantly with a huge bull snake; it has become quite a pet, and I have promised him that he can have a female bull snake as his Christmas present from me ... As you have probably heard, we have finally decided to close the Long Island Studio, and Hector will be transferred to the Coast about the end of January. They both hate to go west but so far I do not see that there is much that can be done about it. Blanche has taken an office in my 57th St. Building and has a great scheme of developing original stories with authors, and selling them to picture companies I think she will make a great success of it, and that is another reason why she does not want to go west....

I am in pretty close touch with Mannie Cohen's activities and I feel he is accomplishing a great deal in smoothing out the organization, and I was happy to learn from Mr. Schulberg that he is working well with Mannie....

I saw 'Frankenstein' and 'Possessed' with (Clark) Gable and (Joan) Crawford, the other night—both great box-office pictures, although entirely different....

December 7, 1931
JESSE

WHILE TALKING WITH SCHULBERG....HE SPOKE IN HIGH TERMS OF YOU AND SAID A PLACE HAD BEEN MADE IN NEW ORGANIZATION SET UP WHICH WOULD MAKE YOU ASSISTANT TO HURLEY WHO IS SCHULBERG'S RIGHT HAND MAN STOP SCHULBERG MOST CORDIAL TOWARDS YOU AND YOUR TRIP TO NEW YORK IS NOW DEFINITELY SET STOP SCHULBERG STATED YOUR NEW POSITION WOULD BRING YOU IN VERY CLOSE CONTACT WITH HIM AND YOU WERE GIVEN THIS OPPORTUNITY BECAUSE THEY BELIEVED IN YOUR ABILITY AND FITNESS FOR JOB I AM MUCH PLEASED STOP WIRE ME WHEN DATE IS SET FOR YOUR DEPARTURE. LOVE FROM ALL. DAD.

So Jesse's short Christmas break was spent in New York with his family; then he returned to the West Coast on a learning curve about the part of the business that didn't really interest him: producing. His father remained in New York, more worried about his personal jeopardy than he was willing to admit to Jesse.

January 8, 1932
Dear Jesse,

...It will undoubtedly be very hard for you at first to adjust yourself to the new position and to executive work, but please remember that whether or not you like this type of work, it will prove a valuable experience in your future career ... You no doubt noticed that the stock has been slowly rising and this has put everybody in a better frame of mind. Also, as long as the stock is ten, or above, you can feel my affairs are in a more secure condition. I think Hertz and his crowd are going to support the stock, which means it ought to gradually rise higher, but don't be discouraged when it goes off, as it is bound to do at times. I am sure the general direction will be upward.

As I wired you, I like 'No One Man' very much indeed. It is really a fine picture; daring, and splendidly produced, and Carole Lombard was gorgeously gowned and beautifully handled. After seeing her performance in 'No One Man', I am convinced that she is the next Joan Crawford, and in a short time we will have a real valuable star in this girl....

Mannie Cohen had dinner and spent the evening at the house the other night. We had a general talk but did not get anywhere in particular...(He) volunteered the information the other night that he thought you were in a fine spot and that he had recommended putting you there, which, while not true, surprised me, because I did not know that he was aware you were alive. He apologized for not talking with you while he was at the Coast, but spoke very nice about what he had heard of your ability and character.

Jack Emanuel just 'phoned me that he made some money for me today in the stock market, and I believe I can operate through Emanuel and really make a little extra money. He is very conservative and seems to have good information....

Under Zukor's policy, the company owned chains of film palaces from coast to coast and into Canada and Europe, controlled by their own exhibiting subsidiary, Publix. The man in charge was Sam Katz. Publix had purchased numerous giant circuits, partly with cash and partly with stock. Before the Depression it had appeared a wise move to control exhibition with their expanding programs of films. But stocks were dropping, capital was shrinking, box-office receipts were falling, and tensions were mounting. Stocks were redeemable upon demand at a fixed price, and now they had plunged far below that. The cash cow had run out of milk and the company was immediately forced to redeem its pledges at full value.

Who was to blame? The finger pointed to the top. Lasky and/or Zukor! In an effort to re-establish unity between the distribution and exhibition departments, Lasky suggested a cosmetic repair: changing the corporate name to Paramount Famous Lasky. When this didn't get a response, he proposed calling the company Paramount Publix, and the name was finally given to the exhibition arm. Peace was briefly restored and the new Board voted in Sidney Kent and Sam Katz as equal vice presidents. Katz, who had brought in the private investment from Chicago, Yellow Cab magnate John Hertz, was appointed chairman of the finance committee—a strong voting arm.

Lasky's strongest friend at the studio, Sidney Kent, had declined the vice president position, reading trouble ahead. He hastily resigned, having been offered the presidency of the Fox Company. He asked Lasky to join him as head of production at Fox, but the last remaining founder of the original company proposed to stay and fight.

It was the wrong move. Lasky was forced to sell over $1,500,000 in shares bought on margin for a paltry $37,000. He gave away his empty New York office buildings rather than jump from one of them.

Jesse watched his father being wiped clean of all he had built. Years later, he wrote, 'My preparations for life had fitted me to order dinner in several languages, drive cars too fast, play polo and tennis, and open champagne bottles. I returned to the Beach House to watch our fleet of Rolls-Royces being driven out of the cavernous garage by our creditors.'

When Harry Warner heard that Lasky was in financial trouble, he sent him a personal check for $250,000. In exchange, Lasky handed Warner his Paramount stock, signed over the deeds to the Beach House and contents (sans Rolls-Royces) as security for the loan.

The stock had now fallen from $80 a share to a few pennies, and Paramount's new board of directors called an emergency meeting to deal with the crisis. Before the upheaval, Lasky had taken on the eager young Mannie Cohen as his personal assistant. Mannie, always full of questions, was a quick learner and was aware of every move Lasky had made over the past months. Lasky felt he had picked someone with a future in the business. Now he asked Mannie to back him up with facts and figures at the meeting. Facts that would establish Lasky's position in the rush of charges and counter charges.

Any film that had failed to bring in profits was blamed on the production department's extravagance, bad judgment, and miscalculation. Mannie Cohen, who had read confidential files and familiarized himself with studio operations and the intricacies of production, could have refuted the charges hurled at his boss, but to Lasky's surprise, he didn't *join* the attack, he led it.

The vice president in charge of production, the last of the original three pioneers, was unceremoniously sacked. And although they couldn't fire Zukor, he was not immune. He was exiled to an outpost in South America. But Zukor would return to rise again, seemingly to go on forever. In fact, he lived to 103 years old. On his 100th birthday he is often reputed to have said, 'If I knew I'd live so long, I'd have taken better care of myself.'

Mannie Cohen was appointed as head of production. The stars were now Paramount's real assets, and as contracts for Gary Cooper, Mae West, and Bing Crosby came up for renewal, Cohen, with a highly original agenda, secretly negotiated personal contracts for their services.

When the East Coast board of directors got wind of his duplicity, they kept their discovery to themselves. A testimonial dinner was organized in Cohen's honor at the Ambassador Hotel in Los Angeles for an array of Hollywood bigwigs. After enjoying a night full of speeches and praise (not by Lasky, who did not attend), the next day Mannie Cohen boarded the Santa Fe Chief heading for a similar function planned in New York. On the train somewhere nearing Chicago, a telegram was brought to Cohen. It was simple, direct and concise, with a touch of Donald Trump's *The Celebrity Apprentice* television series, about it. It simply read: 'You're fired.'

But Cohen wasn't too worried. He still had those personal contracts with the Paramount stars. He'd pulled a fast one, but the studio was faster. Paramount offered Cohen a glitzy independent production deal, which he hastily accepted. But the board of directors retained final approval on all his projects—and such approvals were never granted. Since the stars found themselves unemployed, it was not long before they broke their contracts with Cohen and signed once again with Paramount.

In the midst of all this upheaval, Lasky's sister, Blanche, always his closest friend and ally, suddenly contracted pneumonia and died. She was forty-nine. Hector took to the bottle and Lasky sank into an uncharacteristic depression.

The Laskys were now the nouveau poor and were all living at the huge beach house. Betty and Bill shared one nanny, who Lasky couldn't afford. Jesse was given the chore of selling keepsakes that Lasky couldn't be seen selling himself. He filled an old valise full of baubles such as a jeweled gold cigarette box signed, 'To my esteemed boss. Rudolph Valentino.' Another was signed, 'To the man who set my feet on the road to success. Buddy Rogers'; and Lasky's collection of silver hip flasks, some still full. Bess had already sold her valuable pearls and an emerald ring for a fraction of their value. She handed the money to her surprised husband, who was embarrassed that she had felt it necessary. It was. There were no parties to wear them to.

Next afternoon Jesse found himself standing at the corner of Hollywood and Vine with his travel-worn calfskin valise, empty of those treasures he'd been able to flog. As was the fashion, his travel bag was decorated with brightly colored stickers from all the great hotels across Europe where he had stayed in plusher days—the Adlon Berlin, the Donaplota Budapest (from that journey, one city behind his father), the Ritz, London, and hotels from other luxurious memories in Vienna, Prague, Marrakech, Egypt, and Palestine. Jesse stood on that corner with a pocketful of cash for his dad and a head full of worries about what the future held for the family.

A voice interrupted his self-pity. A bird-like man, rather shabbily dressed, was standing beside him asking in a rather thin voice if Jesse had really been to all those places—Paris, Vienna, Prague, Marrakech, and the rest. A 'yes' brought the next question: did he have a job? Of course he didn't—nor a place to stay without sponging on his parents. 'Nobody wants to hire writers at the moment.' Jesse sighed.

'You're a writer?' The thin man's eyes lit up. It was fate, he said! Because, would you believe it? He was a writer, too. Before Jesse could make excuses and run, Jack Preston explained that he had a contract for a series of books. Fiction. Potboilers, really. For the McCauley Company. $500 advance against royalties. His stories were always set in exotic places—places he'd never seen except in his imagination. Preston wrote about a world of glamor and intrigue. He wanted, yes, needed someone to describe those places and the people who inhabited them. Someone who'd actually been there. As a matter of fact, his wife owned some apartments on Vista Street and one was empty. What was his name?

Reluctantly, Jesse gave him only his first name.

Jesse? Well, Jesse could have the apartment and they could feed him in exchange. That was, if they got along all right—if it all worked out. Would Jesse consider taking the job? At least try it out for a while. Jesse accepted perhaps a shade too quickly; but these were perilous times.

A few days later, he found himself at work in Jack's office, a rusting automobile chassis parked on tireless rims in a vacant lot behind his apartment. Jack sat in the front seat, a wooden board holding his antique Underwood. In the back sat Jesse, a board on his lap for his Underwood and a thesaurus and dictionary by his side. (No spell-check in those far-off days.)

As months passed and each new book was churned out and on its way to the McCauley Company, Jesse's contribution grew, and soon he was actually getting co-writing credit. Now Jesse spent week days at Jack Preston's and went to the beach house on weekends. He was anxious about his parents. His father was unusually quiet, and Bess was looking worried. She offered her son a warning: 'Watch Dad, Jess. Just keep your eye on him! In all the years we've been together, I've never seen him depressed.'

Then one Sunday Bess frantically called upstairs to her son, 'Jess, Jesse...! HURRY! He's gone! Out there! He's swimming—way beyond the waves!'

From his bedroom window upstairs Jesse saw his father swimming steadily in the direction of Japan. He rushed down, kicking off his shoes and trousers as he flew across the sand in his shirtsleeves, jumped in, swimming desperately towards his father. Was this the kind of death his dad would choose? To vanish in the ocean without having caused anyone and trouble? Yes, maybe, thought Jesse as hard strokes brought him abreast of the older man. He seemed detached, deep in thought as he stared out to sea. Then he turned and squinted at his son in surprise. 'Jess! What are you doing here?'

Jesse tried to hide his fear as he called as nonchalantly as he could, while breathless, 'Hi, Dad. Thought I'd swim out and join you.'

'Oh...!' Lasky said, realization hitting him. 'You're dressed, aren't you? I see. Well...! So you thought I was going to...?' He broke off, glanced at the now distant shore. 'Didn't realize I'd swum so far. You see, I have the greatest idea for a new picture about a romance in a zoo!'

Treading water, Lasky proceeded to tell his son the idea for the movie. 'What do you think, Jess?' he asked as a wave broke over the two of them.

'I think we'd better start for shore', Jesse said.

By the time they got back on the beach, Lasky was full of excitement. He had reached a decision. He would set up his own production company. Start all over again, and his first film would be called *Zoo in Budapest*.

His friend, Sidney Kent, now heading Fox Studios, came to the rescue. That head of production spot he had offered some months before was filled by Winfield Sheehan, so Kent invited Lasky to become an independent producer at Fox with a six pictures a year deal, $3,000 a week, and a percentage of profits, with a no-option three-year contract. Kent built him a special building on the lot, with offices and a private screening room. *Zoo in Budapest* with Loretta Young and Gene Raymond was the first of eighteen films he would make there, and it was a great hit.

ZOO IN BUDAPEST

Lasky brought in Hector Turnbull as associate producer in the new setup, and one day Hector arrived with an American writer who brought him an original story. The producer expected Preston Sturges to pitch his story, but Sturges explained that he'd rather put it on paper. Expecting him to come back with a synopsis, Lasky was stunned when Sturges returned with a screenplay, complete with technical instructions for director and camera. Lasky thought *The Power and the Glory* was the most perfect script he'd ever read, and he was keen to produce it.

Sturges was asking $62,475 for his script, but since he was working on a shoestring budget, Lasky designed a deal in which Sturges got only $17,500 up front, with 3.5 percent of the first $500,000 in receipts, 5 percent of the next $500,000, and 7 percent of all receipts over $1,000,000. Percentage deals were rare, and Lasky's agreement caused much discussion among current film makers.

The deal in place, Lasky knew just the actor to play it. Spencer Tracy was under contract to Fox but was out of favor at the studio. The actor had been given an earlier opportunity for a starring role and went on a 'lost weekend' instead. Holding up production is still the one unforgivable sin in Hollywood, and Fox had been forced to replace Tracy.

Sensing what the actor was capable of, Lasky felt it was worth the risk, and he was determined to have him for *The Power and the Glory*. So he sent Tracy a message saying that he would never ask what had happened on his last assignment because it might have happened to him instead. There were plenty of good parts waiting for an actor with Tracy's talents, but not until he pulled himself together. If he could do that, Lasky was offering him the part of his life.

Tracy accepted. But then first, Mother Nature and then the aftermath of The Great Depression intervened.

'The Palisades will fall on us!' somebody screamed. That March, the Lasky family and celebrity guests were in their private solarium theatre at the Santa Monica beach house watching a screening of *Ecstasy* (*Ekstasy*), the romantic Czechoslovakian drama in which Hedy Lamarr's nude frolic introduced her to Hollywood. But Hedy was not the only earthquake that struck the California coast that day. As the first shock waves of the Long Beach magnitude 6.3 quake subsided, wild-eyed neighbors came running with news: Santa Barbara and Long Beach were practically demolished.

The damage was soon repaired, but a quake of a different kind had finally reached its zenith, after which nothing would be the same for Jesse L. Lasky or his family or his film *The Power and the Glory*. In 1933, all Hollywood was forced to postpone any filming and tighten belts. Lasky wrote to his brother-in-law, Art, who was still in France and suddenly in declining health. This letter gives a report on the situation.

March 13, 1933
Dear Art,

...Since the Moratorium was declared, things have been in a chaotic condition here (at Fox) and, due to shortage of cash, my production 'The Power And The Glory' has been postponed. Today all the studios are closed, and while we expect them to reopen tomorrow, we have all had to go on a four-week's lay-off without salary. This is a severe blow to me but there is nothing else to do but accept the situation, and we will continue to work on our future productions so that when we can start them, we will be well prepared.

The closing of the Banks hit the industry very hard and box-office receipts fell off so rapidly that the Fox company could not keep up its production schedule. To meet these conditions we had to suspend all salaries in the studio for four weeks, as stated above, but the studios are now at grips with the labor unions ... I will put off bankruptcy just as long as possible, and when it comes time to pay out any large sums of money, it will be time enough to file a petition.

Loyd Wright[38] seems to be busy with his various clients' affairs and outside of an occasional telephone call, I have not seen him ... While all this upset has been distressing, I do feel it has postponed any crisis in my personal affairs, and for the present I think the policy of 'watchful waiting' is the correct one to adopt.

Jesse Jr. is now located at the Fox Western Avenue studio as Sol Wurtzel's assistant. He seems happy enough, although he is a little distressed at being off the payroll for a month.

Bessie and the children are fine; no doubt she wrote you about the excitement of the Earthquake - that was an experience indeed but fortunately, aside from the nervous shock, we were in no way involved.

My best to you –
Jesse

With Lasky teetering on the edge of bankruptcy, *The Power and the Glory* was finally put into production. The film begins with the protagonist's funeral and follows the story through flashbacks of a man who rose from menial railroad jobs to become head of the company, but loses his family. Film critic Pauline Kael later considered that Sturge's script served as a prototype for *Citizen Kane*. (Her idea is possibly strengthened by the fact that co-writer of the Welles film, Herman J. Mankiewicz, was a friend of Sturges). It was directed by William K. Howard and costarred Colleen Moore. Tracy's powerful portrayal in a boardroom scene is considered one of the highlights of a lifetime of magic performances. Great critical reviews, but no Oscar. Spencer Tracy always acknowledged that he would never have become a film star if it hadn't been for Lasky.

With Paramount now his past, Lasky looked to the future and was sure of one thing: he may have lost his money, but he hadn't lost his touch. He would have been proud to know that in 2014, *The Power and the Glory* was deemed 'culturally, historically, or aesthetically significant' by the Library of Congress and was selected for preservation in the National Film Registry.

But while *The Power and the Glory* was something of a critical triumph, although it didn't win an Oscar, it didn't make Sturges rich. Outside of New York City, whose theatre-going audience enjoyed more serious film fare, it did poorly at the box office. By the end of 1940, it had grossed only $563,323.88, paying Sturges' profits share only some $2,000.

---

38 Lasky's lawyer.

LASKY, SPENCER TRACY, COLEEN MOORE

As for Jesse, he had just co-written a pot-boiler novel with Jack Preston,[39] and on the strength of it had been given the job at Fox's B-picture Western Avenue Studio, run by Sol Wurtzel. The studio was considered such a lowly place that when anyone went to work there, it was said they'd gone from 'bad to Wurtzel'.

The budding screenwriter began in the reading department, where his job was reading unsolicited submissions, and writing reports of them that nobody would ever read. He was delighted when his father invited him for a golfing weekend across the border at Agua Caliente, the film colony's 'away day'.

On the golf course, Lasky drove his ball three hundred yards down the fairway and then set off after it with Jesse. He was annoyed to see a blonde with a man moving ahead at snail's pace. But as they came closer, he recognized that the blonde was 'The Bombshell' Jean Harlow, number one Hollywood star of the day. The nattily dressed man with her was her stepfather, Italian Señor Marino Bello. Lasky greeted Harlow with great enthusiasm, introduced his son, and the quartet played on together.

That evening Jesse was thrilled to find himself at the craps table next to Jean in a white satin gown with cleavage to her navel. She was unsuccessfully throwing dice

---

39 *Curtain of Life* by Jack Preston & Jesse Lasky, Jr., The Macaulay Co. 1934

and paused, thrilled when Jesse hit a winning streak and scooped up his winnings. 'Basta!' she cried, turning the full power of her presence him. 'You roll great dice and you play good golf. Perhaps we could have a game tomorrow in town? We can meet at the Riviera Country Club—one o'clock.'

At twenty-two, Jesse was an especially presentable young man, but for all his worldly travels he was shy with the ladies; a quality that can be intriguingly endearing to a glamorous woman. Harlow threw him such a cataclysmic smile he thought it must be aimed at somebody else.

'That is, if you don't mind playing with an old lady', she added.

He stammered something resembling a yes as she disappeared in a cloud of men, chaperoned by Bello. He'd heard the gossip: Harlow had broken with her current paramour, actor William Powell, and maybe had even been romancing her co-star, Clark Gable. The following day (and he'd been thinking about it all night) back at his desk at Monogram, Jesse decided that the most important star in Hollywood wouldn't remember a carelessly made date with the lowest reader at Western Avenue, so there was no point in his turning up at the Riviera and looking a fool. At 1:15 pm his phone rang. 'Not very nice of you to stand up an old lady!' came the seductive accusation.

'Is this . . . Jean?' he stammered. Of course it was—and it was the beginning of a fantasy experience for Jess. Harlow had no desire to hide from press or public. She loved the adulation of her remonstrative fans. For the next few weeks she and Jesse went everywhere together, in flashy restaurants—slumming at Venice Amusement Park or on the Santa Monica Pier, or just hanging out. Jesse dared to hold her hand, kiss her hello and goodbye, but did not presume further. Perhaps that was his attraction: a highly presentable pal with no complications.

Then one day Wurtzel shattered his dream world. 'Junior…! You don't work no more on nights?' he snarled. 'And half asleep! You don't go to bed any more neither, huh? Are you still on my payroll?'

'Oh, yes, sir', Jesse assured him.

'Tonight then!' Wurtzel roared. 'I got to select stock film. Projection room number one—eight o'clock. Be there!'

Jesse phoned Jean. He would be fired if he didn't appear for the screenings with Wurtzel. Unperturbed, she said she'd come to the studio and wait in his office. She could work on her script for her new film, *Bombshell*. They could go out together after.

When she arrived that night, he took her up the rickety wooden stairs to his room with his cluttered desk and pointed through the window to the building where he'd be working with Wurtzel. She would see him emerge and could come down to meet him.

Jesse joined Sol in the projection room, finding it difficult to concentrate. It seemed like—and was—hours later when he and Wurtzel stepped out into the dark quadrangle. The parsimonious Wurtzel spotted Jesse's lighted window and glared up at it with incredulity. 'Jesse! You…you left a light on?'

'Well, you see, sir, a lady is waiting there', Jesse stammered. 'I didn't think you'd mind if I let her study her script while we were…'

'Junior's got a dame, huh?' Wurtzel snorted. 'Saturday night he gets laid?'

Suddenly the office light went out and Harlow emerged, swaying down the stairs. Wurtzel stared, then gawped in disbelief as she came closer. 'Junior…! She looks like Jean Harl… She can't be!' But there was no mistaking the hottest blonde in a world that had not yet met Marilyn Monroe.

'May I introduce Miss Harlow, Mr. Wurtzel?' Jesse asked, not without a certain inhalation of triumph.

Next morning, Jesse arrived at the studio to find himself promoted to Wurtzel's assistant, with a salary hike from $25 a week to $250. His new main job: casting stars that Wurtzel might borrow for a guest appearance in one of his films. Then he got a call from the head of Fox, Winnie Sheehan, inviting him to 'a party…and bring Jean.' To Jesse's surprise, Jean accepted and their entrance made quite a stir. Even his father suggested he bring her to the house for dinner. Jesse and his date were in unbelievable demand.

One day Jean called: 'You're taking me out to the Trocadero tonight. I feel like dancing.'

He was thrilled at the thought—until he thought about his height. Jean was only five foot three but she'd mentioned that she liked tall, dark, athletic guys. Jesse was athletic and dark, but he was five foot six and painfully aware that his father had called him Shortie when he was a kid. That night he stuffed his shoes with paper to add two solid inches, although he had a little difficulty keeping them on.

When he picked Jean up, she didn't seem to notice his sudden growth. 'We'll have fun. I want to have a lot of fun tonight', she announced.

He drove her to the Troc in his wreck of a car. When the doorman opened the door, the handle came off in his white-gloved hand. A bad start, but Jean thought it was hilarious.

After charred steaks and Waldorf salad, he led her onto the dance floor and into an impressive tango.

'Did you learn this in the Argentine, Jess? Traveling with your father?'

Jesse had learned it from a dance class with Arthur Murray, but wishing to project his image as an international *homme fatal*, he replied, 'I did most of my tango dancing in Paris. And Spain. Traveling alone, Jean.' As she swayed into his arms, he began a graceful glide—and slid out of his overstuffed shoes to fall flat on his face. He rose inches shorter, the center of the room's laughter and Jean laughing the loudest.

When he drove her home, she led him into her white bedroom, which had been called by gossip columnists, 'the platinum house that hair built.' She sprayed a bottle of perfume on Jesse, saying, 'I like my perfume straight and my liquor strong. But somebody's got loose with a hammer in my head.'

JEAN HARLOW AND SEÑOR BELLO

Jean stepped into her dressing room, leaving the door ajar so he could glimpse a flash of white flesh. She came out wearing a peach-colored silk negligee.

'Think I should lie down. Why don't you relax, Jess? Stay a while', she asked, stretching out provocatively on her bed in a voluptuous pose. Any pose with Jean would have been voluptuous, but Jesse was slow on the uptake. Instead, he hurried to her bathroom, returning with two aspirin and a glass of water. 'For your head', he said.

'How old are you, Jesse?' she asked, peering at him.

'Twenty-two.' It was an apology. She was twenty-three.

She told him she had married at sixteen—and he noticed she hadn't taken the aspirin. 'Would you like me to read you to sleep?' he asked.

'Beds are not for reading.' She studied him a moment longer. 'Be a good boy and go home, Jesse.' He realized the moment had passed when he might have been any other kind of boy.

The next day he phoned Jean and she did not take the call. Nor the next ten calls. Then gossip maven Louella Parsons reported that she'd gone back to William Powell.

Wurtzel wasn't the last to hear. The following day Jesse was back in the reading department, his salary returned to $25 a week. No explanation was needed and none given. Jesse never saw Jean Harlow again.

Writing of it years later, he said, 'No one would remember that for a brief moment in her life, Miss Harlow had amused herself with an altar boy in the temple of her fame.'

SCENE FIVE
1935 – 1939

PICKFORD-LASKY PRODUCTIONS

When his contract ended at Fox, Lasky was asked to stay on. Instead, he accepted an offer from diminutive super-star Mary Pickford to partner her in Pickford-Lasky Productions, Inc. The actress/producer owned 50% of United Artists Studio and it sounded like a judicious move.

It was and it wasn't. The partnership lasted for only one year, during which time the company made four films. Their second film in 1936, *The Gay Desperado*, was a musical comedy starring another Lasky discovery, Italian opera star Nino Martini. It was a great financial success.

In 1929, while attending a concert in Paris, Lasky had first heard Nino Martini sing. He was wildly impressed by the handsome tenor's fresh voice and elegant looks. Although he was leaving for the states in the morning, one look was all the star-maker needed. As usual, he had a contract in his pocket and signed Martini on the spot. As soon as his concert tour was finished, the singer was to report to Paramount by the 29th of August to begin filming on Lasky's all-star revue *Paramount on Parade* (which also featured Maurice Chevalier). In it, Martini sang 'Come Back to Sorrento' in one of several unique Technicolor sequences.

Under the supervision of production supervisor, singer, actress, songwriter, Elsie Janis, various sequences in the film were directed by different people: Edmund Goulding, Dorothy Arzner, Ernst Lubitsch, Rowland V. Lee, A. Edward Sutherland, Victor

POSTER: GAY DESPERADO

Herman, Lothar Mendes, Otto Brower, Edwin H. Knopf, Frank Tuttle, and Victor Schertzinger.

Martini was to become one of Lasky's favorite singing stars. By the time he was ready to film *The Gay Desperado* at Fox, Lasky had already featured him in four movies at Paramount, including *Night in Venice*, *Moonlight and Romance*, and *Clair de Luna*.

The Gay Desperado[40] featured the flamboyant character actor Leo Carrillo as a Mexican bandit with a musical soul. He stole the picture from singing star Nino Martini and everyone else. Ida Lupino, a British actress from a famous theatre family, was the female interest. She was to become an American star, director, and writer. The director, Rouben Mamoulian considered the film his masterpiece and it was a runaway financial success.

http://www.tcm.com/mediaroom/video/239472/Gay-Desperado-The-Movie-Clip-Senor-Troubadour.html

Jesse was still attempting to become an employed screenwriter, the one part of the industry where he felt he could fit. In 1935 he took an assignment in London working at British Gaumont as the 'American dialogue' writer on a Hitchcock film, *Secret Agent* (also called *The Hawk*). American and British English were truly an ocean apart before television leveled the idioms.

Lasky, on a whirlwind European scouting trip hunting new film properties, discovered a French actress, visited his son, and returned stateside to problems with America's Sweetheart, having shared those problems with Jesse, whose toe was now firmly dipped in the business (with the help of introductions from his dad).

On board the Santa Fe Chief:
October 16, 1935
Dear Jesse,

...We arrived at Quebec after a most uneventful voyage, and left for Chicago the same night. In the meantime, Miss Pickford had telephoned me at Quebec to remain over in Chicago as she was coming to meet me on her way to New York - also, my New York attorney, Mr. Panuch, was jumping on to Chicago to meet me, so Mother boarded the train from Chicago alone (for California) and I remained behind in the windy city.

Then I got an inspiration, and the next morning instead of waiting for Pickford, I boarded a TWA plane and had a marvelous flight to Albuquerque. I left Chicago at one o'clock and reached Albuquerque at nine o'clock. Mary's train came in an hour later at 10 o'clock, and I returned to Chicago with her, giving us a day on the train to discuss business. I arrived in Chicago at 8.45

---

40   *The Gay Desperado* has been restored by the UCLA Film and Television Archive.

Monday morning and left on the 'Chief' the same morning at 11.15 o'clock - and I am now on the last lap. It is a gorgeous sunny day - and Oh. Boy! California looks good. . . .

Pickford seemed pleased with all the deals I made in Europe. We won't exercise the option on 'Black Eyes' until we see the picture, on account of the fact that we only get the British and American rights. It is quite likely I will return to New York next week as matters are being fixed with the lawyers so I can go there now, (Lasky was in danger of being sued and was still on the edge of bankruptcy.) and I will join Mary as she is still working on the financing of the company and I think needs my help to bring this situation to a satisfactory conclusion.

The fact that you are working at British Gaumont has been publicized to your advantage, and I only hope you can stick it through and try and make a go of it. It is going to help your prestige here enormously; however, if things don't work out to your satisfaction, you have your transportation and do not hesitate to pack and come home. I cannot tell you how anxious I am for news from you so do write often.

I do not want to let this opportunity slip by without telling you how much I appreciated the help you gave me, sacrificing at times your own pleasure. I was just telling Randy I do not know what I would have done without you, not alone for your companionship and help but your judgment and moral support. I miss you like the devil and would give anything in the world if you could be on this train with me - but we did a smart thing in having you stay behind, so do make the most of your opportunity and we will look forward to giving you a real welcome at the United Artists Studio in the new Pickford-Lasky offices, when you arrive well before Christmas.

Mother and Grandma are meeting me at Pasadena and maybe I won't be glad to see the children. Randy tells me our offices are just too wonderful. With all the best -

Your Pal - Dad

Lasky wrote to his son, who was living on his own in London, and signed his letter 'Your Pal'—an indication that Jesse had grown up, but equally a sign that Lasky was not 'growing old'.

October 28th, 1935
Dear Jesse

. . . Needless to say we were glad to learn you are comfortably settled at No. 8 Dorset Square and that you have reported to the studio for work. Your description of your first day there is typical . . . I think you are going to need endless patience because they do things very slowly in England; however, I trust things will work out okay.

... I like my new offices very much, in fact, the lay-out, physically, is perfect. Miss Pickford has been in New York since my arrival, consequently, I cannot tell how we are going to work together as she does not arrive until tomorrow. She, as well as everybody else, liked 'Monsieur Sans-Gene'. I probably will use Harry D'Arrast to direct it, and Morrie Ryskind to write it—you will remember he wrote 'Of Thee I Sing'.

I could not arouse much enthusiasm in anyone over the 'Black Eyes' picture. Looking at it here, the censorship problems seem too great. It is curious how different things appear in Hollywood than they do in the atmosphere of Paris, or even London, and, as I knew from past experience, you have to make great allowances when making deals abroad for America.

Miss Pickford likes Ariane Borg very much and we are signing her up, in fact, she arrives tomorrow... Mother is thinking of leaving for New York in another week. It is difficult for her to get settled here. She is lonesome for Louise (her sister) so probably a dose of New York will do her good and make her more content to remain in California.

... Hanline and Phil Friedman are functioning splendidly and I like the United Artists... Our big problem will be to get on a working basis with Mary. She is changeable and uncertain and worries like the devil, but time will cure that no doubt. The Writers' Club is giving her a dinner on Thursday night and I am going to be one of the Speakers at the Speakers' Table, and Mother has consented to occupy a front table with Francis Lederer and a few people...

This is Monday morning - one should never try to write a letter on Monday morning, but my conscience bothered me for not having written you, and I determined to start this week right, so get what you can out of this letter.

Your Pal - Dad

November 2, 1935

We have just received your most interesting letter, the one in which you described your experience in writing the Mexican dialogue. I enjoyed your letter so much that I brought it down to the office this morning and read it to Phil, Randy and Hanline, and this afternoon I read it to Mervyn LeRoy and L. Wright, who were visiting me in my office.

... I found on my arrival that Mary had not completed the financing of the company. This was rather disturbing, but I finally got her to agree to put up enough money to finance the first picture, which would give us time to negotiate for the rest of the capital we need. Seeing she was very slow, I suddenly got an inspiration and sent for Mervyn LeRoy who, when he finishes directing 'Anthony Adverse', wants to leave Warner Bros. and get into business for himself. I told Mervyn of our set-up, and we are now trying to arrange a deal to take Mervyn into the company as a partner, but not change the name of the company Pickford-Lasky Productions, Inc. Mervyn, through Harry Warner, his father-in-law, could get a lot of capital, and I think it will be a marvelous set-up as he and I will work together and he will direct some of the pictures. We are also considering taking in Jay Paley, or if not, it looks as if we can get some capital from the East through Mary's connections . . . Everyone who saw 'Sans-Gene' thought it was simply a marvelous purchase, and everybody is crazy about Ariane Borg, the little French girl, so my European trip is considered a great success. I have engaged Harry D'Arrast to direct, and Morrie Ryskind to write, 'Sans-Gene', and they start Monday on a six-weeks' writing schedule, and the picture will definitely go into production on December 16th, with the most brilliant cast I can assemble—pretty good, don't you think?

On the whole I think things are going very well and I have never been happier in any spot than I am in my present set-up. Our company seems to have the respect of everyone and they look for great things from us, and I feel we are going to succeed. Lederer is delighted with his part in 'Sans-Gene' so there are no unusual production problems. Guy Endore is still working on the Casanova treatment and doing a pretty good job. I like him very much and I think he was a good choice and that you are right about him. He just brought me a copy of his book 'Werewolf of Paris' which I promised to read in my leisure moments.

Mother is fine, and leaving for New York Tuesday, November 6th to visit with Louise . . . she will be installed at the Sherry Netherland Hotel . . . Billy and Betty are well and happy, and struggling with their very difficult studies at school. I tried to help Betty last night in some of her arithmetic problems, and they were really too much for me, and as for Billy, with his Latin and Algebra, he is pretty nearly burning the midnight oil.

This is Saturday afternoon and I have been in the office all day, even giving up golf on account of a meeting with Pickford, Wright and LeRoy. Tonight, however, I am going to a party at the Trocadero, given by the John Cromwells (character actor) to welcome the Freddie Marches. Nothing ever changes in dear old Hollywood, and after Europe, I like it more than ever. . . .

I cannot tell you how thrilled I was over your experience in writing the Mexican dialogue for Peter Lorre. I know you will lick the tough old Hawk, if you have to put it over a camp-fire and cook and eat it. Use your good old American sense of humor, and your Lasky patience, and everything will turn out okay for you.

Mother will look up Frances[41] when she gets to New York, which I know will please you ... At home we have a new cook, a new butler and a new chauffeur, but as the new butler is an expert masseur, I am very happy over the change. (This was cutting down from 12 servants.)

I have been elected President of the Divot Diggers Club, and next weekend we will have a swell meeting at an out-of-town golf club. Tomorrow, Sunday, I am going to spend the day with Cecil at Paradise as I have not seen him since my return.

This is about all the news, except I intrigued Mother into going to a dinner at the Writers' Club, given to Mary Pickford, and she sat with me at the Speakers' Table, and I made one of my usual eloquent speeches which they tell me was pretty good....

Pickford-Lasky's story editor, Maurice Hanline, who had become a friend, wrote to Jesse in London.

November 4, 1935
Dear Jesse,

...The smiling cloudless skies of Hollywood greet the fogs and miseries of London. Pickford-Lasky Productions, Inc., in the slightly stout and bald-headed shape of its Story Editor, greets BIP in the shape of a 'spat'ted-monocled' writer of genius, no doubt by this time surfeited by the horse-faced buck-teethed damsels of London. You never know what you leave, do you my son? What would you give for a corner of Hollywood Blvd. and Vine Street—all of Leicester Square—I wonder?

Well, I will try to bring Hollywood to you as best I can and give you some idea as to how we are functioning.

First I want to tell you how delighted I was with MONSIEUR SANS-GENE, it fits Lederer better than the proverbial paper on the wall and I am sure we would not have done better if we had searched the story market for the next five years.

I am crazy about the little French girl and you know me well enough to be sincere and I say that I believe her to be most important among the feminine screen personalities since Dietrich. To me it seems that her possibilities are unlimited. My only regret is that your father insists she has to go out with no one in Hollywood, not even with his own Story Editor. Joking aside, I believe she represents ultimately one million dollars in cold cash to the company.

We have two sets of writers working on the Casanova script. Samson Raphelson (Raphaelson) on his own and Guy Endore with Hanns Schwarz (aka Hans Schwartz) on another. Ernest Pascall is working on a Martini

---

41 Frances Hackenberg was a dancer, (as Donna Drake) Jesse's newest conquest.

original and you can gather that I am kept rather busy and believe I have been of appreciable aid in the development of their stories. Your father is pleased with the progress of the writers. I hope by this time you have contacted Pollinger and Kyllman (agents). Kyllman especially is the most charming man I met in London, the best type of Englishman, which after all is synonymous with the best type of man no matter how much we hate London and the lesser English fry ... Here at the studio everything is progressing excellently. The morale of the entire organization is hundred percent perfect.

When you have a minute time drop me a line, meanwhile take my best regards and good wishes

Yours,
Maurice [Hanline]

And there was more news from his father:

November 8, 1935
Dear Jess,

...Mother got away safely for New York on Tuesday night, after a wild ride to the station during which I had to stop the car and 'phone to hold the train fifteen minutes, Mother having given me the wrong time at which the train departed—a typical Lasky getaway. The next day your fascinating letter arrived and after reading it at least three times, I have forwarded it to Mother.

Things are moving along in Pickford-Lasky although still in the formative stage. Due to the death of his father, Harry Warner will be in Hollywood for the week-end and we are then to discuss the Mervyn LeRoy situation to see if Warner will put in the money Mervyn requires to join with us. In a word, we are still going ahead on Mary's financing which will carry us through one picture, but I have no doubt at all as to the success of our completing the financing of the company as we have several other propositions in case Mervyn cannot make it.

...I saw the most thrilling picture recently—'Mutiny on the Bounty' - it is one I will insist on your seeing when you get home; a gorgeous romantic picture, the kind we both like.

I see in the paper Mickey Balcon[42] will be arriving here in a few days and I will of course see him. I am just leaving for a cocktail party at Pickfair[43] given in honor of some United Artists executives from abroad. Mary doesn't come to the studio very much - which is a blessing; confidentially, she doesn't know what it is all about. I have never worked in such comfortable quarters; our projection room connecting right with my office is a joy and the studio

---

42 Michael Balcon, British film producer.
43 Mary Pickford's home with Douglas Fairbanks known as Pickfair.

personnel seems to be splendid. Worked all day yesterday and last night until midnight and seem to be full of my old pep.

I can see by your letters that you are having an invaluable experience, one that will stand you in good stead for many months and years to come, so no matter how tough it may be, stick it out. I am convinced that your prestige has been enhanced enormously by this adventure abroad, and all my agent friends assure me that you will be much easier to place than you were before, and at a higher figure; if not, there is always a spot in Pickford-Lasky....

P.S. Ariane Borg looks better than ever. I am having her trained by George Hadden, a stage director from Fox—the man who directed the Berkeley Square dialogue for me—and he thinks she is the greatest find of recent times. This girl is positively going to be a sensation, and we are grooming her.

November 21, 1935

...It was nice to receive your letter this morning, the one in which you told me about the young composer, Mr. Potsford. As long as he is coming to Hollywood in a couple of months, I think that will be time enough as we will hardly be selecting numbers for Martini's picture before that time - but I certainly want to get a chance to hear his numbers.

...We aim to start the 'Sans-Gene' picture December 16th - just think, we do not have a title yet, and we are experiencing the usual troubles in getting a worthwhile cast. All the department heads on the lot here, including the Art Director Captain Day, and Newman, Musical Director, saw the picture and think it is a wow. Harry D'Arrast and Morrie Ryskind are doing good work on the script. I must say, Jess, the purchase of *Sans-Gene* saved my life.

For the time being we have abandoned 'Casanova' because the story developed only fairly well and the picture promised to be altogether too expensive, so we would have been in a spot if it had not been for the good luck of our finding 'Sans-Gene'. Ariane Borg, the little French girl, has won everybody who has seen her, and we are making her first test today, after having had her coached in English until she speaks quite fluently.

Unfortunately we have been handicapped through the fact that we have not completed the financing of the company as yet. I have had to accept $2,000 a week instead of $2,500 which is going to make it just a little harder for me to navigate, but there is a provision that if we make more than four pictures during the year, my salary will be retroactive and I will be paid at the rate of $2,500 ...I met Mickey Balcon yesterday and he asked about you - also told me he surmised you were getting along quite well. He knew all about your writing the Mexican dialogue. He is a nice chap. Noll Gurney sent me a copy of your last letter to him - he is a good friend of yours.

Mother is in New York but will be home for Thanksgiving, and I will be glad to have her back as it is a bit lonesome at times. The children are fine and great company for me. I took them to the Brown Derby the other night for dinner, and to see 'Metropolitan' afterwards.

...It was great to hear that there is a prospect of your novel being published - if this should come off, send me the news quickly.

All the boys, I mean my staff, want to be remembered to you - they ask about you all the time. Billy, Betty and Grandma join me in sending you our love.

There was still a large audience for opera in the 1930s, and Lasky was particularly fond of it since the days when he attempted to make a silent film with the great opera singer Enrico Caruso and had successfully made several with Geraldine Farrar. *Metropolitan* was a picture about the opera and starred a well-known opera singer, Lawrence Tibbett.

December 3, 1935
Dear Jess,

...Last night, when I arrived home, Billy and Betty eagerly read me your last letter to them, the one in which you devoted a paragraph to each, and I must say you are developing an amusing style in your letters, which have handed us many good laughs, Incidentally, I enjoyed your November 16th letter so much, the one in which you described your experience with the London Rowing Club... Mother and I met Michael Balcon last night at Tai Lachmann's one of Tai's typical dinners - and Balcon told me that they were much pleased with you according to the reports he had; that you were working on 'The Hawk' and that he understood the treatment was very well liked. He is a very agreeable chap, and really thinks he did a smart thing in engaging you... The other day I met Gladys Unger. She told me she had cabled you as she is very anxious to get on with the story, and later I met her with Major Bodeley from whom I think she was getting some military advice. At any rate, I imagine there is nothing you can do about it until your script is finished and you can speed home. I don't think there will be much trouble in selling the Sudan story at a good price once you and Gladys get together and finish it.

As the Holidays approach, I realize you won't be able to be here for Christmas, and I imagine not for New Years either. Well, it is too bad we shall all miss you more than you realize, particularly your Dad - who would be glad to discuss some of his story problems with you.

Since your last letter, Morrie Ryskind fell down on the Sans-Gene story and I now have Steve Avery on it; you remember he did 'The Gay Deception'. Harry D'Arrast is not too pleased with Avery's work so far and yesterday I think we had a break. Ben Hecht, whose dialogue is particularly brilliant -

there is no better writer in the business - is visiting out here and due to his friendship for D'Arrast has agreed to write the script for us at a nominal sum, providing we don't use his name, as he has turned down offers of exorbitant sums and will not write a picture for any company out here. At any rate, if all goes well, I am sending D'Arrast to New York with him on the train so they can finish the script, and we will go into production on December 26th instead of December 16th. Fortunately we have made no commitments so the slight delay doesn't cost us anything. So far we have cast, in addition to Lederer, Ida Lupino for the lead, and Edward Everett Horton for the girl's suitor.

Thus far we have not solved the problem of financing the company but we expect a capitalist from Montreal this week who Loyd Wright feels sure will supply us with the needed capital. If not I am sure we can get it from New York - it is only a matter of time.

December 9, 1935

...This is a hasty note to wish you A MERRY CHRISTMAS, and to enclose a very modest Christmas present. Hope the Gods will smile on us and l can do much better for you next year. I am just catching the Chief for New York to spend one week there talking to bankers and others about completing the financing of the company.

December 17, 1935

... Randy and I are in New York for a week. While visiting here I am giving testimony in the lawsuit of the Paramount Trustees against the Board of Directors, having arranged a truce with the lawyers so that I can come to New York without being served.[44] The real object of my trip is to raise money for Pickford-Lasky; we are seeking to raise $2,000,000 and it looks as though we are going to be successful...I find that my prestige is as big in New York as it ever was, and the whole trip has pepped me up enormously - meeting all the old gang and going to shows has been fine for me. We are leaving Friday for home as we start our first picture a week after we arrive in Hollywood. Harry D'Arrast came with me, also Ben Hecht, who is writing the script; it is now nearing completion and in Hecht's best style, which means it ought to be very good.

... New York is very exciting, also very tiring, and the more I see of New York, outside of the temporary exhilaration it gives you - very much like champagne, great while you drink it but not so hot the day after - I prefer California. Miss you like the devil but don't forget - everyday you are away you are gaining in prestige because they seem to judge one's success away from California by the number of days one is absent ... MERRY CHRISTMAS!

---

44 Lasky was still in financial difficulties in New York.

and all that sort of thing - write me a long letter - I will write you again when I reach Hollywood.

Your loving Dad

December 31, 1935

...My trip to New York was fairly successful inasmuch as I got a subscription of $350,000 from one source and made some very fine contacts, however, we are still up in the air due to the difficulty of getting Mary Pickford to stay put. She is a handful as a partner so that nothing permanent has been settled yet, however, we are having a meeting in a couple of days which will, bring matters to a head and probably a successful conclusion ... In order to get permission to go to New York, I had to agree to give testimony in the Paramount Trustees' suit against the Directors, which means I had to go through several severe cross-examinations; on top of all this, constant meetings with prospective investors, brokers, bankers, two trips in the subway to Wall Street - all in the space of a week; some holiday, I don't think.

We had to delay the starting of our picture, which is now scheduled to start January 6th. You would not think it would be hard to adapt that charming French picture but it proved a real tough job, and worst of all, I got into trouble with Harry D'Arrast, the director; we could not see the story eye to eye at all - he wanted to change it so that it would lose its simplicity and charm and I not agreeing to it, result: I had to let him out, and good old dependable Rowland Lee is now set to direct it, and we have the last minute rush of finishing the script. Tonight is New Year's Eve, and I have persuaded Mother to go with me to a New Year's Eve party at Sam Goldwyn's - not much fun for either one of us but we must do these things occasionally. Sunday afternoon we attended a huge party given by Basil Rathbone and Ouida Bergere (his wife)—everybody present from Billy Buckland, Ruthie and Mac (Mac Capps, Ruth Goldwyn Lasky's husband) to the top stars and celebrities. Saw Gladys Unger who is still anxiously looking forward to your return so that the writing of Sudan can proceed.

Needless to say we missed you on Christmas and will miss you this New Years ... I only wish you could have been here to work on the Monsieur Sans-Gene story. The more I work with other writers, the more I realize how much you have got to contribute, if properly placed....

Billy has grown about three inches since you left and Betty grows brighter and cleverer every day. I know Betty has written you, also they were pleased with the presents you sent them. I suppose some day the script of 'The Hawk' will be finished and we will be receiving word of your early return home. Needless to say you will receive a warm welcome.

Well, here's wishing you a Happy New Year in which all the family joins....

January 13, 1936

...We have enjoyed your letters so much, particularly the one about the Boxing Day Shoot...I met Sam Marx, the story editor at Metro, at lunch the other day and he asked for you most cordially. I gave you the proper boost, but told him nevertheless you were trying to break away and that when you returned he could expect a call from you....

We finally got 'One Rainy Afternoon' started...Have been shooting three days and the rushes look good, although the script even now isn't quite finished. Hanline and Steve Avery are working on it and, by the way, Hanline has proved a very valuable man. I hated to start the picture without a finished script, but the Ben Hecht script did not work out well at all; too sophisticated and it got too far away from the original story we bought. In a word, we have had the usual producers' problems, but the picture will probably in the end turn out okay.

...Regarding the financing of Pickford-Lasky, that is still up in the air, but two men are arriving from New York the end of this week and then the matter will come to a head. One of the men is Nate Spingold, an executive in Columbia who wants to put his own money in the company and become an officer in it. He is a very able man and if this goes through, it will give me just the kind of partner I need as Mary has proven worse than useless; by that I mean she is seldom around and cannot offer any help—on the other hand she wants to be consulted and doesn't know what it is all about.

John Otterson is here from New York and I am meeting him this week to discuss my possibly returning to Paramount in case our financing should not materialize in Pickford-Lasky. Had a talk with him in New York and he is most keen to have me in a top executive position in Paramount so, for the moment, my future seems to be in the lap of the Gods...My Mother celebrated her seventy-fifth birthday last week and Ruthie gave her a lovely tea party. She is feeling fine and is full of pep and enthusiasm; really Grandma is a wonderful woman. Billy and Betty are thriving and you will find them amazingly changed when you return.

Went to the Fights the other night with Nigel Bruce[45] and saw Art Lasky[46] make his come-back and win—and I won about fifty bucks...Needless to say I miss you like the devil; your counsel and advice would be very welcome if you were here....

After making *One Rainy Afternoon* with Francis Lederer, Ariane Borg had been considered for several other roles. But she lost out to Dolly Haas in the 1931 remake of *Broken Blossoms*, and although Lasky had such high hopes for her, she returned

---

45 The original Dr. Watson with Basil Rathbone's *Sherlock Holmes*.
46 No relation to Jesse. Professional heavyweight boxer.

to France where she continued to work. She lived to the age of ninety-one, but was never seen again in Hollywood.

It wasn't all work for Jesse in London. He became an enthusiastic member of the London Rowing Club at Putney Bridge during his early years in England. He no longer rowed when we lived there together in the 1960s, but he would stand on the

DOUGLAS FAIRBANKS JR.

bank of the Thames at Putney with a nostalgic look in his eyes, and proudly wore the Club's silver buttons on a series of navy-blue jackets for the rest of his days.

In 1936, after a taste of exciting country weekends at stately homes with tennis and pheasant shoots and dressing for dinners, when his job was finished, he was reluctant to leave. But having spent more money than he'd earned, he sailed home on the SS Ile de France, second class. It turned out to be a memorable trip.

Standing at the railing at Cherbourg, he watched with casual interest the arrival of a silver-grey Mercedes Benz. From it emerged a spectacularly handsome man wearing a Homburg, half hidden in the immense Astrakhan collar of a vicuna coat. It was Jesse's childhood chum, Douglas Fairbanks Jr., and with him, wrapped in mink and masked behind giant dark glasses, Marlene Dietrich stepped out to share a farewell embrace that hinted of a passionate affair. While the voyagers gawped, having no trouble recognizing both legendary stars, Doug ascended the plank to reappear on the first-class deck in time to blow a kiss to his hardly incognito amour.

As the ship took sail, Jesse called up to Doug, who stared down in amazement, surprised to see Jesse traveling second class. Questions were tossed between decks.

'Conserving the pocket, old man', Jesse confessed in a loud stage whisper.

'Good God! Come on up at once. We'll have a drink', Doug called.

There was iced champagne and an insistent offer to share Doug's huge Royal Suite. A grateful Jesse readily accepted. Doug was fencing in his next film and Jess had been captain of his fencing team at Hun School; so for the rest of the journey, they daily fought a duel on the promenade deck and nightly wined and dined in a flurry of international society.

When the Ile sailed into New York harbor, Jesse, standing at the railing with his pal, had to tell him how much the trip had meant to him and how deeply moved he was at Doug's generosity.

'Not another word about it, old man', Doug insisted.

But Jesse insisted. 'I certainly wish I could pay my own share', he said, knowing he had just enough money to get himself back to California.

'If you feel that way, old boy, of course I'll send you a bill for your half', Doug assured him, considering that he was doing his chum a favor.

When Jesse got the bill he borrowed the money to repay every penny. Doug, like most people, assumed all the Laskys could afford anything.

Jesse was home again and his bosses at Gaumont wrote to him c/o his agent, Myron Selznick, David's brother.

February 3, 1936
My dear Lasky,

First of all I want to offer you my apologies for failing to give you the farewell lunch we planned: there has been an excessive activity in this department during the last ten days, and the time passed without my realizing it.

Mr. M.E. Balcon has asked me to thank you very cordially on his behalf for your letter of January 26th. He wishes me to tell you that he fully appreciates the work you did for us over here: I join with him in expressing the hope that we may have a chance of renewing our association with you again later on.

Meantime, please accept every possible good wish both personal and professional.

With kindest regards.
Sincerely yours,
Angus McPhail

The trade papers heralded the return of the prodigal son, although in this case, perhaps not so prodigal. He had stopped off in New York for a few days to see the young ballet dancer his mother had visited for him, Frances Hackenberg. They decided to marry later that year. Jesse was twenty-six. His dad wrote to him in New York.

February 6, 1936
Dear Jesse,

...After waiting all day Wednesday for news of your safe arrival, your wire finally reached us this morning and, of course, we are very happy to know that you are on American soil and will be coming home in two weeks... Mel Shauer is anxious to discuss with you collaboration on that play about the movies for which he says he has a producer. He is quite excited about it and wants to see you as soon as you arrive. Jack Kirkland wants to see you about something when you arrive here, and Rian James, whom I ran into at a restaurant, wants to discuss your joining him to write some original stories, after his contract expires at Radio (RKO). He wants to take a period of time and write originals as he thinks there is a big market for them, and wants you in on it. Gladys, of course, is waiting for you to start work with her on the Sudan story. She has a play opening tonight at the Show Case Theatre in Beverly Hills, called 'Three Sheets in the Wind'; I have promised to attend. I think you are going to be very busy and very happy. After London, Hollywood will seem like Paradise.

...We have a gorgeous home, nicer than Tower Road, but being a brand new house, never before lived in, it takes time to get it properly furnished. We have a lovely tennis court, which I hope you will find time to use, and the grounds are just being landscaped.

Things are only going so-so at the studio. 'One Rainy Afternoon' is slowly nearing completion; it should be finished about February 17th. Rowland Lee is very slow and not doing as good a job as I would like, although the boys seem to think it is going to be a good picture. Hugh Herbert, who plays the prompter, is very funny, and Eric Rhodes, who plays the suitor, is grand; in fact all the cast are excellent, but the script is not very good. I honestly believe you could have written a better script in two weeks than we have gotten out of the combined efforts of Stephen Avery, Maurice, etc.

... By the way, be sure and see 'Dead End' which we have been trying to buy. I want your expert opinion of the play, and I wish you would meet a very swell young writer, Sidney Kingsley, who wrote the play. We had some grand talks in New York. Al Rockett, who is leaving New York today, and I were going in partnership on the play, if it could be purchased, and Kingsley would write the script. He wrote 'Men In White', and is the type of fellow you would like enormously; I believe he is only a year or two older than you are. Enclosed is a letter of introduction ... There is a European writer out here by the name of William Wilder who is a marvelous idea man, but his English isn't good enough for him to write good dialogue. He is crazy to collaborate with you on a couple of originals, and it might be a swell tie-up. I think there is a big field for originals and you can make some real money if you get tied up with the right collaborators ... You should see many plays because the studios will, be discussing them ... I am really very optimistic about your prospects. ...

February 13, 1936

... delighted to learn that you are leaving on the 19th. Glad to know that you planned to meet Jack Salter and Nino (Martini), also that you enjoyed 'Dead End'. I think I told you we tried to buy it offering up to $100,000 advance against a percentage proposition, but they are holding out for much more money ... We went to the Chaplin opening last night with George Putnam and Amelia Earhart; it was the usual gala affair. The Putnams had dinner with us first. George and I hit on a swell idea for a story to be called 'The Mission Inn', the whole thing laid in the Mission Inn at Riverside, California.

The last time I wrote you I told you I was going to see Gladys Unger's new play. It turned out to be pretty God-awful—inexcusably bad. I would place most of the blame against the chap Armitage who collaborated and staged it.

There is nothing new on the Paramount situation, except that I am lunching with Rothacker tomorrow which will be a preliminary discussion before meeting Otterson again. Things are in terrible shape over there; Lubitsch has left and Bill LeBaron was put in temporary charge.

Am sorry to tell you that 'One Rainy Afternoon' doesn't look too hot. Rowland Lee is just the wrong director for a comedy of this type. The picture will be roughly assembled by the time you get here; we are still shooting.

We had a charming dinner at the house the other night—among the guests were G. B. Stern, Rachel Crothers, and Mr. and Mrs. James Hilton who wrote 'The Lost Horizon'. He brought me one of his earlier autographed books - we seemed to hit it off very well at a previous meeting and I like him very much. Am lunching with G. B. Stern today and showing her 'Here's To Romance', as she wants to have a crack at writing a Martini story.

I think we are beginning to lick the Martini story. We have a strange contraption in a story, which presents Martini against a rural background in which Chic Sale carries most of the comedy as a quaint old postman. It sounds crazy but it really will be a somewhat different musical if the treatment finally comes through as now seems likely....

So far, all the people whom his father thought were so eager to hire Jesse hadn't appeared. He had seen DeMille's latest spectacular *The Crusades* in London and had written the director telling him how much he would like to work for him. The great man had telegrammed, 'Come see me when you return.'

Cecil, at the top of his career, and Jesse who had known him since he was a child, had been flattered at the praise Cecil heaped on him for his three books of teenage verse.

At twenty-six, entering DeMille's vastly dark, high-ceilinged office, Jesse could believe the joke currently going around: Heaven had sent for a psychiatrist because God thought he was DeMille. The style of a DeMille film was larger than life, and to Jesse, irresistible. Impressive pageantry, panoramic scenic effects, lavish costumes and sets offered audiences visual inspiration and vast spectacle. Many images were drawn from the works of classical painters. The stories had complex plots and sub-plots with plenty of suspense and twists, which was what DeMille's target market demanded.

Cecil cared nothing for the critics, who anyway, considered his work insignificant. The box office results proved there was a worldwide devoted audience who would be watching DeMille spectacles into the 21st century. These were the kind of films that Jesse craved to write, and finally, DeMille called him to his office.

A clutter of objects filled long shelves, each of vital importance to some phase of the forthcoming film. In this instance, it was the first *The Buccaneer*. The walls were lined with magnificent storyboard drawings for the current film. These were not just sketches. DeMille actually used large, colorful paintings by Daniel Sayre Groesbeck. He'd discovered the artist had a remarkable talent for visualizing the drama of a scene and putting it on paper. The producer said, 'He always knew what I wanted and he could capture character and drama in a few strokes of his brush.' Groesbeck was to create thousands of drawings and watercolors for DeMille, including the eight films Jesse worked on as a writer.

But that first day as Jesse walked the length of the vast imposing office and perched nervously in the indicated chair across the gigantic desk, placing him squarely in the sharp beam of a spotlight—like a suspect, DeMille moved around his desk to take his seat opposite. Certainly, Jess thought, the director was the only man who could swagger while sitting down. He was not prepared for the first question fired at him from beneath those sharp, steely-blue eyes. He may have failed as an actor, but that voice was theatrically commanding. 'Do you believe in God, Jesse?'

Jesse stammered a tentative mumble. When the great man seemed unsatisfied, he added, 'I believe in *you*, sir.'

He was aware that three other writers were already assigned to *The Buccaneer*. Nevertheless, DeMille's secretary had sent him the screenplay treatment and one first draft scene in preparation for the meeting. He was expected to bring a sample of suggested dialogue changes to improve the scene.

The director received the pages from Jess's hand like Zeus accepting a burnt offering, and proceeded to read the scene aloud with just the edge of a sneer in his voice. In the glaring spotlight, Jesse cringed. Then, with a menacing look, DeMille reached into his desk drawer and pulled out a pistol. For one brief moment Jesse thought his offence so great he was about to die on the spot. But DeMille shoved the revolver toward him, butt forward, growling, 'If you want to destroy me, Jesse, use this. It's quicker!'

Having abstained from shooting DeMille, Jesse watched as the director resumed reading his proposed scene. Then quite unexpectedly, the pained expression changed to a smile of surprise and pleasure. Jesse had written a line for Akim Tamiroff, the Russian character comedian playing a pirate. A girl is forced to walk the plank with her dog. Jesse's added scene read:

The dog barks.

Tamiroff: You hear that, boss? A barking fish!

'Barking fish…' DeMille said thoughtfully and then looked up, a smile lighting his thin lips. 'That's a DeMille line, Jesse! Not just words, but an original way of moving a plot. I can use ideas like that!'

But there was no job. The budget for writers was all used up. However, he would use the line—send Jesse a present—and make him a promise: on his next picture, Jesse would have a place on the writing team.

The present? One of DeMille's chauffeurs delivered it the next day. A case of champagne—Bollinger 1928. It went down well with the hamburger diet Jesse was on at the moment.

That April, with hopes for the future high in his heart, Jesse got married to Frances, the ballet dancer he'd met in New York. They were married quietly in the living room of his parent's home. By October, he had finished a book, sent his father the manuscript, and was back in London, this time with a wife and an assignment.

And Lasky was hot again. His musical, *The Gay Desperado*, starring Nino Martini, Leo Carrillo, and Ida Lupino had proved to be a huge hit. Breaking his agreement amicably with Pickford, he accepted what sounded like a substantial offer from RKO.

Radio-Keith-Orpheum, RKO Radio Pictures, had been suffering like the rest of Hollywood and had teetered into bankruptcy. In their recent reorganization, there had been a shifting of many chairs. In the east, Leo Spitz had been elected president, and on his first trip to the West Coast studio he appointed Russian-born Sam Briskin as vice president in charge of production.

At thirty-nine, slender bland-faced, bespectacled Briskin, who started as a CPA, had made a name for himself working for the Cohn brothers as general manager of Columbia at their Independent Studios on Sunset and Gower. This area was known as Poverty Row or Gower Gulch because it had a reputation for harboring seedy, fly-by-night film companies. Briskin's former boss, Harry Cohn, had a reputation as the most hated executive in the film business. Columbia was known as 'Corned Beef and Cabbage' Productions. But, no matter his roots, Briskin had one major talent: he could hold his temper and was tactful in negotiating contracts, a quality that the crude and explosive Harry Cohn did not possess. As a moderating force, Briskin had been credited with the success of Columbia. With his move to RKO, he announced that he intended to bring RKO into the 'A-' picture market. He was quoted in the press as saying he was looking for quality. Lasky liked the sound of that and was optimistic about his future at RKO.

But things were not all they seemed, although producer Pandro S. Berman was number one on the studio's 'A-List' having turned out four hits in a row. The most recent, *Follow the Fleet*, with the sparkling combination of Fred Astaire and Ginger Rogers, was box office magic.

Jesse, now in London with his new wife on another assignment from Gaumont British, received a letter from his father filled with multiple enthusiasms.

October 21, 1936
Dear Jesse,

... I like Sam Briskin very much, and it looks as though we are going to sign (Rouben) Mamoulian and buy 'The Woman Marches'; in fact, I will probably turn Phil Friedman over to R.K.O. to become the Casting Director for them and will take as my assistant, Carl Winston ... I am also taking Hanline as Story Editor, so am looking forward with real enthusiasm and a great deal of happiness, to conquering R.K.O. I am feeling very well, am full of pep, and I am positive the Lasky Star is in the ascendant ... All that I want to see happen is for you to get a writing job to justify your trip to London, and then back to Hollywood and a job with R.K.O ... We have a nice set-up and were received most cordially, as you can imagine. One of the men who is in charge of the physical end of the studio, something like Fred Harris—is Dave Garber and he said he is a friend of yours; an awfully nice chap. Randy and he hit it off immediately. We both feel we are going to be very happy at R.K.O. and things look very bright.

Mother and I are going to Palm Springs Friday to get three days' rest before I take on my new duties.

I forgot to tell you I started to read your book and while I have not gotten very far, I like the new opening very well although it seems to me the other opening was more original; however this opening is extremely well written and really interesting. Good luck with the book....

Jesse's draft manuscript, as yet unsold, would become *No Angels in Heaven*, which was finally published two years later.

Oct 26, 1936
The Desert Inn, Palm Springs
Dear Jesse,
  ... We are all installed in our nice new office ... they think I'm a Tin-Jesus at R.K.O., and all due to 'The Gay Desperado', which continues to be the talk of the industry here ... I will finish your book, this week–and write you about it—all the luck in the world to you and Frances. If you need any money or anything just cable ... I only implore you on one thing—<u>don't worry</u>! Life is short—and in the end everything will turn out all right, and then how you will regret the needless days and nights of worrying—that doesn't help a bit, anyway....

November 4, 1936
  ... On Monday I took possession of my offices here at R.K.O. and they are very nice and comfortable. My office is in the Administration Building right next to Mr. Briskin's office and across from Pandro Berman. My staff consists of the following: Charles Woolstenhulme, Production Assistant; Maurice Hanline, Story Assistant, and Joe Roos as his assistant; and Randy. I have been here two and one-half days and feel I am going to like it very much. I am devoting all my time now to trying to find our first story.
  Today we are all excited over the outcome of the Election as we were all rabid for Roosevelt - and what a landslide it proved to be. Even Mother went to the polls and voted, and towards the last we had a Roosevelt placard on our automobile. Today everyone feels that America is in for a long period of peace and prosperity under the Roosevelt Democratic Administration ... 'The Gay Desperado' has taken the country by storm and is doing enormous business throughout the United States. In many cities it is being held over for second week's engagements. This has naturally given me a lot of prestige so I really have a lot to be thankful for....

Although Briskin had announced to the press that he intended to up the 'A' list product of the studio, Lasky was encountering a very different agenda.

November 18, 1936
Dear Jess,

...I have accepted an assignment to make a big musical revue - 'Radio City Revels'—the story to be laid in Radio City, something like 'Big Broadcast' or 'Broadway Melody'. I have taken Alex Aarons, a former musical comedy producer, as my assistant on this assignment. Aarons only gets $200 a week, but he has had a couple of years' experience under Sam Katz at Metro and I think will be helpful.

...Briskin who runs the studio is accustomed to 'B' productions and doesn't like spending money and, consequently, is not too easy to work with and is very busy and very difficult to see, so, of course, it is not easy but I think we can make a go of it...I lunch with Mamoulian every week and we are great friends. He is getting ready to start a picture at Paramount...last night, Schumann-Heink[47] died. The 'old guard' are passing on. Mary (Pickford) is engaged to marry Buddy (Rogers). She came over to see me a few days ago; had a story idea she wants to sell....

We will be thinking of you and Frances on Thanksgiving Day and will drink a toast to the English branch of the Lasky family...

P.S. —Many hours later:

...Randy and I are sweating in my office in the studio, but I cannot go home until I tell you both how happy your letters made us. Of course your letter will now be passed on to Grandma, and Randy will also peruse it; in fact, I doubt if you will ever write anything with more emotion, and as interesting as your account of your first days in London.

I hope to heavens you had the courage to take the lease on the flat. $80.00 for six months is no commitment to worry about. The worst that could happen would be that you would have to leave before the six months were up in which event you could either sub-let it, or forget it, and we would pay the balance. I shall certainly be anxious to know that you did not lose the flat, but if you did, you will find another somehow, and don't be afraid of the lease. That is exactly what I mean by having courage—make the commitment and everything will work out all right...

After reading your letter I made up my mind that Mother should come over and join you, if all goes well, for the King's Coronation.

I was fascinated by the number of friends you have made and the various invitations extended to you, and while you are not working, you ought to take full advantage of them...I would rather see you write another novel, while you are freezing in London, than do a picture job. It is true a picture would give you an immediate income, small though it may be, but the novel would build you prestige for the future...

---

47 Ernestine Schumann-Heink (née Rössler; 15 June 1861 – 17 November 1936) a German Bohemian, later American, a famous operatic contralto.

(Still later;)

I wish you would find out if Agatha Christie, the author of the detective stories in which Hercule Poirot, the Belgian detective, is the principal character, is in London and manage to meet her. I am about to negotiate the picture rights for her book, the A.B.C. Murders, for which we want Leo Carrillo to play Poirot, the Detective. She is very jealous of these books; she nearly sold them to Metro and then the deal was held up because they wanted options, and the right to have a love story with Poirot which she objects to. You could see her on my behalf and tell her the fine production I would give her stories and how faithfully I would produce them, and maybe some good would come of it. I only mention this on the chance that you might run into her— (Edward) Knoblock or G.B. Stern might know her... We understand perfectly that you will not send us cables, unless it is very important, on account of the expense, so don't worry on that score....

November 30, 1936

...Things at the studio have been moving very slow - too slow to please me. We have been working on the 'Radio City Revels' story line with not very great success so far, and I am about to abandon the other story I was working on for Lederer. Briskin has been in New York for about ten days and the studio has been very quiet; however, things will work out all right it needs time and patience.

...Physically I am feeling very fit - mentally a bit worried over the slow progress. As I size up this studio, they are pointed too much in the direction of 'B' pictures. They think and function in the terms of small pictures. I could not sell them on 'The Woman Marches' - they are afraid of it....Last night we took the children and Grandma, and John Burton, to see a Federal Theatre play - not very good... Thanksgiving night we went over to the Paleys and took the children, and they ran 'The Devil is a Sissy', a very interesting picture, directed by (W.S.) VanDyke ... This is blue Monday morning and a bad time to write letters. I hope Frances is enjoying London as much as ever. We miss her. With love to you both.

December 9, 1936

... I think you acted correctly in the Bellman situation. There is no reason for you to work on 'spec', as he suggested; in fact, such a move would have lowered your standing, and they would not have appreciated it anyway.

I am mailing a letter to Irving Asher today, copy of which is enclosed, and I want you to immediately present my enclosed letter of introduction at his office. I know him and I am sure my letter will provide the key to his August's presence.

The nicest thing about your interesting letter was the line in which you stated you were really not discouraged thus far and that you thought things would be better after the first of the year ... I just won't be jockeyed into making an ordinary little picture for my first at R.K.O., and that is the reason it takes time to get started. I distinguished myself brilliantly the other night. They gave a dinner to Adolph Zukor in celebration of his twenty-fifth year in the industry. I was one of five speakers, including: Louis B. Mayer, Joe Schenck, Darryl Zanuck and Frank Lloyd. I was the last speaker called upon before Mr. Zukor spoke, and received almost more applause than the rest of them put together. As I arose to speak, the reception was so prolonged and enthusiastic that it was commented upon in the papers the next day. I was fortunate in making a swell speech and the whole affair I am sure rebounded to my credit. Mother was present, I having to drag her there by sheer force, and I had the following guests at her table, as I sat at the Speakers' table: Pandro Berman and his wife, Mary (Pickford) and Buddy (Rogers), Mamoulian, Dorothy Arzner, Mr. and Mrs. Giannini, Dave Rose and his wife and Edgar Selwyn—it really was a very nice affair ... Mentally I am very much like you, one day up and the next day a little down, but my common sense always prevails, and I know that things will turn out all right if I only give them a chance.

Lasky wrote to producer/director Irving Asher in London hoping to find his son an open door.[48]

December 9, 1936
Mr. Irving Asher;
Warner Bros. Studio,
Teddington, Middlesex,
London, England.
Dear Mr. Asher:

My son, Jesse Lasky, Jr. is freelancing in London, and I would greatly appreciate it if you would grant him an interview.

Jesse is a brilliant young writer and his salary is within the schedule of what you pay writers for British productions. He has some splendid credits over here but insists on living in London because of the fact that he is completing a novel with an English background, and prefers cloudy England to sunny California. I have taken the liberty of giving him a letter of introduction to

---

48 Decades later (1977), Jesse and I interviewed the affable Asher when we wrote *Love Scene*, the biography of Vivien Leigh and Laurence Olivier. Asher had filmed *Elephant Walk*, when Leigh had a complete breakdown.

you, which he will present about the time you receive this letter, and I hope you can spare the time to grant him a brief interview.

Thank you for this courtesy, and with kindest regards -

Sincerely yours,
Jesse L. Lasky

December 14, 1936
Dear Jesse

...Last night Mother and I, with Billy and Betty, went to the preview at Grauman's Chinese of (Charles) Laughton in 'Rembrandt'. Artistically we enjoyed the picture very much - of course, Mother loved it, but I am afraid, it will never get any business over here, and I doubt if it will do too big in England. Tonight I am going to a dinner at Edwin Knopf's house, the dinner being given to Blanche Knopf who is here from New York. She came in to see me yesterday and told me there was a terrible dearth of coming authors in the publishing field as Hollywood has swallowed them all up. I immediately pounced on her and told her of the budding young author, Lasky, Jr. and his promising novel, and she asked me to send a copy to her hotel, which I did this morning, and Maurice wired your Agent in New York to send Alfred Knopf a copy in New York. Maybe something will come from it....Cecil has invited us to go to Paradise for New Year's Eve, with William LeBaron and Al Kaufman, and I may stay up there for a couple of days, as Mother doesn't want to go out New Year's Eve. We have a lovely Christmas tree, which the children decorated last night - it is standing in the very spot where you were married. So much for family matters... in the meantime, I am drawing my salary so should not complain....

December 23,1936
Dear Jesse Junior:

...I spent New Years Eve at Cecil's—an honest-to-goodness stag party—with Al Kaufman, Jack King and two of Cecil's staff, and I had a real rest. Last night Sonya Levien and Carl Hovey came in with Stokowski and we had a grand evening at the house, as Stokowski is a very interesting and friendly man.

...We are well into the script of 'Radio City Revels' now and will have the first draft continuity finished by January 15th when we will select our Director and begin to do serious casting. The story as you can judge by the first synopsis I sent you, is going to be very funny, and I think the picture will have a chance to succeed. It is the toughest kind of a picture to cast and we are having the usual casting problems, but somehow or other we will lick it. It will be quite a big production. We are now casting around for the right Director and, believe me, good Directors are scarce... Blanche Knopf returned the book (Jesse's *No*

Angels in Heaven) to Hanline with some message that it was not right for their publishing house....

January 7, 1937

We were so glad to receive your letter announcing the good, news that you are engaged for the treatment of the story for Marcel Hellman and Doug. Well, that is a beginning at least, and I hope and feel sure will lead to more and better assignments ... I see in the trade papers that Korda has announced some 'B' pictures for London Films. If this is true there ought to be a chance for you, although I suppose for the time being you are occupied with your present script ... there has never been such a scarcity of story material in the history of the industry. There are no good plays on Broadway; very few novels, so that more and more the industry is compelled to turn to originals.... We were all so interested during the last few exciting days before the King abdicated.[49] I think we have the next idea for Martini worked out in a very rough first draft - the last 'India Desert' story that you once heard me talk about, in which Martini is captured and sings from the slave block. Unfortunately this studio is not an inspiring place at all which doesn't make it any easier, however, one good picture and things will seem brighter.

The American papers just teemed with news and it was the one topic of discussion out here. I listened in on the radio to his farewell address and it certainly was thrilling and I thought very touching. We are anxious to hear your account of how the news was received in London. I wonder if you realized the papers had been carrying on the front pages full accounts of the situation long before the English papers printed a word about it. ... Ran into dear old Jack Preston who talks big and seems to be prosperous - what a friend and admirer he is of you. I think he is going to write you a letter as he asked for your address ... According to the Hollywood papers, the motion picture industry in England is a big flop. Korda's company showed a tremendous loss for the year and other companies are hard pressed for finances, and the banks are not going to finance any new ventures. This means that there will be a great many small British pictures produced after the first of the year, which might be favorable for your situation at that time. Everything that we foresaw would happen in England is now happening from all that I can gather.

By the way, Billy is developing into a fine boy. We saw three pictures together last week and his taste and judgment are just like yours and mine. He is swell company and always ready to jump out after dinner and see a

---

49 Edward VIII, later The Duke of Windsor was King from 20 January 1936 until his abdication on 11 December 1936.

picture with me, or anything else for that matter. Betty also is developing splendidly and is becoming a really excellent pianist. Mother is again living in the painting world and is consequently quite happy. She is a guest of honor tomorrow at a painting club downtown - no doubt she will write and tell you all about it . . . I shall be anxious to hear how and where you spent your Christmas. . . .

January 25, 1937

. . . today your letter dated January 12th arrived, the one written after your return from Naworth Castle.[50] . . . I appreciated your letter in which you gave a general criticism of the 'Radio City Revels' treatment. We are still working on it, having started the last draft today, and if we can cast it, I think it will be funny in a screwy way. There is a regular epidemic of screwy comedies on now, so ours is at least quite in the mode. Now, music and lyrics must be written, and a Director selected, and if all goes well we should be in production the middle of March . . . Our treatment of the Lederer story has finally been finished, but now Mr. Briskin informs me that the Sales Department do not want a picture with Lederer; that he is not a drawing card and, if anything, keeps people out of the theatre, so we shall have to hunt for a new star to replace him - not a very bright prospect as this particular story was written to suit Lederer and his type is scarce. The Martini story is coming along slowly and I think we are on the track of something pretty good—and that about tells you the studio situation . . . I was a guest at the West Side Riding and Asthma Club meeting at Frank Morgan's[51] house a couple of weeks ago. It was an uproarious party; when I left everybody was getting exceedingly drunk, but it was amusing. Your name came up many times and it seemed to me that you must be a popular member of the gang and that you were really missed . . . Enclosed is an article from the Sunday Examiner. Your Press Agent is trying to keep you before the Hollywood public and I think, generally speaking, this publicity is good . . . From what I read in the trade papers the British industry has all but folded up, and from a motion picture production standpoint, things are going to be very bad in London.

This means that your chances for a job are narrowed down to possibly Korda and one or two other spots at the most; therefore, if by the time this letter reaches you, you see no prospects of a writing job and your original story is finished, it might be a good idea for you to start for home, as things are booming in the industry here and I think your chances for a job will be much better now than when you left . . . You mentioned in your letter about returning via Panama Canal. If the trip is just as cheap, and I imagine it is, or even

---

50 Jesse had been hosted by the Duke of Norfolk on several shooting weekends.
51 The actor best know for his later performance as the gatekeeper in Wizard of Oz in 1939.

cheaper, I see no reason why you should not do this . . . I have stumbled on something that might prove very interesting. Some young men have developed a method of animating small figures so that they can produce short subjects with all the facilities of a Disney cartoon.[52] It is too complicated to explain the process, but I have had it thoroughly investigated and. . . .have decided to invest a few thousand dollars for a half interest in the company. They are now engaged in making the first short subject in Technicolor and if it turns out good, as seems most likely, we hope to make a deal with a major company to release twelve short subjects a year, and I will have a ready-made business to step into if I need it. We call the animated figures 'Humanettes' and the hero of the first series of cartoons is a very cute little figure called 'YEABO' (Yea-Bo!). The idea is to popularize 'Yeabo' the same as Mickey Mouse . . . The first short subject will be finished in about six weeks and then I will know its true value.

That reminds me - I made a broadcast for Walt Disney the other night in celebration of an award he received from the United States Junior Chamber of Commerce and afterwards I attended a banquet at the Roosevelt where he was Guest of Honor, and I made a speech in his behalf. . . .

February 1, 1937

. . . Have set Joe Santley to direct 'Radio Revels', as he is on the lot, and two song writers, (Arthur) Freed and (Burton) Lane, to start on music and lyrics . . .

As Lasky noted, Knopf had turned down Jesse's novel, 'No Angels in Heaven', but it had been accepted by The Macaulay Company, N.Y., to be published the following year. Jesse hoped it would kick-start a serious writing career. Following an earlier suggestion of his father's, made before the Depression when Jesse was first in England, he was again considering attending Oxford University's writing course.

February 2, 1937

. . . Frankly, things are not going any too well at R.K.O. However, the contract was signed recently. This studio seems all wrong for me; the whole atmosphere of the place and the method of doing business is demoralizing to my personality . . . The point I want to make is that it might not be safe for you to consider the two-year academic course in order to increase your mental stature and give you a better foundation for fine writing. While I do not think it is a crazy idea by any means, it is not entirely practical due to the uncertainty of my affairs . . . and they are starting to make one feature which, if it is good enough . . . would put us in the short subject business in a very good

---

52 This was a use of 'stop frame animation' developed by Ray Harryhausen.

way, because the Humanettes are not drawings, but actually little figures … (that) work in miniature sets. Now, when you come back, what is the matter with your taking hold of the business, learning the process, writing the stories … you would be a partner in the business, be independent and maybe make a Walt Disney out of yourself … and you will find yourself quietly working in a company called Jesse Lasky, Junior's Humanettes, Inc. starring 'Yeabo'—so come home, my son, and let us see if we cannot lick this Hollywood bugaboo together. Don't forget, your novel coming out this Spring is going to be a great help to your prestige in Hollywood, apart from the fact that it will probably be sold for pictures the moment it appears … I urge you to return immediately to this land of opportunity … I am investing $7,000 in a half interest in the short subject company—'Humanettes' which I wrote you about recently. We have moved the outfit in my building on Sunset Boulevard.…

This project was a non-starter, but Lasky soon found his next discovery. Her real name was Joan de Beauvoir de Havilland. She took her stepfather's name because Olivia, her older sister, was already under contract to Warner Brothers in 1935 when

FONTAINE, LASKY, MARTINI

Joan had just turned eighteen. In her autobiography,[53] Joan relates that she was playing the ingénue in Henry Duffy's *Call It a Day* at Duffy's Theatre on Hollywood Boulevard when Lasky was ushered backstage to her dressing room.

She wrote: Mr. Lasky was noted for his good taste, the quality of his films ... I was extremely flattered that I had caught his attention. Soon Mother and I found ourselves in Mr. Lasky's paneled office. I affixed 'Joan Fontaine' to the bottom of a seven year contract ... Mr. Lasky shook our hands as we were about to leave and smilingly promised that Olivia's little sister would be a big star under his management ... After the run of *Call It a Day*, 'Little Sister found herself a run-of-the-mill player at RKO, for Jesse Lasky sold them my contract almost immediately. I had nothing to say about it.'

She also later noted that she was, 'disillusioned with Hollywood after Mr. Lasky had sold me to RKO like so many pounds of meat....' But in fact, after Lasky produced her first film at RKO, *Music for Madame* in 1937, opposite his favorite singer, Nino Martini, Lasky was forced to relinquish her personal contract with him as part of his separation agreement from RKO. What Fontaine did not mention in her biography was that she had a short but fairly serious affair with Lasky in the beginning, after which they remained friends.

Fontaine went on to appear opposite Fred Astaire in *A Damsel in Distress* that same year. She told this on herself: At the premiere, a woman in the audience seeing her dance with Astaire cried, 'Isn't she awful?' She called it 'run-of-the-mill' that RKO featured Fontaine in eight more films in the next two years, including *Gunga Din*, opposite Cary Grant. As Lasky had predicted, she became a great star. Her somewhat irascible nature caused her to be at permanent loggerheads with her sister, and often with her daughter.

Decades later, in 1978, Jesse and she were appearing on the same American TV interview shows on their separate book promotion tours for their autobiographies. (Jesse's autobiography was *Whatever Happened to Hollywood?*) On New Year's day, Joan invited Jesse and me to lunch at her vast and gloomy New York apartment. Joan was a terrific cook and served us homemade blintzes with sour cream and Beluga caviar, washed down with vast amounts of chilled vodka to start the new year. She and Jesse exchanged books. She signed hers to us:

> To Pat and Jesse—
> Without Jessie Lasky Sr.,—
> This Book would have
> Been about how to make curtains and mow the lawn.
> Joan–

Forty years earlier, in 1937, Jesse's career was finally getting a boost in London. His father wrote from Hollywood:

---

53 *No Bed of Roses,* Wm. Morrow & Co.,1978 the autobiography of Joan Fontaine.

February 3, 1937
Dear Jesse,

...Just received your letter in which you advised me that the little independent script you did has been accepted and that you have picked up a few extra dollars.

I enclose two letters, which please present immediately to the respective parties. Ben Goetz is an old friend of mine, and I think you have met him at the Fights here and would know him by sight. He will grant you an interview the moment you present my letter, and so will Mr. Hanbury on account of my connection with R.K.O — so get busy and see both men quickly and let me know the result of the interviews.

I am glad you have an idea for a new novel that you are enthusiastic about - go to it, and Good Luck...if you think you have any prospects and want to continue the battle to make your own way in London, then ignore my letter. If, however, nothing turns up, then you know how I feel about your returning ...I think your plan to test England until May when your lease expires is reasonable and sane, and if you do not have something pretty good by that time, come right back to Hollywood where I am certain your prospects are much better now than you realize...As I wrote you, I had a siege of flu which left me weak and depressed for about two weeks afterwards; however, that is all behind me now and my mental state is excellent....

February 20, 1937

Played poker at Myron Selznick's house recently with a nice crowd of fellows - Bill Powell, (Adolph) Menjou, Robert Riskin, (Gregory) Ratoff and (George) Kaufman—I did not win and I did not lose. I am still struggling with 'Radio City Revels' for a start about April 1st, and a Martini yarn which I hope to put Herman Mankiewicz on next week, to start in May...Had a week-end with Cecil and Hal Roach and a couple of men from the East, at Paradise, but it rained the whole time we were there, and we had to dynamite the road to clear it of land-slides to get home....

The theme of 'Radio City Revels' has been changed from a Peace Essay to a competition for a love song, and we really have a very funny script after much re-writing. Have a good gag man, Jack Mintz, a brother of Sam Mintz. I like our Director, Joe Santley, very much.

The West Side Asthma and Riding Club are after me to give them a night but I told them I would not do it until you returned when we could give those roughnecks a joint evening. I made a nice broadcast a couple of weeks ago from NBC; it was a good experience and I received some very favorable comment.

The most important development that interests me for the future is our little 'Humanette' cartoon short subject experiment. I saw 100 feet of the stuff yesterday and it is coming along great...I hope your new novel is coming along well...I have been having writers' trouble, as usual. I put Herman Mankiewicz on the Martini idea and he flopped miserably. After working one week he could not get a line on paper and I had to let him go. I now have a bright writer named Nat Perrin polishing up 'Radio City Revels' and it looks as though we will start shooting the picture the first week in April. What a tough script to prepare - we are getting some good music by (Arthur) Freed and (Burton) Lane...Tomorrow night is the Academy Dinner. Mr. Briskin has a large table for RKO, and I am literally dragging Mother to it by the hair of her head. She becomes less and less socially inclined as far as picture people are concerned, and looks almost ten years younger than when last you saw her. It must be the simple life she leads because she seems to be blooming....

March 15, 1937

...We were just finishing our script of 'Radio City Revels' when Briskin found he could not get some of the players whom we had cast so we have to postpone the start of the picture until the middle of May when all the cast will be available. As this delay is not my fault, I am not letting it worry me....

The new Martini story opens with Martini singing at the Hollywood Bowl. The camera stays on him for a song which runs about a minute. We hear the applause and bravos of one man, and the camera pans out over the Bowl to discover that it is empty, that the symphony orchestra accompaniment is a Victrola, and that Martini is trying out his voice at midnight because his landlady has turned him out of the boarding house where he is living in Hollywood, trying to break into the movies...We are trying to tell the yarn of a singer who doesn't want to be a movie actor but who wants to sing, and the story ends with his singing at the Hollywood Bowl with a symphony orchestra in back of him and a crowded audience in front. It sounds very trite as I tell it, but we have the bones of a pretty good story in between the beginning and the end which I have attempted to sketch all too briefly.

Mother and I went to the opening of 'The Lost Horizon', Columbia's $2,500,000. production, directed by Frank Capra, and the picture proved a disappointment. It simply isn't right, and I doubt if it will prove an eventual success.

The budget of *Lost Horizon* eventually was estimated at $4 million. It was nominated for 4 awards and won two: direction and film editing. It was certainly a succès d'estime.

March 22, 1937

...Mother gave a very interesting Tea last Tuesday and a couple of days later a description of it was broadcast by the Society Editor of KHJ, and I think you and Frances might like to read a copy of the broadcast which I am enclosing.

I showed George Schaefer of United Artists the workings of the 'Humanettes' and he was definitely interested in it and thinks we have something.

I went into an oil proposition, investing $2,000, which I can ill afford, in a set-up that might make some money. Just six men went into the deal—Sam Wood, Jack Conway, Bill LeBaron, myself, and two other men I know, and as they all think this oil proposition has a great chance, I followed a hunch and made the investment.

Just learned Warners don't own 'The Amazing Dr. Clitterhouse' and I am now trying to get RKO to buy it. I won't have any production activity until the middle of May when we start 'Radio City Revels' and, a week later, the Martini picture.

...Just received a present of a gorgeous electric clock from NBC broadcasting station on account of my appearance at one of their broadcasts recently....

Lasky's magic touch did not extend to The Humanettes nor was investing in an oil proposition.

April 1, 1937
Dear Jesse,

I just received your letter in which you advised me that it looks definite you are sailing on May 3rd...It is funny, but I suppose you regard your letter as containing bad news inasmuch as nothing very important happened in London, but to us it came as a letter of cheer and good news, because it means you are coming home.

You said you need about $700 - I am enclosing a draft for $800, and before sailing time, if you find you are going to be short, for heaven's sake, cable me and I will wire you whatever additional money you need. I envy you that trip through the Panama Canal...I have accepted the assignment of a Lily Pons picture to be made about August 1st, and am now looking for the right story idea....

I don't regard your trip as a failure at all. It is no different than my return from Honolulu, when I came home broke, or from Alaska, also broke - but I would not take a million dollars for those experiences...next to money, experience is the most desirable thing one can acquire...After I finished the

'Radio City Revels' script, Briskin did not like it or, at least, did not like parts of it, and we are forced to re-write it...this studio has a tough customer in Briskin; we don't speak the same language and, consequently, as he has the last say, I will have to do some changing and re-writing until he is satisfied. However, I am accepting all these problems philosophically - I can stand it if he can, and it doesn't affect my morale or my disposition . . . I think you could lick it in a week. The writers I have had are all written out, and I am now looking for a new writer or two to do the final job.

We have a thrilling idea for Lily Pons that I am crazy about. I am now wondering whether Briskin will be able to see it . . . Billy had his 16th birthday the other day and is really a young man, and Betty is fast becoming a very attractive girl. Their intelligence and common sense at times simply bowls me over. My heart grows warm when I think what a swell little family we are....

April 6, 1937

. . . Here is some interesting news that might turn into very good news indeed. The oil well I invested in struck oil and yesterday I went down to Bakersfield with Sam Wood, taking Billy along.

We looked into the whole situation and it seems almost certain that the first well will be flowing in a week and will bring in a sufficient amount of money to permit the little company to sink more wells in what we think is our very rich field. We are in the center of all the big oil companies and all around us wells are flowing, and the man who is doing the job for us is one of the best oilmen in the State.

He told me yesterday that we have a very fine proposition indeed, one that ought to make a lot of money, and the beauty of our proposition is that if all goes well and our oil wells turn out okay, we should have an income for years to come, as the wells in Bakersfield keep producing for many, many years. At any rate, by the time you return, we will have our second well down, and if that produces, we are really in the oil business.

I wish I could give you some good news about my pictures but Briskin is against the script I have prepared for 'Radio City Revels', and . . . so, here we are, after months of work, starting almost all over again. . . . Keep your fingers crossed for the oil wells - and what I really wanted to say was 'Congratulations - with all my love on your first Anniversary.'

April 13, 1937

. . . by all means plan to move right into your flat on Bonita Terrace. Rents have gone up since you left, and your rent of $75.00 per month is very reasonable . . . it won't be long before you will find yourself on your feet, and we will all be glad you did not give up your nice little flat . . . Went out to

Bakersfield again last Sunday to see the oil well. They have struck oil sand and we expected the well to come in yesterday or today, so any minute I may hear good news.

Have had several differences with Briskin over 'Radio City Revels', so nothing is settled yet on that picture. The Martini picture starts May 31st. The 'Humanettes' short subject will be finished by May 1st and then I will know if there is anything in that. I have a feeling with more irons in the fire, the better the chances for something to come through.

There is also a possibility of a radio broadcast program for me. George Putnam is working on it in New York . . . Ned Marin just joined the Feldman-Blum Agency as Vice President, having left Metro. I am going to get Ned to work on placing you, and you might want to let that agency handle you because I am sure Ned, and Charlie Feldman as well, will make a special effort on your behalf.

P.S. If, for any reason, you cannot move into your flat the day you arrive, we have two spare rooms and would be delighted to put you and Frances up until you get your flat in shape. . . .

April 19, 1937

. . . I just sent you and Frances a cable from the family, Grandma and the kids, on the occasion of your first anniversary. We were all talking of you last night, and we realize that while it has been a tough year for you, nevertheless, it has been a happy one. . . .

Yesterday Sam Wood and I went to Bakersfield, taking Billy with us, to look at our oil well, which was on the verge of coming in. We expected to hit oil a week ago, but struck water, and the water had to be pumped out which held up the proceedings. It was a beautiful day; Mother and Betty drove out, and we picked huge baskets of wild flowers in the vicinity of the well, and spent the afternoon watching it, expecting every minute for it to spout. They were still pumping the water when we left, late in the afternoon, but this morning at 3 o'clock Sam Wood called me stating that he had a long distance call from Bakersfield and that the well had come in. During the next 24 hours we will know how many barrels a day it is going to run . . . If all goes smoothly, seems most likely, we have a fine proposition which will bring us an income for many, many years - how large, depends on the size of the wells, but our oil driller is positive we have rich oil land and our prospects certainly look good . . . It looks now as if we are going to postpone the 'Radio City Revels' picture as Briskin and I don't agree on the treatment . . . a musical revue of this kind is very tough to make unless you have a lot of personalities, and we have not got them, but we have in our Martini story the greatest story I have ever had to handle in my life, and that will probably be my first picture and is destined for positive success ... we will look up the route of your steamer and will probably cable you at your first stop - so enjoy yourselves, my dear ones, and look forward to a wonderful home-coming and a warm reception....

Ever the optimist, Lasky had been sure he could make a success of producing at RKO, but he and Briskin were never on the same wave length.

May 3, 1937

...we are now concentrating on Nino's picture which starts June 1st. At this moment, it looks as if Jack Blystone will direct it ... He has made a couple of good pictures, one was a comedy which Sam Goldwyn produced, which really is quite good.

Nino had a concert here last week and I took Briskin - it was the first concert that Briskin had ever attended, and he was very much impressed by Nino's reception. The stage was jammed with people, the same as last year, and the concert was very successful. I told Nino and Jack Salter the story we have for him and they like it enormously ... Lynn Starling has been on the script a week and is making good progress, and seems like a good writer. It looks as though I am going to make a small picture 'Mother Carey's Chickens' by Kate Douglas Wiggin, to fill in and reduce overhead. In the meantime, I am searching for a Lily Pons story to start August 1st so there is no time to lose and, as you know, a musical of this type is the toughest kind of picture to make. However, one good picture and things will look much brighter here, and that good picture is going to be the Martini ... Mother is doing wonders with her painting ... She will ship four paintings to Nordlingers in London today and has an exhibition at Nordlingers in New York in September ... We are talking about building the house on our plot of ground, as the bank will loan us the money we need for this investment and it will reduce our expense about $450.00 a month. Billy and Betty are planning a trip to Mexico City by automobile. Miss Allen, the nurse, is going along to take care of them and our driver will take our car. It will be a very wonderful trip and very inexpensive ... Betty's band turned out for a May Day holiday with about 100 kids in the band, and she tooted her flute, and came home with sore feet after marching in the sun....

Bill and Betty, now self-reliant teenagers, probably saw more of their father than their mother, who was waiting for them to grow up so they could become her 'friends'. There was still a nanny or a nurse to stand in for 'mom', and Lasky was still hoping to make things work at RKO.

Wednesday, June 2, 1937
Dear Jesse,

... Well, we finally shot our first sound track on the Nino Martini picture today. We have a script of over 160 pages that must be edited and tightened up, but we really have a grand story—one good enough to follow 'The Gay Desperado'. We will be well into it by the time you arrive.

I think I have finally licked the Lily Pons story which starts August 1st... Have one other story in work called 'Main Street Goes To Town', but we have no production date or cast as yet. It has been an awful tough grind here at RKO but I think we see daylight at last. Just now Mother is working with an architect trying to contrive to build a mansion on our limited budget, and somehow the two just don't go together; however, this time the budget is going to win out, and we will probably have the architect's plans finished when you arrive... I have so much I will want to talk to you about - at last I will have somebody to tell my troubles to, however, maybe there won't be any troubles when you and Frances sail into the harbor.

Here's a startling surprise for you - but, thank God, it all came out fine. Just three weeks ago Billy was stricken with pains in his tummy, exactly the same as you had. We rushed him to the hospital in an ambulance and had his appendix out in a hurry. However, his recovery was perfect, and he came home in ten days and is starting back to school tomorrow looking and feeling almost his normal self. Billy was very matter-of-fact and brave about the whole affair and had little Miss Allen for his nurse, in fact she came home and took charge of him for several days after he was out of the hospital. As he had no after-effects whatever, his recovery was quicker than yours, and we have all forgotten the whole affair, except maybe I will be reminded of it by the accumulated bills - however, that is all in the game. Betty is fine and eagerly awaits the arrival of Frances. They will do nothing definite about the Mexican trip until they confer with Frances and if she wants to go, they will be overjoyed and it can be arranged.

Now for a personal word to yourself. I don't want you to worry about money matters. As soon as you arrive I will give you a substantial check to take care of you for several weeks, and don't feel that you have to dash into looking for a job the next day after arrival. You want to get nicely settled, take it easy, hold up your head, and, of course, you will have money in your pocket, and the job will be forthcoming at the proper time. Ned Marin is the backbone of the Feldman-Blum Agency - he is now a partner in that concern - and I think will go out of his way to try and place you; and, strange to say, Jack Emanuel, who is practically running the H. M. Swanson Agency, will work his head off to place you. Maurice still insists there is an opening waiting for you at Warner Bros, that he can arrange, and I have a hunch, if nothing develops in a week or two, we can get you in RKO - so enjoy the remainder of your trip and don't worry about the future - things always work out right in the end.... Mother will probably spend a couple of weeks with Aunt Louise at Lake Tahoe in

July, and if Frances is in Mexico with the children, you and I can cover a lot of pictures, fights, etc. together. I hope you have a manuscript of your novel as there is such a demand for original stories now that one of the agents may be able to sell it even before publication - I mean at a good stiff price.

Well, I have rambled along sufficiently I guess to give you a hint of how the land lies, and the next event will be a mighty handshake to you and a walloping big kiss for Frances from

Your loving Dad

Jess and his bride were home again and things were looking up. When the McCauley Company, true to their promise, published Jesse's second book *No Angels in Heaven*, DeMille, true to his word, hired him as part of his writing team for *Union Pacific*. It would be the first of eight films he would be assigned to for DeMille. The writing team peripherally included plump, aging Jeanie Macpherson, ex-mistress and ever-present fixture in the DeMille stable, who had evolved from actor to writer. There were three other writers on the team and DeMille told the nervous newest addition, 'You're here to get some poetry into this film, Jesse!'

The story was epic Americana—the saga of steel rails being laid across the sweeping grandeur of the vast continent. Each writer was assigned a section or scene. As Jesse soon discovered, the system was lethal and there was no safety in numbers. Each would have a go at polishing the other writers' latest versions. On and on, days into nights, rewrites could cover thirty attempted overlays, and only when DeMille had finally okayed and labeled the section would they move on. Too often the team considered the 'Final Revised Final Revision' no better than the first draft, (and once they'd actually slipped in the first draft as a final, which got approved) but it satisfied C.B. that no stone had been left unturned to satisfy him and his audience—if rarely the critics.

Through the following years, Jesse was to learn the DeMille formula. He called it the 'peculiar combination of glorious hokum, history, and suspense that C.B. called drama. A circus salted with history in packages larger than life.'

1937 had been the lowest point in Lasky's career. The Humanettes hadn't worked out and the anticipated oil wells gushed water. Getting *Radio City Revels* up and running had dragged on far too long. The producer found himself forced to squeeze into RKO's 'B' (for Briskin) budget and was reduced to using recycled sets and costumes and keeping dance numbers and assorted production values to the total cost of $810,000. The picture's plot involved a song-writing duo who steal songs from a music student who creates swing tunes in his sleep. It featured jokesters of the day Milton Berle, Jack Oakie, Bob Burns, and introduced a dazzling eighteen-year-old dancer, Ann Miller. After all the hassle, Lasky's name did not appear as producer—only Edward Kaufman's name. Ultimately, Lasky was happy about that.

Thoroughly frustrated with his position at the studio, by the following year the producer had managed to arrange his contract to include an outside assignment. He had an offer to broadcast a radio show and approached it with his usual high spirits and optimism. He even tried to drag Jesse into the project.

September 21, 1938
The Chicago Blackstone Hotel
Tuesday night, 11 p.m.
Dear Jess,

...Well it seems that the Lasky Luck, which has never failed me, is once more asserting itself. After more or less exhausting the possibilities for the elusive sponsor, having covered all the ground possible in N.Y. Det(roit) and then Chicago, I called on P.K. Wrigley[54] yesterday morning, the last shot in my gun and I think, found just what I was looking for!

Wrigley who seems a swell chap (my kind) gave me an hour and a half of undivided, rapt attention and swallowed the program hook, line and sinker! Then a meeting with his financial and advertising and radio executives, and they went for it also!

Another meeting this a.m. and I gave them a 30 day option in writing, and they immediately appointed a top executive to go to N.Y. with me, to meet Spitz, and check up on all details! We leave on the 'Century' tomorrow, and I phoned Spitz this afternoon, and he was most cordial and is holding himself available for a meeting on Thursday.

The understanding is that if everything holds up satisfactorily, and I see no reason why it won't, they will sign contracts with me for the show having agreed already to spend $10,000 a week, on the show, without including the misc. charges. (Another $10,000). The show can just about be handled for that amount allowing $3,000 a week for me, less commissions.

The executive is to <u>stick with me</u> until every detail is worked out. He is a fine chap admires me, and will work fast to clean up his end. There are a lot of details to be worked out, but nothing insurmountable, so 'Jesse L. Lasky's Gateway to Hollywood' looks like it is going to become a fact!!!

What a break for us all, if or rather when it goes though.

It's been a tough period for me, but the old spirit, that climbed Double-Top[55] with Cecil and explored Tiburon and the Balsas with you, just wouldn't be licked. What a tale I will spin for you my son, when next we sit around the festive board!

Now here is more pleasant news, and you may have noticed, I wouldn't write you, until I could say pleasant things! I have made some really valuable loyal friends.

---

54 American chewing gum manufacturer and executive in Major League Baseball.
55 Doubletop Mountain, Maine: Baxter State Park.

I just returned from dinner with Robt. Lee, the Editor of the 'Chicago Tribune', the greatest News Paper in America! What a man, what brains and ability and how we have <u>hit it off</u>. And Marion Claire and her husband Henry Weber, what hospitality and Geo Bates and his bride. A young man with <u>Millions.</u> And others here too numerous to mention, but these Stories will keep.

What I want you to do is '<u>study the radio</u>', listen to broadcasts <u>every chance you get</u>!! There's a great field for writers - Robt. Lee and his Chicago Tribune are in Radio up to their necks! I will need numerous, one act ten minute sketches; and all my talks have to be written - what a chance I see. The agency's in New York and here are looking for writers, I know of several spots for you. Robt Lee would do everything to boost you, and I have learned so much about the inside of radio, that I can see great opportunities ahead for you.

Anyway when you finish with Cecil, I feel sure we can spot you somewhere in Radio. It is the coming thing for writers.

I showed the 'Gay Desperado' to a small group last night at the United Artists Projection rooms. What a hit it made. I am a lion, or big-shot, away from H'wood,

I certainly have Chicago at my feet. Marion Claire's husband runs the whole musical end of the biggest Radio station here - and I have watched him broadcast. He conducts about five radio shows a week, and is the top musician in Chicago - Conducted the Chicago Opera with Flagstadt[56] and all the great artists. He is going to read 'No Angels in Heaven', so is his wife and Lee tried to buy copies today, bookstore getting them from the wholesale house - none in stock at the store.

If anything happens to your job, wire me, and I will have you join me, if I have not returned so you can get a new viewpoint on things! Can't tell how long I will be in the East; should clear up N.Y. Thursday and Friday, then a short time in Chicago. Will keep mother posted.

... Sorry I missed your Birthday but it was on your Birthday morning that Wrigley said - 'You've got a very great show, Mr. L.' That was your Birthday present!! The rest has pepped me up and I am rearing to go, and teeming with ideas!

All the very best old fellow and again love to Frances and the whole Lasky Tribe that can't and won't be licked.

Your loving Dad

Having survived his assignment of *Union Pacific*, Jesse was now working on a documentary for DeMille for the 1939 New York World's Fair, as the official exhibition for the Motion Picture Industry. *Land of Liberty* was to use stock film from every picture ever produced that dealt with American History. Annie Bauchens, DeMille's lifelong film editor, had already begun a rough assembly of film clips.

---

56 Kirsten Malfrid Flagstad, Wagnerian opera singer.

Jeanie Macpherson had been given the assignment for the narration script by the boss and had asked for Jesse to work with her, although no one had asked Jesse if he wanted to. Typically, DeMille informed him, 'I want the history of the United States stressing the theme of liberty on my desk by five o'clock today.'

Naturally they had a technical adviser, a Dr. James T. Shotwell, Chair of History at Columbia University and author of *The History of History*. Somehow, the film was successfully put together and even admired. To Jesse, the highpoint was Charles Laughton's[57] reading of the Gettysburg Address over shots of the Gettysburg cemetery and the soundtrack from the film of *Ruggles of Red Gap*.

For Lasky, 'The Gateway to Hollywood' was getting off to a queasy start touring cities, auditioning unscreened amateurs in front of live audiences, who were vying for a crack at the forthcoming radio show where someone would win a one-year Hollywood contract.

August 25, 1939
Dear Jesse,

... In the first place, financially, our show is a flop; by that, I mean I have lost the investment irrevocably, and, in addition, every week has shown a loss. The reason, our show was geared up too expensive for the kind of theatres we are playing. We are doing good business, according to the average business of the houses and the size of these cities, but not good enough to break even.... The talent we are finding is only fair, due to the fact that they have to appear on the stage (without being screened) ... I have made a deal with the Wrigleys ... seeking the talent through private auditions in halls or small ballrooms, etc. Two talent scouts will go ahead of me, preceded by publicity men, and when all the towns are rounded up and weeded down I will step in and make the final selections ... I will be on the road not quite a month, and Wrigley will pay me pretty well for the job.

What a summer! I will never forget it.

Confidentially, and this is for your ear alone, Saturday night an officer was driving Edmund Lowe[58] and me out to Randolph Field for an officers' dance. Our car was hit by a drunken driver, and both cars were pretty well demolished. I received a cut on the nose and had the wind knocked out of me, and was pretty generally shaken up. Two days later, my ribs pained me, so I went to the doctor and found I had two small fractures. So, I have been strapped up, and doing four shows a day, under these conditions in a very hot climate, is work for a he-man. I am feeling quite comfortable now, and there will be no ill effects whatever - in fact, the bandages will be removed in a couple of weeks. Please do not mention this to mother or grandma; they

---

57 American audiences knew Laughton best for his performances in *The Private Life of Henry VIII* and as Captain Bligh in *Mutiny on the Bounty*.
58 Hollywood star.

would only worry needlessly, and there is nothing to worry about, although I did have a very narrow escape from a very serious accident; so, you see, I have a lot to be thankful for, after all.

I haven't had a bit of fun. This week I made two broadcasts between the shows, and addressed a Rotarian Club luncheon today, making a very successful speech as usual. I have become utterly adept at impromptu radio broadcasting. In fact, my radio work next Fall should be much better.

To add to my troubles, there were serious differences between the Wrigley outfit and the RKO outfit, and, at one time, I thought the whole thing was going to blow up ... However, Schaefer came through in fine style, and now all is harmony in both camps and the 'Gateway to Hollywood' will be on the air October 8th, bigger and better than ever.

Tonight, after the last show, we grab a train for Dallas, open there tomorrow about one thirty, play seven days, and then I hope to fly home to see the family and have a brief rest.

Fortunately, the hotels are air-cooled, so we escape the heat by never going outdoors. There isn't time, anyway, as I only have about an hour and a half or an hour between shows. What a life! ... Glad you are still on the job with Cecil. ...

In 1939 the 'Gateway to Hollywood' talent search awarded one-year contracts to a few contestants who had mildly successful careers, and to several who became stars. With Lasky's love of changing other people's names, his winners accepted his screen monikers, among them, Josephine Cottle became Gale Storm. The show aired on CBS for fifty-two weeks and introduced Rhonda Fleming. Though the fifteen-year-old lost in the final audition, Fleming went on to become 'The Queen of Technicolor'. Another non-finalist was sixteen-year-old Linda Darnell, who won a place in film history as the voluptuous heroine in *Forever Amber*.

Now promoted to a permanent member of DeMille's staff, having followed *Union Pacific* with *Northwest Mounted Police*, Jesse was not tempted by the idea of working in radio. He had, however, agreed to write his father's biography and had written a few chapters. With the war in Europe looming closer to America, Jesse had joined the California State Infantry and was spending one night a week, in 1940, training at the Los Angeles Armory as a buck private in the 2nd Regiment.

His father's career was about to make a drastic change. For the better.

SCENE SIX
1939 – 1943

*PRESIDENTIAL RECEPTION 1941 the opening: Sergeant York
Behind Roosevelt, L to R, Congressmen Gore and Priest, Gov. Prentiss Cooper, Representatives Este and Kefauver, Senator Kenneth Keller, Sergeant York, Miss Gracie, and Jesse L. Lasky*

In 1939, when *Gateway to Hollywood* ended, Lasky was still at RKO. On his next trip east, he was granted a private audience with Franklin D. Roosevelt. The president discussed Hitler's progress through Europe and made a pointed suggestion to him to produce a film that would sway the hearts of isolationist America into entering the war on the side of Great Britain.

Back at RKO, Lasky was wracking his memory for a suitable subject when an executive reminded him of the inspiring story of a conscientious objector-turned World War I hero. The subject had been dormant in Lasky's mind since May 22, 1919 when he had leaned out of an eighth-floor window in the Famous Players-Lasky offices at Forty-First and Fifth Avenue and watched the hysterical demonstrations for Sergeant Alvin C. York. This American soldier unbelievably, and practically unassisted, had wiped out a machine-gun battalion in the Argonne Forest in north-eastern France, and with just twenty-eight bullets in his rifle, had killed twenty-eight German soldiers, captured 132 more, and had taken possession of thirty-five machine guns. As war heroes went, nobody could top Sergeant York.

Back in 1919, the spectators had gone wild as the car carrying York and the young representative from Tennessee, Cordell Hull,[59] rolled down Fifth Avenue. Lasky, seeing the potential for a film, had tried back then to buy Sergeant York's story. But the sergeant was adamant: 'My life is not for sale.'

York's life story would be the perfect choice, but there was no question in Lasky's mind that it was not a picture he would ever want to make under Briskin. The producer decided to leave RKO and get on with his life and the creative work he wanted to do. He later wrote, 'I can't make a picture until I reach the state of self-hypnosis, and when I reach it, I have to make a picture.' Twenty years had rolled by since he had approached York, but he decided that he would tackle him once again, and this time, not take no for an answer.

Sergeant York lived in the Valley of the Three Forks o' the Wolf, Fentress County, Tennessee—real backwoods country. Lasky wrote him an inspiring letter, appealing to the hero's sense of patriotism.

York didn't even reply.

He next sent York a telegram, imploring a meeting to discuss 'a historical document of vital importance to the country in these troubled times', reminding him that President Roosevelt had proclaimed a limited national emergency.

York agreed to meet at a small hotel in 'Jimtown', as Jamestown was known locally. The flaming-haired giant arrived with a quiet little wife whom he called 'Miss Grace'. With no hotel lounge, they relocated to Lasky's room. The two men sat on the bed, Miss Grace taking the only chair. They talked and talked and got nowhere.

Back once more in Hollywood, the showman felt it was a time to be inventive—so he fabricated a telegram to York:

---

59   Cordell Hull: longest-serving Secretary of State, 11 years (1933–1944) under President Franklin Delano Roosevelt, during much of World War II.

I HAVE JUST AGREED TO PLAY THE PART OF SERGEANT YORK FOR THE MOTION PICTURE PRODUCER JESSE L. LASKY'S FILM OF THE STORY OF YOUR LIFE. I HAVE GREAT ADMIRATION FOR YOU AS A MAN, AND I WOULD BE HONORED, SIR, TO PLAY YOU ON THE SCREEN.

GARY COOPER.

As yet, Lasky had not actually approached Cooper—although he fully intended to. A few weeks later, he traveled to Nashville to meet Sergeant York once again, this time at the Andrew Jackson Hotel, which had a lobby. He had arranged to have lawyers present for both sides, but York was still in refusal mode. A little more showmanship was required. Lasky asked him, 'Sergeant York, you risked your life for your country in the first World War—and you'd do it again if your country needed you, wouldn't you?'

York nodded, tight-lipped against this fast-talking Hollywood film producer.

'Then, Sergeant York', Lasky proclaimed with his most theatrical passion, 'that need exists right now! I know you'll give your life to your country through the powerful medium of the screen! Because this country is in danger again—and the people don't yet realize it. It's your patriotic duty to let your life serve as an example to this nation. It's the greatest lesson to American youth that could be told!'

York sat for a moment, taking this in. 'Maybe we do have somethin' to talk about', York conceded. Lasky offered him $50,000 for the exclusive rights to his story, plus a small percentage of the gross receipts. The price was right—but for several days the lawyers argued over clause eight: determining whether the contract should be interpreted under California or Tennessee law.

At an impasse, Lasky suddenly recalled that he'd met another Cooper: Tennessee's Governor was Prentice Cooper. He hurried out to make a phone call in private. It was the Governor he phoned, to ask him if he would witness the signing of his contract with York, pointing out that it was a great coup for his state. Delighted, the Governor suggested they come immediately to the State Capitol Building. He was leaving soon for the weekend.

'There'll be no signing of the contract with that clause eight!' York's lawyer decreed.

'I don't think it's wise to offend the governor', Lasky declared with a slightly worried brow, adding, 'But we don't have to sign the *real* contract. We can let him witness a dummy contract. Then if we do sign the contract while the governor's away, we'll have a photograph of him as a witness. That would please him and be very good publicity for the picture—and of course, for the state of Tennessee.'

Sergeant York thought about it. 'We could tear up the photograph if we don't sign the contract', he decided. 'The governor is a good man. Let's don't keep him waitin'.'

Photographers from the national press services and the local Nashville papers hurried to record the ceremony. Later that evening, with an agreement still to be reached about clause eight, York heard newsboys in the street shouting, 'EXTRA! EXTRA! CONTRACT SIGNED FOR SERGEANT YORK MOVIE!'

York sighed and shook his head. 'Mr. Lasky, I guess we'll have to sign it now!'

Regretting the subterfuge, Lasky hurriedly handed over a $25,000 deposit. Unfortunately, he had no money in the bank to cover the check, much less the rest of the $50,000, due in 60 days. Worse still, the only person who was perfect for the part was his earlier discovery, now a star, Gary Cooper, whose name he had used in vain. More trickery was called for.

Before boarding the plane, Lasky hastily sent Cooper a wire from the Nashville airport: I HAVE JUST AGREED TO LET THE MOTION PICTURE PRODUCER JESSE L. LASKY FILM THE STORY OF MY LIFE SUBJECT TO MY APPROVAL OF THE STAR. I HAVE GREAT ADMIRATION FOR YOU AS AN ACTOR AND AS A MAN AND I WOULD BE HONORED SIR TO SEE YOU ON THE SCREEN AS MYSELF. SERGEANT ALVIN C. YORK.

Back in Hollywood, Lasky borrowed $25,000 on his life-insurance policy to cover his kited check. Then he got the good news. Cooper was willing—and that worried Lasky just slightly. Cooper's salary was now the highest of any actor in the States. He'd have to find a major studio to finance the production before the second payment became due, and it seemed nobody had made a war picture for ages, nor wanted to. The consensus was that the president may have wanted one, but not the public.

As a last resort, Lasky approached his friend, Harry Warner, whom he knew to be a great patriot and offered him a slate of three pictures, *Sergeant York* being the first. Harry got his brother Jack on the phone. 'Jack, I want you to make a deal with Jesse for a story he wants to do. I believe in it, so do it for my sake.'

Jack Warner signed Lasky to produce three films for Warner Brothers, *Sergeant York* to be followed by either *The Adventures of Mark Twain*, or possibly a story about Lord Baden-Powell, founder of the Boy Scouts, or *Rhapsody in Blue*, a biography of George Gershwin. Lasky was back in business, all with 'A' picture budgets. It was the way he functioned best.

With a contract for the first film granting him twenty-five percent of the gross proceeds on *Sergeant York* after negative costs, Lasky's next step was the script. He returned to Tennessee with writer Harry Chandlee to fill in the story gaps, taking along his youngest son, Bill, now an able cameraman.

York staged a typical turkey shoot and hillbillies came from miles around to win prize steers, provided by Lasky. York was somewhat surprised and impressed that the producer was an excellent shot. Bill photographed it all in 16 mm. He would later work as an apprentice assistant director on the film, renewing an acquaintance with Cooper and introducing him to his trained hawk.

When director, Howard Hawks saw Bill's footage of the turkey shoot, he was intrigued by York's characteristic gesture: wetting his thumb and touching the sight of his rifle before aiming it. Lasky explained it reduced reflection of the sun, permitting more accurate aiming of the old-fashioned rifle. Hawks established this gesture

BILL, COOPER, AND HAWK

early in the picture with York at a turkey shoot, as a symbol of a perfect shot: a dead turkey. And subsequently, those twenty-eight perfect shots that day in the Argonne.

The final script collaborator was a young film director/screenwriter/actor, John Huston, who contributed some outstanding scenes. With the script finished and clearances obtained, the immediate problem was to sign Lasky's earlier discovery, who was now under contract to the ubiquitous Sam Goldwyn.

'Cooper? You're crazy!' Jack Warner exploded. 'Don't waste your time asking Goldwyn. Look for another actor!'

'Cooper is the only actor who's right for it', Lasky replied, 'and I'm going to get him if I have to remind Sam who made it possible for him to go into the picture business!'

Initially, he had approached Goldwyn about the project, but he'd turned it down. However, Lasky had heard that his ex-brother-in-law wanted Warner's star Bette Davis for *The Little Foxes*, so with Warner's cooperation, Sam agreed to loan Cooper in a trade for Davis—and everyone was happy.

BETTY, SERGEANT YORK, BESS

York was brought to Hollywood as an advisor. Bess served him tea and Lasky took him to meet Gary Cooper, who lived across the street. The actor came to the door in his stocking feet for a meeting of two of the three most taciturn men Lasky had ever met. He later wrote, 'If we'd had Calvin Coolidge there, it would have been a three-ring wake.'

Sergeant York came to New York for the world premiere and sat beside Lasky as their fleet of automobiles paraded down Broadway to the Astor Theatre with an American Legion band, a drum corps, and assorted bigwigs. The producer considered it the third lofty moment of his career. His first: as a young producer and competitor of Flo Ziegfeld's, riding down Broadway with Bessie to the glittering opening of his ill-fated Folies-Bergère Theatre. The second, when he rode in state down Broadway to the opening of his newly built Paramount Theatre. Both had ended in disaster. This was a procession of honor down that same fabled street to the Astor Theatre for the screening of *Sergeant York*, and it was third time lucky. Once again, the intrepid showman had floated to the top.

Later, he heard York tell the governor's wife, 'All that talk you heard in the picture when I said goodbye to Miss Grace was just what I said when I went off to war.' John Huston even made Sergeant York believe that scene had happened just the way Huston had filmed it. Lasky was to learn that York donated his full salary to complete a Bible school that he had started in 'Jimtown'.

At the White House, the producer and the others were shown into President Franklin D. Roosevelt's office. The president greeted everyone cordially, then turning to Lasky, seeming to take the producer to task. 'Lasky, I saw your picture last night and you made one unforgivable mistake.' Roosevelt paused for effect and with a roar of laughter added, 'You should have got old Cordell Hull to play himself.'

Once again business was booming in Hollywood, and between DeMille assignments, over one weekend Jesse had 'knocked out' an original Western story called *Bull Train* and sold it the next morning for $25,000 to Dore Schary at Metro. It was Jesse's birthday and he and Frances were in England. Now he could celebrate being an established Hollywood screenwriter. His father, planning to finish his film at RKO, took the opportunity to pontificate just slightly:

January 25, 1937
Dear Jesse,

...today your letter dated January 12th arrived, the one written after your return from Naworth Castle.[60] ...I appreciated your letter in which you gave a general criticism of the 'Radio City Revels' treatment. We are still working on it, having started the last draft today, and if we can cast it, I think it will be funny in a screwy way. There is a regular epidemic of screwy comedies on now so ours is at least quite in the mode. Now, music and lyrics must be written, and a Director selected, and if all goes well we should be in production the middle of March....

But money matters were intruding on the profits due on *Sergeant York* and diplomacy was required with the Warner family, who had a lesser-known brother, Albert Warner. Not as much of a public figure, Albert (known as Abe) was treasurer of Warner Brothers.

December 4, 1941
FROM JESSE L. LASKY
TO: MAJOR ALBERT WARNER
  Warner Bros. 321 West 44th Street
  New York, New York
Dear Abe:

I am in receipt of your letter of November 24th and I am indeed sorry that while I was in New York you did not take advantage of my presence there to discuss the subject matter of your letter. As it is, it will take a somewhat

---

60 Jesse had been hosted by the Duke of Norfolk on several shooting weekends.

lengthy letter to express my feelings about this situation—so bear with me and read the following:

First, as an old friend, I do not hesitate to disclose my present personal situation to you. You will remember that when I left Paramount in 1932, I lost my entire personal fortune. As a matter of fact, when I arrived in California my affairs were so involved that I retained Loyd Wright, who has been my attorney ever since, and by the time we were through settling with all my creditors, I had not only lost my fortune and my home but I had to borrow considerable sums on my life insurance. Since that time I have cleared myself of all indebtedness, but this effort has left me without any cash reserve whatsoever.

About this time, I conceived the idea of acquiring the picture rights to Sergeant York's life. This cost me six months of negotiation and four trips to Tennessee, during which time I was not drawing salary from any company—a considerable investment on my part, you must admit. When I finally persuaded York to sell his life story, I had to make the first payment. I did not hesitate to do this because I knew that I was acquiring one of the most valuable properties available to the picture industry.

When I contacted Harry Warner with the object of producing the picture for your company, I did not attempt to make a profit on the resale of the picture rights which I might justifiably have done. Instead of that, having absolute faith in the timeliness and box-office appeal of this subject, all of which Harry immediately sensed, and my ability to successfully produce it, I determined to gamble, and so was willing to make a deal so that I would not get any profit until after the picture grossed $1,600,000.

Your contention that Jack Warner estimated the picture could be made for approximately $1,000,000 is true. He should not be criticized because of the fact that the picture went over this amount, as many unforeseen elements caused this overage—for instance: we were delayed for several months in starting production waiting to secure the services of Gary Cooper. Let me say, even then it would have been impossible to secure his services if Jack had not very wisely offered Bette Davis [for Goldwyn's The Little Foxes, 1941] in trade for Cooper, which gesture on his part I deeply appreciated. Also, we were producing the picture during the rainy season and lost about three weeks due to extraordinary rainy weather when we had nothing left to shoot but exteriors—battle scenes, etc. Other unforeseen conditions arose which further increased the cost of the picture. However, this is not a new situation. We, who understand the exigencies of picture production, realize it is not unusual for occasional big pictures to exceed their budgets by a very large percentage.

During the years I served Paramount as its First Vice President in Charge of Production, we had many instances of pictures exceeding their budgets from $500,000 to as much as $1,000,000. These very pictures, however, proved in the end to be our greatest moneymakers—and I was always able to face my Board of Directors courageously because the eventual profit on these pictures that exceeded their budgets justified their enormous additional expenditures.

It seems to me, that is the situation that now confronts you. Instead of apologizing or explaining the fact that Sergeant York [1941] cost approximately $600,000 more than was estimated, you should ask for a vote of thanks and confidence for first, having had the foresight to make the deal with me, and, finally, for the amount of profit that it will bring to your company even in spite of the percentage that will accrue to me.

How I would like to have a chance to face your Board and justify this deal. I would tell them that, in the first instance, they should have paid at least $150,000 for the Sergeant York picture rights alone, which would have reimbursed me for my six months of time and financial outlay in acquiring the story—but I didn't ask for this sum because I was willing to gamble for my profit on the outcome of the picture itself. But why go on—I know you follow my thoughts…

I can't help but smile as I conclude this letter because I am thinking back to the many times I was compelled to do the very thing, under similar circumstances, that you are attempting to do in order to placate your Board of Directors and serve the best interests of your company.

Please have no regrets over having written me as you did -and please do not blame me for turning down your request that I give up $120,000 soon to accrue to me. I am very glad that this matter came up because I feel it will create a better understanding between us - and, anyway, it is well that matters of this kind are brought out in the open for frank and honest discussion.

With kindest personal regards, I am
Sincerely Yours,
Jesse L. Lasky

P.S. I would appreciate it enormously if you would pay me the compliment of reading this honest expression of my thoughts and experiences to your Board of Directors.

This Warner brother and the board were placated and Lasky was to receive his due. But the world was not doing as well.

Three days later, the surprise attack by the Japanese on Pearl Harbor, Hawaii's U.S. naval base, on the morning of Sunday, December 7, 1941, finally propelled the United States into World War II. Jesse, who had now established himself as a screenwriter in demand, had been completing the screenplay of *Omaha Trail* at MGM, based on his original story. He found himself immediately activated as a second lieutenant in the U.S. Army Signal Corps.

In April, 1942 he was first assigned to the Long Island studio his father had built so long ago, which was now commandeered by the Army to make training films. He left his wife, Frances (Donna) in their new home on Veteran Avenue in Brentwood, CA.

The army needed training films. The following letters give an insight into how the war affected Hollywood. Film editors, cameramen, directors, actors, producers and writers were 'turfed out of civvies' and into uniforms doing what they did best: making films. George Cukor, famed as a 'woman's director', told Jesse, 'I'm doing the same old thing, except instead of Joan Crawford in *A Woman's Face,* now my star is in a gas mask.' Diverse themes were covered in those training films, like *The Loading of Box Cars, Kill or Be Killed*, and *Disposal of Human Waste*, starring fake turds. Jesse's first assignment was to script a film on rigging and maintaining barrage balloons. His father kept up the flow of Hollywood news.

Jesse's first assignment was to script a film on rigging and maintaining barrage balloons. His father kept up the flow of Hollywood news.

April 28, 1942
Dear Lieutenant Lasky,

...I am thrilled to death over your getting the commission in the Signal Corps and am anxiously awaiting details. How little we thought, when I saw you off at the plane, that it might be some time before we see you again - but you are lucky in getting this commission and I would not have it otherwise for anything in the world...I asked our Publicity Department to get a line in the trade papers here so the industry will know what became of you, and am writing Jack Alicoate of the New York Film Daily to also mention your presence in New York. No doubt you noticed the President's Message to Congress which may limit all incomes to $25,000 - that's a tough break for me as it means that all the vast sums of money I would have gotten from 'Sergeant York' will now go to the Government; however, it's a great cause and if it will help to end the war that much sooner, I am for it - but it leaves me with a real problem and that is how to reorganize our living to get along on $500 a week when it has been costing me three times as much during the past years. However, we have met other emergencies and will surmount this one with chins up and flags flying...What a quirk of fate that you will be working at the Long Island Studio that your Dad help build, and where you worked before...Julius (Evans) and Randy join the family and me in saluting Lieut. Lasky - the first soldier in a long line of Laskys.

May 1, 1942

...Frances was over for dinner Wednesday night and read us parts of your very interesting letters and we had a very pleasant evening. She is well and not worried and you need not worry about her. We will see that things go smoothly … Things are going along splendidly on 'Mark Twain', however, we won't start production until the end of June. …

Lasky was busy at Warner Brothers, happily working on the second of the three films he had contracted to produce: *Mark Twain*. But with greatly diminished earnings.

May 5, 1942
Dear Jesse,

… As soon as Frances received your wire last week she told us of your being sent to Tennessee and we are now awaiting more details. Tennessee ought to be a lucky State for you as it was for me, and although I know it isn't all fun and there is naturally a certain nervous strain in invading new fields, nevertheless, I envy you the adventures that you are having.

… The first draft of 'Twain' has been distributed around the studio and everybody likes it very much, including Jack Warner.

Somehow it makes me feel good that you are in the U.S. Army. I don't hesitate to let everybody know and you may be sure you did the right thing in volunteering, regardless of temporary financial embarrassments that may ensue. …

Frances discovered she was pregnant and Jesse, now in Tennessee, wrote to his mother by hand. Although Bess had hardly been a hands-on mother with the three children, she expected to be friend and confidant when they grew up—and she preferred her children to call her Bess. They accepted their mother the way she was, which was not unlike arresting a hummingbird in mid-air, long enough to appreciate its iridescence. Jesse wrote to her.

May 10, 1942
Dearest Bess;

I know you will forgive me if I write you in pencil. I'm out of ink, and it's evening in a great wooden barracks, and no one has any ink. If I could dip my pen into the soft Tennessee night, I would write for a better world … This is a pretty desolate section of Tennessee. The camp is of plain board buildings - spreading over a rolling country. Red dirt and green forests - one little town neighboring is indescribably filthy but I spend my entire time at this post - eat in the officer's mess - at long tables … Mother's day I sent you a wire from a little town in Kentucky - I went - invited to stay over night with another officer who lives there. It was my first night off the little iron cot and army blanket - and I certainly slept! He bought a couple of drinks - I haven't yet received the many small sums due me from Uncle Sam, so am slightly broke.

I must say the officers here are grand. Everyone is friendly and helpful - but discipline on a post is strict, and clothes - these summer uniforms are a problem! Put them on in the morning and their filthy dirty by night - also we shine our own shoes - sew on buttons etc. It's a great experience - and if Frances is happy - I will be - I know I can count on you and Dad to help keep the homes fires burning.

Much love to all, and write me often - I'll be photographed in uniform when I get back to New York...

Worlds of love - Jess

Working as an apprentice assistant director on *Sergeant York* at a salary of $75 a week, Bill Lasky had met and fallen in mutual love with Margery Lowe, Howard Hawk's personal assistant. They decided to marry, although neither of his parents thought it a good idea because Bill was 22 and this was his first attachment to anything other than snakes, hawks, and creepy-crawlies. But they were soon married and rented a little house in West Los Angeles.

In the middle of *Mark Twain*, Lasky had begun researching the possibility of following it with a film on the Boy Scout movement, which he had earlier discussed with his eldest son.

May 12, 1942
Dear Lieutenant,

...In the studio we are having all kind of restrictions. Only $5,000 is allowed for materials on sets; they are about to limit the use of trucks and motor vehicles on locations; manpower is getting short - but we are taking it all in our stride. I feel I can play any game as well as anyone else as long as I know the rules, and if war imposes these hardships, we will do the best we can without kicking or complaining, and will get a good picture. Alan LeMay is doing some cleanup work on the script and we are in the first phases of getting the physical production ready.

I may fly to St. Paul on Sunday for an important Boy Scout meeting, otherwise I was supposed to be at Angels Camp in Calaveras County (calaveras county) for the Annual Frog Jumping Celebration and to look at some locations.

Billy has been so busy on his picture I have not seen him for a week but he is coming to dinner tonight with Margery, and Frances is picking up Grandma in her car, so we will all drink the usual toast to you. We had to let William[61] go and Grandma is getting along without a car.

Betty has been busy with her various war activities; she has even enlisted as an air raid warden in the day time and has an arm badge and insignia for her

---
61 Another chauffeur.

car, and they are now issuing her a steel helmet. It seems they cannot get men for wardens in the day time and so they take women and Betty volunteered and is being well trained and, strange as it may seem, takes a hold in her quiet way and knows what it is all about.

If you don't hear from us often it isn't because we don't think of you - you are constantly on our minds and we are proud of you - don't let us down....

Jesse replied by hand:

May 13, 1942
Dear Dad,

Just a quick hello before I go over to the officers' mess. It's been a hot day in many respects. The request has just been made by the commanding General here, to my Signal Corp - that I be retained for two weeks longer - as it has been decided to prepare four training films.

Anyway they seem to like having me around - and this is an interesting experience from my standpoint. The work is very difficult - I can't explain what it is, but some day I'll tell you the whole story. I'm not worrying, however, because I can't do better than my best, and I have a kind of half-born faith that it's going to come out well for me.

Tennessee was good to one Lasky already - so perhaps it will be a habit. I've completed one script and am deep in the 2nd - what complications - if only I were a mathematician, a chemist, an astronomer, a mechanic and an electrical engineer!!

It's no place for poetry - but hard work will have to make up the difference. Exactly how much longer I'll be here - nobody knows - or how long I'll be in New York when I do get back.

I don't think Frances should make any drastic steps - like getting rid of the house just yet. I don't think any definite decisions can be made just yet. Everything is uncertain. The ideal arrangement would be to have her east with me, but Louise didn't think that would be wise before the baby is born. I would rather wait, at least have the grasp of things I'm sure to have when I get back and have spent a normal working month in Astoria - this field assignment has put me in loops!!

PS. Please address mail to me 2nd Lieut. J. Lasky Jr. Publications Division Barrage Balloon School Camp Tyson Tenn.

And write soon!
Jess

May 21, 1942
Dear Jesse:

... Briefly—I flew to Minneapolis and St. Paul and attended a meeting of the National Council of Boy Scouts and then went on a speaking tour with Dr. West and a group of the Scout executives - and also participated in the dedication of a canoe base north of Duluth, a real jumping-off place for the wilderness. I even got into a canoe with a guide and astonished the Boy Scout executives by the way I handled the canoe. We stopped at schools and colleges and addressed thousands of kids and had a marvelous time, and I flew back from Chicago ... After you are definitely stationed in New York, I will probably find an excuse to jump east when we can have a visit together.

By the way, I had James Street, the novelist, meet me in St Paul and he accompanied me on the trip with the Boy Scout executives to pick up data, and is now starting out to write the Boy Scout story ... The Mark Twain script is finished ... We start shooting in about four weeks and the script is simply great - I am really happy over it now.

Billy is worried about being drafted but is hard at work - and Betty and Mother are up to their ears in USO work. I am feeling fit....

All the Laskys send their love—Keep'em Flying....

May 26, 1942

... We start shooting 'Mark Twain' in about a month as we are waiting for Irving Rapper, the director, to be finished with his current picture. All the department heads in the studio who have read the script think it is extremely fine. By the way, I helped Phil Friedman get a job as Assistant Casting Director here. He told me of meeting you in New York. He is a fine chap and I am glad he is added to the Warner Bros, forces.

Billy is working very hard here at the studio. He seems worried about his future. I suppose he will be drafted any time now and he is not very enthusiastic about the Army. Betty is developing beautifully; becoming an extremely pretty girl ... I loved your reference to my favorite phrase in your recent letter - and Keep Up Your Good Spirits!

We all send best love.
P.S. Hope the enclosed certificate from Uncle Sam for ten bucks reaches you safely.

June 3, 1942

... When I was on my 'Gateway to Hollywood' tour, I spent an evening on the roof of the Hotel Peabody in Memphis. I little thought at that time that you would be dancing on the same roof in the uniform of Uncle Sam, which only goes to prove you cannot out-guess destiny and, as I used to say 'you never know what is just around the corner waiting for you.' ... We have just started casting 'Mark Twain' and what a tough job it is trying to get good players to play bits. We will probably start shooting on the 25th of this month. James Street is working on the Boy Scout story in New York; I haven't received his first draft as yet so can only hope for the best. I have told Julius Evans that I will give him screen credit as Associate Producer and that has made him very happy. Send him a postcard sometime. I am wondering how you prepare your script concerning the barrage balloons. Do they give you anyone to type the script or do you have to hammer it out yourself? By the way, they have put up barrage balloons along the coast. We can see a flock of them from our porch protecting the Douglas Aircraft plant at Santa Monica. I never expected to see such a sight in peaceful California. Betty read Billy your letter. He seems confused and worried. He is working so hard on his picture that he is worn out nights and lacks his usual spirit and gaiety. I am hoping we will get an inspiration so we can tell him what to do. I understand that when he is drafted he can immediately apply for assignment to the Air Corp or some other branch - is this correct?

I was all set to go to Paradise with Cecil on Friday night but Cecil was notified that he would have to remain near his telephone for forty-eight hours, over Decoration Day, as he is an Air Raid Warden and they expected an air raid over the weekend. The entire community was aroused to this expectation because all air raid wardens, etc., were notified to stand by and gas masks were distributed to many of the wardens - but nothing happened and I personally do not look for this kind of trouble for a long time. The rumor around here was that they had sunk an aircraft carrier, which contained no planes off the Mexican Coast, and the mystery was - what became of the planes? However, Hollywood is filled with rumors and we do not know what to believe....

By the way, Betty, without saying much, is very proud of her Lieutenant Brother. She meets so many soldiers in her war work and is so active that she is a constant source of surprise to me. She is an air raid warden and very active in our district. On certain days she has to remain by the telephone from 7 am to 7 pm and she has done all the typing for her little group so that the women in her immediate neighborhood have come to depend on her....

June 12, 1942

...I am enclosing another one of Uncle Sam's greenbacks so that you can paint that town red - the town that is near Camp Tyson - and from your description of it, you won't need much red paint either.

Your last letter of June 7th, written on the back of the military order, shall be preserved as a souvenir. Seeing the name of Lieut. Lasky on the list of officers gave us all a great kick. I was astonished to see that you were used to drill a squad of regular soldiers, which only goes to prove that nothing you learn in this world is ever wasted - and, thank the Lord, for your State Guard drill nights. I was much interested in your explanation of how you function and what you are supposed to do...

I was surprised to learn that Cecil wrote you a letter. As it happens, we are making our deferred trip to Paradise tonight, so I am going to <u>read</u> him much of your letter; of course, I will leave out the part that refers to him.

...Betty and Mother are getting a great kick out of their war work, in fact, Betty says she would like to be a social worker, and Mother's enthusiasm for the U.S.O. doesn't seem to wane. We are going to Hillcrest Country Club for dinner again next Sunday. Mother was not with us last Sunday, and she called Frances this morning to ask her to join us. I hope she will be free as I have not seen her in some days, but she seems fine on the telephone.

We are really in the midst of preparations for 'Mark Twain' now and our starting date is June 25th. The casting is extremely difficult because the parts are all so small but still we want fine actors for them. Just came from the stage where we are making a test of a beautiful girl, Alexis Smith - a new Warner Bros, leading woman who some day will be a great star.

Billy is still unduly worried over his nearness to the draft. They are picking up the boys awfully fast now....

Lasky was a founding member of the beautiful Hillcrest Country Club. It was formed because The Los Angeles Country Club did not allow Jews or showbiz people, although Harold Lloyd and DeMille, (being half Jewish and all show-biz) somehow slipped in.

Jesse wrote to his mother:

June 12, 1942
Dearest Bess

...Today a great storm came thrashing out of the sky - lightening exploded almost into our faces - rain churned the dust into red lather - thunder exploded - thus ended the heat wave for moments at least. I have just been scraping Tennessee off my shoes. Two rooms away an officer is whistling 'Over There' otherwise it is wonderfully still.

All your words are wonderful to me - there is a great deal of self meditation - sometimes at noon I skip lunch in the crowded, stuffy mess hall and find a patch of wild grass - and lie - face staring into the sun. I try and let its strength and confidence - its surety fill me. Many phases of my work have been tremendously difficult - some still are - I can have no idea if I have done a good job until I get back to Signal Corps headquarters and hear their opinion. But the Coast Artillery seem well satisfied. One more long difficult assignment, and I can return....

What work you are doing! Thrilled with it all, and thrilled to be a snap shot in your purse. Life has become quieter here, but never stagnant. Up always at six thirty and working at eight. Major Pamplin, my immediate boss and friend has become Lt. Colonel. Many of my other good friends here have left for destinations unknown. This has quieted the social happenings. Also I have had to work several nights this week and will have to work many more to conclude the last assignment.

Well, my wonderful Bess I must trade this conversation for sleep. Soon radios will be silent and I can close my eyes and see 507 Veteran Ave - or Paris, 1929. Dreams flutter through one's head like imitation snow in a paper weight ... Now then, my friend of the heavenly paint brush ... I seem far from creative writing, even reading, if the snake is unaware of losing its skin - I might hope that some of the Hollywood scales are wearing off.

In the meantime, Darling Thanks again for the letter and all it contained - write often - to the wild-eyed young man with the double chin, but much love -

Jess

Lasky had reason to write his son with a glimpse of what the war was doing to the film industry, aside from whisking away talent.

June 24, 1942
Dear Jess,

...First, thanks for your Fathers Day telegram which warmed my paternal heart more than you can realize ... Last Saturday Billy received his classification which is 1-A. He was a bit upset as that means within the next two or three weeks, maybe sooner, he will receive his induction notice ... I remember writing you that I thought it would be a short war and you didn't agree with me. I hate to admit it but I am afraid you are absolutely right. From present indications, one can only conclude that we are in for a long fight - God only knows how long.

At this end things are tightening up very fast - I mean in the motion picture industry. What with conserving film and materials, and the gradual disappearance of our manpower, particularly actors, it is going to be most difficult to make good pictures. As a matter of fact, my hunch is that within six months the industry will be only turning out half of the features they are making at present.

... (We) start shooting montages next Monday for a week, and on July 6th the picture actually starts. We have tested Freddie March in the older Mark Twain make-up and he is simply magnificent, breathtaking, perfect! There is every indication that he is going to be great in the part which is all important to the success of the picture.

I have had some encouraging correspondence and a vague draft of the first part of the Boy Scout story from James Street; as you know, he is writing it in New York. This story must be licked as it is timely and important—at least, my instinct tells me just that and I won't let up until I get it on the screen.

We spent the weekend at (playwright) Gwen Baer's Yucca Loma Ranch at Victorville. There is an aviation camp of several thousand men close by and I met a lot of the young officers and have never come across a finer bunch of boys. Every one of them say the same thing - they are only living to get a crack at Tokio (sic)!

June 26, 1942

...Nothing much has happened here except I cannot help but be impressed over Betty's general improvement. She shows a quiet but definite authority. Just now she is trying to gather a huge bunch of girls to go to an U.S.O. affair in Indio on the Fourth, of July. As the temperature in Indio will be about 130°, the job of getting the girls is a difficult one. Mother is splendid and very much interested in her U.S.O. work and, in her quiet way, accomplished splendid things - but she is keeping up her painting and doing some beautiful work, the finest she has yet turned out. In fact, due to Mother's calm and sane outlook on things, our house is very peaceful and happy. Naturally we try to conserve gas and rubber as much as possible, in fact, Mother has learned to drive and is today taking an examination to get her operator's license. I suppose I will have to take up driving again but that won't be hard for me due to my past experience as a driver.[62]

...I was just out on the stages and saw our first big sets going up - the huge interior of an early Mississippi steamboat and an exterior of the boat - very impressive. Alan (LeMay) spent yesterday afternoon in the studio trying to help us to cut the script, which is still too long. I find Alan most friendly, agreeable and cooperative. He is a fine chap when you know him, and he and Julius get along splendidly.

I am going to take a chance and put the usual 'ten' in this letter; in fact, now that you are in New York I must write you oftener as I know the 'tens' are going to be needed more in New York than in the wilds of Tennessee .
.. Forgot to tell you that Cecil said at Paradise that if you were available he would be sending for you. He did speak as though you have a very warm place in his affections....

---

62 Lasky was losing his chauffeur to the Army.

July 2, 1942

...Billy has been more cheerful lately and more like his old self. He received his Notice of Selection last Saturday, and the notice read that he would receive his Order for Induction on July 16th. It looks now as if there is a good chance of getting him into the photographic division of the Air Corps under Lieut. Col. Jack Warner. The Air Corps are taking the old Vitagraph Studios here to make their training films, and after Billy gets his six weeks of training at some camp he would be located at the Vitagraph Studios which means he could live at home. This would be a great break for Billy - better than being sent east in the Signal Corps, so we are keeping our fingers crossed.

... Billy, by the way, is Second Assistant on 'Mark Twain' and has been with the montage unit since Tuesday as we have been doing montages all week. Monday we start the picture and Billy, of course, will stay with it until he is drafted.

... We are beginning to line up a pretty good cast for 'Mark Twain' and have cut nearly twenty pages out of the script. Irving Rapper, the director, is an enthusiastic young man and Julius is all over the place doing a swell job - so between us all we ought to get a fine picture.

... Last Saturday afternoon I made a trip with mother to Terminal Island, San Pedro, where she is decorating the U.S.O. rooms. The place was teeming with sailors - the Navy headquarters having formerly been the Federal Prison. I was surprised to see the way mother was received and how well she functioned. The Navy Chaplain took charge of her and she was surrounded by sailors helping her in her work. ...

July 11, 1942

... At the last minute Mother, Billy and Margery and I decided to go away on the Fourth and we finally found accommodations at the Miramar near Santa Barbara. We had two lovely days and Betty and Frances met us at the Beach Club on our return on Sunday and we all had dinner together. We thought Frances looked particularly well and she certainly is cheerful and seems quite contented, and I believe is managing things very well.

Billy has received his orders to report for induction so is quitting his job so that he can report next Thursday. After he is sent to camp, I expect to have a letter written requesting that he be assigned to the Photographic Division of the Air Corps, with headquarters at the Vitagraph Studios in Hollywood, where training films will be made for the Air Corps under the general command of Lieut. Col. Jack Warner. ...

Alan LeMay has joined Cecil again and I believe is working on the 'Dr. Wassel' picture. We have been shooting a week on 'Mark Twain' and I like the young director, Irving Rapper - and our rushes look very interesting. We have a tough ten weeks' shooting schedule with the usual problems, but the general feeling is that we have in the making an outstanding picture. Freddie March as Mark Twain - we are shooting his sequences as a young man - is extremely good. I haven't a doubt but what he will score a big personal success. He has just the right qualities to play Twain and his makeups are wonderful.

... Betty is off this afternoon with two busloads of girls who she gathered to entertain the soldiers at Palm Springs and Indio. As they report a temperature of over 125°, I persuaded Mother to abandon the trip. She was going along as a chaperone but I know she could not stand the heat.

'Sergeant York' is playing a return engagement at Warner Bros. Hollywood Theatre and is in its second week and doing good business. Jack Hostetter came in to see me and told me that you had written him about 'Ox Train' and the advisability of taking your name off the picture. He was rather vague and said there wasn't much he could do about it. I wouldn't worry about it if I were you - you have such a good credit on 'Reap the Wild Wind' which, by the way, is cleaning up.

... Yesterday we had three of the boys for lunch who bombed Tokyo. I was introduced to one of them, a young Lieutenant, who said: 'I guess you don't remember me, Mr. Lasky—but I served you gas at the gas station near your house.' The boys were not permitted to talk much, but what these three fellows told us about the Tokyo raid was mighty interesting....

July 18, 1942

... Well, Billy reported to his Induction Board last Thursday; passed his examination, but on account of his eyes he was put in the non-combatant class, and then given a two-weeks' furlough. He reports to Ft. MacArthur for training a week from Thursday. His whole attitude has changed and now that he knows what is going to happen to him, he is very much his old self....

The concerts are on at the Hollywood Bowl and we have two seats in a box. The concerts start at 7.45 o'clock. I went with Mother on Thursday night and Betty and Mother went last night. It is a beautiful sight to sit in the Bowl and listen to the concert and watch the night gradually enfold the whole Hollywood Bowl....

We are constantly being warned to expect an air raid along the coast due to the numerous airplane plants in the vicinity. They even have big triangular gongs hanging on posts in various parts of Beverly Hills, with a sign stating they are to be sounded in case of a gas attack.

Betty is coming out to the studio with a young flyer from the Air Corps to visit on the Mark Twain set this afternoon. She works daily now at the U.S.O. headquarters and is doing some splendid organization work. She gathers girls to visit the various camps; answers the telephone, and really is becoming quite an efficient little executive...I am going to do some betting and if I win any money, you will get the winnings....

Jesse wrote to Bess from New York, where he had finally been moved.

July 20, 1942
Dearest Bess;

I hope you won't mind if I talk to you on the typewriter today, but it is literally so hot, that if I set pen to paper, the heel of my hand would soak it to pulp. Perhaps you have been reading in the papers about the heat wave that has submerged New York. It is the worst I've ever seen - so wet that I had to change my clothes three times yesterday...what a place. Since it was Sunday Louise and Ben invited me to dinner, so we went to an air-cooled restaurant into which the panting, sopping population of New York had wedged itself for a few gasps, then we went to see Gary Cooper in 'Lou Gerig', in an air-cooled theater. I was so glad they rescued me from my oven of a room.

Of late there has been a new series of night events in the way of classes, and courses in various subjects. These keep me in Astoria till quite late at night, on several nights a week, and others are getting organized. I hope some of the subjects, are part of a preparation for active duty in some other locale. There's no way of knowing, but rumors are always rife, and it seems possible that the younger officers, of which I am one, may sometime be sent into more active fields; anyway its fun to hope for...I am so thrilled about the approaching baby event, and shall try and get a furlough in early December or late November. There might be an excellent chance of getting it, but that, too is impossible to tell in advance. Frances sounds brave, happy, calm, practical, and her letters have been reassuring and inspiring. I know you and Dad have had a big hand in keeping her in such good spirits, and you know how much I appreciate it. What a good thing I didn't bring her into this hellish eastern summer.

Well, Darling this was short and sweet but I did want to get a few lines to you, and - Now to finish this off in pen - a personal touch for beautiful Bess - I'll write soon and longer again. Kiss goodbye,

Jess

Through all the difficulties that war had brought to making films on mini-budgets with loss of staff in every field from actors to technicians, Lasky was producing some of the finest pictures in his long career and found time to keep up a steady stream of letters to both his sons.

July 28, 1942
Dear Jess,

...I was glad to receive your letter yesterday, Monday, even though I had talked to you on the 'phone Sunday night.

Let me first, compliment you on your typing. Necessity is making you a fine typist indeed. From what I can gather, a lot of the fellows in the Signal Corps are not too happy with their assignments. Frank Capra is now stationed in the Taft Building!!! And, from these headquarters, is supervising the making of training shorts. Major Bob Lord had lunch with us recently and I gather from his remarks that making pictures for the studios is child's play compared to the problems that have been confronting him in his Signal Corps efforts. Hal Roach was a Reserve Officer; he went in the same time I did, but while I resigned a few years ago, he neglected to do so. He suddenly received a notification for active service and although he explained he was the head of his business and tried to get a deferment or postponement, he found himself in the Army before he could turn around. I had a swim with him Sunday and chatted with him at his Beach House, and you will be seeing him at Astoria next Monday. He seemed a little dismayed by the suddenness of it all.

Billy closed his house and has moved his things to a little apartment to cut expenses and he reports to Ft. MacArthur on Thursday. He quit his job here about ten days ago in order to move.

...We have been shooting three weeks on 'Mark Twain' with all the usual problems. Trying to get a good script on the screen is like an obstacle race. The company, the director, the actors, the weather, the budget, the war restrictions, become hurdles and if you can persist and jump them all, maybe you get a good picture. Our rushes look very interesting. We have shot the Mississippi sequences and the Jumping Frog and most of the Western sequences, but until they are assembled, one can only hope that the rushes which look good will go together as the pieces of a good picture puzzle should. The principal members of our cast are Fredric March; Alexis Smith, a very interesting new young leading woman; Alan Hale; Donald Crisp, John Carradine; Bill Henry, and a host of lesser names.

I am still waiting for the treatment on the Boy Scouts from James Street, so cannot tell you anything about that as yet.

August 1, 1942

...It was so nice to talk to you again on the telephone and Frances was tickled to death to hear your voice and very appreciative of the opportunity of talking to you from our house.

Billy was inducted at Pt. MacArthur on Thursday but they would not accept him for transfer to the Air Corps on account of his eyes so he decided to state the Signal Corps as his preference…Jack Warner is anxious for me to undertake the production of the 'Life of Winston Churchill'. The Warners have acquired the picture rights to this subject and, of course, will have the cooperation of the British Government - but it is a terrific undertaking and I am not very enthusiastic about it. There is a vast amount of material to read, and at least I will explore it for a while. By the way, this Churchill matter is confidential - don't want it to get in the papers.

Enclosed is your $20.00. For safety's sake, if it is all the same to you, next week will send a check - let me know which you prefer.

…Went with Mother to the Hollywood Bowl to see the Russian Ballet. It was a perfect evening; full moon over the Bowl and, except for the distant drone of an occasional airplane, it is impossible to sit there in perfect peace with simple music-loving people and realize a war is going on. Sometimes I think the whole thing is a nightmare and I will wake up and find it was all a dream - but I guess millions of others have the same thought….

P.S, Since dictating this - Billy telephoned in from Ft. MacArthur that they had been informed they are being sent away today, but he doesn't know where. He thought he might get a 24 hour furlough but nothing doing. As soon as we hear what Camp he has been sent to - I still think it will be Camp Crowder, Missouri - I will let you know. Margery said he was in good spirits; his hair was cut; he had just received his uniform and a lot of shots in the arm….

August 8, 1942

…Margery has had long amazing letters from Bill which she read to me Thursday night and he has been thrilled by his experiences thus far…. His two days on the troop train impressed him greatly and he has made some wonderful friends - fellows who have the same tastes as he has. The Photographic Division of the Air Corps at the Vitagraph Studios is beginning to get active and I am sorry that he missed getting in this division….

We attended the world premiere of 'Tales of Manhattan' the other night. If you get a chance to see the picture, I am sure you will enjoy it as it is different and makes one forget the war.

The 'Mark Twain' picture is progressing slowly. My private opinion is that our young director, Rapper, has been over-rated but Julius sticks with him all the time and keeps him as straight as possible. It is a tough picture to shoot and we haven't enough stuff assembled - due to the fact that our cutter has been tied up on another picture - for me to express a definite opinion on how good it is. This much is certain - Fredric March is going to be excellent, and our leading woman is very fine. The thing I cannot tell is whether the story is holding up and whether it is going to be too episodical as it unfolds…I finally received my Boy Scout material from James Street - five chapters written like a novel, and the rest more briefly sketched out - and to my great disappointment he has missed the whole point of the story. Very little of his material can be salvaged and it leaves me rather up in the air. It is undoubtedly the toughest subject that one can tackle and I am liable to abandon it, for the time being at least, and turn to something else. Jack Warner wants me to do the life of Winston Churchill, but I am very much afraid of it. It is a tremendous undertaking, and one fraught with endless dangers.

I sometimes feel like taking a lay-off when the Mark Twain picture is finished and coming to New York to make a quiet search for material for a couple of months. If I could pick up two good stories, or even practical story ideas, it would be worth the trip - I am getting very stagnant here and lack inspiration. The change is probably what I need and a couple of months without salary would not make any difference as I am in such a high income tax bracket that the loss of salary would be a very little personal loss to me at best. . . .

In a curious twist of fate, Bill, who had been so worried about what he would do in the war, was given an assignment he never expected.

August 13, 1942
Dear Jesse,

. . . Billy seems to have found just what he is looking for and undoubtedly will be attached to the carrier pigeon unit, for which I must say he is well qualified. He is happier than he has been in years and hopes he will never have to come back to studio work again. He is urging Margery to give up her job and join him at Crowder as they have told him he will be stationed there for some considerable time. I think as soon as Margery can wind up her affairs with (Howard) Hawks she will go to Crowder, and it may be she could get a job there.

. . . We have a few reels of 'Mark Twain' roughly assembled and the stuff looks pretty good. I feel more encouraged about the picture. I am thinking now of taking over 'A Connecticut Yankee in King Arthur's Court' and giving it a modern treatment. One of the writers here has a swell idea as to how it should be treated and I may set it as my next picture as I am not sure how long it is going to take to lick the Boy Scout story now that Street has fallen down on it.

Betty and I attended the premiere of 'Yankee Doodle Dandy' last night. It was a very gala affair and the picture made a sensational hit. I have seen it three times and liked it better each time . . . When you see it, you will know why it is my favorite picture . . . I am going to start driving a car again and will try and get a license very soon so that I won't be dependent on chauffeurs so much. They are getting scarcer than hens' teeth.

Next week we are going to have a dim-out area all through Hollywood and this will last until the duration, which means we will have to drive 15 miles an hour with dimmed lights. Slowly but surely things are tightening up as is to be expected....

Letters from Jesse to his mother seem to have been better preserved than those he wrote to his dad. Bess preferred hand-written missives in the flowery, pseudo-poetic style he reserved only for her. He wrote her the sort of letter he knew she would like.

August 17, 1942
Darling Bess

'Tis an age since a letter from you, but I know you are busy, and so have I been - my life - a tremendous momentum of work, with little free time - and seldom a moment alone to drink the pools of silence. This I shall have next week when I move to a very pleasant Hotel and have my own tiny room - I won't give you the address till I'm positive I can get a niche there - but write me care of Signal Corps. Photographic Center, Astoria, Long Island, New York - Mail finds me there always.

Good news is that I have made a preliminary stab at getting leave in November and it seems certain I will be successful!! Also I may soon be sent on another interesting trip, this time to some Camp in Pennsylvania I do believe. New York is terribly hot and wet - sultry heat - It keeps us changing uniforms every time we turn around - and oh those laundry and cleaning bills!! Alas a poor officer must pay for everything - next war I want to be a private - and speaking of privates - our Bill sounds like the happiest man in the Army, and I'm so glad he is - I took steps toward getting him here and he turned the proposition down cold - and I think he was right - the pigeon fancying is a much better job for him, and he seems so happy where he is, why come into this, where there is much he might not like - it's more like a studio grind.

Wonderful letters from Frances, and I'm so happy when you and Dad write me how well she looks, and how her spirit is calm, and never depressed, never lonesome.

...Well Bess, it's a strange thing being here, I still can't believe it - or that I'm nearly a father - or that I'm mixed into a war - I feel most like an overworked picture writer in a strange city but its less strange now - New York is more friendly - beginning to be familiar – Hot - fearfully expensive, but not strange and frightening any more - nor big. I have no feeling of oppression as I pound the hard pavements - I'm beginning to be quite fond of New York ... I liked the new Orson Welles picture - have you seen it?[63]

Well dear Bess - I've enjoyed this talk with you - I feel you always very close to me - somehow more than ever - I often think of Art[64] - I have even almost seen him - hurrying beside me - somehow past present and future are strongly etched together - I have a sense of timelessness - destiny or what?

I'm lonesome - busy, and yet happy all at once - but always I feel this is right - the direction and work are right - A lot of love to you Bess - and write soon - Jess

Lasky tried to keep Jess abreast of studio news. As usual, daily life was eventful.

August 21, 1942
Dear Jess,

... I just got through touring the studio with Harry Warner, entertaining General Hsiung-Shihfei, Chief of the Chinese Military Mission to the United States and one of the most important military figures in the world. We had lunch with the General and his staff and it was a thrilling experience. These modern educated Chinese are as brilliant as any men I have ever met and after hearing them tell us the inside dope on China, I feel that we have a greater ally than we realize in the wonderful, heroic Chinese people.

I am glad you are moving to the Belmont Plaza Hotel on Lexington Avenue... Mark Twain is progressing pretty well but we are having the usual troubles - particularly because our script is long and every time we cut it we hurt the picture. After eliminating the character of General Grant from the picture, we are breaking our necks trying to get him back ... Frances spent last Sunday night with us and she was in fine spirits. We'll probably see her this weekend ... You will notice Bill sent Mother a Signal Corps pin. If you should come across one, send it to her as she would be awfully proud. Well, if you read my letter to Bill and his letter to me and the enclosures and consume the twenty dollars enclosed herewith, my conscience will be clear until I get time to write you a longer and newsier letter....

And Jesse had some news.

August 25, 1942
Dear Dad,

... Once again the wand of adventure was waved near my head, a big new medical project to be written, but it was decided not to interrupt or speed

---

63 Jesse is referring to *Citizen Kane*.
64 Bess' brother Art had recently died.

the work I have yet to complete on the very long barrage balloon project . . . Finally got around to seeing 'Yankee Doodle Dandy' and liked it tremendously. As for 'Mark Twain', was horrified to hear that you had cut the General Grant stuff. That happened to be the part of the script that made the deepest impression on me, and the part I best remembered. Certainly hope you can get some of it back in, I think I loved your Twain more for having struck a blow for a tired, beaten, financially licked old hero, than for writing Tom Sawyer. That selfless act gave the picture of the man a tremendous dimension. Hope you get it back. This world is bulging with cannibals, who eat each other alive. They are here and everywhere, the madly ambitious hard riding, steel shod folk who are too busy going somewhere to see anything but the golden swimming pools. Their present to this world was the war, and every war. Personal ambition for glorification will keep feeding humanity wars as long as it exists. Twain was greater for me in that single act, because he was doing it for someone else than himself, his life, his future, or his present!

. . . Spoke to Carl Brandt on the phone, and he promised to call me some time. I haven't lost one iota of my ambition to finish your life story, in fact I have the first half with me, and I may find a little time late nights to do some polishing on it. Wish we had got to the end of the recorded research. The book must be finished. I read some of it over and was thrilled with what it can and will be. Looking forward so very much to my trip west in November. I don't know the date of the baby, and neither I suppose, does anyone, but it will be shortly after that that I make my big effort to go west for ten days, and from all indications I will be granted this wish. Have had a few photos made in a little shop on Broadway, and will . . . send them to Frances for distribution.

Bill's letters are a real inspiration. Glad somebody is really happy. Not that I'm unhappy, but this somehow is not what the Army should be for a writer. It's useful important work, but it's far from war, I feel.

love to all of you. affectionately, Jess

And Lasky wrote to Jesse about a subject he had become interested in.

August 27, 1942
Dear Jess:

When talking with Frances on Sunday morning, she mentioned that you had asked her to send you a Bible. I told Frances I would like to send you one and, after thinking about it, I decided to send you a set including a Bible, and Science and Health with Key to the Scriptures by Mary Baker Eddy.

The reason I am doing this is because, in my own experience, I never could get very much out of reading the Bible until I studied Mary Baker Eddy's interpretation of it, which is contained in Science and Health.

Now that you have a room of your own, you will have a little more time, I hope, to read - and just for the sake of knowing something about it, if for no other reason - read the Preface to Science and Health, and the first chapter on Prayer. If you do that, I have a hunch that you won't stop until you have read Science and Health from cover to cover - a little every day - and, after that, the whole Bible will take on a new and fresh meaning for you.

I also included in the set I am sending you a Christian Science quarterly. This contains one lesson each week which all students read and study. Just as an experiment, so you will know what it is about, try doing one of the lessons which consists of reading designated passages from the Old or New Testament and their interpretation or explanation in correlative passages in Science and Health. Julius Evans and I occasionally do these lessons, particularly when our minds are confused and we are worried, and the result has always been like magic.

I am not trying to make a Science student out of you, but I do say that it is just as interesting and important for you to read and know something about the book, Science and Health, as it is for you to read Shakespeare or a current popular novel.

The fact that you are away from home and that we are all going through such a trying period, brings home to us the necessity of leaning on something besides our human hopes and desires. You always had a leaning and, I think, a yearning for some kind of spiritual help and belief, and I sense now more than ever that you have this desire. It is my hope that my little gift, which I am sending you by parcel post today, will answer this urge....

Our Mark Twain rushes are really beginning to get very interesting and some of the cut stuff looks fine. Two more weeks of shooting, then some editing and probably a few retakes, and the picture will be ready for music and sound effects. What a long grind it has been!

The Draft Boards out here are taking our boys awfully fast now; pretty soon there won't be a young man left in the studio. With every day that passes, I am more happy than ever that you are in it. You couldn't have held your head up if you were still walking around Hollywood. You would be amazed at the number of people that ask for you. Even Jack Warner the other day asked me how Lieut. Lasky was doing in the Signal Corps.

Frank Capra is in charge of the Signal Corps out here. Would you like me to look into it and see if you could be transferred to Hollywood - or would you prefer to let Army procedure take its course?...

Still posted at the old Astoria studio, Jesse found himself being given more executive work and was beginning to wish he would be sent into action. Mom and Dad were each sending him pocket money to ease his days.

August 28, 1942
Darling Bess

... A sudden, violent change has come to my job. I am - for the time – appointed - Officer in Charge of the Scenario dept. This is busy difficult work - It means I am a department head - not writing now - but rather in charge of writers.

I am like a writer's head at a studio - with a million problems – difficulties -

Against it, is the fact that it means no more field trips to camps - it means being nailed to one desk indefinitely - longer hours - harder work - a basket of worries - but also it is an important position - a private office - secretaries, Sergeant assistant - and the chance of quick promotion, so I'll do it, and make the best of it. Then, if I am pulled out and put back as a writer I'll be glad that I am.

Now - let my insides give you thanks for those heavenly cookies - the envy of the post - and the joy of the scenario dept. Those few that I offered to others (I tried hanging on to most of them to be gorged in my hotel room) anyway those that I did give out were enjoyed and some of the officers asked for the recipe.

It was sweet of you to remember my tooth for such things. Your last letter and back pocket encouragement was a great lifter up -Your words came very close to my mind - you seem to catch the spirit of my thoughts sometimes - very closely - and I am thrilled to have your words.

Am happy with my room at the Belmont Plaza that looks like the cabin of a ship – bunks - and brass lamps - very original and unhotelish - and thank Heavens - alone - I can read again - and write verse again - without the perpetual clatter of voices in my ears. It's a happy location and I'm delighted with it, but of course it isn't as inexpensive as sharing a box with my two military sardines!

Well Bess, I don't know how I'm going to like being 'an executive' - but in the Army one does as directed, and 'liking' has little place in things -

Had a sad bit of news from England - Gerald James - in the Royal Canadian Air force - reported missing. Only pray this leaves the door open to hope - I am writing his mother and father - there just isn't anything one can say - His mother writes - I hope we will never forget what the Nazis have done to us - I hope we will never go soft on the subject of Germany - and I join her in this hope - I add another hope - that my own war life won't be always behind a desk!

I know you don't agree with me - with my wish for overseas service - and I only tell it to you because there seems small chance of getting it - I'm Astoria bound – tied - for the duration I guess - safe and restless - so it will be. More on this tune later—for it is late. My love to you - beautiful Bess - and write soon - To your Jess.

It was Dad who wrote back from the studio.

August 29, 1942

... After several days of really great rushes, I am actually beginning to get excited about the picture and - hold your breath - I almost dare say it is going to be pretty fine.

By the way, here is an amazing thing: Monday I began to worry about the elimination of General Grant and, finally, we got Harry Chandlee in and we wrote Grant back into the picture in a magnificent pathetic scene, better than the one you remember - and the scenes have already been shot and are great.

Imagine, therefore, my emotion when your letter arrived on the day we were shooting the Grant scenes, and I read your wonderful paragraph explaining why you were horrified to hear that it had been cut, and the reasons why it was one of your favorite scenes. Believe it or not - I had argued with the director and with Julius that the scene had to go back, and gave the very reasons that you later gave me. It is almost as if, through mental telepathy, you had wirelessed me to put back the scene and the reasons for doing so. I read your paragraph to the boys and they were amazed that you should have sensed the dangerous mistake we had made and why it was such an important element in the story....

I really worked terribly hard this week, leaving the studio at seven or eight o'clock exhausted, but it has been worth it and I am really in a much happier frame of mind than a few weeks ago.

... Billy keeps sending us the most cheerful letters. He won a medal for marksmanship and apparently is happier than he has been in many years....

It was finally sinking in to Lasky that Jess had an excellent story mind - and a shortage of cash.

September 6, 1942
Dear Dad,

... I had a very nice dinner with Henry Salsbury and his new wife. He took me to a magnificent place and we had a good talk, he was tremendously interested in the little I could tell him of my work, and incidentally I believe I am making quite good progress in my departmental job. How long it will last no man knoweth and wouldn't tell if he did, but its an important spot while it lasts, executive for a change in my life. My imagination still runs out to the fronts of action and I suppose it always will, but I'll have faith that the Army knows best where it wants me.

The weather has changed for the better at last. It's cool air, and fresh. Soon we will change back to winter uniforms, which of course raises the necessity of acquiring several new items that I didn't need when I joined last year because of the lateness of that season. A long dress overcoat for New York wear, a short heavy overcoat for day wear, another complete uniform perhaps. Heavy shoes. The Army is ever a clothes problem, and it takes years before men are fully outfitted. The enlisted men have things issued them, but we buy every article of clothing we wear. Don't take this to be a hint which it isn't, as your weekly assistance will enable me to manage. I only tell you about it as a point of interest in the life of an Army officer stationed near New York.

Frances writes cheerful encouraging grand letters, always mentioning that you have called or taken her to dinner, so I know that you are keeping track of her, and I have no worries. She mentioned that the baby will be some time around the end of Oct. or beginning of November, and that she would be laid up in bed for about four weeks afterward normally, that is about two in the hospital and two at home, so that she would enjoy my visit and I would enjoy my visit more if I made it the end of December or beginning of January. What I will try to do is to make it just over Christmas and New Years. I'll try for two weeks, but will probably get ten days. Unless something far fetched happens before then, there should be no difficulty earning this well-earned furlough, as I have not yet requested as much as one hour off, and don't expect to. It would be perfect if you came to New York for a visit sometime before then.

Have already read some of the bibles you sent me, and enjoyed the clear cool reason of Science and Health... but don't celebrate a convert to the fold just yet ... Best to Randy and Julius, and all my friends, and love to all at home.

Jess

September 9, 1942
Dear Jess,

... I spent Labor Day with Cecil at Paradise. We had a very pleasant evening, being served for the last time by Arthur, his butler and Man Friday for many years, as Arthur left the next morning to be inducted into the Army. Cecil asked with much interest about you and I told him all I knew. He is becoming more mellow with the years and we really had a fine long chat.

Was very much impressed with the news in your last letter that you are functioning as the Officer-in-Charge of the Scenario Department ... I think you were right in advising that I do not attempt to pull any strings to get you out here. Matters like that usually work out if not forced but left alone.

We are in the final stages of shooting 'Mark Twain'. Freddie March will be washed up next week and we will be finished shooting on the picture around September 19th. In the meantime, the Montage Department are shooting some very difficult montages which will hold up the final assembling of the picture somewhat. I have looked at nine or ten reels assembled (rough cut) and the picture shows real possibilities. I am hopeful that it is going to turn out to be pretty good after all.

Jack Warner ran the picture John Ford made, 'The Battle of Midway' for us yesterday. It is in two reels and will be playing in all the theatres. It is very thrilling and you will no doubt get a chance to see it.

It looks as though Colonel Warner will have to follow in Zanuck's footsteps and devote all his time to the Army. He expects to transfer over almost any day, but he has a good assistant who can keep things going. It is positively frightening the way we are losing men now; every time you turn around another chap has gone.

Frances is coming in this week for dinner. Mother had a nice talk with her on the 'phone yesterday and she is well and cheerful as usual.

Enclosed is copy of a letter we just received from Bill which will bowl you over. We are quite excited over his prospects; it looks as though his whole life, will be changed for the better as we are convinced he will never come back to the picture business. Margie is leaving to join him in about ten days and, judging by his letter, he is well set for the duration and doing the kind of work he was born to do and loves the most.

I understand you tried to get us on the telephone the evening we were both away. Do 'phone us again when you are in the mood and reverse the charges. We were so sorry to have missed your call.

By the way, here is a good suggestion: we will all be home Sunday night which is my birthday. Suppose you call me for a chat on Sunday evening.

Will write you again the end of the week and we look forward to your next letter. With all the best -

As ever, Dad

As Jesse noted in his letter, training films were a vital part of educating the new Army, and he was in the thick of it.

THE BELMONT PLAZA
Lexington Ave. and 40th St. New York City
September 9, 1942
Dearest Bess:

Your long nice letter cheered one of those occasional empty spaces that can come to one strongly in New York. I manage to keep fairly cheerful, In fact I am generally <u>too busy</u> to have time to know <u>how</u> I feel, but there are moments when the stress of this city seeps through into one's soul. I have been going to a few plays on free nights and much enjoy them. This and work is about all of life here.

Work is exciting! The new job seems to be growing rapidly. It abounds with difficulties of every nature but I like it. Colonel Gillette, our commanding officer, had a nice talk with me today and expressed pleasure with the way things are going. He also told me he hoped Dad would visit New York and tour the Astoria Post. Dad will certainly be amazed with the changes in his one-time studio. Hardly a thing is familiar. The Colonel can be extremely warm and friendly and he certainly was today.

My Job is amazing - I can't find its boundaries but it embraces everything connected with writers and scripts. I have a private telephone in my office now which is a singular distinction in the Army.

Will certainly try hard to get results, I can't feel that it is permanent. Nothing is. One of our most important officers is leaving for special training, and from there to - heaven knows where! But we are growing fast - training films are a vital part of educating the new Army.

... Tomorrow night is a farewell party to our Major - Stag event at the Sherry-Netherland Officers Club. Tonight I have studies and scripts to be read.

... Frances' letters are ever encouraging and full of cheer, the baby draws near and I can hardly believe it! I'm thrilled, and thrilled with the wonderful things you mention getting the 'essential layette' and the 'Bassinette' - I scarcely know the meaning of the words! But I'll learn them in December - Will come west for Xmas if possible, or soon after.

Your beautiful philosophy brings much happiness. Between this and Dad's Christian Science book, I shall be the most spiritually evolved soldier in the Army! This is a short hectic scrawl, but I wanted to chat, darling Bess, so will write more coherently next time.

Love,
Jess

September 12, 1942
Jess...

Although your birthday is not until next Saturday, I thought you wouldn't mind my recognizing it in advance because I wanted you to get my birthday present as I know you will need it for your winter outfit.

Enclosed is a check for $100.00 - with all my love and affection - and this is what I want you to do. I want to actually give you, for your birthday, your complete winter outfit, including shoes - so when you line up all your purchases, let me know the balance that you need and I will send you an additional check airmail. Please don't think I took your letter as a hint; I am only too glad to help as long as I can and as long as you need it.

...I think the decision to postpone your arrival until the Christmas holidays is wise. By that time the baby will be born and Frances will be up and about and you will have a much pleasanter time. As the blessed event draws nearer, Mother and I are as excited as you are over the advent of the beginning of another generation of Laskys - and I have an idea that this new generation will grow up into a much more peaceful and sane and happier world than the one we are living in now. While this present conflagration seems very terrible, I am utterly convinced that in the scheme of things, it is for eventual good and out of it will emerge a better world.

Frances and Margie are dining with us tomorrow night for my birthday . . . Another interesting thing has happened in the family. He is a fine looking chap - 24 years old; a Jew; about 5'11' tall; extremely well educated - he went to college in Palestine and speaks all kind of languages and Mother and I like him very much, so, while nothing has been settled, the probabilities are you will have a brother-in-law and one you will be proud of, before the war is many months older.

Now, a word about Mark Twain We have 80% of the picture assembled and what with intelligent editing and the addition of occasional scenes, it is coming to life and is going to be very fine...and while it is too soon to go overboard or express too much enthusiasm, I won't be surprised if it is a very fine picture and a popular success. If that should be the case, I will be awfully happy. Harry Chandlee has been helping us with little additional scenes and editing, and is also working on a new angle on the Boy Scout story. Harry is very helpful as we speak the same language.

I am also definitely committed to do 'Connecticut Yankee in King Arthur's Court' which I am really enthusiastic about. I am only waiting for a writer named Arthur Horman. He is finishing another script after which we will get ours underway. We have a great idea of taking a man of today, fully conscious of world events, back into King Arthur's Court. With a treatment like this, I sense a very timely picture as well as a novel and interesting one.

'Mark Twain' will probably be released about November 30th. I will go east for the world premiere, which may be Hannibal, Missouri, in which event I will visit for a day with Billy and then go to New York and try to plan so we can return on the train together, fitting my time with yours, if possible . . . we are doing some wonderful shots of Mark Twain's death and the materialization of his spirit as he meets Huck and Tom and their dog and walks with them into Infinity. We are liable to have one of the most inspiring endings ever seen in pictures—and this is a good place for me to end my letter.

All the best from All the Laskys—

P.S. I didn't mean to gyp you out of your 20 bucks this week so consider my gift as $80.00 and don't forget to send me the bill for the balance of your outfit.

Dad

Jesse found time to write every member of the family, this one to his sister, continuing the story of the motion picture industry's place in the war.

September 13, 1942
Dear Betty,

Some time has elapsed since receiving your nice letter but don't think I've forgotten you. Was much interested in the account of the Desert Battalion and also your persistent winged gentleman. Did he get his silver wings - and rejoin the Jerry command - and did you accept the engagement ring?

Well now, as you may have heard, I am an executive - my belly bulges against a fat desk - private telephone, name on the door: Lt. Jesse L. Lasky Jr. Officer-in-Charge Scenario Dept. I have in it some sixty or more people - Enlisted writers; civil service employees; secretaries; civilian writers; asst. project officers; non-commissioned officers; privates; assistants; Chief of Section, and even three commissioned officer writers, one of whom ranks me, being a Ist Lieut!!

My wall is covered with progress charts, graphs, etc., and I lead a wildly busy life interviewing, recommending transfers, hiring and firing - a confused, bedeviled and exciting life, while it lasts, for nothing in the Army is permanent, and I'm hoping that Dad comes to New York sometime while I'm still in this job. Of course if I can hold it long enough, I'll be in line for a promotion, though promotions in the Photographic Division of the Signal Corps are very rare unfortunately I'll explain why at length when I see you.

My real hope is to be sent for training and then shipped out with troops to some combat zone, but this is a difficult thing to get since the present work of training film production is tremendously important in the building of the vast armies and we are considered a lot more valuable doing this than we would be in the war zone. Still, a few officers have been sent out and my chance may come in the Spring.

I plan to request a ten-day furlough in December and will try and get home for Christmas and New Years. I'm thrilled at the near prospects of being a father - and though thirty-two years of existence will be my score by next Saturday, September 19th, I still don't look old enough to have an offspring.

Keep a sisterly eye on Donna whose cheerful happy letters are so encouraging.

Love to you, Jess

Lasky wrote to his eldest son, noting changes the war was making on the film industry.

September 18, 1942
Dear Jess,

This is Friday night—and I wish you were here to go with me.

Tomorrow is your Birthday and I trust you received my birthday letter which was written last Saturday . . . Frances is dining with us on Sunday - it will be Margery's last dinner as she leaves Tuesday to join Billy. She is going to motor to Camp Crowder and I think another soldier's wife is going with her and will share the expense. All reports from Billy's front indicates that he is very happy . . . Just think - some day the war will be over and there will be a get-together of all the Laskys - three ex-soldiers and three brides and the grandchild - what a reunion!

. . . We are losing men now very fast - producers, directors, writers, technical men, etc. The latest news is that Col. Warner has had to go over to the Army and give all of his time to the war job. Before he left for Washington, he asked me to take over an Errol Flynn picture - a wild melodrama out of the Adventure Magazine - about a Royal Mounted Police Officer's search for some escaped Nazi prisoners from a concentration camp in Northern Canada - sleds and dogs and snow and blood and thunder - the last yarn in the world I would ever choose for myself. Due to the fact that the studio is short of Producers, I could not refuse to make this picture - so I now have in preparation: the Errol Flynn picture; the Boy Scout picture; 'Connecticut Yankee in King Arthur's Court' and 'Winston Churchill'. We finish shooting the 'Mark Twain' picture Monday. In a couple of weeks I will be able to tell you more about it. We have a tough editing job ahead of us . . . We have many interesting visitors at the studio these days. Today we had an Admiral from the Navy and two British Generals, the latter had just come from the desert inspecting our tank troops around Indio, Calif., and were burned to a crisp. I took them out on the set and had a very interesting talk with them.

And there were changes to Jesse's position.

September 25, 1942
Dear Jesse,

. . . Congratulations! Congratulations!! and Congratulations!!!

I don't remember ever being more thrilled than when Mother 'phoned me about your wire which notified us that you had been promoted to the rank of First Lieut. That is making good with a vengeance. Keep up the good work and you will come out of this war at least a Captain.

Met a Lieutenant on the lot yesterday who said he left you in Long Island two days ago. He said you had made good in a big way and was there when you were promoted, in fact, he mentioned that you were his superior officer... Due to the story in Variety and the Reporter - it was on the first page of the Reporter - and the second page of Variety - a number of people have spoken to me about your promotion.

... We finished shooting 'Mark Twain' and as Col. Warner gets back from the east on Sunday, I am showing it to him at his house on Sunday night, minus montages, inserts, etc., which have not yet been completed.

... Margery is due to reach Camp Crowder and - hold your breath - the latest news from Bill is that he is singing in a choir in the local church.

I had some fine reproductions made of your two heads, larger than the original and they are simply splendid. I am having then framed for my office and Betty has two in her room; Mother has two in her room - also Grandma was sent two of them - so you are well distributed through the family. I also sent Billy one of your photographs. He seems to be extremely proud of his brother, the First Lieutenant...

This will hand you a laugh. I took my examination to get a driver's license this morning; flopped on the first one and had to take a second exam, before I could pass, but I got my license and am now independent of chauffeurs. What a feeling of relief it gives one although we will keep our present chauffeur until he is drafted or until we get gas rationing which is in the cards in the not distant future....

October 2, 1942

... I bet two-to-one that the Yankees would win the first game of the World Series and also participated in a pool on the first game - and won both my bets, so I am increasing my bribe this week to $25.00.

Well, I ran 'Mark Twain' for Mother and Alan LeMay and his wife and several others last Saturday night, without inserts or about 1,000 feet of montages that were not ready; no music; no sound or sound effects - and, in spite of all this stuff being missing, the picture made a fine impression. Alan was very pleased with the way we had handled it and Mother was thrilled. The following night, Sunday, Jack Warner returned from the east and I ran it at his house in the same condition for him, his assistant and the chief cutter of the studio, and they also liked the picture very much.

At last I dare tell you I think we are going to have a really fine picture and I am very happy over the outcome. It will be nearly two months before the montages are in and the musical score has been done, and the picture finished.

Jack Warner is going in the Army on full time duty and will be stationed in Washington, so he held a dinner the other night at which all the Producers were present – and, during the course of his talk, he said: 'You know, we all have to make sacrifices and that is why I am doing my part.' Then he turned to me and said: 'Look, here's Jesse – his two sons are in the Army and others of you have sons in the Army' – and we checked up and found that several of the men had one son each in the Amy – but I led with my two, and felt quite proud.

I am enclosing some additional publicity and I must say you have been mentioned many times this week on account of this publicity, and the word seems to have gone abroad that you have made good in a big way, and the men here say that your heading the scenario department at the Astoria Signal Corps Photographic Center is a great honor and great experience. I am sure you will come out of this war with more prestige than when you went into it and I can underwrite all the writing jobs you want at Warners.

... As I write this, I am looking at your picture which adorns a prominent spot in my office, and everyone who comes in the office admires it, so you are constantly before me.

I secured my driver's license over a week ago and now drive to and from the studio; in fact, I have not used the chauffeur since. Yesterday we bought a Chevrolet 1941, convertible top, for Mother and she is practicing driving as we expect to be without a chauffeur any day now and will not attempt engage a new one as, with the coming gas rationing, we won't do much superfluous driving anyway. I find I enjoy driving and it seems now as though I had been driving all my life.

Betty is making plans for a very quiet wedding in December, although, naturally, things are uncertain until we see what happens to Buddy (Barasch) in Florida, but it won't be long now before the old folks will be alone – but if we know that you and the others are getting along well, that is all the happiness we need. . . .

October 9, 1942

... I foresee real difficulties ahead in making good pictures but we will have to make the best of everything and, somehow or other, one can always manage and can overcome handicaps when they have to be overcome. . . .

'Mark Twain' looks good. Our montage and inserts are gradually appearing from the various departments and are being incorporated in the picture so that, in about two weeks, it will be ready for the music department. We still have to squeeze five or six hundred feet out of it which is difficult because the picture now seems very tight and plays very well ... How strange to find Mannie Cohen in the Army; your account of your meeting with him proved both interesting and amusing. Give him my best regards when next you see him. . . . .

Although Mannie Cohen had let Lasky down badly when he was ousted from Paramount, it was typical of Lasky's philosophy not to harbor ill feelings.

October 16, 1942
Dear Jesse,

...We are making the most of the weekends because when gas rationing becomes effective next month, all pleasure driving will be out; as a matter of fact no one knows here just how we are going to manage with limited gas rationing, but we will cross that bridge when we come to it, and try to enjoy ourselves in the meantime.

If you haven't heard from Billy, here's some news. He was transferred from Camp Crowder, Missouri to Camp Robinson, Arkansas, into the Medical Research Training Corps, and the day after he arrived, he was called out of line and promoted to a Corporal and I understand has been hard at work drilling rookies ever since, Enclosed is a letter from him written apparently the day before he was made a Corporal.

I haven't seen Frances this week although I had a nice talk with her on the telephone yesterday. She said the doctor doesn't expect the baby for about three weeks. I loaned Grandma our car and this gave her an opportunity to visit with Frances yesterday afternoon, which she did, and Grandma was very much impressed with Frances' neighbor who is helping her so much.

Betty is wearing her engagement ring and seems to be very busy with, her U.S.O. and other activities. Tomorrow she is taking two busloads of girls to a camp deep in the desert many miles beyond Indio. The tales she tells when she returns from these trips are amazing, and somewhat depressing. The boys who are being trained for desert warfare are going through a physical ordeal that is indescribable and, as they never see a petticoat, when these girls arrive you can imagine their excitement.

By the way, Mother and I visited the U.S.O. in Indio last Sunday while at Palm Springs and it was an interesting experience. Mother took along books, fresh vegetables, a crate of lemons, etc. If you could see a hot dismal town like Indio, and the boys on leave walking around looking for fun where none exists, you would appreciate more your luck in being stationed in a big city. When I think how well situated you are and how wonderful things have broken for Billy, I am truly grateful.

...We have decided not to undertake the Churchill picture for the present; it is too dangerous as it would mean an enormous investment and no one knows what the world's attitude toward Churchill will be a year from now. It really is a subject for after the war, if Churchill survives and comes out the great figure he is at present.

... As I dictate this to Randy, we are both wondering what the outcome of the great battle now raging in the Solomons will be. I pray to heaven it will be a decisive victory for our side. ...

The Philippines had fallen to General MacArthur in May of 1942, followed by a series of stunning victories for the Americans. At Midway, U.S. forces sank four Japanese carriers, allowing them to take the offensive in the Pacific. By August they attacked Guadalcanal and the battle was still raging as Lasky wrote of it.

Jesse was as yet unaware of how soon he would be involved in the crucial island-hopping attacks being led by MacArthur.

October 22, 1942
Dear Jesse,

 ... Frances was in for dinner last night. She is looking and feeling fine and we had a very pleasant evening. Mother picked her up in our car as we still have a chauffeur hanging around - although he will leave the end of the week - and Mother also took her home.

 ... It is evident that Julius Evans will be drafted before the end of November so I have decided to take as his successor, Carl Dudley, who says he knows you well. He worked with Jack Chertok at Metro and is related to your former writing partner at Republic. Please let me know what you think of him, as it is important I do not make a mistake, but he sounds like just what the doctor ordered ... I have a writer started on 'Connecticut Yankee' which will probably be my next picture. I also have a story in preparation for Errol Flynn but due to his trouble[65], no doubt you have read about it, he may not be here, so this story, which is being written for him may have to be laid aside. Incidentally, the studio is loading me with scripts to read - productions that have been abandoned by other producers after first drafts were finished, so I am plenty busy.

 ... We are all dreading gas rationing but we don't know the actual details yet - how much gas we will be allowed, etc. The rationing doesn't start until about November 22nd.

 ... Tomorrow night I am taking a table at the famous Hollywood Canteen. Each night they have what they call an 'Angels Table' which they sell for $100 and I am the 'Angel' tomorrow (Friday) night. . . . .

And with all the film subjects Lasky thought he might be doing next, a new one appeared which seemed to be leading the rest.

---

65 The swashbuckling film star's illeged sexual assault of two underage girls.

October 29, 1942

Last Monday, Col. Levinson brought several officers to lunch and one of than - a Colonel from Washington who is in charge of your outfit - when he was introduced to me, spoke up and said in a loud voice so everybody could hear him: 'Mr. Lasky, I want to compliment you on your son, Lieut. Lasky. He is a fine boy and a fine officer - so good that we recently promoted him; as a matter of fact, he and I speak the same language. I wanted to change the method of making certain pictures so that we would talk the language of the soldiers, and when I conferred with Lieut. Lasky, I found that he had the same idea and was eager to do the very thing I thought should be done. We are very proud of that boy and I want you to know that he has the respect of all of us.'

Well, my boy, this was said loud enough so that the entire executive staff heard him; in fact, it embarrassed me and I think I blushed . . . I am very proud as I constantly hear from different fellows such swell reports of you and your work.

. . . The Government has passed a law, effective immediately that if, during 1942, you have made a net of $25,000 or more (which means between $64,000 and $67,000) then no more salary will be paid you for the rest of the year, regardless of contracts, etc. This means that a lot of us will receive no more salary for the balance of the year. The order means that from October 27th, you will not be permitted to earn more than a net of $25,000 during any one year, until the Presidential order is rescinded. Of course, no business or industry is hit as hard by the order as the motion picture business, whose salaries are higher because the salary life of a motion picture wage earner is shorter than any other industry. It is all very confusing and somewhat drastic, but, strange to say, it has not depressed me in the slightest. We can manage beautifully; in other words, if this is to be our contribution to the war, Mother and I are ready to make the necessary sacrifices in our personal comfort and adjust our affairs accordingly. We have already had to turn in our four almost new extra tires, by order of the Government, and in a few weeks gas rationing begins - and without much gas and without a chauffeur, we are certainly going to have to live simply, I would not be surprised if we ended up by taking a little place in Hollywood where we could see an occasional picture, have an occasional meal in a restaurant and enough gas for me to go to and from the studio. From what we know now I will only get four gallons a week which would allow me two round trips from home.

Of course we will double up with other fellows living in our neighborhood, but it is going to be difficult, as we will all have to leave at the same time in the morning and return at the same time in the evening and once we are home, we will have to stay home. Betty and Mother will use the buses a lot and the rest of the time will have to remain home. So you see we are all beginning to share the burden of the war which, of course, is as it should be.

... next week I am making a transcription which will be short-waved to our armed forces in every part of the world, I am telling fourteen minutes of human interest stories about the movies; the early days in Hollywood and stories about the Sergeant York picture....

I am all excited about 'Rhapsody in Blue' - the life of George Gershwin, and am trying to get Mamoulian to direct it - and I just finished a long conference with Sonya Levien who will undoubtedly write it. We already have a script of 350 pages written by Clifford Odets. I think we have an angle on the story, and it can be one of the finest musical pictures ever made.

'Mark Twain' won't be released until long after the first of the year and that is the reason that I am not making any plans to come east now. There is a slight possibility of a quick trip almost immediately as Loyd Wright[66] is working on a plan to try and save me some taxes and will go to Washington to confer with the powers-that-be, and may want me to go with him, in which event I will see you in New York. I will let you know about this very soon - it is only a chance, but we shall see.

When you get your furlough, by all means take the plane. You are sure to save a couple of days even if you are put off enroute.

If you see Carl Dudley again, try and size him up as an all-around assistant: contacting all departments, functioning in every respect as an Associate Producer - and then let me know whether you think he has the proper qualifications. This is an important move and I don't want to make a mistake.

I started this letter yesterday. Went to the Fights last night and had a wonderful evening; sat next to Eddie Cantor and lost, as usual...I am running 'Mark Twain' for the last time with the cutter who has been away ill. The picture will be ready for previewing in a few weeks and it looks mighty promising.....

Lasky was cautious. In his bones, he could feel he had a winner; however, he was already gearing up mentally for the next exciting project. He had found an ideal home for his talent at Warner Brothers.

In the late '20s George Gershwin had been a regular visitor at the Lasky's New York apartment, and Bess had even given him painting lessons. That the producer knew him so well was part of his excitement of planning to make this film. He kept Jess abreast of his news; the taxes and the government restriction on his earnings.

November 7, 1942
Dear Jesse,

---

[66] Lasky's California lawyer.

...I appreciate your style in writing; you can make the dullest things interesting due to your definite ability as a colorful writer. I make it a rule usually to have Randy read your letters, as he is one of the family, and then I mail them on to Grandma - so you see your literary efforts are appreciated and your circulation has at least three paid subscribers.

It is now lunch time in the studio, and the most beautiful day that one could imagine - a typical sunny California day, I shall have lunch and then either go to a football game or to Edgar Selwyn's for the afternoon.

Attended the Fights last night and had a swell evening, although I lost five bucks to Preston Sturges and five bucks to Dave Butler, nevertheless, I am going to enclose you an extra $5.00 because I sense how much you need this extra change to make life bearable in New York. You don't have to tell me how expensive New York is. When I used to do a couple of night clubs in an evening, with drinks, it was nothing to consume $25.00.

By the way, everyone was scared stiff by a Wage Stabilization ruling that no more salaries would be paid for the balance of the year to those who had earned a certain sum this year, however, the ruling has been rescinded so that I will get my salary every week, as usual. This is a great relief - although, in the end, the Government would get it in taxes anyway and it would not make much difference in my final financial condition, which is too complicated to attempt to explain.

You will be interested to know that the Warner Company estimated that my share of 'Sergeant York' will be well over $1,000,000.00 of which over $600,000 will be paid to me this year - which means that if we were in normal times I could have retired, having made one more fortune. As things are, however, the taxes will take practically all of the money and I will have nothing left but enough to live on and a very slight surplus. What a world! - and yet I thank God every day for all our blessings and do not worry or complain about having made and given up in one year another great fortune. When I can give you the full details, it will make the best chapter in our whole book. How many men at 62 can make over $1,000,000.00 in one year. Randy estimates that I will probably pay the largest income tax of any executive or actor in the picture business, not excepting Louis B. Mayer. This means that my tax will be so large that I will be one of the top ten men in the United States who is paying the Government huge taxes.

Col. Levinson left for New York yesterday. He may visit Astoria; if he does, make it your business to look him up. He is a great friend of mine and has expressed himself as being proud of your record, which I still can see you don't fully realize - but you have explained why very clearly in your letter.

I had a nice afternoon at Ira Gershwin's house yesterday discussing the details of George's life and getting his support and help on the picture, which is the most difficult undertaking imaginable - more difficult than York or

Twain - but if I can achieve what I see in it, it will be one of the great musical pictures of all time, and it is a cinch it will cost over $2,000,000.00 ... I am glad Billy sent you his picture; when you think of him, see him as the happiest soldier in Uncle Sam's Army, because his letters just glow with enthusiasm and confidence. Of course, having Margie with him makes his life complete.

... By the way, we are all thrilled over the news of the great desert victory over Rommel. Maybe that will prove the turning point in the war. ...

It is worth noting that General Rommel, called by the British 'The Desert Fox' because of his great skill at desert warfare, and known to the Germans as Hitler's esteemed 'People's Marshal', was finally defeated by British General Montgomery at El Alamein in 1942. Hitler had him immediately recalled from his post before his corps was wiped out in May. But when in July of 1944, he was implicated in the plot to kill Hitler, he was ordered to take poison to avoid standing trial, and thus destroying his heroic image to the German people. Meanwhile, the war in Hollywood moved forward with little inconveniences.

Liberty Magazine was quick to note Hollywood's share in the war in a key article, 'They Fight with Films'. Lasky was proud that both his sons were serving, and that Jesse was part of the film industry's particular contribution, and despite restrictions on almost every sector of film making, Lasky was producing some of his best films.

November 13, 1942
Dear Jesse,

... our gas rationing has been postponed until December 1st which gives us another brief breathing spell and was most welcome news to everybody.

Col. Warner is out of uniform, he having been retired after doing the work the Army wanted him to do. I am going with him tonight to a preview of Desert Song.

... Betty is getting excited as the time for Buddy's return approaches - he is due here in about three weeks. She has been shopping all week for her trousseau, and I do so hope everything will work out for her the way she wants it. She seems awfully young and inexperienced to live away from home as the wife of a young officer, but that is probably the way it will work out as Buddy will want her to live near whatever camp he is stationed.

... Thursday night I went over to Cecil's house and we ran a picture 'I Married a Witch' (Fredric March and Veronica Lake), directed by Rene Clair, and I enjoyed it very much. Charles Bennett was there and asked to be remembered to you. He is working on 'Dr. Wassell' with Cecil. ...

By the way, one of our executives just phoned that there is a nice mention of you and me in this week's issue of Liberty, November 21st, in an article entitled 'They Fight with Films'. They are sending over a copy to me but be sure you buy one in New York if you have not already seen the article - and as it is all about Long Island, it is possible you have already seen it...

Loyd Wright, my attorney, left today for New York and Washington to discuss my tax problem with the Government. There is just a chance that something may be saved from the wreck. Keep your fingers crossed and pray as you never prayed before, because if Loyd Wright can put over what he is after, it will mean everything in the world to the Lasky family. I will let you know how things come out...By the way, I made such a hit at the Hollywood Canteen as Officer-of-the-Day that they persuaded me to act in the same capacity next Monday night. It is a thrilling experience and during your furlough I am going to take you in to give it the once-over. Being an officer, you would not be allowed to mingle with the boys, but I brought in Zukor and another naval officer when I was on duty and the Officer-of-the-Day is permitted to admit anyone he pleases....

Sonya Levien is hard at work on the Gershwin story; although it is almighty tough, it interests me more than my other stories. We are starting our first draft screenplay of Connecticut Yankee, and are about two weeks away from the exciting preview of 'Mark Twain'. I will wire you what I hope will be good news after the preview.

The other day the Hays Office reviewed the picture, with music of course, for the usual censorship purposes, and after they screened the picture, they all liked it so much that they sat around talking about it for some time; and later, Geoffrey Shurlock[67] sneaked to a telephone and told me most enthusiastically that I had another hit....

Much of the job of making training films was top secret. The Army recognized the importance of actual filmmakers doing this job, and Jesse had been thrown into the thick of it. He was beginning to recognize the weight on his shoulders in providing training for service men to wage war. In this next letter, Jesse calls it 'the biggest film organization in the history of the world.' The title, *'They Fight with Films'* was apt.

Nov. 15, 1942
Dear Dad:

I've managed to borrow a typewriter from the hotel so that I can give a late answer to your wonderful letter received earlier in the week ... There is so much to talk about that I scarcely know where to begin. In the first place Lt. Col. Lanham was here from Washington and spoke of enjoying meeting with you on the coast. I had long talks with him and even told him my heart burning desire to get into the war zone, overseas ... He said that I was too valuable in this work to be moved, but sympathized heartily with my anxiety

---

67 Production manager who was to become head of the Motion Picture Production Code.

to see at least a fringe of the actual war. He said if he had a regiment he'd take me as a G2 in a minute, but right now my services here were of tremendous importance and my work is becoming well known and thought of in many quarters. We are very close friends, and I admire the fire-eating West Pointer very much. He left next day for Washington again, but not before having told me things that bulged my eyes, and things which began to happen right after he left. I'll tell you as much as isn't secret about all the things that are going on.

As you probably had gathered there was a terrific struggle for power between our post and certain other groups, one of which we shall call a west coast crowd under a man whose name has been connected with polo. Well, our Colonel Gilette seems to have won everything and we are now the sole producing agency for the U.S. Army and every branch! We will prepare every scenario and such pictures as cannot be made by this outfit will be farmed out and produced under our complete supervision. You realize this makes us the biggest film organization in the history of the world, and the implications are tremendous. It means expansion on a scale undreamed! I have had many talks with Colonel Gilette alone last week, and my guess is that he will soon be a general. We are very close, and I know he trusts and depends on me in fact he has told me this.

I have been working closely with a Dr. Arnspiger who is the Vice President of Erpi and a man of tremendous importance in the field of visual education. Col. Gillete has assigned me to work with him on a big program of educational courses to train the writers who will soon be coming in to meet the demands of our vastly increasing program. Dr. Arnspiger is an important educator, aside from being an executive of Erpi and many other affiliations and the work with him has been thrilling. We hit it off very well, and he praises me so highly to the Colonel that I find myself blushing. If it weren't for the sixth months period needed in each grade I honestly believe I'd be a captain right now!

You must understand that as head of writers and the scenario dept. I will soon be responsible for several hundred men including officers, civilians and enlisted men. The training of these men to write training films is a big field in itself, and we've had to plan a course, lectures, and faculty to cope with it. Also the space problem enters the picture and my guess is that we'll soon have a floor of some big building in New York, just for this dept!

In line with all this excitement and sudden growth you won't be surprised to hear that I now have a personal assistant, a brilliant young 2nd Lt. O'Harra fresh out of officers school, and formerly head of Columbia's East Coast story Dept. Well Dad, who would have dreamed that I'd ever be thrown into an executive job!

Last night Major Lord took me to dinner and we went to a picture together. Carl Dudley who is a good friend of his also had dinner with us. I like Dudley very much, and he might well have the qualities you need. I think he has a good grasp of the technical side of pictures and would also be a very pleasant fellow to have around. I'm very fond of Major Lord and of course we are working together as he was connected with signing many writers who will soon arrive.

Lt. Col. Sloane and some other officers have left for the coast and you may see him out there. Looks as though we'll have a big setup out there as well as in other spots, so who knows, I may yet manage a trip west in line of duty. Whether I do or not, the furlough will be applied for just as soon as I hear from Frances that Baby has safely arrived. This is stretching out into a long time of waiting and I'm trying not to be worried as they say first babies are often late. I shall plan to leave around the nineteenth of December and be home for Christmas. Will travel by air if I can get reservations, or otherwise take the Super Chief. Its faintly possible I may make this trip under orders which would be marvelous, but if I don't, I'll need financial help on the ticket situation. We'll call that my Christmas present if you are agreeable. Will let you know more about the trip as soon as I hear the baby news. I'm superstitious about applying for the leave before hearing the news, also seeing the baby will be given as one of the reasons for the trip. How thrilling it will be to see you all again. Can't think of any greater excitement on earth.

Show this letter to Frances and Bess and Grandma, but the news about our activities should not be discussed with anyone else. It's not secret or I wouldn't tell you, but nevertheless there are many reasons why it would be very bad to say anything about it outside the immediate family, so please be careful about this.

Well, Dad its a tough week ahead, and in addition to the many activities I will be officer of the day with gun and flashlight again tomorrow. I have to go to bed very early every night as it requires strength and sleep to cope with the things that are happening. Will write Betty very soon also her Buddy. I've meant to do this a thousand times but always too busy or exhausted for anything. Someday I'll be able to describe the job and you'll understand. Love to Bess, Betty, Grandma, and I know you are in close touch with Frances. . . .

Affectionately your overworked but so active young exec of a former poet,
Jess

November 20, 1942
Dear Jesse:

I just put down the 'phone after having a long chat with Frances. She said she feels normal in every way and so there is no news yet as to when the Lasky offspring is to arrive. When she saw the Doctor Tuesday, he said the baby might come within a week but was not sure...

Incidentally, she mentioned that she thought it best for you to come two months after the baby is born. I suppose she wants to be up and about and well so as to fully enjoy your visit. Let us know what you decide....

We are becoming very excited over Betty's approaching marriage. Buddy will have only four days leave of absence; he graduates as a 2nd Lieut. on December 9th and has to go to Brooks Field, San Antonio, Texas, for further training, but at the end of eight or ten weeks, I forget which, he will be promoted to a First Lieut., and then hopes to be stationed with the Ferry Command on the Coast....Buddy will fly from Miami, Florida, to Phoenix. We will meet there on December 10th, have a quick marriage by the Justice of the Peace, and they will leave by train on the night of the 11th, arriving at San Antonio on the morning of the 13th...Betty is...a little awed at the prospect of arriving in a strange city, San Antonio, and eventually getting an apartment and setting up housekeeping - but she is learning very fast and has developed a lot of latent ability that we never realized she possessed...'

Some of the 'Connecticut Yankee' screenplay has come through and looks very promising—and Sonya is plugging along on the Gershwin story which, of course, is very difficult. Jack Warner told me yesterday that he is going to give me Michael Curtiz to direct it, and if you saw 'Yankee Doodle Dandy', you know what a fine director Curtiz is.

Loyd Wright is in New York and will be meeting with the powers-that-be in Washington by the time you receive this letter. If the matter is settled favorably - and I have the strangest faith that it is going to be—I will send you a wire; anyway, by the time I write you next Friday, we will know the best or the worse. What a dramatic situation—as what happens in Washington may mean a mere $500,000 for me—so if you ever prayed, my lad, pray for the successful outcome of Wright's trip to Washington....

November 27, 1942

...You will be interested to learn that Billy called up yesterday to tell us that he is transferred to the Army Hospital in Denver, Colorado, and that he was made a Corporal with a 'T' on his sleeve, which I suppose means Technician. He was very much excited as he believes Denver will be a wonderful place for his further training. Margie leaves by automobile today, and Billy leaves by train on Sunday—so his problems are solved for a while. I think he said he will be there for ten weeks.

Bob Lord arrived yesterday and immediately called Frances and told her that he considered you—in fact you are generally considered—the best officer in the outfit and, by far, the most popular with the rest of the outfit....

Col. Levinson called me the day he got back and told me that he had seen you and that you were looking fine and full of pep, and said that you were making good in a big way. If all they tell me is true—and I am sure it is—you have at last hit your stride. The thing I see for you, when you get back is to become a Producer, and I will underwrite getting you a production to do right in this studio. It seems that the best Producers are those who can work with their writers and who can write themselves. For instance, we have Robert Buckner and Jerry Wald—two writers who are now Producers in this studio and they have both made good —so you ought to feel very optimistic over your future prospects when the war is over.

Frances is still waiting. She told me this morning on the 'phone that the doctor said it would probably be next week before we could expect any news.

In case you have not heard, Tony Quinn[68] had another daughter. You might, want to write him a letter; enclosed is a little article referring to it.

After dinner on Thanksgiving I took Betty and Jane Allen to see Jack Benny in 'George Washington Slept Here', as I have practically decided to use Jack Benny for 'Connecticut Yankee'. Our script is coming along in splendid shape; we have over one-fourth of it in excellent screenplay already finished... Our gas rationing starts Tuesday and we are all terrified by the prospect of this new ruling, although I have just been assured that I will get a 'B' ration card next week which, in addition to my 'A' card which I already have, will give me another four gallons a week. After much effort, Randy just secured a three gallon empty can which we are going to keep full of gas in my car. This empty can was more difficult to secure than front seats at a championship fight. Whoever thought we would be fighting for Gasoline as we never fought for liquor.

Some of the boys in the studio have bought little Austin cars and we look at them with the same eyes of envy that they used to look at me when I would arrive in America with a new English Rolls Royce. I tell you, my boy, the world is changing right under our eyes. What a period to live through! I am so grateful for the breaks that you and Billy have received... I appreciate just how you feel about not being able to get over into the thick of things on the other side. If I were in your place, I would feel exactly the same—but I am glad it is not up to you—and my paternal feeling gives thanks to God and prays that you will never be permitted to get in it.

I was so interested in your description of how you had to prepare a course for the civilian writers. You must feel like a veteran when you stand in front of these newcomers.

We all send love -

---

68 Anthony Quinn married DeMille's adopted daughter Katherine, with whom Jesse grew up. They became lifelong friends.

P.S. I will be happy to send Christmas Cards to any Officers whose names you may give me—for instance: your roommate Hopper; Col. Gillette; Col. Lanham, Washington, etc.—so send me a long list of names and addresses.

Jesse had worried that he would not be able to be with Frances when the baby was born. No one had expected any problems, because Frances had seemed so cheerful and so well throughout the months of pregnancy. Then suddenly, the baby was stillborn. His father, who had tried to phone him the sad news, wrote.

December 4, 1942
Dear Jesse,

    We tried to get you on the 'phone last night but could not get a clear line and so finally wired you instead. Mother spent more than an hour with Frances and found her feeling so well and in such fine spirits that we felt we could explain it to you better over the 'phone than by wire.

    Frances accepted the situation very philosophically, the doctor having told her before Mother arrived. The doctor also told Frances that he had wired you. Frances said she felt so well that she would probably write you a letter, and she understood that we had telephoned you - so there is nothing more to be done now but to put the matter out of your mind, and devote your full energies to your duties until you come out here.

    There is not the slightest cause to worry about Frances - she was almost sitting up. She has a nice room and has had a special nurse to take care of her. Mother is writing you today and giving you full particulars. We have all accepted the situation philosophically and I am sure, knowing- you as I do, that you are doing the same.

    As to your coming out here, there is no occasion at all to rush out now. My suggestion is that if it is convenient, you try to arrive for the Christmas Holidays. On the other hand, if Frances suggests that you wait a little longer so that she will be stronger - take her advice. It would be mighty jolly, however, if it turns out that you can spent Christmas with the family, or what's left of it. . . .

December 22, 1942

    . . . It is Tuesday morning and I have just reached the studio as our train from San Antonio was thirteen hours late. My first and immediate thought is to mail your Christmas present, which is enclosed herewith. I want this to be a happy Christmas for you and Frances, and I will tell her on Christmas morning of this gift which, of course, is to you both.

    . . .I want you to know that I am sending Billy and Margy the same gift as the enclosed and that I gave Betty and Buddy a check for $1,000.00 for a wedding present.

Mother and I will miss you this Christmas but we will be happy in the thought that we were enabled to contribute materially to your joy on this historical Christmas.

Please, God - the war will be over or near a successful finish by next Christmas, and my hope is that we can all be together a year from today.

P.S. If you can get through on the 'phone Christmas morning, 'phone me Collect.

Jesse managed to get a compassionate leave to visit Frances, but was not allowed to stay for Christmas. Frances was depressed but put on a brave face. But Jesse missed seeing his parents, who had gone to San Antonio, Texas to see that Betty was properly married. From this leave, Jesse was assigned directly to Dallas, where he received this letter from his father, who was back at Warner Brothers.

December 24, 1942
Dear Jesse,

... It is Christmas Eve and I just came from the dining room where Jack Chertok[69] was telling the boys how he met you in Dallas. He made quite a story out of your meeting and I got a great kick out of hearing about Lieut. Lasky as Jack told the story. He is a swell fellow and admires you enormously.

... On Tuesday evening I picked up Grandma and we had a long visit with Frances. Spent over two hours with her, during which she told me all about your visit; how happy she was - and I told her all about Betty's wedding. Frances was looking and feeling splendid and, incidentally, she gave me the lovely letter you left for me which made me understand how you feel and which made me very happy.

With the family all away, Mother and I will spend a quiet Christmas. We are going to visit with Frances tomorrow, Christmas Day. Mother sent her a lovely gift and I told her my Christmas gift to you was, of course, also to her - I refer to the body-blow check.

Needless to say we shall miss you tomorrow but we are happy in the thought that you are doing so well and making us so proud of you. Just exchanged Christmas Greetings with Cecil on the 'phone and he sends you his best.

Will write you a more coherent letter next week—but I wanted to get the bribe off in this mail.

With affectionate greetings, Dad

---

[69] Chertok was to produce the critically acclaimed film *The Corn is Green* in 1945. He later become a successful TV producer.

Having had a taste of home, seeing his bride again and sharing the loss of their child, Jesse tried to imagine what the future might hold for them. He wrote to his 'ethereal' Bess, whom he always treated like a fragile child—one who must never be indulged with too much reality.

December 30, 1942
Dearest Bess:

The beautiful card - with that magnificent tie and socks just arrived. These are most useful gifts, and the words on your card were aimed squarely at the beast. It is a busy and yet lonesome time, and I will be glad when the holidays are over as I know, will you. It must have seemed a strangely lonesome Christmas with the family scattered like salt - about the country. We can hope that the next one will see at least some of us together. These are strange times, and there is little to hang on to, but the love of each other. I shall be happy when Frances can join me in New York - have spotted an apartment that will be perfect - I know how much I miss her now, and this sloppy hotel existence would hardly be bearable unless I were certain that she'd arrive with the signs of Spring.

How much I appreciated all the things of home - and home itself. Every tree - the sun shining through our curtains into our rooms - the shelves of books, pipes, pictures, furniture - all the implementation of a happiness that I had hardly appreciated, but once seen, know how much I missed it - With Frances in New York, we can build a temporary world.

In the meantime I shall keep busy, an easy matter from dawn to dusk. How I loved your description of the wedding - I could live though every moment, what a splendid stage manager Dad became - he really is wonderful - and it takes a lifetime to appreciate him. Well, I'm proud in my bright new socks and tie. Louise gave me a scarf for Christmas, and my roommate did too, so I shall have the best-dressed throat in New York. Dear Bess, what a wild breakfast we had in the sun - I'll never forget it.

Donna tells me of a beautiful gift to her from you - you've kept Christmas alive for us - and next year the war may be near enough over so that we can see some clear vista of our future lives -

Love to my wonderful Bess.
Jess

Lasky and his wife had become 'best friends' with the children away, and while he was no longer the highflier studio executive, as a producer he was creating the sort of films he loved. Keeping up with the times, he had bought a little Austin car and had rediscovered the love of driving for himself.

December 31, 1942
Dear Jesse,

...Last night with two or three people we ran the first finished print of Mark Twain...I had Mother see it and she thinks it is one of the finest things she has ever seen on the screen. The others were equally enthusiastic and there are indications that we have an outstanding picture of supreme importance - a super feature - that is bound to cause favorable comment. I don't want to compare it with 'Sergeant York' - but the last ten minutes of 'Mark Twain' are as fine as anything you have ever seen and will leave the audience choked up with emotion and in a mood that will stay with them for many hours.

Through consistently driving my little Austin, I have saved enough gas for Mother and me to go to Palm Springs this afternoon. She is going to remain there quietly for two weeks as she needs a rest and quiet - and I will remain until Sunday night. We plan to have a quiet dinner when we arrive, and spend the New Year's Eve in bed reading. This will be a new experience for me - I don't want you to think I have slowed up, but after our strenuous experience in San Antonio, a few days spent conservatively and quietly, will also do me good. ..We are plugging away on Gershwin and Connecticut Yankee....

January 8, 1943

...Mother telephoned me last night from Palm Springs and said she was feeling so well and rested and, incidentally, so lonesome, that she wanted me to come down tonight and bring her home Sunday night - so I am rather looking forward to driving down this evening all by my lonely - having a nice dinner and a cocktail along the road, and playing the radio. After torturing myself all week in the little Austin; having every car pass me on the road; going up hills at about 12 miles an hour - my Cadillac which I will use tonight, is a real joy.

Had a nice visit with Frances Wednesday evening. She is beginning to make plans for getting away March 1st. She is up all day now and there are no signs of the invalid as far as her external appearance is concerned. Monday night I am going to take her a nice selection of avocados, some of which she can share with her neighbor.

...Bill is making a valiant struggle to pass very difficult examinations in competition with older men who have had fine college training. Enclosed is copy of a letter just received from Betty which will show you how she is maturing; it is hard for me to realize that Betty is married and on her own far away in a strange city.

I have seats for the opening of 'In Which We Serve'[70], January 27th, and look forward to seeing it. The other night I saw 'Random Harvest' which you surely do not want to miss - it is a fine picture.

---

70 Directed by Noël Coward and David Lean. War film about a British destroyer.

Things have been quiet at the studio. Am getting very excited over the possibilities of the Gershwin picture, which can be made into a terrific box-office attraction. I wish I could find someone more interesting than John Garfield to play Gershwin - talk this bit of casting over with some of your friends - they might suggest someone I have not thought of.

I rather dread the 'Connecticut Yankee' subject but I suppose it will all work out in the wash.

Had a wire from Jack Warner telling me that he ran 'Mark Twain' for the executives in New York and they pronounced it a <u>very important picture</u>. We are holding up the preview until he returns, in about ten days, as there is no rush to preview it seeing it cannot be released for several months on account of a backlog of several pictures dealing with the war which must be put out as soon as possible.

I went to the preview with Hal Wallis of Howard Hawks' picture 'Air Force' and it is magnificent, except for the ending which they are re-editing and which I imagine will eventually be all right. That is another picture you will want to see when it is released.

How I wish you were not in the Army at this moment. I would grab you, if you would agree, as my assistant and associate producer and, in a year or so, I could step out of the picture and you could carry on the Lasky Productions. As a matter of fact, when the war is over, what would you think of the idea of joining up with me, if I am still in the business, as my associate producer, which means that you could supervise the writers and collaborate on scripts, as well as produce - we would have a lot of fun and you would find yourself a top a producer in a year. If you like the idea, pray a little hard for the war to end - and keep working hard to maintain the prestige which you have achieved in the industry through your Long Island activities.

I hope you heard or read the President's speech - I thought it was very fine. . . .

With Hollywood's place in the war efforts well established—to enable the reader to be aware of what the war effort meant in terms of military production, it is worth quoting from President Roosevelt's 10th State of the Union Address:

'. . .In 1942. . .we have. . .stepped-up production of new, deadly field weapons, especially self-propelled artillery. . .produced 56,000 combat vehicles. . .670,000 machine guns. . .21,000 anti-tank guns. . .10 ¼ billion rounds of small-arms ammunition. . .181 million rounds of artillery ammunition. . .three times greater than our total production in the first World War. . .I think the arsenal of democracy is making good.'

And more news from Lasky:

January 15, 1943
Dear Jesse,

Your last letter dated January 5th was much appreciated. It was the one in which you recommended that we read 'A Time For Greatness' by Herbert Ager - Mother has ordered it.

An interesting event happened which I forgot to write you about in my last letter. Two or three weeks ago, Col. Lenehan came to lunch with Col. Levinson. When I entered the dining room, I hardly recognized him, nevertheless, he arose and came around the table and shook hands with me as if I were an old friend, and said: 'I want to tell you that boy of yours is certainly making good. We think a great deal of him; he is not alone a fine officer and a fine executive but a very popular chap and is doing a great job. You can be very proud of Jesse Jr.'

Col. Robert Lord was sitting next to me, and the other executives around the table all heard what Col. Lenehan said, as he apparently spoke not alone for my benefit, but for theirs. I watched Bob Lord's face, and he was beaming. He is very fond of you.

All these little incidents are indications of the background that is being built up for you, and I am confident that when the war is over, as a result of the record you are achieving, you can take your proper place in the industry.

...I had a nice trip to Palm Springs and brought Mother back Sunday night. It is so restful and peaceful down there, in spite of flocks of soldiers on the street day and night, that I would have given anything if I could have remained a couple of weeks - but even the two days' rest did me good - and Mother is blooming like a rose and never looked better and is full of pep and energy. Last night I took her to see 'Moon and Sixpence'. (You should see this picture. It will never make a dollar at the box-office - but remembering how much you loved Irving Stone's 'Lust for Life'[71], you will eat this one up.) . . . .

January 22, 1943

... We finally previewed 'Mark Twain' last Tuesday night at the Warner Bros. Theatre at Huntington Park. Jack Warner admitted, before the preview that it was the toughest audience we could get for a quality picture like 'Mark Twain'. The house was crowded and, incidentally, Warner said: 'Let's go by ourselves with just the executive group, and not take any of the producers, as we will have a second preview when we will notify the other producers.'

The picture went on at 8.50 and was finished at 11.03 - two hours and thirteen minutes - and the audience never moved. Laughs were plentiful

---

71 Based on Somerset-Maugham's novel about the painters Gauguin and Van Gogh's years together. It won many awards.

- tears were plentiful - and, when the preview was over, one knew that we had another great picture. Warner congratulated me; Charlie Einfeld could hardly speak from choked-up emotion, and the others were simply beaming with delight.

We waited a few minutes for the preview cards which had been turned in as the audience left the theatre, and then we stood in a group while Warner read them aloud. When he was finished reading them, I said: 'What are you trying to do kid me? Where are the bad cards?' He said; 'There aren't any bad cards - I read you everyone that has been received.'

Well, the cards are so good that Randy has made a copy of them for your perusal . . . I expected we would have a lot of cutting and editing to do, although, personally, I could not find anything to cut, and, to my amazement, Warner could only suggest a couple of little deletions - and he said: 'What's the use - the picture is perfect; let's leave well enough alone - and what's more, we won't have another preview - we don't need it - the picture is in the bag!'

Yesterday, I began to worry, and I said to him at lunch: 'I think it is a mistake not to have another preview. The picture is so important that it needs every attention that we can give it. This was his answer - 'Jesse, I would preview it five times if I thought it was necessary but you have a great picture, one that will make a fortune; its distinguished and fine - and a picture that we can well be proud of. We don't want any suggestions from the other Producers - the picture is great and we know it - let's leave well enough alone.' I readily agreed and there the matter ended - so, at the moment, my stock as a Producer is still above par.

. . . We are having one of those terrific rains that usually occur out here this time of the year. It started yesterday and has been pouring ever since. Mother and I are going to the opening of 'This is the Army' tonight - the Irving Berlin show - and we are looking forward to it with considerable anticipation. Seats are $11.00 per, and the demand has been terrific, but I secured a fine pair well down in front. The show will run for ten days at the Philharmonic.

I am getting quite excited over the Gershwin picture and am determined to make it the greatest musical yet produced. As a matter of fact, I am planning to take a three or four months' layoff when the Gershwin picture is finished - and loaf and rest, and visit you, Billy and Betty. This, however, won't occur until the middle of summer. . . .

January 29, 1943

. . . I am still laughing about the names of your two assistants: Pvt. L and Pvt. S. Don't worry - I shall not breathe these names to anyone because I can understand how quickly it would get in the papers - and what a story it would make - but it is a strange quirk of Fate that has brought this combination about...[72]

I don't know whether I wrote you that I have arranged things with Jack Warner so that I am rid of 'Connecticut Yankee' and another terrible story they wanted me to make, and am to devote all my time to 'Gershwin' - and, as a matter of fact, make only one picture at a time, which means about one picture a year. Naturally, if you were with me, I would, make two or three pictures a year but, until that time comes, I am determined to do only the biggest pictures in the biggest way - and, after finishing Gershwin, I will have a unique record of three outstanding <u>Box-Office Champions.</u>

...I have temporarily taken Alex Aarons, who produced many of the early Gershwin shows, as a kind of advisory assistant on the 'Gershwin' picture. He is not too bright or too aggressive but will fill in well enough for the time being.

...You should devote all your spare thoughts and take advantage of this tough experience you are having, to build yourself in the direction of production. A producer's life is so much happier and so much more permanent than that of a writer, and, besides, you will perpetuate your name as a writer by finishing our biography...

Glad to say the Government decided not to take over the Ambassador Hotel and make it a hospital, so Grandma's mind is at peace again and she is feeling and looking very well and full of pep.[73] Again she called me yesterday to say she had a lovely letter from you - what great events your letters are in her life, you will never quite know.

Wednesday night Mother and I went to dinner at the Brown Derby with, Sonya Levien and some of her friends and then we all attended the opening of 'In Which We Serve' at the Carthay Circle. It was a wonderful opening and a wonderful picture although the first two reels were rather crude and terribly confusing, but once the picture got underway, its emotional impact was terrific.

...Sonya finishes her Gershwin treatment today and goes back to Columbia, and I am now negotiating with several writers, so we can get the first draft screenplay started. At the moment we have a great chance of securing Albert Hackett and Frances Goodrich - $3,500 a week for the team—but what a team! I pray that I get them....

Jack Warner was well aware of the quality Lasky could bring to films when working on subjects he felt were important. The producer was partial to biographies because they dealt with the choices real people had made to create their unique and special talents. Music was Lasky's other focus. As a reward, the films that Lasky had no desire to make were wisely removed from his slate.

---

[72] Jesse's assistants, Private Long and Private Short got a few laughs.
[73] Grandma Sarah was not to be kicked out of her penthouse apartment.

February 5, 1943
Dear Jesse,

... Such a nice long letter from you this week. Again I have to tell you that you achieve such a style in your letters that they are good enough to publish—which reminds me that there is an article about Cecil in this week's Saturday Evening Post which you might enjoy reading. My friend, Irving Hoffman, asked me to send him some stories about Cecil for his column in the Reporter, whereupon, I sat down with Randy and whipped up a few interesting items which I am sure he can use.

I have been out nearly every night this week; to a Philharmonic concert with Mother last night; to a dinner (Walter) Wanger gave for about one hundred men in honor of Dr. Gallup[74] at the Beverly Hills Hotel ... in fact, I am a little tired and am going to pass up the Fights tonight and dine home and turn in early....

'Gershwin' progresses slowly. Sonya is finished and is back at Columbia, and Harry Chandlee is re-editing and improving her treatment. I didn't get Hackett and Goodrich after all but will soon find the right 'top' writer for this important job. How you would have enjoyed working on this picture - it is right down your alley.

Col. Smith, the Commander at Brooks Field, has been after me to send them a star when Buddy's class graduates on February 16th. I think I have secured Alexis Smith for the trip and Mother and I are planning to go to San Antonio as we had promised the Colonel we would be present for Buddy's graduation.

February 12, 1943

...I talked to Frances several times this week and no doubt she told you I got her seats for the Ballet which she thoroughly enjoyed ... I am going to get her railroad transportation and will pay for it myself as a farewell present for her.

There is an article in the Reader's Digest, February issue, condensed from the article in Liberty, called 'They Fight With Film', and it mentions your name and Carl Laemmle, Jr.'s name.

I have taken Irving Rapper, who directed 'Mark Twain' to direct 'Rhapsody in Blue'.... 'Mark Twain' turned out so well that maybe we are a good combination. Just now, Nelson Poynter, the head of the Motion Picture Division of OWI called me to tell me that he and his staff ran 'Mark Twain' last night, at Jack Warner's suggestion, and he considers it one of the finest

---

74 Dr. George Gallup, creator of the Gallop poll, who said, "If democracy is about the will of the people, shouldn't someone find out what that will is?"

pictures he has ever seen and is recommending that it have its world premiere in London because of the wonderful propaganda it contains.

Mother and I saw the Ethel Barrymore (stage) show 'The Corn Is Green' the other night and enjoyed it very much. We are making a test today of the boy who played the lead opposite Ethel Barrymore, for 'Gershwin'. Have been testing him all day and he looks awfully promising - he may turn out to be a great discovery. I would much prefer an unknown, like this boy to John Garfield, or any actor who is already typed. Harry Chandlee is doing some inspiring work on 'Rhapsody in Blue' and I am keeping him at it until we can get a final important writer. Good writers are awfully scarce as you can imagine....

February 19, 1943

... Mother received such a nice letter from you, which she answered at length last night, and read to me this morning. She is such a happy person - her life is so full, with her painting and her shopping, and she really enjoys keeping house. I think her letter was very amusing and so typical of her.

... At the moment the studio is overrun with soldiers. The entire troupe, including Champion Joe Louis, are rehearsing the numbers for 'This is the Army'.

'Gershwin' proceeds slowly; Chandlee is plugging along, and in two weeks Howard Koch will join him as collaborator and do the polishing which the screenplay is going to need. Only having this one picture to prepare makes it comparatively easy for me at this stage of the picture. Later on it will turn into a very difficult and exacting job....

Jack Chertok poured out his troubles to me today and asked me to read the script he is working on for a general criticism, which I promised to do. He is such a nice fellow that one wants to help him.

Last Saturday night we had a gathering of a lot of fellows in the business to form a club something like the old Asthma and Riding Club. A number of boys whom I had not seen recently were there and they all asked for you. It is surprising how constantly I am stopped by people who know you and who inquire about you.

Tonight is Fight night and I am staying downtown for dinner with Jack Emanuel...The Hollywood Legion Stadium is packed to the doors in spite of the war. There is a smattering of a few soldiers - but there are still plenty of fellows not in uniform.

... By the way, I wonder how well you got acquainted with Walter Doniger.[75] He calls on me a lot and I think he is an extremely bright boy. We

---

75 Doniger became a successful film director.

have been exploring together the possibilities of doing a picture on Luther Burbank,[76] an idea which has fascinated me for a long time.

Enclosed is copy of a letter I received from Nelson Poynter. He saw 'Mark Twain' and is urging Warner Bros. to release it in England as soon as possible. Poynter called me on the 'phone and congratulated me and said it is one of the best pictures he has seen in a long time…There won't be any more weekends for the duration as they have stopped cars going to Palm Springs and to all summer resorts.….

February 26, 1943

… Frances called me yesterday morning and read me your letter which positively thrilled me. As I understand it, you are becoming a Project Officer and will produce training films, for the Medical Corps and the Military Police. Frances was so excited as she read me your long letter that I may not have it all straight—but it is quite a coincidence that you should have anything to do with the Medical Corps inasmuch as Bill is so involved in it himself. Immediately my imagination got the best of me and I saw you actually visiting at Bill's next post, wherever it is. In any event, you should sit right down and write 'Dr.' Lasky a long letter, telling him all about your new duties. I am sorry to report that Bill is hospitalized again. After he got over the measles he got some kind of streptococcus infection in his head and a temperature, and I am a little anxious about him. He is supposed to graduate next week, but I think he finished all his examinations in spite of his illness. A letter from you at this time would cheer him up enormously.

From the other front, Betty reports that they have found a little apartment in Harlingen, Texas, and as it is a sleepy Mexican town, thirty miles from the Border, Betty seems to like Harlingen after the hectic life of San Antonio.. .Buddy has started his gunnery practice and will soon be transferred again.. .Harry Chandlee has hit his stride and is doing a good job on the Gershwin story, and in a week he will be joined by Howard Koch who will collaborate on the screenplay. Harry, however, has already turned in about 50 pages of first draft screenplay that looks very good…I want to emphasize again that all this experience you are having, and will have, will be invaluable when you join me as Associate Producer:

Production by Jesse L. Lasky
Associate Producer Jesse Lasky, Jr.

… I have my eye on a nice bungalow in the studio which would give us marvelous headquarters and, boy, what pictures we will turn out. When I think about it, I get so enthusiastic about it that I would like to join the Marines to end the war that much sooner.…

---

76 Horticulturist who developed the Burbank potato and over 800 new strains of fruits and flowers.

March 5, 1943

... Last night, Mother and I attended the Academy Award Dinner as guests of Jack Warner, at the Warner Bros, table. As luck would have it, Mother found herself sitting next to Col. Robert Lord. Mother looked so young and beautiful, not a day over thirty, that at first Bobby Lord was embarrassed, and when he finally asked me if she was actually your Mother, and I confirmed the fact - Bobby, who as a rule is very quiet, started to talk to Mother and the two of them had a great conversation. I overheard enough of it to realize that he was eulogizing you. He explained that your orders had been approved, making you a project officer, which was the same as a full-fledged producer - and that, beyond question, you were one of the finest officers; serious, conscientious, with great ability and a wonderful personality - that you had handled the most difficult office imaginable with tact, courage and patience - in fact, no one ever gave another human being more generous praise. Needless to say Mother was thrilled and impressed beyond words and no doubt will write you about it herself.

The Academy Dinner was at the Ambassador in the Cocoanut Grove, and the place was packed like a can of sardines. I could not help but think of our excitement last year and how close we came to winning the award ... enclosed is an item cut out of the Hollywood Reporter today. We don't know how it got in, but it is good to keep your name in front of the industry.

As a little going-away gift, I am going to give Frances $50.00 in cash for her to have on the train - and Mother is giving her a present of some stockings....

March 8, 1943

Just a few lines - which I am writing at Frances' suggestion, to tell you not to worry if you have not heard from her recently. She is busy closing up the house - also, her brother arrived; in fact, I am having Frances and her brother in for dinner tonight....

Mother had a talk with Billy on the long distance phone, and he will be discharged from the hospital in a couple of days. He has had a pretty tough time - and as Margie was also down with the measles for a couple of days and they both sounded so forlorn, Mother has decided to pay them a quick visit as Denver is not very far. Bess will leave here Friday night and will arrive in Denver at 7.30 Sunday morning; will spend a few days and come home.

Betty, on the other hand, is getting along grand, as is evidenced by the letter enclosed herewith.

With Mother and Frances out of town, I will be the 'Last of the Laskys' in California, except for staunch and courageous dear Grandma, who will be with us tonight to speed Frances on her way. I advised Frances to let her brother remain in your house for a few weeks as his presence will be in the nature of a caretaker. When he leaves, he will turn the keys over to Randy and we will look after everything, including the garden - so please don't worry about your house.

Oh. before I close, I must tell you about the greatest picture I have ever seen. Jack Warner invited Mother and me to see Saroyan's 'The Human Comedy' at his house. Never have I seen such a wonderful picture. Mother and I were literally bathed in tears when it was over, but we came away from this experience uplifted and purified, as if we had been under the influence of a prayer with the soft accompaniment of an organ in church. The picture is beyond description, but it is an emotional experience that you will never forget. See it—see it quickly—and revel in it—and then write me how you feel about it.

There is a scene where two little boys go into a public library - neither one of them can read - which stands out as a gem, and the kind of scene I want you to invent and write some day. After you see 'The Human Comedy', you will want to take off your coat and really write for pictures again. What a medium of expression! What possibilities for constructive good! What an influence it can be in this war-torn world. It is a 10-1 shot "The Human Comedy"[77] will win the next Academy Award - my vote is already cast!

March 12, 1943

...When this letter reaches you, Frances will be with you - and I know you are both very happy. Randy said Frances looked so pretty when he put her on the train; he was quite proud of her - and she will have told you of the nice evening we spent together before she left...I think I wrote you about Mother planning to pay a quick visit to Billy and Margie - well, at the last minute today I decided to go with her. It is a very easy trip... so I will only miss two days at the studio, and I am not very busy as my two writers, Chandlee and Koch, will keep plugging along.

Bill wired us he was discharged from the hospital, and when his Captain heard that Mother was coming, he told Bill he would have a three-day furlough, so that will make it very nice for all of us. Believe me, I won't mind a nice restful train ride...I just had a talk with Ruth (Goldwyn/Lasky) and Mac (Capps, her husband). I was going to spend Sunday evening with them and they were going to have Sam and Frances (Goldwyn) over, but we have postponed it until a week from Sunday. I shall be most anxious to hear of your adventures on your first trip as a Project Officer to Ft. Custer....

Now that Blanche was gone, Sam Goldwyn had reconciled with his daughter, Ruth, and the Laskys played happy families with Sam and his charming wife, Fran-

---

[77] Starred Mickey Rooney from a story by Wm. Saroyan.

ces, on various occasions. Many years later, in the 1980s, when Jesse and I were visiting Hollywood from London, we were surprised when Sam Jr. phoned Jess out of the blue and invited us to his house. It seemed he wanted to ask Jesse about his Aunt Blanche, his father's first wife.

March 19, 1943
Dear Jesse,

...Your most cheerful and interesting letter arrived this morning - also Frances' very nice letter. I was so glad to receive them as I was really anxious to know whether you had returned from Ft. Custer in time to meet Frances' train. I think Frances' first night in New York was grand and I can see that life will not be too dull for her....

I paid my respects to General Quade, the Commanding Officer of Fitzsimons Hospital, and he proved a charming man. He left his office and his busy affairs and devoted himself for two hours showing us through the hospital from the basement to the roof. It was a fascinating experience and one that I shall not soon forget. Bill had never even seen the General - you know the gulf between a Corporal and a General - it is pretty wide. Well, Margie and Bill were waiting in the outer office, and when the General heard that they were there, he stepped out and said; 'At ease, Bill, you and your wife must accompany us' - and Bill nearly died of excitement...I just returned from the funeral of Alex Aarons. He assisted me for a couple of weeks on the Gershwin story - as he was the producer of many of Gershwin's musical shows and the discoverer of Fred Astaire. The poor guy died penniless and practically friendless at the age of 54 - but, as usual, when it was too late, all his old friends turned up at the funeral.

As Mother was away, I had dinner with Grandma in the Cocoanut Grove at the Ambassador last night and she got a great kick out of it. I left her at ten o'clock and she went into the card room where they were impatiently waiting for her, and she tells me this morning she played gin rummy until after midnight and won first prize—what a marvelous character she is. I had taken a cocktail in the bar before I went up to her room and she smelled liquor on my breath and gave me h—l, as if I were twenty years old....

March 26, 1943

...Spring has come to California and the days are beautiful - and our garden is just too lovely. We have cut down a couple of dead avocado trees and have planted an enormous amount of vegetables including watermelons and cantaloupes...

Here's an interesting item of news: I have been talking with Hamilton MacFadden for about a week with the idea of making him my assistant to replace Julius Evans. While Hamilton is not a very good director, he knows every phase of production - has a good story mind and a nice personality and he should work out extremely well . . . Incidentally - and this is very confidential - I wouldn't even want Julius to know it - I am buying on my own account all the rights to 'Singing in the Wilderness' (the life of Audubon). I have re-read this material and a treatment that Peattie wrote for me a few years ago - and I know I have discovered the possibilities of one of the greatest pictures that could be made. The story has everything. Later on I hope to sell it to Warner Bros, at a good profit and make it my big picture to follow 'Gershwin'. Fredric March could play 'Audubon' perfectly and, anticipating his success in 'Mark Twain', he will be very big for 'Audubon'. Here's something else that's interesting: Jack Warner has asked all the Producers to make one moderate priced picture as we are short of medium pictures. I suddenly became inspired to look up 'The Apple Tree' by Galsworthy, which you may remember that I considered at various times in the past. It is a little gem of a tragic love story and I know just how to modernize it; bringing it up to date, and it can be produced at about a cost of $500,000. I hope to put it into work immediately and by taking on this extra production, it will permit my securing MacFadden as my assistant . . . A banquet is being given to Madame Chiang Kai-Shek[78] at the Ambassador Hotel next Friday night. The whole city is trying to get tickets which are very scarce, but Mother and I were invited and we are really looking forward to it.

Also, next week there is a George Gershwin Memorial Concert at the Philharmonic; Paul Whiteman will conduct and prominent artists like Bing Crosby, Dinah Shore will appear, and, of course, we are attending as this will be a great inspiration for the Gershwin picture. . . .

April 2, 1943

. . . I have written some of the theatre circuits in New York and will have some theatre passes for you in a few days. I also wrote my friend, Irving Yergin, who is now in Publicity at Warner Bros. New York office, to arrange a showing of 'Mark Twain'. Freddie March and his wife, Florence Eldridge, are anxious to see it, and I wrote Freddie that you and Frances would see it with them. Yergin will contact you either at your hotel or at Astoria to try and arrange a mutually agreeable time.

It will have to be late in the afternoon as Freddie is at the theatre every night. In case you cannot coincide your time with Freddie's, I suggest that you ask Yergin if he could not run it for you some evening - and you might want to take a couple of your friends along - or better yet, Louise and Ben. If you don't

---

[78] Wife of President Chiang Kai-shek, she played a prominent role in the politics of the Republic of China.

hear from Yergin, call him on the telephone and talk it over with him. He knows all about you, and is a very close personal friend, and will go the limit to arrange things the way you want it. I am anxious for you to see our 'Mark Twain' masterpiece ... That reminds me - we are attending a banquet for Mme. Chiang Kai-shek at the Ambassador tonight. It is a very swanky affair - and Cecil and Constance will be at our table, along with the Mervyn LeRoys; the Dick Wallaces (actor) and the Mark Sandrichs (director). Then on Sunday we have a box at the Hollywood Bowl where Mme. Chiang is making her only public appearance. They are planning a great show around her and it will be a very interesting occasion.

Wednesday night I took some of the boys from the studio over to Pasadena to attend the George Gershwin concert conducted by Paul Whiteman. It was so good that I took Mother last night to hear the same concert at the Philharmonic downtown, and also took Jack Warner and his daughter - so I have had a lot of Gershwin music this week.

Along about April 13th, our friend Albert Rothschild is going to communicate with you. I think I wrote you all about him. He is a very fine man and a member of the famous Rothschild family. We entertained him beautifully while he was in Los Angeles, and he just wrote me a letter from which I will quote - as follows: 'Will you write little Jesse about my coming to New York; one of the first things I will do is to contact him and tell him about you, the house, and the lovely time I had with you.' He will undoubtedly invite you and Frances to dinner and entertain you nicely, and I am very anxious that you meet him as he is a very useful man for you to know.

...I was very much interested and impressed by the amazing ratings you received in your examinations. Isn't it curious - you never could have gotten ratings like that in any of your studies at school, which proves that your mind has developed, as it naturally should, since your school days....

Lasky had forgotten that years before, Rothschild had ordered copies of Jesse's books of verse and had sent them to Jesse to autograph.

April 9, 1943
Dear Jesse,

... Well, we had a very pleasant surprise, which occurred just after I mailed your letter last Friday. Betty wired that Buddy somehow achieved a ten-day leave of absence between his transfer from Harlingen, Texas, to Godman Field, Ft. Knox, Kentucky, which is near Louisville. They jumped in their car on Saturday and drove 1800 miles in 2-1/2 days, arriving here at 11.45 o'clock on Monday night. They were pretty exhausted, as you can imagine, but they were in great spirits and have been enjoying themselves ever since.

Buddy is flying back to his new post on Monday afternoon and Betty is remaining over a week and will leave the following Monday by train to join Buddy... Mother had herself painted by a very great artist - Henrique Medina - he is probably one of the greatest contemporary portrait painters we have and has painted notables of many countries. The portrait is finally finished and I am to see it at his studio for the first time this afternoon... Billy has been transferred to another department at Fitzsimons Hospital and will definitely remain in Denver now - at least long enough for Margie's baby to be born there. They like Denver, but due to his transfer, he has been unable to secure a furlough, as he had hoped...

'Gershwin' continues to progress. We made a test of John Garfield and discovered that he is definitely wrong for the part, so now we are reconsidering Ethel Barrymore's leading man whom we previously tested. He would be a new personality on the screen at least and, consequently, would get over the illusion of the real Gershwin more than any well-known actor could....

April 23, 1943

... I had a very interesting experience last night. California Shipbuilding Corporation at Terminal Island, Wilmington, launched the S/S George Gershwin, and Ira Gershwin, his wife, Lee; Paul Whiteman, myself, and some others were the guests of the Calif. Shipbuilding Company. They sent a car for us and we reached this amazing place at about 9.30 pm. First, we were met by hostesses and press men, who entertained us with coffee and sandwiches; then we had a brief look-see at the marvelous things that are going on - and promptly at 11 o'clock, we assembled on a platform for the launching.

A master-of-ceremonies presided at the mike and introduced us to the crowd who were assembled below, and even while he was talking, the noise of the welders and the indescribable racket that accompanies the building of these ships, never ceased. Suddenly Mrs. Gershwin was told to smite the bow of the vessel with a bottle of champagne encased in a red, white and blue covering - the whistles blew and down the ways to the water the great ship slid as smooth as a canoe on the lazy Colorado.

... Marc Connelly[79] was with us and we didn't reach home until 2.30 am - but I shall never forget participating in the launching of this ship, which is named after the hero of my new picture - the picture which I hope is going to make new history in the world of the cinema.

If I ever had any doubts that a war was going on, these were dispelled by seeing 40,000 workers hard at it twenty-four hours a day, and the marvelous organization that turns these 10,000-ton ships out in a matter of fifteen or

---

79 Best known for his Pulitzer Prize winning play The Green Pastures (1930), a fantasy of biblical history seen through the religious life of the Southern Afro-Americans of the period.

sixteen days. Even as the ship rolled down the ways, men way up on the superstructure continued their work.

...I had another interesting experience this week. Jack Warner invited me for dinner and took me to a sneak preview of 'Mission to Moscow'. It is a magnificent documentary type of film, different from anything that has yet been done. It will probably be much discussed and it seemed to me that the subject matter will cause considerable controversy - but certainly it is the most courageous film ever produced. Warner did not have any of the producers accompany him except me. He said I was the only one whom he wanted to see this picture, and whom he could trust seeing it in this studio. He is a swell chap and our relations are very cordial and pleasant.

On Tuesday night I took George Schaefer[80] home for dinner and, later, to see some British war pictures at the Filmarte. We spent a very pleasant evening, and I enjoyed his company as we are very good friends....

April 29, 1943

...Had a letter from Billy this morning. He was all excited over the fact that President Roosevelt visited his hospital, and he stood six feet away from him. His account of the excitement occasioned by the President's visit was most interesting and amusing. Billy has found a lovely little house which he has just moved into, and seems happy and contented.

...Gershwin proceeds slowly. Chandlee finishes his version of the script this week, but Howard Koch has about four or five weeks more to go - and it seems that his script is the best. It has been a tough story to lick as you can imagine, but I see daylight.

May 7, 1943

...The thrilling news of the capture of Bizerte and Tunis has just come over the radio and the whole studio is excited over the news. This might very well mark the real turning point in the war, and the end is that much closer in sight.

I think we have finally found our George Gershwin - a newcomer brought out here from the east who has never been on the screen - by the name of Robert Alda. I have just seen with Jack Warner a test we made and we both think he is it.

Warner leaves for New York tonight, and this afternoon we closed a deal for my next picture 'Singing in the Wilderness' - the story of John James Audubon. I am going to prepare it for Errol Flynn who has become extremely popular and I believe can do it very well. If all goes well, and we can stand the cost, we plan to make it in Technicolor. Hamilton MacFadden is going to

---

80 Uncredited Executive Producer: Citizen Kane (1941), The Magnificent Ambersons (1942), Journey Into Fear (1943)

work on the script with a writer who we still have to find, so Hamilton joins me officially on Monday, which pleases me very much as I have had a chance to study him and he has real ability and is an extremely pleasant person to work with.

I am going to the Fights tonight with Alan LeMay. I tried to get Alan for 'Audubon' but he can't get away from Cecil. He had read our treatment and was crazy to do it but it looks as if he will be on 'Rurales' (the old chestnut that you worked on) for many months[81].

I am so glad you saw 'The Human Comedy'. You can see why I raved about it - it is just the kind of picture that I like. It opens here next week and I am going to see it again, as I originally saw it with an audience at Jack Warner's house.

We just had wonderful news from Billy. He was transferred back to the laboratory and he could not have been more excited if he had inherited a fortune. I guess you knew that after he passed his examinations, he was put in sort of a public relations job, the very thing that he wanted to get away from, but now he is back in his beloved laboratory work and all is well with him. I enjoyed so much your description of the work you are doing and the duties of a Project Officer. I know you are taking it all in your stride ... Well, I wish I had you here to start work with Hamilton on the 'Audubon' script - and what joy you would have in co-producing it. It is going to be an Academy Award picture or I am daffy - and you will have to admit I was not crazy when I got excited first about 'York' and, later, about 'Twain'.

The 'Gershwin' picture is going to be all right too, so the Lasky Banner is still waving proudly at the masthead - and may it continue to wave until you join me - after that, you will keep it flying! ...

May 14, 1943

... I have had a very exciting week devoted mostly to getting 'Audubon' started - and what a story it is. I have never had any picture, including 'The Covered Wagon' excite me as much as 'Singing in the Wilderness'. ... Mother and I saw the MGM picture 'Cabin in the Sky' last weekend enjoyed it enormously - I hope you get a chance to see it. I also went to the opening of 'Porgy and Bess' - a couple of numbers from which we hope to use in 'Gershwin'. So far we have only been able to clear the rights to use 'Summertime' ... Just heard Churchill's speech on the radio. We are all thrilled by the successes in North Africa, and I think you must feel a little more optimistic about the progress of the war ... I know you will be seeing 'Mission to Moscow'. Don't fail to let me know what you think of it. I went to the

---

81 DeMille's *Rurales* was never made.

preview and I was left with mixed emotions: admiration for the production, direction and acting, but a little bored by the subject matter....

May 15, 1943

...I noted that you had breakfast with Albert Rothschild and I laughed heartily over his remark: 'I say worse things to your face than I say to your behind'...I have just finished a long session with my writer, Philip MacDonald, an Englishman with real ability. Hamilton and I and MacDonald are so excited about 'Audubon' that we are literally walking on air. If this picture doesn't win the Academy Award, I should retire forever.

Jesse in all my life I have never had such material to work with. The story has everything that one could ask for. It is 'a Producer's dream come true' - and we are going to make it in Technicolor, with a magnificent music score - well, remember my words - the Academy Award is our goal!!

Jesse saw quite a bit of Albert Rothschild and described him in his diary:

Diary: Thursday, April 29, 1943,

Went to dine with Albert Rothschild. He is most like the German actor Viedt[82] in both voice and appearance. One of the most elegant individuals I have ever encountered. The room, the food, the conversation were quite in accord with his presence. One had the feeling of participation in elegance and perhaps a final dance to the strains of an old and courtly music. He came back to our apartment and conversed far into the night. Being with him made it possible to imagine an interview with Disraeli. But such men cannot actually leave the world – for without them an essential richness would be gone. They are the icing to the cake.

And Lasky wrote:

May 21, 1943

...I just came from an Academy luncheon at the Beverly-Wilshire, which was addressed by Hilary St. George Saunders, who has been recording the history of the war, as he is the Librarian of the British House of Commons. He made a thrilling speech and told us some amazing things about the way the British Government goes about getting the history of all the incidents in connection with their battles and campaigns. I wish you could have heard it.

Our first week on 'Audubon' develops a story that is thrilling beyond words. Hamilton and I took our writer, Philip MacDonald, to Santa Barbara on Sunday and we had a very pleasant day with Mr. and Mrs. Donald Culross Peattie. What a wonderful person Peattie is - and what a writer! I wonder

---

[82] Conrad Viedt.

if you ever read his 'Almanac for Moderns'. He has a beautiful home, high up in the hills of Santa Barbara, overlooking the Santa Barbara Mission. It was a perfect day and we spent the afternoon on his piazza, overlooking this beautiful scene and drinking mint juleps, such as you have never tasted, and discussing 'Audubon'. By good luck, John Baker, the executive head of the National Audubon Society was present, and Bert Hartwell, who is the Pacific Coast representative of the Society. Hartwell, through many years in the field, has come to whistle and imitate all kinds of birds so perfectly that I got the idea of having Audubon whistle, using Hartwell as the sound track, through many silent scenes in the picture. It is hard to keep my mind on 'Gershwin', with this world of material on 'Audubon' coming to life so rapidly.

Hamilton is grand to work with and is just the inspiration I need, and I find his viewpoint on pictures sound and practical. After all, he has had a vast experience in his own right. 'Gershwin' is within a week of being finished, and then another week of re-writing and the script will be ready for all departments. It is going to be a difficult picture to produce as there are endless big musical montages - like 'Yankee Doodle Dandy' - and important production numbers, but I begin to sense a really fine picture...Monday night I was invited by Louis Mayer to attend a small dinner at the Metro Studio, and I met a number of my old friends.

I wish you could see us on Helen's (the cook) night out. Mother cooks the dinner and we eat it on the kitchen table; then she washes and wipes the dishes - and I read the evening paper - all in the kitchen, and I get a very comfortable homey feeling out of the experience. Think of this scene a moment - and then remember 910 Fifth Avenue - with two butlers and a couple of maids and a chauffeur - and the Beach House and its retinue. Late in life though it is, we are learning how to live. Of course, the big events of the week are the arrival of letters from you, Betty and Bill. If they are particularly interesting, Randy makes copies of them and sends them to Grandma.

We are all somewhat cheered by the war news which certainly has been encouraging. I hope you heard Churchill's speech - I thought it was magnificent...

Saturday Morning.

...I can see by your letter that you really have a tough job, but it won't last forever, and studio work by comparison will now seem like a cinch....

May 28, 1943

...While you were looking out of the window at the rain, I was looking out of my window at the lovely California sunshine and listening to the birds who, since I have announced that I am going to do the Life of Audubon, seem to take special joy in singing at my window.

Speaking of 'Audubon', I have had the greatest break imaginable in securing at last the right writer to work with Donald Culross Peattie. I wonder if you know about him—Elliott Paul, author of 'The Last Time I Saw Paris' and 'The Life and Death of a Spanish Town' - and endless other fine novels. Here's a man so modest that it is hard for him to talk - but what a wizard at his typewriter! I am arranging for him to spend a few weeks with Peattie and then I sense he will give us a treatment that will be memorable. My first writer, Philip MacDonald, could not quite measure up to the subject so I am letting him out today.

...Producing a picture the size of Gershwin is like first planning a campaign in North Africa and then carrying it out - but we shall win the campaign in the end and be decorated accordingly. The darn trouble with my mental attitude at the moment is that I am simply mad about 'Audubon'. Believe me, Jess, with full recollection of the success of 'Covered Wagon', 'Beau Geste', 'Wings', 'Old Ironsides', or even of 'Sergeant York' - and 'Mark Twain' which you are going to adore when you see it - *Audubon* will top them all from every point of view.

...The more I watch the business, the more I am convinced that the successful producer of the future must be a writer; in other words, he has to be able to talk the writer's language and, if necessary, edit and improve his own scripts. Well, once this bloody war is over, you and I will have a chance to test all these theories, because I am determined to stay in harness until you can join me and carry on the Lasky Banner!...

June 4, 1943

...I noticed that you mention the Training Film Program is shrinking. It is funny, but I have been thinking for some time that it is inevitable that the Training Film Program would come to an end because, after all, they can only use so many training films for each branch of the Army, and once they are made - that is it. This makes me feel that it is very likely that you will be transferred to some other field - and I would not be a bit surprised if you were sent overseas. If that should happen, I have the strangest feeling that I would be glad for you to have such an experience. I haven't the slightest fear but what you would come back and, consequently, I would not be worried or hysterical, and neither would Mother....

Our weekend at Del Mar didn't turn out so well. First, we drove down half the way in a dim-out, which is the most difficult driving one can imagine. Then we found the hotel was short of help; no room service; no umbrellas on the beach to shelter us from the sun - and very poor food. So, the day after our arrival, Mother thought she would be more comfortable at home - and I let her have my car and she drove herself back home - but I stayed on alone as

I wanted to get the rest and the bathing, as I personally didn't mind the very slight inconveniences brought about by war conditions. I returned Monday by train which, by the way, was packed, and my good friend, Jack Emanuel, met me at the depot and drove me home.

Tonight will be an interesting evening. Cecil is giving a dinner to W.M. Jeffers, the Rubber Administrator, who is also President of the Union Pacific R.R. Jeffers will have six of his staff with him, and Cecil has invited a number of prominent men in the industry to meet Jeffers, who will give us some interesting dope on what is going on in Washington....

My *Gershwin* script is finished and down to length, however, we are going to devote a few days to polishing it, and improving it, I hope - but it is really very fine....Our tentative starting date is about July 15th. In the meantime, Elliot Paul and Donald Culross Peattie are hard at work on 'Audubon', and my enthusiasm grows apace over that subject...Randy just reminded me that you have been away and in the Army for over a year— how times flies! I still maintain that in another year it will all be over. Wasn't it tough about Leslie Howard being shot down enroute to England from Lisbon? It has caused quite a stir here....

Leslie Howard, most famous for his role in *Gone With the wind*, was flying from Lisbon to London when his plane was shot down by eight German Luftwaffe. It was first thought that the Germans imagined Churchill was on the plane, but it was later believed that the Germans were actually after Howard, who had been involved in certain intelligence-gathering activities. Lasky's letter continues:

June 4, 1943

...Next month our invaluable Helen is going to leave us, but mother doesn't seem to worry about it. We will find someone to take her place - and my most enjoyable times at home are the days that Helen is off; then mother cooks the dinner and we dine in the kitchen and feel very homey, old-fashion and efficient. I'll bet, between you and Frances, you can turn out a good meal yourselves. How the world has changed since 910 Fifth Avenue - and I don't think we will ever see that kind of life in America again. It is going to be a new world after the war - a better world for the masses, but not so good for the idle rich....

June 11, 1943

Bob Presnell called Mother yesterday and spoke beautifully about you and, later in the day, he called me on the 'phone and Randy listened in and made a record of what he said. I attach Randy's memo which gives you exactly his remarks. He promised to call at the studio to see me if he is able to manage it, and I hope he can.

...My 'Gershwin' script is finished and is a beautiful job. We start shooting on July 19th with Irving Rapper directing, and we are now beginning to cast the picture - and I am becoming immersed in the various details of preparation for production. In about a week I am going to send you a mimeographed copy of the script which you will enjoy reading, I am sure.

...I suppose you have been reading about the zoot-suiters[83] our local papers are filled with this terrible situation.

...I had a very nice time at Cecil's party to William Jeffers last Friday night. Cecil called on me for a talk. I followed Jack Benny and got more laughs than Benny did. Jeffers gave us a great talk and told us all about the rubber situation. He said that by the middle of next year the synthetic rubber would be plentiful, enough to take care of all the needs of the country....

June 18, 1943

...I mailed you a copy of the 'Gershwin' script - and to help you enjoy it while reading it, visualize Albert Basserman as playing Prof. Frank, and Oscar Levant, Paul Whiteman and George White playing themselves - and probably Joan Leslie playing 'Julie', the lead. If I give her the part, we will dub her singing voice throughout, using the voice of a fine singer....

A New Yorker through and through, Oscar Levant was of Russian-Jewish descent. He was one of the great popular pianists of the day, having studied under Zygmunt Stojowski. He became friends with George Gershwin and had composed music for at least twenty films; but his true fame for the average American was as a sage and wit, always ready with a sharp, funny remark. He played himself in many films and regularly appeared on the Kraft Music Hall radio show starring Al Jolson, where he not only accompanied the star on the piano, but also ad-libbed and did comedy sketches with him. The two appeared as themselves in *Rhapsody in Blue*. At the time Lasky wrote this letter, they hadn't yet signed Jolson for the film. Lasky's letter goes on:

June 18, 1943 (continued)

...If you have seen 'Mark Twain' by the time this letter reaches you, you will know that such a great picture could not have just happened. Endless people

---

83 A style of men's suit popular with African-American, Chicano, and Italian Americans in the 1940s: high-waist, wide-legged, tight-cuffed and pegged trousers. The long jacket had wide padded shoulders and wide lapels. The zoot-suiters were involved in racial riots.

contributed to its success - but always your Dad was the 'Captain of the Ship'; guiding, placating, inspiring, and knowing the right thing to do every time an emergency arose - and, believe me, there were plenty of emergencies and knotty problems to solve before 'Mark Twain' was completed. I know that Julius' experience, working under me, will mark the turning point in his life, just as I know the experience that you are going through now will bring you back to the studios a much abler and wiser, and better man all around.

Just as you are gaining valuable experience, I can see by Billy's letters that he, also, is forging ahead and developing into a very able person…I am mighty proud of both you boys and it is a source of great satisfaction, now that I am really getting along in years, to have the great joy of seeing you boys develop, and knowing that you are both going to give good accounts of yourselves in the post-war world.…

Thanks to the brilliant mind of Elliot Paul, my 'Audubon' script is progressing splendidly. We are well into the treatment. Paul is an amazing man and I want you to meet him some day. He has lived many years in Europe; he speaks many languages - and is a brilliant musician and pianist. I am having him out to the house tomorrow afternoon for tea. He will look at mother's paintings, play the piano for us and then we will take him out to dinner.…

June 25, 1943

…I was so happy to receive your thoughtful Father's Day cards which arrived right on schedule. As I also received remembrances from the other 'four' of my children, Father's Day was indeed very happy for me.

This has been a terribly busy week for me, and my mind is so engrossed this morning with the thousand and one details of the production - the starting date of which is speeding at us like an express train - that I won't be able to give as much time as I would like to this letter.

I have even had to work nights - one evening until one o'clock at Ira Gershwin's house, going over details of the script and trying to get him to approve certain scenes; another night with my dance director, LeRoy Prinz and the Music Department, selecting and planning how to use the endless Gershwin music we are trying to incorporate in the picture - and so on; and the casting of the picture is always a terribly difficult problem. However, I have had one good break this week, and that is, I think I have sold Charles Coburn on playing the part of Max Dreyfus. He has become so big that he is now starred in every picture in which he appears - and he will be a tower of strength to this picture.

As is usually the case, after my script was mimeographed (you have a copy of the same). I saw many opportunities to improve it - so I took Elliot Paul off Audubon and he is now doctoring and improving, I believe very much, the characterizations of certain characters in the script. If you read the script, Jesse, you will agree with me that the part of Alma can be definitely improved. Also, it is necessary to build the part of Dreyfus to get Charles Coburn to agree to play it. Well, this is nothing new as scripts are never finished until the company is shooting, and even then we make changes as characters begin to develop and come to life on the screen.

...I looked at Frank Capra's picture 'Arsenic and Old Lace' yesterday. It was finished before we started 'Mark Twain' and still has not been released. It is a very amusing and rather mad sort of a picture - I could not tell by seeing it in the projection room how it will be received by the public...

P.S. In the rush of things I almost forgot to tell you how thrilled I was over your and Frances' reception of 'Mark Twain'. I had praised the picture so much to you that I feared, at the last minute, you might be disappointed, consequently, your reactions thrilled me more than I can tell you. Somehow I wanted you Jesse, and Frances, to like the picture as I like it. I think I was more concerned about your personal reactions than I am about the public's.

This week Henry Blanke whom I consider the best producer here, saw 'Twain' and he simply raved about it; to quote him, he said: 'The only way I can tell you the way I feel about it is that I wish to heaven my name could have been on it as Producer. It tops any biography ever made.'

Thanks again for your long and enthusiastic letter, which made the week very bright.

July 2, 1943

...This has been a hectic and difficult week for me, and as our production date draws closer, the problems multiply. Casting; arguments over script; tests, and the endless trouble and details that look like mountains, but soon dissolve into molehills as I tackle them one at a time. For instance: there is a rule in the studio that producers are not allowed personal production assistants. This has robbed me of much help that MacFadden might have given me; nevertheless, it compels me to stand more on my own feet, and maybe it will be a good thing in the end.

I can see, by all that you have written me, that the work you are doing - trying to produce films for the Army - is much more difficult than my job where I have the resources of magnificent departments; experienced men on every side; a capable unit manager; a well-trained first assistant who I use as much as the director does, etc., in a word - once you lick your script in a big studio and assemble a good cast, the problems that occur are inherent in the business and are to be expected and overcome.

. . . I have been hearing endless tales of the intense heat in New York . . . I am wondering how Frances likes the job - at least, Saks is air cooled, as I remember it. (Frances had taken a salesperson job.)

By the way, Mother has painted her masterpiece - no fooling. Last Sunday Elliot Paul spent the day with her and posed for three hours for a portrait. He is a very distinguished guy, with a goatee type of beard; a bit stout - and he must have inspired Mother as his portrait is truly great. He is a great art critic in his own right, and was really bowled over by Mother's skill.

I spent last Sunday at Santa Ana as the guest of General Cousins, a two-star General, who treated me royally . . . I got quite a thrill as we entered the reviewing stand with everyone standing at attention - and the General turned to me and said: 'Mr. Lasky, you sit between me and General Walton', and as we sat down, all the officers and spectators resumed their seats. Immediately the review of the student pilots started and 15,000 boys passed in review, drilling in companies, like the well-trained West Point cadets. It took nearly an hour for the parade to pass - and it was an unforgettable experience . . . It gave me a queer feeling as I watched the review of the flower of American youth, and realized that soon they would be trained pilots, bombardiers, navigators, etc., and that many of them would never return to their homeland.

. . . This one field turns out 4,000 student pilots every six weeks. At one phase of the proceedings, the General turned to me and said: 'It is the constant stream of pilots that we are turning out from all our fields and schools that is going to win this war, and, Mr. Lasky, I am telling you that Germany will be out of the war before the first of the year.' Please, God, he is right. . .

By the way, Mervyn LeRoy phoned me the other day - he and his wife, and a couple of others, had seen 'Mark Twain' the night before at Jack Warner's house. Mervyn went crazy over the picture. He said: 'Jesse, this is one of the great pictures and must be a candidate for the Academy Award.' He also said: 'I have been talking about it all over the Metro lot - and I told Jack Warner if he doesn't roadshow it, two-a-day, like *Gone with the Wind*, he is crazy.' Every few days some individual sees the picture and invariably they praise it as much as you did. Of course, whenever this happens, I take another notch in my belt and swear that I will surpass it with 'Gershwin'. . .

Billy is getting along great. He is in charge of his particular Laboratory and is wallowing in blood transfusions, germs and whatnot, and has never been happier. They expect their baby the end of July and Mother plans to leave here on the 20th so as to be with them when the baby arrives. . . .

July 10, 1943

...First, I had a nice little visit with your friend, Anton Dolin[84], who came over to the studio to see me - and tomorrow, Sunday, he and Alicia Markova are coming to the house about 5.30 o'clock, and Rouben Mamoulian is going to join us at 6.30 - and I am taking them out to dinner to Romanoffs, and will give them a swell evening. I have also invited them both on the set when we are shooting 'Rhapsody', which definitely starts on the 19th.

You wrote such a beautiful criticism - or should I say, eulogy, of the Gershwin script that I read that part of your letter to Rapper, Oscar Levant and Ira Gershwin - however, much as you liked the script, I dare say we have improved it 25%. Elliot Paul, in three weeks, has done a wonderful job, and it is now really ready for shooting.

What a busy week! Oscar Levant arrived from New York and I gave him a little dinner at Romanoffs; then we went over to Ira Gershwin's house and stayed up until 1.30, talking and playing Gershwin. Last night Oscar was the guest soloist, in fact, he was starred at the Bowl, and gave an electrifying rendition of 'Concerto in F' and 'Rhapsody in Blue', also played a Grieg Concerto magnificently. The Bowl was packed and he received a tremendous ovation. I went backstage to congratulate him and took Irving Rapper with me, and he insisted we join him for supper afterwards - so, again, I was up until 1a.m. We had quite a supper party of various music lovers and Levant worshippers, including dear old Sonya Levien.

I have been casting the picture all week - and everyone is cast but George's mother and Bill Daly. I am getting terribly enthusiastic about 'Rhapsody in Blue' - and am quite excited over doing a musical, which, I modestly confess, I have a special talent for.

Well, yesterday, Betty called up rather excited. Buddy had been on a cross-country flight and on reporting back to Ft. Knox was put on 'alert' - which means he is about to be sent overseas. They would not allow his group to return to their homes anymore, in fact, he was supposed to be out of communication - but he got Betty on the 'phone somehow and explained the situation to her and told her to pack his things and her things, and plan to go home...We all hate to see him go, but it is War - and his case is no different than thousands of others.

We also heard from Billy that Margie's baby is expected in two weeks, so Bess will get there just in time....

---

84 British ballet dancer, choreographer. With frequent partner balarina Alicia Markova, founded the Markova-Dolin companies and London's Festival Ballet.

July 16, 1943

...I had quite an adventure getting Mother on the train. We arrived in front of the Union Depot at 6.15 pm - the train left at 6.30 pm. We unloaded from the car enough bags and packages to fill a huge compartment, possibly fifteen pieces, only to learn that no porters could be had for love nor money. The station was literally a bedlam - troops of soldiers marching in one direction—troops of sailors in another direction - a mass of humanity surging like cattle in a stampede; mothers with babies; women in tears bidding 'good-bye' to their loved ones - and I had 15 minutes to get Mother on the train.

At first it seemed inevitable that we would have to miss the train - then I got a brainstorm. I saw a Corporal and two Privates, Air Corps boys, chatting nearby, and I rushed over to them, saying: 'Fellows, if you have a few minutes, will you help a lady out who is in real distress - and save my life?' They answered: 'Sure, Boss - lead us to it.' So I grabbed the three soldiers and, at the same time, spotted an empty luggage cart which had probably been abandoned for a moment by an overworked porter, and said: 'Grab that cart and come with me.' They followed instructions, and we rushed the cart over to Mother's baggage, loaded it all in and then, with the Corporal going ahead with the cart and a soldier on each side of it - and Mother and I following - we rushed it through the surging crowds, wending our way through the labyrinth of the depot to our train.

With three minutes to go, another mass of humanity was surging around the train - but the soldiers and I went to work and passed the baggage from one to the other, in longshoreman style, and got all the bags into Mother's small bedroom just before the train left. How she will ever find room to sleep, I don't know - but, at least, she is on her way to Denver with all her baggage.

Needless to say, I thanked those soldiers profusely, and offered to buy them a drink. Imagine my astonishment when they replied: 'Mr. Lasky, someone told us who you were; we haven't time for a drink but we would appreciate your autograph.' So, I autographed each one of their notebooks; shook hands all around, and they went on their way - and I left them with a new respect for our American boys.

So much has been happening. On a moment's notice, Buddy was ordered to report to the 106th Reconnaissance Squadron, Chatham Field, Savannah, Georgia - the jumping-off place for overseas but, of course, we don't know where. He only had time for a brief 'good-bye' to Betty, and she was left high and dry with all his civilian baggage and her own baggage. She called me on the 'phone and I advised her to try and get to Denver - so she found her way from Elizabethtown, Ky. to Louisville; secured transportation in Louisville to Chicago, where I wired a Warner Bros, man to meet her and try to secure transportation for her to Denver - which he apparently did, as I received a wire last night that Betty had arrived safely in Denver and was domiciled with Margie and Bill. Poor Betty was feeling pretty distressed over the fact that Buddy is about to be sent overseas and must have had a very difficult trip to Denver. We will no doubt hear of her adventures later ... I am moving into the Roosevelt Hotel today and will remain there until Mother returns, as it would be too lonesome in our big house - and as our picture starts Monday, I will have to be in the studio every morning at nine o'clock, and living in town will save a half hour each way.

Just received a note from Jack Warner which is so nice I am asking Randy to put a copy of it in this letter.

The big picture is all ready to go on Monday and we have a magnificent cast and wonderful plans for brilliant production numbers. Monday night we are going to record our first sound track - Paul Whiteman directing 'Rhapsody in Blue' which we have cut to 6-1/2 minutes, with Oscar Levant at the piano recording the solo piano part which, of course, will be played in the picture by George Gershwin on his first appearance at Aeolian Hall. Our script is now so much improved that you would hardly recognize it - and I am more than usually excited over the prospects of a super-great picture! The 'Rhapsody in Blue' cannot fail!! ...

July 23, 1943

... I was really excited over the news that you might be sent overseas. No doubt Frances will forward this letter to Ft. Dix, and I shall eagerly await further news of your adventures. I am awfully glad that you are going to get combat training; it will build up your health and morale and will be a great experience. I am looking forward to our first letter from Ft. Dix.

... We have been shooting 'Gershwin' for five days and our stuff looks very good. We recorded the sound track of the 'Rhapsody in Blue' on Monday night; Paul Whiteman was inspired and conducted a great orchestra, with Oscar Levant at the piano - and I just heard the assembled sound track, and it is out of another world. It is the greatest recording ever turned out by this studio, and the whole studio is buzzing about it...I think of you both constantly and hold good thoughts over you for your future—and send you both my devoted love....

From Jesse's diary on July 26, 1943:

Back to the wooden barracks - I bought a GI raincoat for $3.00 as there were patches of rain, and the earth was muddy. Thus went the day and I dreamed of overseas travel - while headlines blare Mussolini's probable imprisonment.

On the 27th, he continued:

Practice dry firing- practice drill – calisthenics - map reading - old training films shown to a tight-packed audience in humid darkness - flesh smelling fragrant of the day...It seems hard to believe that this fragmentary training is in fact the preparation for overseas. That possibility had always seemed too distant. Too unlikely to have any other shape now - but this is me - in leggings, fatigues, and steel helmet, touching other weapons than pencil or typewriter key.

His father wrote Jesse news of Bill and Margie:

July 30, 1943
Dear Jesse,

...They expected the baby before this, but it has not arrived yet. Due to the fact that Mother has had her transportation for a long time, and it is impossible to get transportation for several more weeks, she will have to leave on Saturday even though the baby has not arrived. I don't want her to risk being stuck in Denver for a couple of weeks, as the transportation problem is simply frightful as you know only too well. I will save your letter and photographs and will give them to her as soon as she arrives... We have had a terrible heat wave, so much so that after moving to the Roosevelt Hotel I found it was so hot there that I have gone home nearly every night.

The picture is going quite well. Rapper, as I knew from the beginning, is not the ideal director, nevertheless, he is catching the spirit of much of it, particularly the intimate scenes - and it is bound to be an outstanding, successful - I almost wanted to use the adjective 'stupendous' production. Next week we are shooting the 'Rhapsody in Blue' - the scene at Aeolian Hall the first time it is played. Fortunately our many production musical numbers and orchestral setups are being handled by LeRoy Prinz; he seems to have a great feeling for it and we talk the same language. I must say I have a definite talent for musical pictures; I understand them and enjoy doing them very much.

I just signed the great colored artiste, Hazel Scott, who has a fine bit in a French cafe in Paris, the first time George goes abroad. She sings 'The Man I Love' in French and English, and plays a medley of Gershwin airs on the piano as a compliment to George who is sitting in the little French cabaret.

This afternoon Anne Brown is coming in for a conference. We have signed her to sing 'Summertime' in the 'Porgy & Bess' sequence. She created the role of Bess in the original production in New York. We have added the famous dancer of the former 'George White Scandals' - Tom Patricola - to do a dancing bit in the Scandals sequence.

Oscar Levant is here and I have been seeing a lot of him. He is the most nervous human being I have ever met; the unhappiest man I have ever associated with, and difficult to handle but his playing of the 'Rhapsody' makes up for everything. Paul Whiteman, on the other hand, is a grand guy and cooperates beautifully.

Today we are shooting Albert Basserman's scenes which will be marvelous and we start with Charles Coburn on Monday.

This picture is going to cost over $2,000,000 and I feel a sense of great responsibility as a result of this extraordinary cost - but if it comes off, as I hope, I will have three distinguished pictures in a row which will give me a record and a place in the industry that is unique.

... I met Mrs. Presnell last night and she told me that Bob is in Australia. She just had a letter from him and is 'phoning me today to give me his address so that I can write to him. It would be funny if you were sent overseas and turned up in Australia. It would be nicer if you remained in the good old U.S.A., but things have a way of working out and I know that whatever happens it will be for the best and you will be o.k. ...

If the question was 'What did Hollywood do in the war, Daddy?' The answer was, 'A lot'. Mrs. Presnell Jr. was actress Marsha Hunt. Her husband Robert Jr. was a highly regarded screenwriter, like his father. A few short years later, on October 27, 1947 Marsha and Robert Jr. would be an outspoken part of a newly formed group of Hollywood actors, writers and directors to fly to Washington D.C. to protest the Hollywood Un-American Activities Committee (HUAC) who were blacklisting members of the Hollywood film industry whom they considered were secret subversive communists. Industry members found themselves pariahs and unemployable.

Many star names were among the protesters including John Huston, Humphrey Bogart and Lauren Bacall. Actor Luther Adler discovered his name was on the Blacklist and didn't work in Hollywood again for years. 'They couldn't miss my name - it began with an A', he told me and said he had existed on apples.

On his return from the South Pacific (where he was now to be sent), Jesse found himself called up before HUAC and questioned as to whether he was a member of the Communist Party. They said he had attended a lecture with writer Dorothy Parker.

'The Communist Party?' he replied and shook his head. 'No', he said. 'I never attend a party to which I was not invited.' The only thing that stopped them from questioning him further was the fact that he was filming General Macarthur's landings in the South Pacific on the date of that particular lecture.

August 6, 1943
Dear Jesse,

... This has been an exciting week. Mother and Betty arrived from Denver on Monday ... Billy's baby has been named Ronald Charles Lasky and weighed 7pds. 6 oz. at birth. Reports from Denver tell me that Billy, Margery

ROBERT ALDA

and the baby are all doing well. The papers out here have been teeming with stories, labeling me a Grandpa; there were big celebrations on the sets - LeRoy Prinz' unit printed a placard, signed by over 100 of the cast and crew - and the Rapper unit had quite a celebration when I came on the stage. I had to open cigars for the whole studio. . . .

By the time this reaches you, I suppose your combat training will be about ended—and then what? I shall be anxious to hear what your prospects are.

... The picture is progressing splendidly, and if we can keep up the pace we have set for ourselves and the quality that is beginning to appear on the screen, it will top 'York' and 'Mark Twain'. By the way, Bob Alda, as Gershwin, is sensational. I will be responsible for a new young star. ...

I am looking forward to your next letter—and hope this finds Frances well and not too tired from her long days at Saks—and I know it will find you in top physical condition due to your combat training.

My devoted love to you both.

For *Rhapsody in Blue*, Jesse L. Lasky is listed as producer and Hal B. Wallis as executive producer. The film's director, Irving Rapper, was nominated for the 1946 grand prize at the Cannes Film Festival. *Rhapsody in Blue* was also nominated for two Academy Awards; Best Musical Scoring of a Musical Picture: Ray Heindorf and Max Steiner. Best Sound: Nathan Levinson.

As for Jesse, what he wanted to happen, had happened. He was to experience the war with General MacArthur, filming the first landings. His father was involved in his own war at the studio

August 11, 1943
Dear Jesse,

... Naturally we were not surprised when you telephoned as we were prepared for the news. I wouldn't have it any different, and if I had the power or influence to keep you here, I would not assert it. At this stage of your career, to participate in the greatest adventure in the history of the world is a privilege and something that you will remember with pride and satisfaction all your life.

At last a Lasky is really going to be right at the front and actively participating in a war. America has been good to us, and Mother and I feel it is a privilege for you to go overseas to do your bit. We have no fears whatever as to your safe return - our minds don't run in that direction ... We will be with you in spirit, and we will hold up our heads with pride at any and every meeting where the war is discussed. Our first-born is overseas! ... And now about Frances. We will have her met at Pasadena with a car to take all her baggage. Be sure that she plans to get off there as the Union Station in Los Angeles is impossible. She should wire me the day she leaves, and we will have her for dinner the night she arrives. I will talk over her financial affairs with her and see that she is well taken care of, so, when you sail, you are not leaving any problems behind you.

...I am delighted that you were able to meet Buddy before you sail. You can see why we are all so fond of him and how lucky Betty is in getting a husband who is as keen and fine as Buddy is.

Enclosed is a check for $400.00 - the extra hundred is for your birthday, September 19th. Just think - you will be 33 and I, 63 but the way I feel, I can carry on for another twenty years, if necessary. My health is fine; my spirit was never better - and I like the feeling that I am helping out the whole family at a time when they all need help - Billy and Margie; Buddy and Betty and you and Frances - to say nothing of Grandma and Bess. When I think of the help I am able to extend at this critical time, I have a feeling of warm satisfaction - I have not worked in vain....

August 13, 1943

...Was so glad to get your wire on Wednesday advising us that the event had been delayed for four weeks. That was good news because it gives you time to get yourself organized and Frances packed up ready to return home...Just received a letter from Margie telling us that she will soon be moving out of the hospital and that she is getting along fine and that the baby is marvelous...

By the way, in talking with Col. Levinson, I mentioned that you had received orders to sail very soon. He told me he was sure that you would be assigned to Col. Gillette's outfit as he has already sent for many of his officers. Gillette is on General Eisenhower's staff, and I have a hunch that Col. Levinson is right and your destination is North Africa or somewhere in that vicinity. If that should be true, it will be a strange quirk of fate that you should find yourself in the same country that you, Art and Mother explored not so many years ago.

Well, I must bring this letter to a hasty close have just called me to come out to the set.

My devoted love to you both.

August 20, 1943

...this morning Mother read me your beautiful letter to her, which touched her deeply. You will never know what pleasure your letters give us and how carefully we read them...By the way, Major Paul Sloane introduced me to Colonel Whatshisname? I can't remember it - anyway, I think he is the head of the Signal Corps - could his name have been Temple or something like that - at any rate, the Colonel said: 'You have a son who is with us and I am happy to tell you that I hear very good reports about him.' He seemed to know all about you and he is a very important officer.

...The picture is going great. Many of the sequences are assembled and, consequently, I am in a position to say that we are getting a truly great picture. The boy, Alda, who plays Gershwin is doing fine work, as are Charles Coburn, Levant, Whiteman, Morris Carnovsky, Albert Basserman, and the others. Last Sunday we made the sound tracks of the Concerto with an orchestra of 75 men, and Oscar Levant at the piano doing solo passages which, in one sequence will be played by himself, and in another sequence will be played by George Gershwin. The studio is agog over the magnificence of the recording of these sound tracks. Next week we do 'Summer Time' from 'Porgy and Bess', with Anne Brown singing this beautiful number...Nino Martini is here and I took him and Rouben Mamoulian down to a Beach House last night with Mother - and we had a wonderful musical evening. Nino sang like a Greek God.

No doubt you have noticed I am getting a lot of publicity. I sent you a review that appeared in the Sunday Times - and enclosed is one that appeared the same Sunday in the N.Y. Herald-Tribune....I was surprised the other day to have a 'phone call from Sam Jaffe, the Agent, who said that he had a proposition to make to me from Twentieth Century-Fox, and would I consider such a proposition. Of course I answered that I was very happy at Warner Bros, and that my contract runs for another year - nevertheless, it was nice to know I am in demand. As a matter of fact, a few weeks ago, Louis Mayer told me in person that he wished I was at his studio - so my position in the industry has never been as good as it is now - I mean since I left Paramount.

To my surprise, I am enjoying producing 'Gershwin' more than I had anticipated. My early vaudeville training, and experience with musicals at the Folies Bergere, and my own understanding of music, has made me very close to the musical end of this picture - and the crew indicate that for the first time they are working with a Producer who knows what it is all about.

Mother and I attended a dinner the other night at the home of Richard Hageman, the symphony conductor - a group of twenty people, all of them distinguished. The hostess called on me to introduce the two principal guests - Upton Close[85] and Dr. Luckner. The latter spoke brilliantly of the German situation and of his many interviews with Hitler - and Upton Close spoke pessimistically on the general world situation - but it was all very interesting - and Mother, who doesn't read about world politics, was tremendously impressed.

By the way, I read a book last week called 'The Dead Look On' by Gerald Kersh. It is the finest piece of writing I have come across in years. Please buy yourself a copy and read it - in fact, to be sure that you read it, I am enclosing two extra dollars, the cost of the book. Now send Frances shopping and get a copy. It is terribly realistic - I wouldn't let Mother read it for worlds - but you should not miss it.

---

85 Explorer, adventurer, journalist, author, and radio commentator.

Well, they are 'phoning me to come out to the stage so I must bring this to a close....

August 25, 1943

...I have the strongest kind of hunch that your destination is Australia and that you will be under Col. Bob Presnell's command. If this hunch should prove true, I hope we will get a chance to see you...my hunch is based on information which I cannot divulge and which I believe will come true.

I met Mrs. Presnell recently and she asked me to write Bob, which I am glad I did - and in my letter I said there were rumors of your being sent overseas and that I hoped Destiny would put you under his command.

...By the way, Peter Keane gave me a snapshot of you in full regalia - rifle and helmet - which I am going to have enlarged. Whoever thought, when your hobby was playing with soldiers as a little boy at Hillside and La Brea, that I would have in my office a picture of you as a real soldier, fully equipped for battle. I am afraid your Dad is still romantic, and somewhere in my youthful interior there is a slight feeling of envy for the adventures that are ahead of you....

September 2, 1943

...The picture is moving along satisfactorily, as far as I can judge by the rushes. We finished shooting 'Summertime' with Anne Brown singing the number - and we have shot about two-thirds of the script. This has really been a tough picture with plenty of problems still ahead, but when we finally get it all together, it is liable to be pretty damn good. The company has picked three pictures for road-showing: 'Mark Twain', 'Saratoga Trunk' and 'Rhapsody in Blue'.

...The war news certainly continues good. Well they are waiting for me in the projection room so I will have to bring this letter to an abrupt close as I want to get it off so you will have the enclosure by Saturday night....

September 8, 1943

...I was delighted to learn that Betty and Buddy reached New York in time to spend Sunday night with you, and I hope you are seeing a lot of each other. Since Betty married, we seem to be so much closer than we were, even when she lived at home.

This morning, as I rode to the studio, I heard the first announcement of the 'unconditional surrender' of Italy. As the vibrant words came over the radio, tears came into my eyes and I uttered an audible 'Thank God'. I was the first to take the news out on the set and we stopped production five minutes to celebrate. Certainly this tremendous event is the 'beginning of the end'. I don't imagine it will affect your overseas adventure - and, somehow, I hope it doesn't. I have a tremendous hunch that your going overseas is right and will be the most important event in your life. Keep me posted on what you learn about your next move ... My picture continues to progress satisfactorily. Oscar Levant finished his part yesterday and leaves for New York tomorrow - and I am giving him a Farewell Dinner tonight at The Players. I have invited Ira Gershwin and his wife; Oscar Levant and his wife; Irving Rapper, the director; Sol Polito, my pet cameraman, and his wife - and my first Assistant Director, Bob Vreeland. After dinner I am bringing them back to the studio and I am going to show them all the cut sequences of the picture. Oscar has promised to call you at your home after he arrives in New York. ...

September 14, 1943

...Mother airmailed you a package for your Birthday this morning and we hope it will reach you on time - and this letter is my Birthday Greeting to you and may it be a happy day! You know you will be in our thoughts all day, particularly as we just received your letter telling us that you 'take off' on Sunday for the great adventure.

Mother read your letter aloud at breakfast this morning - she choked up a little bit, which is only natural - but we have been prepared for the news and we both know it is the right thing and we wouldn't change the situation if it were in our power to do so. We understand perfectly that you will be out of touch while you are at your port of embarkation and if we don't get any letters, we will understand the reason why. If, by any chance, you should be in the vicinity of San Francisco and could let me know, I will fly up and see you. ...

If you should be in Seattle, think of the time I found myself in Seattle, a second-class passenger on the S/S Zealandia, enroute to Cape Nome. I was alone and only twenty years old; had never been away from home and didn't have too much money in my pocket, and had no idea how I would ever get back to Frisco. It would be strange if you should sail from the same port—on a much greater adventure!

Thank you for your wire which was beautifully expressed and which we read on the morning of my birthday. When I reached the studio, I received many messages of congratulations and, in the afternoon, they called me out on the set and had all the cast and crew assembled - about 75 people. They had also invited Rouben Mamoulian, Sonya Levien and Jack Emanuel - and as I entered the set they played the *Rhapsody in Blue*, and presented me with a huge birthday cake, and served ice cream to the crew. On a long table they had a picture of 'Sergeant York' (Gary Cooper) on one side, and a picture of 'Mark Twain' (Fredric March) on the other end and, in the middle, a scroll, in a frame, with a picture of me and signed by all the members of the cast and crew of 'Rhapsody in Blue'. It was a touching ceremony and I thanked them all in a very brief speech.

So now my birthday is over, and while the calendar says I am a year older, I feel ten years younger than I did a year ago.

Things are going well at the studio. My affairs are in fine shape and I have a lot to be thankful for ... So, enjoy your birthday and don't worry about the folks behind ... one of these days, you will be back with a service ribbon on your chest, and a good old Lasky welcome awaiting you - and you will tell your story from the day you sailed until your safe arrival home.

God Bless You - and Keep You. My devoted love to you both. ...

Lasky also wrote to Jesse's wife, aware of what a difficult time it was for her, and was always ready to offer help. Jesse got to come home for a few days, and his father proudly paraded him around the studio, delighted to show his film to his writer son. The studio photographer recorded the visit, which included director Irving Rapper, and Jesse returned to San Francisco in time to be shipped out.

October 7, 1943
Dear Jesse,

... Just a line to let you know how much I appreciated receiving your letter written last Sunday ... Mother is returning tomorrow night (Friday); she just 'phoned me from Carmel. She was in Frisco on Wednesday and hoped she might locate you at the St. Francis Hotel. It would have been thrilling if you could have run into each other.

You will be interested in knowing that the first draft of my 'Hollywood Canteen' story is finished and it is a 'honey'; I am very enthusiastic about it. In the meantime, the 'Gershwin' picture is coming along great. Rapper will be finished shooting next week. ...

Last night I went to a sneak preview of 'Saratoga Trunk' with Jack Warner and Hal Wallis, and to my amazement it turned out to be a very dull picture. The stars, Gary Cooper and Ingrid Bergman, give good performances, but the story is very uninteresting. I wonder if you read the book—I didn't.

Tomorrow night Mamoulian is giving a birthday party at the Players restaurant which I plan to attend.

Frances and I had breakfast together this morning—and we are wondering if you will be able to communicate with us soon again. If you are free to telephone, why don't you call us on Sunday morning, as I don't think Frances will move into her house before Monday.

All the best and keep your chin up!

LIEUT. JESSE, LASKY, IRVING RAPPER

October 12, 1943

...I just mailed you two photos which I thought you might like to have. They are the ones taken on the set when you were here and I hope they reach you safely. If you cannot take them with you, maybe you will want to mail them back to Frances... Rapper finishes shooting 'Rhapsody in Blue' but we still have some musical numbers for LeRoy Prinz to shoot... Thursday night I am going to Jack Warner's house and show him the whole picture assembled, with everything in it but the few musical numbers... We are a little anxious over the gas situation as we will only get three gallons to a coupon, where before we got four—but my little Austin will save the situation. Mother and I are looking forward to your next letter - and when the letters stop, we will know you are on your way....

First Lieutenant Jesse had hoped to be sent to Europe, but the Army had its own ideas. His regiment was to be shipped out from San Francisco as a replacement to a Signal Corps battalion in MacArthur's South Pacific Army. He kept a diary during the war. This is what he wrote that day:

JESSE'S DIARY – October 15, 1943

Left S.F. Harbor aboard transport Fred C. Ainsworth. Awoke in port, of course - breakfasted well - second call in a comfortable mess. The meals are excellent - served in a dining room or mess - with tables for groups and pairs. There is a salon or lounge - and of course we must wear our life preservers or carry them at all times. Then up on deck to watch us pull out of the harbor. This ship being fast, travels alone and un-convoyed. Moved stately down the harbor, under the first of the bridges. In the distance the tips of the Golden Gate Bridge stood out of a scarf of mist – slowly - by submarines, under many types of planes, we moved out of the harbor - through the great submarine net - the Golden Gate - and out to sea. A single naval blimp circled us nimbly out in the Pacific. There was a considerable ground swell, which rocked my berth pretty violently at times. Read in bed and passed a quiet time - then to sleep early. Shall not forget the last sight of the navy blimp as it curved gracefully back toward the mainland, leaving us alone in the Pacific.

Seven days later his father wrote to him.

October 22, 1943
Dear Jesse:

Not having heard from you for many days makes us believe that you are on the high seas, or about to jump off. Well, I am going to write to you every Friday until I know your destination and then we will send you V-Mail letters.

We met Frances at a cocktail party at Rudy Maté's[86] last Sunday and then we took her to dinner at the smart Savoy restaurant. She enjoyed it very much and seems to be in good spirits.

Today is a beautiful typical California day - and tonight I am going to Paradise with Cecil and spend Saturday there.

We just made the sound track of 'An American in Paris' and it is the most magnificent thing you have ever heard. We only have a couple of numbers to shoot and the picture will be finished, although we cannot shoot the sequence with Al Jolson for some time as he is ill in New York. We are going to start 'Hollywood Canteen' in four weeks and it is going to be a lot of fun working on this one, I have found a boy named Robert Hutton - handsome, six feet tall, and with the same qualities as Jimmy Stewart - shy and bashful, but with a world of personality. He will play the Corporal who falls in love with Ann Sheridan and, of course, Ann will play herself.

I have been going around a lot lately, to dinners, etc., and having a pretty good time, Sunday I went to a cocktail party at Walter Wanger's and then met Mother at the Rudy Maté cocktail party....

---

86 One of the most respected cinematographers in the industry.

October 30, 1943

... It is a strange sensation writing letters to someone who cannot answer - nevertheless, I want to keep you posted on the news at home. Billy, Margie and the baby arrived on Thursday; we met them at the train and had a very happy morning. The baby is adorable and Mother has enjoyed having him in the house. Every time I come home, she is carrying the baby around. Frances, Grandma and Margie's mother came in for dinner on Thursday night, but Bill was taken ill after dinner and had to go to bed. He had a mild touch of intestinal flu which the doctor said he brought with him from Denver; however, he will be up and out tomorrow (Sunday) as he was feeling much better today. It was a tough break for Bill as he had so many things he wanted to do and had been looking forward to this furlough for months - but he will still have a week before he returns to Denver....

We are going to start the 'Hollywood Canteen' picture November 29th. I had lunch with Bette Davis and John Garfield yesterday and they said it was one of the finest scripts they had ever read, and they agreed to play the parts assigned to them. We will have a wonderful cast of stars lined up by the time the picture starts ... needless for me to tell you that you are constantly in our minds. We all send our love.

Out of contact with his family for three weeks after sailing, Jesse marched down the gangplank in Australia. That night the battalion slept under tents on a dog track outside Brisbane, and the next morning he was flown in a C47 across the Coral Sea to New Guinea. On the busy airstrip, Jesse ran straight into a familiar face—Merian C. Cooper, Famous Players-Lasky's great documentary maker (with Ernest Schoedsack), now an Air Force brigadier general. Later, he stopped to chat with Gary Cooper, who was passing through with a USO show. The actor's back problems had kept him out of active service, but *Sergeant York* had been of some small service to the war effort.

Fourteen days later, they were in Auckland, New Zealand. Jesse had served in the Army for one year and twenty-six weeks as they moved on to Brisbane. On the 17th of November, they arrived in Port Moresby, New Guinea. His diary recorded:

JESSE'S DIARY – November 17, 1943

We were routed out at 2:45 in the dark dawn with a hard rain smashing at us. A very pretty Australian girl in uniform drove us in an Army station wagon over rain soaked roads to Archer field—Brisbane's airport. Coffee and donuts served from a Red Cross hut in the streaming rain and one jammed station room in which troops, equipment, pilots, Navy—all crowded awaiting departures. Finally boarded a C47 transport plane sitting along walls ... About four hours to sit down in the bright heat of Townsville where we had what was sacrilegiously referred to as hamburgers. Then up to climb over the Great

Barrier Reef—coral—deep green formations giving way to bright turquoise pools. Four hours, then out of the clouds loomed New Guinea—Port Moresby. Down on a strip and joined the 832nd Signal Service Company . . . Moved into a fine big tent built off the ground... Drove through a fascinating country of coconut palms, loin clothed natives with red dyed bushy hair.

SCENE SEVEN
1943 - 1949

CAPTAIN HIVELY AND LIEUTENANT LASKY JR.

Lasky had written his first V-mail to his son not knowing where he was, nor when he would receive it. For the time being, all correspondence would be via V-mail. The government advertised the parchment thin letter service as: V-MAIL IS SPEED MAIL. You WRITE. He'll FIGHT!

November 27, 1943 – V-MAIL
Dear Jesse,

... I was thrilled to receive your Signal Corps postcard; your letter to Mother which is already on its way to New York where she is still vacationing - and most exciting of all - your first letter from some coral reef island in the South Pacific. I know now that when you return, my days as a storyteller are over and you will hold the center of the stage every Sunday night until the end of time.

First - let's talk of Frances. I keep in close touch with her; her allowance goes to her every week - we had dinner with Grandma and she had breakfast with me, and I loaded her with avocados and persimmons from the garden. I am taking her to the Ballet Russe on Monday night and, at her suggestion, have invited Mrs. Presnell. With two such lovely girls, both dancers, I should have, a thrilling evening at the Ballet.

'Hollywood Canteen' starts in two days. I am having a h--l of a time getting stars for the 50 or 60 star bits in the picture - but we will pull it through to a grand success. 'Rhapsody in Blue' is nearing completion and 'Mark Twain' opens in March, with the greatest exploitation campaign for road-showing that any picture ever had.

Mother expects to return from New York Dec. 6th and seems to be enjoying the change; seeing many shows and concerts. Betty just advised me that she and Buddy will be moved again from Raleigh, N.C. to some destination unknown thus far. Billy is doing swell work in Denver and he, Margy and the baby are getting along fine.

... Mother has written you many letters but I am afraid she must have misdirected them and I am not sure you have received all my letters as I have written regularly every week. I find it difficult to express myself when I don't know where you are or when you will receive a letter - in other words, my routine of studio happenings seem trivial when I think of the great adventure in which you are sharing. I am so grateful that you have this opportunity of participating and being near the heart of things - well, don't worry about things at home. My job is to keep everybody happy and the home fires burning - and some day we will turn out en masse to welcome you home....

Lasky began a steady stream of V-mails with the hope that Jesse would receive them. Betty's husband, Buddy, was still stateside.

November 22, 1943   V-MAIL
Dear Jesse,

...Am having a tough time securing stars for HOLLYWOOD CANTEEN, which starts November 29th but we will pull it through to a grand success. MARK TWAIN Is all set for road-showing next March. We are still shooting musical numbers for Rhapsody—and that is all the studio news.

Compared to your marvelous letter, this letter seems very dull, but V-Mail cramps my style... If you get to any of the cities mentioned in the list, please call on the representatives who may know me.

With devoted love. Dad

It was not until December 13th, a few days after they arrived in New Guinea to film the landing, that First Lt. Jesse and Jack Hively found themselves heading in a landing craft to Milne Bay, which had recently been captured from the Japanese. Hively, a film director in civilian life, was Jesse's superior officer and became a reliable friend. With a combat photographic detachment, they had been sent to join the 'Confederates', the 112th Texas Cavalry, who were staging on Goodenough Island for the invasion of New Britain at Arawe Bay. They were immediately made honorary Confederates, to join MacArthur's 'reconnaissance in force'.

As they were about to embark, Jesse saw MacArthur for the first time—squinting benevolently—and smoking a curious corncob pipe. When the general didn't address the men, Jesse decided what MacArthur needed was a good scriptwriter. He wrote in his diary:

DIARY: December 13, 1943

Up in the hot insect crawling day to make final packing and policing of area. We learned that Gen. MacArthur would be over from 6th Army to watch the last force takeoff. Was as close as five feet from the hero of Bataan, a soldierly form in a tarnished gold-encrusted cap—the civilian's dream of the perfect general, but strangely enough, he is ignored or disliked by the soldiers who refer to him as 'dugout Doug' and even go so far as to cast aspersions on the circumstances of his departure from the Philippines. He smoked a large cigar in a somewhat theatrical manner—with him Generals Kruger and Cunningham. The first wave of Buffalos commanded by Lt. Col. Grant rolled by MacArthur and chugged out to sea to be met by their mother ship in whose pouch they would ride like baby kangaroos, to the mission. They came by with metallic crunching thunder of their caterpillars, moving one after the other past the handsome General. I felt disappointed that he said never a word, nor wish of luck, nor even a salute to these men who would carry his hopes to a new island. I boarded the Westrailia with Swed and Hurda, (his camera crew) found them quarters and then spent most of the evening chatting with war correspondents and Major Weiner. Late in the darkness the Westrailia slipped away from Goodenough. It was too hot to sleep and nerves were like wild wires.

Jesse was attached to the 96th Infantry and in command of this combat photographic mission. Since his officers included lieutenant colonels he had to salute them before giving them orders. His diary chronicles the training period before the actual landing, when the battalion practiced going over the side on landing nets. He shot scenes of the men during the practice landings on White Beach, where there was 'much confusion' getting in between the coral reefs and the 'Buffalos' bumping up onto the beach and troops taking off into the undergrowth. With Swed and Herd, Jesse, as writer-producer-director, filmed incomparable actual scenes of the troops' first landing.

Now, with the sea behind them, there was no place to go but forward. Under fire, they needed reinforcements and soon got them; a detachment of jungle fighters was brought in at night from Finschhafen. By the light of dawn, they discovered that their rescuers were a detachment of Native Americans, an assortment of tribes who didn't share a common dialect. Once traditional enemies, they were fighting side by side in the common American cause. Jesse resolved never again to write a scene 'in which the Army arrived in the nick of time to save the settlers from the redskins.' He wrote later '… But my promise was broken on my first film assignment after the war—*Unconquered*.'

Jesse's personal diary documents these first landings, filming it all. It is a unique record.

DIARY: December 14, 1943

In the harbor of Boona the convoy slowly gathers itself around us and then quietly, suddenly, we were off into the blue sea between New Guinea and the Island of New Britain. Behind and before us were ships all manner of craft—the squat, tight-jawed little destroyers protecting our flank.

We photographed all over the ship, the sprawling ease-taking men of C Troop the day before their dip into history. Part of the 1,500 combat troops to land in the vicinity of Arawe coral reefed, crawling with thousands of Japs. The intelligence reports were frightening. In the evening I joined Major Weiner and somewhat gravely cleaned our weapons. Running through my mind, the words, the thought— 'I hate to see that evening sun go down'—for as it dropped slowly, it brought us nearer into that darkness, from which we would spring upon an unknown beach facing an unknown force, with nothing certain but the impossibility of escape or withdrawal.

But there was no moodiness on the deck where men played cards, cleaned weapons, and even read adventure magazines. It was too hellishly hot to sleep. Lt. Thomas called his non-coms about him in the darkness explaining final details of loading—and ending with a silent prayer, after which he said the words, 'God give us the wisdom to make good decisions tomorrow.'

And then he went to his hot bunk and lay without sleep—minds razor sharp, waiting and waiting—minds pounding, throbbing.

DIARY: December 15, 1943

Wednesday. Landed at Arawe New Britain. Cold, black dawn with a disc of moon behind scudding clouds. Up at 1.30 to breakfast almost sedately with the officers. Little said. Then out on the quiet deck—armed, helmeted, waiting for the Westrallia to become still and the LCVs were lowered into the sea. Then quietly, almost without orders or emotion, clamored down the landing nets into jam-packed boat No.1—took my place with Maj. Weiner and a Scotch burr-tongued medic of the 112th who supplied Lt. Thomas with pills for his headache, remarking on man's fear of the dark; a fear born and inherited from the prehistoric night in the forest full of saber-toothed tigers.

We milled interminably in a circle, started for shore, drew tracer fire—and sparks spraying at us, realized the first wave of Buffalos were delayed. Then saw the naval barrage pour flame and screaming thunder into the beach and hill that was our objective. Collected wounded from a Buffalo, which the doctor treated in the boat, then we moved into the beach, but got stuck on the coral—washed ashore to meet Jack (Hively) and the others. In that moment on the beach at New Britain—it seemed an easy thing—and it was nothing to follow the first line of troops.

Then the bottom dropped out of the world. Flashing Zeros with red suns on their wings peeled off and rolled over us, strafing and bombing. The bombs shoot the earth but the strafing drives us mad. We tried to sink ourselves under our helmets—lay in a shell crater with a chaplain and all three of us praying and blubbing. Jack and I embraced like lovers. Exhaustion. And all the rest of the day the struggle to find our equipment—almost nothing to eat or drink but coconut milk. Finally slept between (Chaplain) Kent and Jack beside our shell crater.

DIARY: December 16, 1943

Thursday. The night was made horrible by Washing Machine Charlie, a Jap seaplane. Actually we learned later 12 to 15 of them leisurely and nonchalantly flew over, faking dives, bombing intermittently, strafing frequently. It kept us awake and huddled frightened in our dugout and it lasted with the full moon all night. No breakfast but what we could pull together out of a K ration and coconut juice to save precious water.

The place stinks of dead Japs one of whom was carried or dragged down the hill by the arms to be buried in the valley. Up only a few moments when a crashing, smashing, strafing cloud of Zeros descended and once more we huddled in the crater, in stark terror of falling coral and sandstone which the earth heaved up and shook under the stabbing bombs and machine gun fire. Later, pulled ourselves together sufficiently to take a Buffalo up to the first hospital collecting point at the front. The way was through ragged, wrecked coconut palms. We photographed dead Japs and wounded receiving first aid treatment, then back with shock, hysteria and prostration cases—to deliver them to the evacuation hospital tent. Then came a terrible raid, bombing and strafing and the operating tent was destroyed 50 yards in front of our hole—a mess of burning rubble, debris, dead and wounded, screams for litter bearers, etc. 2 or 3 wounded went up the hill to our dugout and I held one machine gunner in my arms, trying to calm him—they were evacuated later.

The heat came down hard and we spent most of the day ducking strafing, watching dogfights and trying to improve our hole in the cliff. We knocked down overhanging rocks, hacked down a palm with our machetes and forced ourselves to eat the cold, unpalatable food that was left of our rations. Also walked to the beach to wash in salt water but threatened bombing raids drove us to the vicinity of our hole. The boy at the 50 caliber who fired all night was taken away screaming that the trees were full of dead and certainly the smell, the sick warm smell of dead was in the air. The wounded were evacuated but another rain in late afternoon sank a craft or barge in the hospital, and there were more of our dead brought up the hill. Worked desperately alternating photographs and fixing our hole for the night. A council agreed we would take out the boys. Our morale is bad. Darkness and a sick-eyed medical captain sharing our biscuits and coffee brewed over a handful of palm cuttings. Night long the terror of the planes gives us no sleep and trigger-happy men firing at shadows, trees, each other and perhaps a few legitimate targets as there were more Jap dead by morning. Another morning raid and the American dead were brought up the hill on a Buffalo.

DIARY: December 18, 1943

Saturday. Washing Machine Charlie again. But no morn raid so we arranged transportation and went up to the front line. Heavy artillery fire day all night now, from our own guns—105s, I think. The passage to the front took us through a long shell-pocked stretch of plantation—deserted—empty and terribly silent. Got the creeps driving alone between the lines—knowing there were Japs about us as several had been killed in the area and one Texas Farmer on patrol had actually killed four with a sub-machine gun he had never previously fired. At the front Col. Grant and Major MacMahon were as cheerful as boys in summer, sporting captured Jap rifles and a Texas flag under which they posed—with boys from Brooklyn. The front line itself is quiet. Men sit in craters facing the tangled near distance where there are Japs no more than 200 yards away. At night they jabber and patrols clash and a Jap armed with two blade razors was killed when picking up a hand grenade to toss it back. 'That'll teach him to keep his hands off things that don't belong to him', commented a Texan who had thrown it.

DIARY: December 19, 1943

Sunday. An LCT (Landing Craft Transport) almost tried to push the sun down while our craft circled maddeningly awaiting other LCTs to form the convoy. At last it did, and without appearance of Zeros, thank God. So for the first time, relaxed, we climbed into a Buffalo and slept on a stack of life preservers and didn't mind the rain. Awoke in Red Herring, the supply point on the New Guinea coast and had lunch—the first hot meal in how long?

With no idea that Jesse had just survived a shattering first taste of war, his father V-mailed, thinking his son was safe somewhere in Australia.

December 7, 1943 – V-MAIL
Dear Jesse,

... Mother is still in New York; she just wired me that she ran Mark Twain for Gilbert Miller and a number of distinguished guests and it caused a small-sized sensation. Betty is still stationed at Raleigh, N.C., but is going to join Mother and come home with her for a brief respite from Army camp life.

I am in the midst of producing 'Hollywood Canteen'; it is the toughest job I ever tackled, principally an account of the difficulty in getting the many stars our script calls for. Good old Al Jolson arrived here at last, after a long illness in the east, and we are now shooting 'Swanee', which will wind up ' Rhapsody in Blue'.

I still have the funniest sensation in writing to you—I wonder if and when you get my letters, and I try to picture the circumstances under which you receive them. You said in your letter to Frances that you were in Nome-Honolulu, and other experiences—and I knew exactly what you meant....

We were shooting scenes in a jungle yesterday for the opening of our 'Hollywood Canteen' picture. One scene showed the soldiers sitting outdoors in the rain watching a motion picture. It was exactly as you described seeing pictures wherever you are. By the way, I was thrilled to see the picture you sent Frances of you and your brother-officers taken in an Officers' Club before you moved to your present base.

... I feel our spirits are very close. If the going gets tough, imagine your adventurous Dad by your side. Randy joins me in sending you our very best....

Jesse's mention of Nome-Honolulu referred to his father's adventure as one of the first men in the gold rush to Nome, Alaska, and a second adventure where he went to Honolulu as the first white man to be leader of 'The Royal Hawaiian Band'. Lasky had no idea that Jesse had been in the thick of it filming first landings in the Pacific.

Jesse, back in Australia, wrote to Frances, concerned that the folks back home would be worried. He made it sound a bit like an adventure from *Pirates of the Caribbean*.

December 27, 1943
Darling Person,

It is still hard to write, and my stomach is doing slight 'nip-ups', but I am forcing myself to get off a letter, which I hope you will share with Bess, Dad, Grandma, and all other interested parties. Eventually words will pour out on paper, and I'll be able to write everyone, but they must understand, that while the things that happened are still so large and strong in the imagination, it is hard to translate them into words. The base censorship officer has kindly offered to personally go through this letter, and I'll be careful not to mention anything that would not be permitted.

Well, Donna (Frances), whether you guessed it or not, and I somehow feel you have, I have been on a combat mission. Am now back in a city in Australia, safe as Westwood Village, and have not even a scratch aside from the fox-hole digging calluses on my hands to show for the adventure.

I am permitted to tell you, that we participated in the first American landing on New Britain. Our mission, of course, was to make a picture on the operation, and it was certainly one of the most exciting things I ever expect to live through. It was also a wonderful experience, an intensification of emotional reactions - always fear - yet a kind of sense of privilege at being at last in the arena of war itself rather than viewing it from a distant seat on the grandstand.

We accompanied a Task Force and landed upon a beach. The first time under fire was a sensation almost of exhilaration. I saw the tracer bullets flying toward us, looking like sparklers on a Fourth of July evening - or the light of a city - harmless pretty little blobs of death, and the surprising reaction of not being afraid - being rather fascinated by their streaming toward us. I had to be told firmly to get my head down - and when the landing was first accomplished I got another thrill of exhilaration. Here we were - the first troops to land on the Island, the Japs dead or driven back before us - war seemed the glorious adventure encountered in novels about British officers on the frontier of India.

We wanted and started to follow the advance, indeed I felt capable of leading it, with my camera in one hand, film and grenades bulging my pockets, weapon in the other hand, ammunition dragging my belt half way down to my knees, jungle pack – machete - extra canteen. Well - shortly after that the plumes and glory and bugling had completely left my mind - we were bombed, (an endurable sensation) and strafed—machines flying low - pumping machine gun fire into the shell-packed earth. Jack Hively (the only member of our original group to share our experience) and your loving husband hit a shell crater at one and the same time - and lay in each other's arms, unashamed to pray out loud, and knowing that strange sensation of wanting to tuck our entire bodies under our helmets - every inch of skin, bone, and gut, sucked up under the steel helmet - where perhaps an exaggerated sense of security was present. I don't and couldn't say how long it lasted, nor how many raids we had - nor how successful our own air cover was - nor what was dropped, nor when, as all this would come under the head of military information - but I may say that death flew down upon us quite frequently, with tremendous impact, and plenty of teeth chatter effects, but perhaps somewhat smaller than expected actual damage.

We crawled and groveled up the side of the crater after this first air to earth activity - I was down off my white horse, and interested in little else than survival - exhaustion set in, as I was not of course as physically conditioned as the combat troops.

From there on, all visions of glory disappeared - and I felt like a very frightened and dirty civilian who had accidentally stumbled upon a moment of Judgment Day. Yes, I think a lot of men learned to pray - and they learned other good things. They learned interdependence, cooperation, and the sense of being a team - caught in the same grip of things - working, trying, surviving together - in the most intimate terms, that human relationship might ever achieve.

I saw more natural politeness - more brief sacrifices - more share and share whatever ration you have – water - or a taste of coffee brewed over cross-sticks in a tin can. There are no tough guys, and no wise guys and no heroes and no cowards, for everyone is a little bit of a coward and a hero, but most all those who are not casualties, physical or mental, do their job - fighting exhaustion, heat, discomfort, sleeplessness - but they do what they had been brought to do, which I suppose is the reason we were successful. That, and the fine careful planning that preceded the operation.

It is curious that in combat, you learn to like men more than you ever have - you share food and dirt, and sweat, but you are as stripped of hypocrisies, and the complex clothes of civilized living as a skinned rat. You talk and think of little things that are big - you are grateful for the brief loan of an entrenching pick, as you would not once have been grateful for three cases of champagne. You draw comfort and solace from each other - and I've seen tough - flint-fisted guys, who might beat up a man on a Saturday night for a dime, caring for wounded and shock cases more gently than mothers for sick children.

Well, we saw plenty, as we were there for several days - and I shall be grateful all my life for the experience though never actually look for another. Nor will there be others for us for a while, as we are assigned to the more quiet work for which we came, and I am safe, if thinner as ever in my life.

I must close now, and you'll forgive me if words have been stiff and detached. I'll get back my laughter, and my stomach will stop being an acrobat, and my letters will be warm and personal, and I'll not say any more about the thing, until I can tell you all when I come home again.

So much love, and I hope you'll take care of yourself, and your housemate is with you, and you are fat and happy and not missing me too much - for the days go by and each of them brings fragments of news, that when finally completed will be me at a boat rail - and us at a fireplace - or in an open car, or having ice cream sodas, or reading, and collecting stamps - or seeing our good friends such as Beth Ullman, the wonderful Landis, the warm Moores - and the family at Sunday night dinners - and picture shows - till which time I'll write more letters, which could not be fuller of my love. Be gay as a lark - and I'll be messing about the house one soon day - and leave you never again.

Jess.

Before Frances received Jesse's letter, Lasky wrote the following to his son.

December 28, 1943 – V-MAIL

...You can imagine my emotions when I picked up the newspapers and found that in a dispatch from General Mac Arthur's headquarters you had landed at Arawe with the American forces. As this was an Associated Press article, it appeared in one New York paper and in the Los Angeles Herald-Express, Times and Hollywood Citizen News. I am saving the articles for you as I understand Frances mailed you the Herald-Express clipping. The result of these articles was that friends sent us wires and many people called up. More important, yesterday Frances received your cable saying you were safe and well. Mother and I didn't talk much about it but we were both anxious over your safety, so your wire to Frances was a relief to all.

I was laid up with the flu, which is very prevalent right now, for six days, but recovered in time to have Christmas dinner with Frances, Grandma, Bess and Betty. Frances is fine and very proud of her Jesse, as are we all.

Betty is home as Buddy is on maneuvers somewhere in the South, but we expect he will be sent overseas at any time.

My picture 'Hollywood Canteen', due to a row with the Screen Actors Guild over payment of salaries to stars, has been stopped and may not be resumed. We were shooting for about two weeks when the trouble occurred... Gary Cooper called on us the day he arrived home and spent an hour telling us how he met you on two occasions; how you looked, and all about his trip. Gary was wonderful - and the fact that he had seen you only about two weeks before his arrival home, made us feel very close to you. Una Merkel[87] also telephoned and told about her meeting with you....

---

87 Female British comedy actor.

January 10, 1944 – V-MAIL

... You will never know how thrilled we all were over the letter you wrote Frances on December 27th. Frances immediately copied it on her typewriter and sent it to me - and I immediately made copies for Grandma, Bill and Betty and Buddy, and Bess sent several copies east.

In the meantime, last Thursday, January 6th, your friend, Lt. Col. Whitehair called on me at the studio, accompanied by Col. Moyer and Col. Eastman. The three had just arrived from Australia, and I was completely spellbound over Col. Whitehair's description of you and your adventures. He told me of the night you spent in his tent, and gave me the manuscript with the little note on it from you, which I read with the deepest interest. Thank God you will be in Australia for the next couple of months, as I understand it - and what an experience you have behind you ... I refer, of course, to Arawe. If you ever get on the screen that script I read - and I know you will - it should be instructive, interesting and exciting. I was so charmed with Col. Whitehair that I personally escorted him and the other two Colonels through the studio, introducing them to many stars and leading players - and as they had the evening open, I secured them three front seats at El Capitan Theatre where a great musical show is playing.

Last night was Grandma's 85th birthday and she gave a dinner at the Ambassador to which she invited Mac, Ruthie and little Blanche, Frances, Bess, Betty and myself, and Mrs. King. As I had to go to Jack Warner's house from the dinner, and needed an extra car, I picked Frances up on Veteran Ave and drove her to the Ambassador and then Mother and Betty drove her home. Frances looked very nice, in fact, quite smart, and we had a very pleasant evening.

I ran 'Rhapsody in Blue' at Jack Warner's house last night and the picture created a very fine impression. It is two hours and forty-five minutes long, and the music and sound have not been dubbed in it yet, but it will be ready for preview in about four weeks, and there is every indication that it will be an outstanding smash hit.

The 'Hollywood Canteen' picture has been cancelled for the time being due to a controversy with the Screen Actors Guild over the salaries of the various stars, and it may never be resumed.

No doubt Frances wrote you that she had Christmas dinner with us. You can imagine how we all thought of you on Christmas and New Years. I was at a wild party on New Years but when the clock struck 12, I drank a silent toast and uttered a prayer for you ... Buddy flew in from Camp Ellis, Illinois, on New Years Eve and Frances and Betty met him at the Burbank Airport, but he had to return to his headquarters two days later. Betty is living home with us now as Buddy has no regular headquarters; being a service pilot, he is flying all over the place - but I guess he is lucky to still be in this country.

We had Admiral Halsey and General Arnold, also Assistant Secretary Patterson, at the studio the other night and gave them a big dinner and swell entertainment.

Remember me to your pal, Capt. Hively. Frances tells me he wrote a most wonderful letter about you - as a matter of fact I am going to 'phone Mrs. Hively and ask her to read it to me.

We all send our love to our soldier boy. I carry around your press clippings in my pocket, including the photograph of Gary Cooper - which is another way of saying - I am very proud of you....

Jess tried to keep up with the letters to all the family. Of his enormous output, very few remain. At the moment, putting the film together in Sydney, more shaken than he would admit, he was still recovering from the battle at Arawe. This letter was by hand to Grandma, trying to make war sound like a ball game.

January 16, 1944
Dearest Grandma,

It's Sunday in Australia, and I have been playing tennis. This is the second tennis day I've had, and certainly did enjoy it. There is quite a beautiful club, with grass courts and it was fine to get out in the air and sun, in sports clothes and forget the war for a couple of hours. This afternoon I'm working again, as I have every day, and a lot of the nights.

In the process of writing variations and editing film, the great masses of film shot in combat. This has been a very interesting assignment, and I'm over the few trivial after-effects of the campaign - a jumping stomach and nightmares. Am feeling, and I think, looking better than ever although I'm regaining some of the lost weight, I came back to Australia wonderfully thin, but the fine restaurants of this city are ruining my warriors waistline.

Last evening I was entertained by Berney Freeman, who is the MGM distribution chief in this city. Went to a projection room to see a great musical - newly arrived here, called *As Thousands Cheer*. After, we went to his beautiful home for spaghetti and coffee. It is hard to believe that scarcely a month ago I was living in a shell hole in a corral cliff - being strafed and bombed day and night. Shell fragments actually going through my equipment - but God and the love of all of you - or fate - or something brought me out with only a scratch, received when a big piece of sandstone was unloosened by an explosion and hit my helmet so hard it knocked it off and a smaller stone tapped me on the head. It was a strange experience - some day I'll be able to tell the whole story, but I feel deeply grateful to have been in the thing - to have known those great guys - our combat troops - to have lived mainly on chocolate and cocoanut milk, and to be back, to remember. . . .

This is a slow long war, but I do think our feet are on the final road, though it will take much longer than I used to believe. In some ways, I'm looking forward to getting back nearer to it again, but this city life is certainly a soldier's dream - I have a few more weeks here. . . .

Now I must get to work. To Mrs. King my very best greeting, and keep the Ambassador warm for the welcome some day soon.

Love - and to Ruth and Mac

Your devoted Grandson
Jesse

And Lasky wrote:

January 20, 1944 – V-MAIL
Dear Jesse,

I have just returned from a week's vacation which I needed very much after two mild 'flu' attacks. I drove first to Las Vegas, Nevada; didn't like it there, and after stopping over only one night, I went to Palm Springs where I had a marvelous time - and am now back at the studio feeling wonderfully fit.

The first thing to greet me was your letter to Mother and me dated January 9th. As usual, it was fascinating and written in your best style - in fact, your letters are so interesting that every time I get one I feel like having it published - but don't worry, I won't succumb to this temptation.

. . . Last night Randy heard from quite an authentic source that Jack Hively and Bob Presnell were returning to the States; however, there may be nothing to this.

Buddy's father dropped dead very suddenly a few days ago and Buddy was given a fifteen-day leave of absence to attend the funeral and wind up his father's affairs - so he is living at the house. Betty has not been very well and has been consulting doctors - but I think we will get her fixed up in due time.

I wonder if I wrote you that I bought a beautiful Buick Headmaster car, with a collapsible top, as now that Betty is home she uses her Pontiac. Of course, gas is getting scarce but I still save many gallons by using the little Austin about every other day.

Our first sneak preview of 'Rhapsody in Blue' will occur about February 15th - and 'Mark Twain' will be released the first week in April. I am thinking of applying for a leave of absence inasmuch as 'Hollywood Canteen' is indefinitely postponed.

...The Fourth War Loan Drive has started and I am digging up every dollar I can raise to buy my share of these bonds. It seems to be about the only contribution I can make.

...Ye, Gods!—how anxious I am to get on with that biography of ours when this war is over. Incidentally, the kind of material contained in my story is in great demand, and we will be able to sell the book for its picture rights for a huge sum, which should give you something to look forward to - maybe you very first job when you are released from the Army.

We all send out love –

January 31, 1944 – V-MAIL

...Last week the trade papers carried a story that you were in Australia doing an important film for the Army. I will mail you the article in my next regular letter, as I want this one to go V-Mail.

As for news - Buddy has returned to his Post; Betty is remaining with us as she needs several months of treatments by her doctors to get her in good physical condition. Mother and Grandma are fine as usual—and I am looking forward to taking an 8 to 10 weeks' leave of absence for a trip to Palm Springs and I hope in New York to find some new and important material...We have cabled England to try and buy the rights for me to do the lives of Gilbert and Sullivan, with all the Gilbert and Sullivan music. What an assignment - I am excited about it! - but must wait patiently to see whether or not the music rights can be obtained.

...I gave Buddy a farewell party the night before he left, and Frances was with us, and I had pictures taken...Frances and I had several dances together at the Clover Club, where Buddy's party was held. What a good dancer she is - so much so that she made me feel that with a little practice, the two of us could enter a dancing contest....

February 4, 1944 – V-MAIL

...Your letter with the poem attached gave the family quite a thrill. I sent a copy to Gary Cooper - in fact, copies have been sent to Louise, and all the family...It was nice that Cecil wrote you. I have not seen him lately but expect to see him before I go away.

Last night Betty showed me the volume of Gilbert and Sullivan that you and Frances gave her. I was glad that you selected that particular book and I am sure you approve the idea of my doing the lives of Gilbert and Sullivan. We are still waiting to get the music rights cleared.

Warners are beginning to publicize the 'Adventures of Mark Twain' which opens April 7th in New York as a roadshow. They are now working on a plan to give it a world premiere at Angels Camp - and they are going to have a

National Frog Jumping Contest held in Central Park New York, in connection with the Bond Drive. All this must seem trifling to you, one who is passing through such dramatic scenes and living in such a different world - but our motto hero is: 'Business as Usual'. I have loaded up with War Bonds to my last dollar. This Fourth War Loan Drive is a major effort on the part of the country in which everyone is participating. The reports of the atrocities committed on our prisoners in the Philippines by the Japanese has aroused the country as nothing else has since Pearl Harbor ... Write as often as you can - your letters are the brightest spots in our lives.

Your devoted Dad

February 16, 1944

... Edgar Selwyn died suddenly from a cerebral hemorrhage and that the family had chosen me to deliver the eulogy at his funeral. I, therefore, came back to town - and have just been through the terrific ordeal of delivering the eulogy in front of a very distinguished gathering. I spoke extemporaneously and, after the funeral, the leaders of the industry congratulated me and said they had never heard such a touching oration. Cecil was there and said my eulogy was a masterpiece of simplicity, sincerity and good taste —-so, poor Edgar has departed this life.

We held our first preview of 'Rhapsody in Blue' which Frances attended with Grandma and Randy, and it was a sensational success. Jack Warner went on record that it is the greatest musical picture ever produced by his company and that it marks a new milestone in the history of musical pictures. In its final editing it runs two hours and thirty-five minutes and it will be road-showed at advanced admission prices (two shows a day - reserved seats) - that is what they think of the picture.

Today I am returning to Palm Springs to continue my vacation. I have rented Charlie Butterworth's[88] house, which is next to the Racquet Club, and Boris Lovet-Lorski[89] is staying with me. Mother is joining me in a few days—and on March 1st, Randy and I are leaving for New York (partly business and partly vacation).

I am trying to secure the rights to do the life of William Allen White, the 'Sage of Emporia, Kansas'. He founded and made world famous the Emporia Gazette—no doubt, you know something about him. I am also going to visit Orville Wright in Dayton to try and secure the story of the Wright Brothers, for an epic on Aviation.

---

88 Droll British actor.
89 Sculptor, painter, significant in the American Art Deco movement. His sculpture of Lasky, is now in the Hollywood Heritage Museum in the Lasky-DeMille Barn, across from the Hollywood Bowl.

...A friend of mine reminded me that Merian Cooper, now I believe a General, is stationed in Australia. If you are ever in his vicinity, please call on him - as you remember he is one of my closest personal friends....

(And a note from Randy.)

Dear Old Pal:

I will add my bit, although current events are always well recorded by your Dad—and speaking of that illustrious gentleman: he is looking years younger, Jesse, and happier and healthier than at any time in his great career—of course, knockout pictures wouldn't cause anyone to worry very much! Right now we are looking forward to a jaunt to New York and we hope to uncover some new material and do some research on two important subjects —do you remember when we used to 'uncover new material' (shades of Barbizon-Plaza) and our batting average was pretty high!....

Good Luck, Jesse, and make every minute count!

'The Sage of Barbizon-Plaza.'
Randy

March 2, 1944
Dear Jesse,

...I am dictating this to Randy on the 'Chief', as we near Kansas City . ..I drove in from Palm Springs to attend our second and final preview of 'Rhapsody in Blue' at Pasadena. I was with Jack Warner and the gang, and the preview was nothing less than sensational. The picture went over so well that instead of making more cuts, we put some sequences back in the picture that we formerly had taken out, so that it runs 2 hours and 35 minutes. Warner pronounced it the greatest picture ever made by the studio and they are talking about a $20,000,000 gross, as they plan to roadshow it in legitimate theatres for a couple of years before putting it in picture houses - in a word, it will be handled like 'Gone With The Wind', with intermission; reserved seats, and $3.30 top - so you can see what they think of it.

The object of my trip is to do some talks on 'Mark Twain' in New York and possibly some other cities; to generally publicize 'Mark Twain' and take part in exploitation and publicity meetings - and 'Twain' will open on April 7th at the Hollywood Theatre on Broadway for a long run. Incidentally, I have had some fine massages and exercises and never felt better in my life - so this should be a very happy trip.

As to my next story, it is curious that you mentioned in your letter, the Wright Brothers. One of the objects of my trip is to meet Orville Wright at Dayton a few weeks from now. Warner thinks I am the only man in the industry who could persuade Wright to let us do his story...My great problem, of course, is to top my last two pictures, to say nothing of *York*. The industry and Warner Bros, now expect miracles - and I will not decide on a story, unless I can see the greatest possibilities in it...Bess and I had dinner with Grandma the night before I left, and she was fine, and convinced (she having attended both previews of 'Rhapsody') that I am the greatest producer in the world. It seems strange that we should be so well and happy in time of war, when you, Bill and Buddy, particularly you, are in such a different situation, but I guess that is the compensation for age. You make me 33 and I will change places with you overnight!...

March 5, 1944 – V-MAIL

...I have now been in New York for about ten days - and they have been ten hectic days and nights, seeing shows, visiting night clubs, renewing old friendships and, in between, going over to Warner Bros, where they are working out a tremendous campaign for exploiting 'Mark Twain'. I am booked for several radio broadcasts and talks on 'Twain'. Yesterday I turned down being guest of honor at University of Michigan, Ann Arbor, Michigan,

Buddy flew in from Florida Saturday night with his Colonel and, as often happens with him, cracked up the plane, so that he had to stay over two days - but left this morning. Last night I had Buddy, and Louise and Marjorie, and the Colonel, all out to dinner and theatre. The best show I have seen is 'Oklahoma'.

I understand Col. Presnell will be here in a few days and will show me your picture of the Arawe invasion. Betty wrote Marjorie that she had seen the uncensored version and that you were observed in the nude. Needless to say I am anxious to see this picture, which they will show me as soon as it arrives; it may have arrived already. Now that this job is finished, I am wondering what you will be doing next....

March 29, 1944 — V-MAIL

...I will go east, arriving in Chicago April 14th to do a very important Coast-to-Coast broadcast from Northwestern University. The program is called 'Of Men and Books' and I will be interviewed by Dr. John T. Frederick, Professor of Modern Letters School of Journalism. Randy will meet me in Chicago and we will go on to St Louis for a two-day 'Mark Twain' celebration, covering a number of events, including the presentation of a scroll to me by the Governor of Missouri, all of which will be broadcast from St. Louis. I expect to return to New York to participate in many publicity events and to attend the 'Mark Twain' opening....

Buddy just telephoned me from Florida that he has been discharged from the hospital where he has been confined after another crack-up and is flying to

Hollywood to be with Betty for a few days. That boy gets more furloughs than all the rest of the Army put together.

Have not definitely decided on my next story yet but it will come through any time. Every time I talk on the radio, or make speeches, people inform me that the best story of all will be the story of my life in pictures so - speed the end of the war - and we will do the biography and will sell it for a huge sum....

The Audubon project, which Lasky had kept on the back burner, had not worked out for various reasons and he had regretfully given it up. But with his usual zeal he was searching for the next project, although heavily involved with promotional 'events'.

Undated (April 20, 1944?) – V-MAIL
Dear Jesse,

While I have heard from you - you have not had a letter from me in some time. The reason is hard to explain, as you know you are constantly in my mind.

... we visited with Bill, Margy and the baby. You have a very cute nephew in little Ronnie Lasky - I can't call him 'grandson', because it cramps my style. I did about six broadcasts in Denver and was wined and dined extensively. Then Mother returned home, and I went to Chicago where Randy met me, and I did a coast-to-coast broadcast which was very successful. Then we went to St. Louis where I participated in many events. I was presented with a small pilot wheel, with a baseball in the center of it, which had been autographed by all the players of the St. Louis (Cardinals) baseball team. This was given to me by the Mayor of St. Louis on the playing field before the game which opened the baseball season. I was presented with a huge pilot wheel by The Propeller Club of America at a cocktail party. Was given a reception at the home of one of the leading citizens; was presented with a scroll by a delegation headed by the Mayor of Hannibal who came from Hannibal for the occasion. Numerous parties and gala affairs rounded out a most strenuous trip - and now I am on the 20th Century train between Chicago and New York,

Tomorrow, Frederic March and I place a wreath on Mark Twain's statue in the Hall of Fame in New York City; then I go to Philadelphia for a coast-to-coast broadcast on a very popular program called 'Double or Nothing'.

It is amazing how I stand up under the beating one takes - living like a goldfish in a glass bowl, meeting strangers from morning until night; handshakes, dinners, speeches, broadcasts - but guess I was cut out for this kind of thing, as I stand up under it very well. By the way, 'Mark Twain' was shown privately at the various cities and the comments are out of this world. The picture promises to be a great success.

I forgot to mention that I was thrilled to death over the picture which Col. Presnell showed me privately at the studio the day before I left for Denver. We sat alone and he explained everything that I should know I recognized your voice delivering the Lord's Prayer. And I am positive I saw a flash of you in a landing boat - could I be mistaken about this? The picture is simply wonderful and whatever you contributed was good, because the whole picture was splendid. [90]

Before I left Los Angeles for Denver, Frances read me one of your letters - and now I shall await further news of you - and your next letter of course, will be addressed to me at the studio, as I reach home on May 6th.

With much love -Your devoted Dad

April 27, 1944 – V-MAIL

... I am still in New York getting ready for the opening of 'Mark Twain' which occurs on May 2nd. I am taking Freddie March and his wife, Florence Eldridge, as my guests. We are being invited to dinner at the Colony Club by some society people; will attend the opening in a body and, afterwards, Freddie is giving a party to his intimate friends at '21'. I leave for the Coast two days after the opening and will be glad to get home.

... I read your letter very carefully and realize you are a bit fed up with your present situation, and can understand why. After your vital and exciting experiences, another desk job was bound to prove an anti-climax. New York is filled with desk soldiers and I am glad you are not one of them; at least you are in another country. Julius Evans spent the evening with me recently and told me that Officers at Long Island all say you would have been a Captain long before this if you had not gotten yourself sent overseas. ...

I have not settled on my next story yet, which rather worries me—but I usually go around in a circle and then make the right decision at the last moment—and I imagine this time will be no exception. The publicity for 'Mark Twain' is wonderful and everyone is clamoring for seats. I have done many broadcasts and speeches - one with Freddie March at the New York University that was a dandy - so I am much in the limelight as a result of all this publicity.

Betty seems to be getting along well now in El Paso, Texas. Billy is booming in Denver - and I had a nice letter from Frances - and Mother is resting and painting very hard. We are very much excited over her book which will come out in September.

Everybody I meet asks for you and I still have the clipping from the paper containing your photograph and the article of your landing on the beach at Arawe - which I spring on everyone who wants to know about you, with the

---

90 Jesse's war film *The Battle of New Britain*.

usual father's pride in his valiant son's achievements. As I write this we seem on the eve of the invasion of the continent which will bring the war that much sooner to a victorious conclusion - and then for the Grand Day, which will come sooner than we expect - the welcoming of our sons and husbands.

All the love in the world.

May 6th, 1944 – V-MAIL

... Your V-mail letter of April 16th was forwarded by Mother to New York and is now being answered in a drawing room shared jointly by Nino Martini and myself en-route home where we arrive tomorrow (Sunday).

The 'Mark Twain' opening was, in many respects, as triumphant as 'Sergeant York'. The notices were magnificent with the exception of the New York Times all trade papers were great and Jack Warner and Warner Executives are much impressed.

In the face of otherwise consistently excellent reviews and box office receipts, the New York Times review (May 4, '44) was scathing, calling the script 'largely inconsistent with the facts', the direction 'strangely inconsistent throughout'—but admitted March's performance was 'agreeable, especially when he is tossing some of the humorist's livelier quips.'

On Sunday, April 30th, a short-wave broadcast came from Hawaii, describing the world premiere of 'Mark Twain', as shown to the soldiers in the South Seas. 16mm prints of the picture were sent to all the battlefronts months ago and I am wondering if you have heard about it, or if you heard this broadcast.

Col. Bob Presnell called me the day before the opening and I secured two seats for him. He was thrilled with the picture, and the next day he ran the picture you worked on, which is now called 'The Battle of New Britain'[8] for a group of executives in the industry in New York. I attended the showing which was in Warner Bros. projection room, so I saw the picture for a second time. It is truly a magnificent job and it gave me, as nothing else could, an idea of what you and other fellows have witnessed and experienced.

I gather from your letters that you are very comfortably situated for the time being, but naturally impatient for a change - and lonesome. If I were in your place, I would enjoy myself as much as I could when I got the opportunity. We expect hourly to learn that the invasion of the Continent has started, which means a crisis of the war in that theatre and the end of it all a little sooner. I still retain a clear mental picture of our meeting you when it is over, over there....

Jack Warner joined me in New York for the opening, but remains behind for a few weeks. We got along extremely well together so I am not particularly worried over not having my story set. With the 'Gershwin' picture next on the horizon, my stock is naturally above par....

PS If 'Life' magazine reaches your part of the world, the issue of May 8th has an eleven-page spread of Mark Twain.

May 20, 1944 – V-MAIL

...Two weeks have passed since I last wrote you. I just returned from a three-day trip to Angel's Camp, north of Stockton where we dedicated a stature of Mark Twain and also, had a special opening of the picture, including a frog-jumping contest and all the trimmings...Warner is against doing another biography, and as I would like to do something with some significance it may take a little time before I find the right subject. No use telling you the subjects I have been considering as things change so rapidly.

...Mother just telephoned that a letter arrived from you which I will read when I get home to dinner....

Undated - (May 27, 1944 ?) – V-MAIL

You mentioned in your last latter that you had a windfall by way of winning in a poker game. That made me realize that you must be short of cash most of the time - so, today, I cabled you $60.00 as visible evidence that you are still in our hearts and are not forgotten.

...In searching for material, I keep thinking how much better my own life's story would be for a picture than anything I could find. It is needless for me to tell you that with the musical sequences; vaudeville and Folies Bergere, it would have all the elements of a great entertaining picture and, at the same time, the kind of Horatio Alger story only possible in our American way of life....

June 3, 1944 – V-MAIL

... First, I dropped in on Frances a few days ago ... While at the house I conceived the notion of looking up your full first draft of my story, in the two black covers—and it being Decoration Day, a holiday, I took them home and read the story clear through. Jess, you are a fine and colorful writer and have done a swell job, although we both know it is overwritten and too long, all of which you would have corrected if you had had time to edit it.

The reason I read the story was because of Hedda Hopper's[91] article, which was not inspired by me. I think we have a nest egg in this story of ours, and it will be just as good after the war as it would be now.

---

91 Hollywood gossip columnist.

...By the time this reaches you, Rome will undoubtedly be in the Allies' hands, and the invasion probably on the way, which means the war is at least that much nearer its end on the European front.

Bess had a talk with Bob Presnell and will write you about it; she will try to convey certain facts to you and I hope you will understand what she's trying to tell you. We both send our devoted love....

June 14, 1944 – V-MAIL

... Yesterday your friend, Capt. Bachmann telephoned me to tell me about you, as he left you only a few days ago. It was nice talking to someone who had just been with you. Also, Marsha Crocker, a young lady in our publicity department, 'phoned stating her husband, Willie Alcine, is working with you. These incidents make Australia seem nearer than it actually is.

... We are all watching with intense interest the progress of the Invasion on the European Front. The President spoke, on the occasion of the opening of the Fifth War Loan Drive, more optimistically about the war, I thought, than he has ever spoken before...I attended the opening of Cecil's picture 'Dr. Wassell', and although it has been severely criticized by the critics in New York, I enjoyed the picture - a typical DeMille production.

Alan LeMay is working in the studio and has been signed up as a staff writer. This happened largely as a result of my constantly praising him to the front office. Unfortunately he is busy on a picture so I won't be able to get him for a long time.

Not having agreed on various stories thus far discussed, I will probably compromise and do a play which Warner just bought called The Two Mrs. Carrolls.

Have been offered financing in a big way for an independent unit; may consider it later on. The financing was offered when I was in New York, and they are writing me from the east that it is still available. We shall see.

Mother is sending you some books - we didn't realize that you do not get late novels. The picture you worked on, now titled 'Attack' has been getting splendid notices in trade papers east and west, and is about to be released to the public.

As always, we find your letters very interesting. It is hard to realize that you are in the midst of a cold winter - and I shall probably go swimming at the beach this Sunday. I miss my old Sunday hangout at Edgar Selwyn's house since he passed away....

June 24, 1944

Just had a long talk with Frances on the 'phone who read me your letter of June 12th, in which you said that good old Jack Hively is back with you. Please give him my warm regards and tell him that 'Attack' has been extremely well spoken of throughout the industry and also by the public and critics. It is now in general release.

...Yesterday we had a visitor in the dining room - Col. McMicking and when I was introduced to him, he said that he had been with you in the South Seas, and that he is leaving very soon and will be seeing you shortly. I found him a most charming man.

...The last few days I have noticed a perceptible change in the opinions on the duration; in other words, all feel the war will come to a much quicker end than was originally anticipated.

I am finally embarked on trying to lick the New York play success *The Two Mrs. Carrolls*. I have Howard Koch as my writer and will probably do the picture with Bette Davis. It is not the kind of important story I would ever choose for myself but, not having agreed on anything outstanding, I thought it wise to accept this assignment. I previously turned down a number of stories....

Spent a weekend with Cecil in Paradise - a most charming weekend - and he said he would be glad to direct a picture of my life if it could be proved to him that it could be made interesting enough...Cecil's 'Dr. Wassell' has been severely panned by the critics but, as usual with his pictures, it is doing good business......

Critics were invariably unkind to DeMille pictures, but Lasky admired his old partner for following his instincts. DeMille was his own boss from the beginning, and his films were designed for ordinary people who reveled in his visual artistry and pageantry and a more symbolic approach to dialogue. With Giannini behind him, he had the power to do it his way. Sam Goldwyn wielded that same power, as did a handful of men in their time. If Lasky could choose, his path led to music and the meaningful lives of great men. But he had to answer to a higher power—the studio bosses. Now he was being presented with exactly the sort of project he didn't like, and was privately planning his own tribute to a meaningful life.

July 1, 1944
Dear Jesse,

...Referring to the story of my life, I have definitely and positively decided to let it rest until you can write it...I see the ending of the picture in front of a great Hollywood world premiere; over the marquee, stabbing the night in brilliant glittering letters, is the title of the picture: 'The Trumpet Blows Again', and in smaller letters: 'The Life of Jesse L. Lasky'. A first-night mob is surging in front of the lobby; a band is playing in the bleachers; the Press gathers around Lasky who is entering the theatre in evening dress, surrounded by the family—the reporters asks 'What are your plans from here on, Mr.

Lasky?' We cut to a closeup of a trumpeter in the band - cut back to Lasky, and he says: 'Plans? Just to blow the trumpet once more' - or something like that. Anyway, this is a job for after the war - and I will try and keep plugging along until it is all over as I have a hunch I will retire when we finally produce the story of my life.

In the meantime, I am working on the deadliest of deadly chores—a murder-mystery play *The Two Mrs. Carrolls*. Jack Warner paid $225,000 for the play which makes it impossible for me to tell him what a louse it is. I wouldn't have bought it for $1,000....

July 8, 1944

... After experimenting with a couple of writers, I finally secured Tom Job, a specialist in writing mystery melodramas (he is an English playwright), and we are making good progress on the very difficult play to adapt, The Two Mrs. Carrolls.

I took Mother and Betty to a very interesting lecture, at the Beverly Hills Hotel, on the French Underground by a distinguished Frenchman who just arrived from France. I was amazed at the size and organization of the Underground, and what it has been contributing and will contribute to the war effort on the continent.

I don't know if you get much American news, but we have had a series of disasters recently: the Santa Fé Chief went off the rails, and several people were killed and many hurt. The Ringling Bros. Circus burned down at Hartford, Conn., during a matinee performance and the death toll was 150, with several hundred injured ... Mother had to postpone the publishing of her book due to difficulties with the publisher over financial arrangements. It is quite a disappointment for her....

Jesse, in his normally quiet, unassuming way, clearly made an impression on quite a few people. His father received this letter:

July 13, 1944
Mr. Jesse L. Lasky, Sr.
Warner Brothers Studios, Burbank, California
Dear Mr. Lasky:

I served as a kind of aide to Jesse, Jr., at Astoria, when he was O I C scenario. As a result of our daily contacts with each other, I came to think highly of that boy of yours.

He once did me am inestimable favor. I didn't ask for it, but I certainly shall never forget it. In performing it, he had that rare thing in a man: risked his own position for another human being. What could be finer?

I promised myself more than a year ago that I would find him a token of my appreciation and of my esteem for him. Because of the war the article has been unobtainable until recently, but I am now able to procure it and shall.

I should like to have Jesse's mailing address, which I should guess would be somewhere in the South Seas. So if you'll oblige me, I should like to know how I may get the package to him.

Thank you, sir.
Charles Garland

Unfortunately, no one today knows what the mysterious package contained. Meanwhile, second of Jesse's war films, *Briefed for Invasion*, was completed.

July 14, 1944
Dear Jesse:

I stopped in to see Grandma yesterday, and found her writing a letter to you. I had just left Lt. Herb Stein, as he had brought over to the studio a picture called 'Briefed for Invasion' for us to see which, by the way, is one of the finest of all the Army pictorial pictures thus far turned out. Lt. Stein spoke in glowing terms about the work you are doing, and we had a nice chat . . . I also thought you would enjoy having a picture of yourself showing your activities in the First World War.[92] Surely some of your brother-officers will enjoy seeing this picture. . . Here's a piece of news for you. After I came back from New York I developed a hernia and began wearing a truss. I found the truss, at best, awkward and uncomfortable and, yesterday, Jane Allen persuaded me to talk with a doctor at Cedars of Lebanon Hospital, who is a fine operating surgeon - Dr. Chas. Eaton Phillips. He immediately advised an operation, so I am going into the hospital next Thursday and will be there for about two weeks. I am not worried about it - and I would much rather get fixed up than wear a truss for the rest of my life. The doctor said I would be as good as new, and as I like to swim and jump about and be active, I thought it wise to have it taken care of while I can.

Mother had planned an Exhibition of her paintings in Beverly Hills for July 25th, but due to the fact I will be in the hospital, she is arranging today to postpone it for a few weeks.

(later) . . . Just returned from lunch with. Capt. Appleton—what a grand guy! I took an immediate strong fancy to him and would enjoy knowing him better, or even having him work with us, after the war. You can imagine we spoke of you at great length—and he described in detail the work you are doing. I think he admires you, and is as fond of you as your Dad, which is saying a h—l of a lot. . . .

---

92 Jesse's 7 year old photo in The Lasky Home Guard (page 65)

July 20, 1944

No doubt Frances has written you at length about her party for Col. Mixon. Naturally I took advantage of the party to get well acquainted with Col. Mixon and his wife, and I was thrilled when he confided in me that you would be promoted to a Captaincy - he thought within the next six weeks. He spoke in the highest terms about you as a man, and the fine work that you are doing; in fact, for a solid half hour he described to me your duties; how you were handling the newsreel; his efforts in trying to get film from this side of the water, etc., I contributed a quart of scotch to the party, and Col. Mixon and I did our full share in helping to consume it.

. . . I am going to Cedars of Lebanon tomorrow and by the time this reaches you, I will be out of the hospital and back on the job - so, again I repeat, don't let this disturb you.

Mother and I attended the invitational performance of David Selznick's picture which was supposed to be as great as *Gone with the Wind*; it is called *Since You Went Away*. Mother and I were rather disappointed, as were many others - but it was a gala affair; you would never think there was a war on.

Your very fine three-page letter of July 7th arrived - ten days after you mailed it. I was much interested in hearing your account of your activities. Putting it all together - that is, your description, and Capt. Appleton's and Col. Mixon's reports, I feel very close to your activities. I was surprised to learn that you are not getting any of the late pictures in Australia. 'Mark Twain' has been played on every war front months ago - and I suppose Australia won't see it for another year. Fortunately, it is good any time.

Betty could not stand the heat in El Paso; it was 115 in their little house - and she has returned here. . . .

Jesse's friend, Toni Landi, brother of film star Elissa Landi (she was to die four years later at the age of forty-three of cancer) had heard on the grapevine that Jesse was to be moved from Australia to New Guinea. And indeed, Jesse soon found himself there.

July 22, 1944
Dear Dad;

. . . I expect to be on the move quite a bit but the address on the envelope will reach me as it will be more or less my base for a while. I do not think that there is any possibility that I will see Australia again this war. I can't complain. I had more than my share of the good living of one of its finest cities. Now all that is a way back and I'm back into the routine of another kind of living. Jack Hively and I share a tent on a high hillside fringed by jungle that climbs up steep mountains. This place is like a stage setting against which suns go down in unbelievable drama, and the clouds are too good to be real. Nights such as this one are even cool. A faint wisp of breeze plays up the hill. The din of small insect noises beats in at times, almost like a sea, but the insects themselves are in a minority, thank goodness. Nowhere else in the Islands I have been, were the insects so scarce. We sleep of course under mosquito nets, which are carefully tucked under the one blanket on the cot, and take malaria preventative pills which turns us a sickening yellow but keeps us feeling healthy.

Aside from our tent, which by the way sports electric light and field telephone, Jack and I have a hut end for an office that is spacious and airy. Jack whose hair is cropped off close said just now to tell you hello. We are both very sunburned and have the White Cargo look as our 'suntans' are washed without ever being pressed.

There is a good possibility ahead that I might be seeing you somewhat sooner than we could have expected. Lets hope so anyway, and there's a solid chance since a job might bring me to your vicinity.

I suppose by now that your new script is approaching some final form, in fact you are probably discussing directorial assignment and cast. What a wonderful world it all seems from here!

Hope you see Frances often and share some exciting events with her. Aloneness can in itself become a drug in which one draws willingly into a shell which may seem to preserve the shadows of the near past best. Therefore do see her as often as you can, and she so often says of the good events you have shared with her that I am sure there's no need for this paragraph.

Love to the magnificent Bess, and Betty and the ever-vital Grandma.

Lasky had been in hospital long enough to catch up with a familiar nurse.

August 2, 1944
Cedars of Lebanon Hospital
Dear Jesse,

...In a half hour I will be checking out of this Cedars of Lebanon Hospital having been here one day short of two weeks. My recovery from the double hernia operation has been perfect and now the doctor wants me to stay home for a full week - and then I can gradually take up my work at the studio. The last few days - once the pain from the incisions subsided and the stitches and bandages were removed - I really enjoyed myself. I had three wonderful nurses on eight-hour shifts and a lovely big room with double windows overlooking the city. Friends and well-wishers have kept the room well supplied with flowers; many letters and telegrams of cheer and sympathy have enlivened the days, and the last four days I have had quite a few visitors. Cecil has called me regularly, and I promised him to spend the last three days of my convalescent period at Paradise.

By the way, one of my nurses, Miss Altman, is the one who took care of you during your appendectomy. She is a wonderful nurse and I hope you remember her, as we have often talked about you.

By the way, Jack Bachman's son telephoned Mother or Frances that you are to be transferred to Port Moresby. If you write me that you have been transferred, I will be pretty sure that is your destination...

During my stay here I read Somerset Maugham's 'The Razor's Edge' and will try and mail you a copy as you would love it. Will you please request me in your next letter to mail you some books, as this is required by the Post Office.

The war news has been simply wonderful and everyone - commentators, columnists and whatnot - agree the war with Germany will be over long before the end of the year, and not many months afterwards, they expect that the Japanese war will be ended. This must be cheering news for you fellows in the South Seas because at last you can see the beginning of the end, and the possibilities of coming home before the end of another year....

On August 9th, the Americans took Guam after twenty days of bloody fighting. 1,214 American and 17,000 Japanese soldiers were killed. In Europe, General Eisenhower moved his headquarters from England to France for the 'Operation Dragoon' and the Allied invasion of southern France. There was an uprising in Paris by the resistance, and August 25th brought the liberation of Paris.

In Hollywood, they just continued to make motion pictures.

August 15, 1944
Dear Jesse,

....I spent a very pleasant ten days recuperating at home, and returned to the studio yesterday. In the meantime I kept in close touch with my writer, Tom Job, and our script of 'The Two Mrs. Carrolls' is within two weeks of completion, and is coming along very well.

I wound up my recuperation period by going to Paradise with Cecil on Friday afternoon and remained until Sunday afternoon. It was very hot there so we spent much time in the swimming pool, and I came back looking as well, if not better than before I went to the hospital, although I am still about five pounds underweight. Cecil and I had some wonderful talks and we seem to be closer than we used to be. It was Cecil's birthday and I brought up to Paradise a lovely present and surprised him with it. Four of us drank a magnum of champagne (Mumms '28) and had a dinner fit for the Gods; wearing the usual Russian blouses—a wonderful time was had by all.

We are all thrilled by the constant good news from the war fronts. Lloyds of London are offering big odds (100 to 15) that the European war will be over by October 31st, and the radio constantly carries optimistic reports on a much earlier ending than was originally anticipated of the Japanese war. People are beginning to be more cheerful, and I hope some of this optimism is shared by you.

The other night Bess and I attended an invitational preview of 'Wilson',[93] one of the greatest pictures I have ever seen. It tells the story of Wilson's administration and his fight for the League of Nations, and is so timely that it has caused more discussion than any picture ever made.

A week ago Sunday I took Frances down to the beach and we spent a pleasant afternoon together; Jack Emanuel and his wife joined us and Betty was along. During my convalescence I saw a lot of Boris and he and I spent a couple of afternoons at the beach, so I have a very lovely suntan. My convalescent period was so pleasant that it rather spoiled me. I seem to be much more interested in loafing and playing around than in making pictures. . . .

Cecil kept a wardrobe of men's Russian silk blouses in a variety of colors and sizes at Paradise. His male guests were required to wear them for dinner. The ladies, if any, wore evening gowns. After dinner, a tray of rare gemstones, rubies, sapphires, emeralds, and diamonds would be passed around the table as a feast for the eyes. In the ensuing years, as Cecil's chief writer and part of the DeMille entourage, Jesse, like his father, would wear many of those blouses and feast his eyes on that velvet dessert tray of jewels, while struggling to present his boss with the type of dialogue so dear to Cecil's and his audiences' concept of drama—if not the critics.

August 21, 1944
Dear Jesse,

. . . Yesterday, Sunday, I picked up my biography, which I am keeping in my room until you return and read the chapters of our tour of Flynn's Parks. When I came to the last performance - the scene with Bryan and Nadine (seedy summer stock), at the end of the chapter, there were tears in my eyes. I read through many other chapters and, believe me, young fellow, your style as a novelist is comparable to any of the best-selling American novelists. I have a terrible yen to get back to work on the book and that is one pleasant task you can look forward to when you return.

I am feeling fine, in fact, I am feeling my oats again. I must have been to four or five parties since I wrote my last letter. I even danced Saturday night at Mocambo, so you can see I am pretty well recovered from the operation. Also went in swimming at the Beach Club Sunday. . . .

---

93 Played by Alexander Knox, director Henry King, screenplay: Lamar Trotti

September 5, 1944

...While you have been constantly on my mind, I have not written you since I sent you the Tiburon letter. In the meantime, I received your interesting letter of August 15th which told me that within a week you expected to be in a new job in a different city. No doubt by now you are in the new job and I am wondering, without having the slightest idea, where you have been moved to.

This letter should reach you just before your birthday. Good Lord! You will be 34, which is wonderful - but, in the meantime, on the thirteenth, I will be 64, which is terrible! How would you like to be full of life and pep - very romantic - and be a 64 year-old grandfather? The latter title and the romantic tendencies are fighting each other - but I am happy to report that Romance is still winning out.

Enclosed is a bank draft which you can cash immediately if you are anywhere near a bank. I didn't dare cable money this time as I feared it might not reach you promptly due to not knowing where you are stationed. Anyway—HAPPY BIRTHDAY.

Mother is sending you two books which I have read and which fascinated me, and will thrill you. One is, Somerset Maugham's *The Razor's Edge* - and the other, and most fascinating, is *Strange Fruit*. I just finished this book last night - it is a best-seller, and is so powerful, I am still under the spell of it.

...For the first time in my life I have been really campaigning: I am on the Hollywood Democratic Committee and we have been raising funds for President Roosevelt's campaign. To my way of thinking, it is vitally important that he be re-elected as against Dewey who I don't believe is qualified to meet the extraordinary situations that are developing. At any rate, I was Chairman of a dinner that sponsored Senator Claude Pepper Saturday night and was on the speakers' platform next to Pepper, and we had a very interesting meeting - at the conclusion of which we raised a large sum of money - $250.00 of which was contributed by me. I hope you are a Democrat and are for the President. Randy is a rabid Republican - and his pencil is shaking as he is taking this dictation. However, this very difference of opinion, and our freedom to express it, is again what we are fighting for...My script of 'The Two Mrs. Carrolls' is just about finished and it is a wow! It will make a very exciting and mystifying picture—just the kind of escapist entertainment that the public is looking for. I was lucky in getting a young director whom I like very much - Peter Godfrey and we will start casting in a few days.

Last week I had offers for independent production - that is, a lot of capital was offered me, but I put this all aside until after the first of the year when I will decide whether I am continuing with Warner Bros. or moving into new fields. I'll bet you would enjoy being a part of an independent Lasky unit— well, it's in the cards if we want it when you return. Quite a few producers are forming their own companies on account of the tax situation where they are able to retain more of their income....

Jesse's good news prompted his dad's reply:

September 14, 1944
My dear Captain:
Congratulations!! Congratulations!! Congratulations!!

Frances was at the house delivering a birthday present to me - a pair of lovely slippers from her and an after-shaving toilet set from you - when your cable arrived. What a birthday present your cable turned out to be! So the Captaincy came through at last - and I know you are as happy as we are.

Yesterday we were running 'The Battle For The Marianas' with a bunch of officers, some of whom were in charge of the editing of the picture, and Col. Sloane said he had heard some very favorable comment on the narration or commentary that you wrote for a picture that is now being edited by Frank Capra's outfit. I hear so many favorable comments on your work from fellows out here that I am sure you more than earned this promotion.

... There is not much news on my picture, except we have a great script and are beginning to cast it. My Warner's contract expires this year, but I am not worried as I have plenty of opportunities elsewhere if I should not stay here. They are just beginning a tremendous exploitation campaign on RHAPSODY IN BLUE, which Jack Warner says is the greatest musical ever produced by this company. It will open in New York around Christmas for a roadshow engagement and, no doubt, I will go to the opening.

Well, my Captain, I only wanted this to be a letter of Congratulations, so I won't make it very long. Needless to say the news of your promotion is spreading, and by the time Grandma analyzed the situation, she will have MacArthur on your staff as a result of your single-handed conquest of the Philippines. Heigh-Ho - and all the best....

As for *Rhapsody in Blue*, the *New York Times* reviewer, Bosley Crowther, wrote of the film, 'There's slightly more fancy than fact in this lavish film biography of legendary American composer George Gershwin, but oh! That music! Director Irving Rapper had wanted Tyrone Power to play Gershwin, but Power was still serving in the Marines, so Rapper had to settle for Robert Alda—who isn't bad at all, just a trifle over-enthusiastic.'

Although he appeared in a handful of films after that, Robert Alda's career never really took off in Hollywood. Of Italian extraction, he was born in New York, won a talent contest as a singer-dancer in the 1930s, and had progressed from vaudeville to burlesque when Lasky chose him. Alda became personally more successful on

Broadway, where he starred in a series of hits and won a Tony Award playing Bat Masterson in *Guys and Dolls*. He moved to Italy in the '60s, and for the next twenty years starred in many European films, with a few rare appearances in America, particularly on his eminently more famous son, Alan Alda's hit TV series, *M*A*S*H*.

September 25, 1944
Dear Captain Jess:

...I am enclosing with this letter the Foreword to Mother's book, which she wrote and re-wrote until I think it is pretty good. She leaves in four days for New York where she will confer with her publisher on details of the book—also, about an exhibition of her paintings, etc. Bess is full of ambition and is busy from morning to night.

...I am also enclosing a copy of Roosevelt's first political speech which has caused much discussion and which, being an avid Democrat, I think is great. It will be hard for you to appreciate the speech unless you have read (which, of course, you haven't) the various Republican attacks on the President. This speech, very much in the vein of the sarcastic humor of Mark Twain, answers those attacks.

In previous letters I forgot to tell you that Mark Hellinger had quite a chat with me when he returned from Australia, and he told me of his telephone talk with you and, on several occasions, has reiterated that you have made a splendid reputation and are extremely well thought of. Mark told this so all the fellows at our executive table could hear it - and it made me feel quite proud.

In reading over your letter I have come to the conclusion that you are somewhere in New Guinea. Some day you will tell me whether or not I am a good guesser.

...My script is finished, and mimeographed, and has met with hearty approval by all who have read it and we are now trying to cast it, a very difficult job. In my next letter I will tell you who we have cast for the picture.

My contract has expired here and I am working on a week-to-week basis until I decide what I want to do next, but my affairs financially are in good shape so I don't worry....

October 2, 1944

...After an exhaustive search covering the field of big-named players, it looks as though we will have to postpone 'The Two Mrs. Carrolls' for two or three months. In that event I am going to lay off, and take a trip to Palm Springs and New York and, incidentally, search for another big story. My affairs are in very good shape, and my relations with the studio and Jack Warner are very fine, so I can afford the lay-off....the studio will pay my round-trip fare and expenses for me to go to New York and get some publicity for 'Rhapsody in Blue', which opens on Broadway, December 20th, so, if Mother is still in New York that will be a very pleasant part of my lay-off....

Captain Jesse was still occupied filming landings in the South Pacific.

October 3, 1944
Dearest Bess and Dad:

I'm sitting on a beach edge of a small Island - coral atoll I suppose it should be called. On this same island in the Central Pacific 'Mark Twain' had its world premiers in 16mm - played to an audience of sailors, soldiers and marines. They sat on the sand flanked by cocoanut palms, the plumes of which had been mostly severed off by shellfire in the barrage that had preceded the visit of the first Americans. They loved the picture!

I have seen several of these Islands on this trip, mainly from the air; they are incredibly beautiful from above, but hot and smelly in actuality, except when the bright moonlight camouflages the debris and rubble and tents and barracks. I hope soon the plane will come and with high priority I'll be off on the job. Expect to be seeing Bob Presnell soon.

An excellent chance has developed that will get me home, perhaps around the first of the year. I miss you all so much, and miss Frances very much. Have not seen a paper or had news of the war for some days, but I hope that Germany is near defeat, for that will bring a quicker end to our Pacific war.

With all this travel it may be a month before I'm in a place where mail will catch up to me, but I'll keep knowing you are all writing, and keep believing you are all well.

I mentioned to you that I had been recommended for a decoration, but don't say anything about it as there is always the chance it won't go through. I'll know in a couple of months - anyway, my promotion came through and it's good to be a Captain, and feel some slight sense of progress.

I'm more than ever keen to go on with Dad's biography at the war's end. I know that it will be a great long book, a rich symphony in which will be all the varied themes of all our lives, interwoven and mingled in the fullness of a life that has touched so much and so many. I have a positive hunger to go on with that book, and feel that the loneliness and introspection of some of my days here will give me sharper tools of perception. But don't think I've lost any humor - I have stories now that will keep us in stitches around many a fireside.

Love to you two, to Grandma - and pass a kiss to Frances when you see her.
Jess

October 4, 1944
Dear Jess,

...A funny thing happened: a rumor spread around that I was leaving Warners, due to this lay-off, and I have had nibbles from Twentieth Century-Fox and Columbia Studios - and offers of substantial sums to form an independent company. As a matter of fact, I have an appointment to see Joe Schenck at the Fox Studio tomorrow - so one of these days there will probably be a very newsy letter from this world of commerce and intrigue to the theatre in which you are doing your bit to help make it possible for commerce and intrigue to continue ad infinitum.

Thank God I am in wonderful health - played golf the other day and played damn well. Of course always in the back of my mind is the finishing of the biography when you return. Also I have in the back of my mind that any new set-up I make will have an opening for you to step right into - and, who knows, maybe we can squeeze Jack Hively in with us - what a combination of ripe experience, youth, courage and enthusiasm....

October 12, 1944
Dear Jess,

...I talked to Mother on the 'phone and she is very much excited over the fact that she is studying with a very famous painter, and everything seemed well with her....We have just closed my offices at the studio and my vacation is starting. I will spend much time in Palm Springs and, later, will go to New York. Had a talk with Loyd Wright, my attorney, and we are not rushing into any negotiations at present. We think we can make a better deal when 'Rhapsody in Blue' is released on December 20th. We shall see.

Bill, Margy and Ronnie arrive on October 28th on Bill's ten-day furlough and I will be free to help entertain them, and will see that Frances is with us as much as possible....

On October 20, 1944, the Americans landed at Leyte, Philippine Islands, fulfilling General MacArthur's promise, 'I will return', made in 1942 to the Filipinos, after the Japanese took control of the Archipelago. Jesse was part of that landing and was not in communication with his family for about a month. During the Leyte campaign, the Japanese first used their kamikaze suicide planes. On the 21st, Aachen fell to the Allies. In a battle that lasted from the 23rd to the 26th of October, the American invasion forces fought the largest naval battle of the war at Leyte Gulf. It destroyed the Japanese fleet. Jesse had been part of an historic encounter. His insightful observations were filtered through the eyes of a poet.

October 29, 1944
Dearest Both,

This is a letter written before I return to the place where I shall receive the many letters that have accumulated there for me over the past month. I will therefore be out of tune with all your news, but as I may be tremendously busy on my return to my own outfit in New Guinea, I did want to get something in the mail to let you know that I am well and fit and came through en exciting time without a scratch.

Yes, I think the censors will permit me to say that I was in on our first landing in the Philippine Islands. You have probably read about it, and I still know little of what happened except in my immediate sector. It was quite an experience. Some of my friends were wounded, but I guess I was lucky, for although I was in on the first day - and under fire constantly & the snipers' bullets cut holes in the air close to my ears, and mortar fire caused me to take refuge, of all places, in a wrecked cemetery. One of the graves had been conveniently blasted in an earlier barrage, and I fitted myself into it, till the Jap shelling was over.

Will soon know whether the hoped for chance to get home on job will come. At least it is an excellent chance where I go, what my next job rests on - decisions in the next few days. I think whatever happens will seem good to me, and I have the real hope of getting home to you for a while - but do not hold it too tightly for we don't want to be disappointed - however, I may know tomorrow or soon after. I hope I have not painted any noble picture of war; it is dirt and smells & the reek of rotting Japs will always cling to my memory. How strange that amidst all the horror emerges some of the best qualities of men - and the best quality is, I believe, the sharing of everything - a can of coffee, a stick of gum - toothpaste - everyone is short of something, so everyone can find something to share.

In general everything went very well, and my own job came out fairly satisfactory, though there were many difficulties. I'll know more about the results when I return tomorrow. I lived in the ground and with the scorpions, and have no more serious reaction then athlete's foot. It is still too close to be sorted in the mind, but the lasting thought I carry away is the courage and good humor of the civilians, many of whom had endured some pretty real tortures under the Japs. Many were dazed, many were grateful & a few, very few who had collaborated, were terrified. I saw boys down from the hills who had lost all clothing and had only a gunnysack sown on for pants - and their long bolo knives. I met guerillas who had been fighting ever since the fall of their country. I stood in ruined churches and watched the wounded and sick receive treatment, and ever and always our own men & medical officers, administrators, interpreters, working without sleep or the thought of rest. Our troops moving up the dusty roads, hotter and dirtier than can be imagined, yet showing that sublime spirit that I have never seen anywhere else & men from whom everything is stripped but the steady continuing faithfulness to their job. I saw women demented by the terrors of loss - one survivor out of a family whose house - dogs, chickens, everything, had been converted into black debris, the breath of war.

I do not for a moment believe that all these people were individually heroic - but the greater number of them had kept enough of themselves, their humor, their spirit, to be the foundation of a great nation to come. Enough can never be said of them, nor of our own guys whose kindness and consideration to them was amazing.

The presence of danger is a great equalizer, yet fundamental goodnesses survive. These are disjointed ideas that come to mind, burst out of them I will some day make a clearer picture of things - just now it is a mixed dream.

Have had a good rest on shipboard eaten my head off. The leanness of battle is disappearing again....

Jesse and his fellow officers were being transported by the Navy in considerable comfort. During those trips, the new captain made friends with a few high-ranking officers, including Admiral Nimitz. That meeting turned out to be relevant some years later, when Jesse wrote the film *John Paul Jones* (1959) with its director, John Farrow, with some uncredited additions from Ben Hecht (who seemed to like keeping his name off some of his contributions, especially if they were not used). Jesse had many discussions with the admiral during the assignment. Nimitz was a history buff, and presented Jess with a bronze medallion of John Paul Jones. The film starred Jesse's childhood next-door-neighbor, Robert Stack, whose father sold the Laskys additional land for their Santa Monica beach house (today a hotel).

October 31, 1944
Dear Captain Jesse,

...Billy and Margy, with little Ronnie, arrived for their furlough last Saturday, October 28th, and the little fellow is the cutest kid you ever saw. I met them at the depot and we stopped at Grandma's, which pleased her very much, and, of course, she was crazy about Ronnie.

In the evening we picked up Frances and Jane Allen and we all went to the Air Corps show 'Winged Victory', and afterwards to the Biltmore Bowl. Frances looked very pretty and was so gay and lively - we had a wonderful time.

Sunday night I gave a buffet party and again Frances looked very pretty and seemed very happy. She read us your last letter, which was most interesting. We had about sixteen people at the party including Ruthie and Mac. No doubt Frances wrote you about the fun we had the Sunday before Billy arrived. I took her, with Ruthie and Mac and Betty, to the Beverly Hills Hotel for Sunday night dinner—so you see I am following your instructions and see as much of Frances as possible. At any rate you need not worry the least bit about her; she manages very well and is always gay and cheerful.

Had a talk with Bess on the 'phone; she is thrilled with her experiences in New York; working close with the publishers on her book, and studying very hard with a famous painter named Gluckman.

... At this writing it looks as though I might join Columbia as their top producer, with an independent setup. Walter MacEwen would go in as my assistant and associate producer; however, there are one or two other propositions that look good and I may not make a decision for several weeks. The principal thought that moves me is to have a berth for you when you return, and in an independent setup, such as we are planning, you could come in as a staff writer ... I am taking Billy and Margy to Palm Springs for three days as Billy has worked awfully hard and needs a rest. It has been wonderful having him here and he has improved enormously. The work he is doing at the hospital is fascinating....

Wish the devil I knew what you are up to and where you really are. We are keeping our fingers crossed hoping you will arrive back here around the first of the year. I cannot tell you how we missed you at the buffet family reunion Sunday night. Well, let us hope it won't be long now before we have another family reunion with you as the Guest of Honor! ...

Franklin D. Roosevelt was back into office. The news in Europe was hopeful. On October 14th, German General Rommel had committed suicide and there was a massive German surrender at Aachen. The French had reached the Rhine and captured Strasbourg. And Lasky, having completed his deal at Warner Bros., turned over *The Two Mrs. Carrolls*, to Jack L. Warner, who exec produced the film with Mark Hellinger as producer, starring Humphrey Bogart. It was released 3 years later. Lasky was still considering his options.

November 9, 1944
Dear Jess,

... I have just re-read your wonderful letter of October 29th and the shorter one written November 1st ... Betty wanted the original letters which she is putting in a book with all your other letters, and she prizes them highly.

We don't care what the rest of the world thinks, we have a hero in our family and his name is <u>Capt. Jesse L. Lasky, Jr.</u> What talks we will have when you return - and that suggestion of yours of a stag get-together with Jack, his father and you and me, is an inspiration. We will make it the most memorable evening of our lives: a magnificent dinner; cocktails; champagne; cordials, and smokes—and, strange as it may seem to you, I have become a much better drinker than ever, and the stuff agrees with me, seeing that I never felt better in my life, and never looked better. By the way, I have cut out smoking cigars and only smoke cigarettes.

My business affairs are progressing satisfactorily... now have a deal on with Columbia Pictures which I like very much: a three-year contract - two pictures a year; 50% financed by the bank and 50% by Columbia; absolute independence; a call on their stock company, and headquarters at Columbia studio with all their facilities - great distribution terms, and I get 50% of the profits. Loyd Wright is working on the details now, and I will go to work after the first of the year.

In the meantime, however, a proposition has come up that is so wonderful that I might switch back to Warner Bros., as they are anxious to have me, and I can make a good percentage deal there if I find my own material - and I have found a piece of material so wonderful that, for once in my life, I am not going to talk about it until it is all wrapped up in cellophane...I was thrilled over the Election as I know you must have been. I spent Election eve with a big party at Mocambo and danced until four in the morning. Somehow I hate to tell you what good times I am having, when I think of the hardships, the suffering, and death that you have seen and may still see - but life is like that. I guess I was born under a lucky star - maybe I had hardships in a pre-incarnation, and life is making it up to me now.

By the way, the deal at Columbia will be a corporation known as JESSE L. LASKY PRODUCTIONS. Walter MacEwen is coming with me, and we are saving a spot for you to take charge of stories, writers and collaborate on scripts, and assist Walter. If I go to Warners, you go with me there....

November 27, 1944

...We finally incorporated - JESSE L. LASKY PRODUCTIONS, Inc. - and Walter MacEwen and I are leaving for New York on December 1st; I will be in New York when this reaches you. I have not actually signed any deal yet as it seems wisest to first find our material, which isn't any too easy. My New York trip is for the purpose of trying to tie up certain plays and stories and, if successful, my next move will be to sign the contract I described in my last letter, with Columbia Pictures.

'Rhapsody in Blue' was supposed to open in New York on December 20th but has been postponed until May or June. It is too bad as it would have helped my prestige, at least, at that time - but in the end, I suppose it won't make much difference.

I have been working more or less with McEwen for a couple of weeks now and I find him a very able and valuable associate. Randy is also going to New York and among the three of us we should accomplish something. The thing that thrills me about my independent setup is that there will be a place in it for you, as I have already described. In order to get a proper setup for taxes, I am putting $35,000 into the company myself. However, immediately we secure our stories, the banks and the picture company will do the rest of the financing. Loyd Wright is handling the corporate setup...Betty has completely recovered her health and she and Buddy get along beautifully. Buddy flew in again yesterday; his co-pilot crashed while doing a solo-flight, and was killed, and the Army appointed Buddy, as his roommate, to bring the body back to Hollywood - so Buddy and Betty, who knew the boy's wife very well, are handling all the funeral arrangements. It is to be a military funeral and there is a lot of red tape that they are unraveling...I will write you from New York - in the meantime, give my best to Jack Hively if he is still with you - and devoted love to you....

December 19, 1944
Dear Jesse,

... Bess and I were thrilled to learn of the important job you are working on and are anxious to know more detail, which I suppose we won't hear until you finally arrive here. Bob Presnell called me immediately after his arrival in New York and spoke in glowing terms about you and said that you and Jack Hively were in charge of assembling a picture and that very soon you would be sent over here with the picture to be completed in Hollywood - however, your letter contradicts Bob's information, so that we will rely on the information contained in your letter, and will not expect you quite yet.

I am enjoying New York very much. Mother is at The Ambassador, and Walter MacEwen and I are a block away from her at the Waldorf where we have a nice suite of two bedrooms and a sitting room, which I use as an office. We have lined up some interesting material for future productions, and I am now working on securing a release though a major company. I doubt if things will come to a head until after the first of the year—but our prospects are good. Enclosed is one of many notices which will interest you because it refers to you. Sorry that the interviewer forgot to use your title of Captain, but if I can make my ambitious plans come true you won't mind that as you will inherit a title in the new company. I have secured one great story, which is another 'It Happened One Night', popular and down-to-earth, and it will be published as a novel.

I am enjoying the New York shows and the nightlife - the city is crowded theatres packed, and cafes teeming with spenders - God only knows where all the money comes from. Almost every day I run into someone who asks for you - they all claim to be buddies or pals, but I can never remember their names.

This letter will reach you after Christmas, but I can't help that. How scattered the family will be this year: Betty and Frances in Hollywood; Grandma in Los Angeles, Buddy in Texas you somewhere in the South Pacific; Bill, Margy and Ronnie in Denver—and Mother and Dad and Randy in New York. Let's hope that another year will find us all back in dear old California, and some kind of Peace restored to the bleeding[94] world.

Bess and I, and Randy, send you our best, and hope this reaches you by New Years—at any rate, through the Holidays we will be thinking of you. NEW YEARS GREETINGS to You and Jack Hively. . . .

January 16, 1945
Dear Jesse,

. . . Harry Cohn is in New York, and when he arrives here in about a week, we expect to draw the contracts, and I will move into the Columbia Studio with Walter MacEwen, thus establishing Jesse L. Lasky Productions, Inc. One of my reasons for forming an independent unit was to take advantage of a better tax setup. I found, as long as I was working for a straight salary, the taxes were so high that I had nothing left - and did not even earn my expenses. Under this new setup, if we make successful pictures, I would share in the profits, and the tax on these profits would only be 25%; in the meantime, of course, I draw a reasonable salary.

I have bought my first story, which is a dandy, and have several ideas for the second story, as we are to make two pictures the first year. The principal problem these days is casting - but all this must seem far afield from war and the turmoil in the world, and, sometimes, I hate to write about my business endeavors, but someone has to keep the home fires burning.

Now for Frances: I have seen a lot of her since my return. She dines at the house very often, and is in good spirits; looks well, and is quite excited over her studies at the University. We were all hoping, of course, that you would be headed this way early this year, but I gather from your letters that it may be summer before we can look for your return. With casualty lists printed every day from both theatres of war, we must be thankful to know that you are safe and must be patient about your home coming . . . I left Bess in New York looking and feeling wonderful. She leads a simple life there compared to other New Yorkers, but is constantly occupied and is very happy. I think she is going to miss New York when she returns to the comparative quiet of Saltair Avenue. She plans to return home in two or three weeks.

They tell me I am looking, and certainly I feel, very well. I love this life of ease, after working at the studios, and if I could afford it, I would never go back to them - but I imagine in another thirty days I will be up to my ears in preparation for my productions. My only solace is in the fact that by keeping in the limelight and in the picture game, I am holding a spot for you. Walter MacEwen has turned out to be a fine man to work with and you will like him very much . . . Remember me to Jack Hively who, if I remember correctly, is

---
94 Lasky did not use this word in the British slang sense.

now a Major—am I right? Not a day passes but what any number of people ask me about you and they always ask me to send you their regards - and I always forget their names.... I love you and I think you are a great guy.

PS - Enclosed is a notice on 'Rhapsody' from the Solomon Islands.

As part of Combat Photographic, Jesse was in the front line, taking part in the Leyte landing that returned General MacArthur to the Philippines. This unsolicited letter to Lasky expresses the attitude of one naval officer who came across the new Army captain.

1 February 1945
GENERAL HEADQUARTERS
SOUTHWEST PACIFIC AREA
Mr. Jesse L. Lasky
181 North Saltair
West Los Angeles, California.
Dear Mr. Lasky

It has never been my pleasure to have met you, but I know that you will allow me this intrusion, briefly to relate a story and to record a tribute to your son, Captain Jesse L. Lasky, Jr., United States Army.

I met him at the rendezvous point for the Leyte landings. We crossed on the same transport, to play our respective parts in the historic return of General MacArthur to The Philippines. Aboard ship we had many truly delightful conversations, and I became fond of this outstanding young man and splendid officer.

We found we had many mutual friends: Doug. Fairbanks, Jr., Bob Montgomery, Burgess Meredith, Jack (John) Ford, Frank Capra, Willie Wyler, and many another. We found, too, that we had many mutual friends in England, where I served for twenty-six months on the staffs of Admirals Ghormley and Stark, October 1941 to December 1943, prior to being assigned to GHQ, SWPA.

On D-Day we chose to go ashore together as part of the assault waves, and never before have I come to admire more nor to have more sincere admiration for any man. One day you will know the story of our first night and the following several days, but believe me it was rugged, and that is a prime understatement.

In a wide experience in this war, I have never seen displayed more sheer guts, more commendable courage, such cheerfulness and poise as Jesse exhibited. He was an inspiration to us all. Through all the terrible hell of that first night, and the second, and the third, and little relief in the daylight hours, he never was other than during our days on the ship.

Captain Lasky is a credit to you, his father, and to his family; he is a credit to our blessed land, I am proud to call him my friend. And he is doing a highly skilled professional job. To him I say, in the words of the Navy—'Well done Jesse Lasky, Jr., and full marks.'

Sincerely yours,
(signed) ROBERT E. VINING, Commander, USNR

The medals that Jesse was awarded were 1. Legion of Merit. Legionnaire Class (the only class awarded to Americans); for exceptional merit in performance of duties.

2. American Defense Service Medal. For 12 months active duty service during 1939-41 (before Pearl Harbor).

3. American Campaign Medal. For service in the American theater of war.

4. Asiatic-Pacific Campaign Medal. For service in the Asiatic-Pacific theater of war. The arrowhead on the ribbon is for one landing and the three stars for three battle engagements.

5. Philippine Liberation Medal. For service in the liberation of the Philippine Islands between 17 October 1944 and 3 September 1945. Only the ribbon of this medal could be worn in uniform (red with thin blue and white central stripe and two stars), which he has. To wear with civilian clothes, men often added a miniature, as he did, which was un-official.

6. World War Two Victory Medal. For all who served 1941-1946.

7. Armed Forces Reserve Medal. For ten years' service in any service's reserves units.[95]

April was a momentous month in the war. On April 12th, President Roosevelt died at the age of sixty-three and Vice President Harry Truman became president. On the 28th in Italy, Mussolini and his associates were executed at Lake Como. On the 30th, Hitler committed suicide.

And at last Jesse had been sent home. He arrived at his own door, unannounced, and was not delighted to have been greeted by a tall, redheaded major, who it seemed, had been staying with Frances. The major saluted Jesse, packed his bags, and hastily moved out. Than night, husband and wife made love as if nothing had happened. But it was over. They were strangers now.

Still, he could not find it in his heart to blame his wife; it was the war that made these things happen and his family seemed blissfully unaware of France's secret liaison. The deception that all was well would go on for some time, but relations between husband and wife were not to be so easily mended.

Jesse had been home for only a few days when he was sent to New York. It made the split with Frances easier. He would be stationed there as the war finally ground

---

95 These were kindly identified for me by Frank Draskovic President, California Orders & Medals Society'. (fdraskovic@hotmail.com)

to an end in Europe. The U.S. 7th Army had taken Nuremberg; the Dachau concentration camp was liberated—and on May 7th, Germany surrendered unconditionally.

The news, when it came that Frances was pregnant, she was to attribute to the night of Jesse's return.

For Lasky, there was cause for personal celebration. His 'indie' deal was finally not with Warners or Columbia. He had found something better—an offer from RKO, quite different from his prior association, now that Charles Koerner was in charge of the studio. He wrote to his son in New York.

May 7, 1945
Dear Jesse,

Today the war ended in Europe and today, I finally signed my contracts with RKO. Tomorrow is VE-Day and, tomorrow, we move into our new offices at the RKO Studios. I just came from the studio where we had pictures taken with Charles Koerner, the head of the studio, and had the usual warm reception from all the department heads. There is a wonderful friendly atmosphere in this studio, and I feel sure we are going to be very happy there.

It has been a long slow process agreeing on the contracts and getting Claudette Colbert's signature and, at the last moment, the deal was almost upset because we had to give her the right to approve the script - but I don't anticipate any serious trouble with her as she is crazy about the story . . . I attended a lunch today given by Walter Wanger and Sol Lesser, to a small but distinguished group of men in the industry. The object of the lunch was to hear a Lieut. Charles Bolte, who is one of the consultants appointed by the State Department to represent the Veterans of this war at the San Francisco Conference. Lieut. Bolte made a brilliant talk on behalf of the newly formed American Veterans Committee. I subscribed $100.00 to help form the local chapter; some of the men like Sam Goldwyn subscribed $500.00, and some even $1,000.00. I will send you their pamphlet and I know that it is an organization that, when you understand its purpose, you will want to join.

This is certainly a great day in history - the end of the War - and it is wonderful to think that at least in Europe, death is not rampant any more and the guns have ceased firing. Our Victory celebration will come when the Japanese war is over, and may that be soon.

. . .Buddy has been here for several days and leaves tomorrow. He is assigned to-a new post in Utah, and he thinks he is about to get his orders for overseas service in the South Pacific; in fact he is quite sure it will come any day now . . . Betty has been very happy having him here. Am glad to tell you that Grandma is feeling better and is really more like her old self again. I will write a longer letter after we are settled at RKO. The story will break in the trade press and papers on Thursday.

Truman's bombing of Hiroshima on August 6, 1945, followed by the bombing of Nagasaki on August 10th, ended the war with Japan. On the August 14, the peace treaty was signed and the war was officially over. Jesse, in New York, was still expecting to hear if he would be sent back to the South Pacific as part of the 'clean up' campaign. Frances, who had remained at their house on Veteran Avenue, announced to the family that she and Jesse were expecting a baby. Jesse was unusually silent on the subject.

Lasky's next project was to encompass the two themes that excited him the most: biography and music. He had managed to obtain the rights to the life of Enrico Caruso, the greatest opera star of the century, whose silent film Lasky had been forced to shelve so many years before.[96] From New York, Jesse wrote to his mother, having been in the heart of the city when peace was declared. He makes no mention of Frances.

Aug 23, 1945
Dearest Bess

Loved having your letter, written I think the day of war's end. Your feelings were very close to my own. I had been at a small dinner party - or rather had just arrived when the whistles and horns began. The whole air seemed to throb as though with a great beating of wings then we dialed the radio to catch the news.

I could not quite join in the whole-hearted sense of gaiety being expressed throughout the city. I felt a relief and deep gratefulness that the end had come but an unaccountable sadness. The event was too closely related to suffering - and then to be greeted with thoughtless debaucheries.

But still in the historic and sociological sense I wanted to see it. Walked through the streets and into Times Square. Bumped shoulders with the mobs, giddy, should have been. wild-eyed, drunken, depraved - feeling too rarely that sense of gratefulness that

But then it was sometimes there - Somehow the full weight and meaning of the event had not sunk home. People scarcely know what they said, or how they felt or perhaps there was a certain justifiable desire to escape into thoughtless revelry - still it was hard to reconcile the orgies of indiscriminate street kissing, bottle emptying, and vandalism with the portentousness of the hour. My own inner self kept echoing the simple thought, over and over, like a requiem intoned in a church, Thank God it is over.

Well unfortunately, the large and cumbersome mechanism of the Army will take its own time to adjust itself. We cannot now expect, as we had at first widely hoped, a quick exchange of uniform for tweeds. My own chances are

---

96 *Enrico Caruso - His Life & Death* by Dorothy Caruso, republished 2008 by Grant Press:

fine, but it will take time – The job we are on now must be revised and finished to match the changed era – this may take as long as five weeks, and we are now ordered to remain here to the final completion & after that we will supposedly return to the Pacific, but there is a good hope that this may not be too certain.

It is the time of transition, and it's hard to guess when and how soon I can expect to be free – at least there is the satisfaction of knowing that the big changes are over.

Well, Darling, I don't know when you plan to be in New York, but I feel sure I'll be seeing you for a 'garden talk' long before that time. I have Dad's novel and script, and am studying it very carefully before giving him any opinions or verdicts. Believe me if I can be useful, I will be, and I'll have much time here to work on it.

Are you painting, and what about your book? Almost publication date n'est ce que pas?... at least I am comfortable in a nice cheerful apartment at the Beaux Arts – and am alone with no roommate to interrupt work or contemplation – love to my beautifully Bess girl – and write me often again. Adorations to you – Jess

The bulk of Jesse's wartime letters have not survived. Many of them were kept in a scrapbook, which at Bessie's death, was stored temporarily with Jesse L. Lasky's files in the Los Angeles County jail. These files were meant to find their way to a Hollywood museum, which was never built. When Betty checked on them several years later, she found that many of them were missing. Lasky's letters to his son, reproduced here, had been carefully preserved and kept by Jess.

October 4, 1945
Dear Jesse,

...We are gradually improving our script; Colbert came in and has accepted the part, and only had a few little suggestions to make – so that is a big load off my mind. John Wayne loves his part, and so does Eddie Albert who plays Dink. There are still minor troubles in the script, which you could solve in two sessions with me, if you were only here. I am still hoping you and Jack will arrive in time to do a little work in polishing the script. We have postponed the starting date until October 15th and I hope you will be here before we start shooting.

Frances had dinner with us night before last and stayed until 11.30; she was in fine fettle, however, you must be prepared to see a very big girl. It looks as though you are going to have a son who could make the grade as a heavyweight prize fighter.

Walter is all excited today; his wife had a 9-1/2 pd. Boy at the Hollywood Hospital – she had a Caesarean operation, but everything went perfectly. You might drop him a line of congratulations....

France's pregnancy was farther along than the family knew, which accounted for her size, and ultimately a 'premature' birth. Jesse returned from New York, but did not return to Veteran Avenue. He arranged for an immediate divorce. Wishing a quick settlement, he gave Frances everything she asked for: the house, his collection of first editions, several valuable paintings, and half his salary, until such time as she remarried. While he was overseas, she had sold his treasured gun collection, saying she needed the money.

Although in the years that followed several men approached Jesse, entreating him to stop paying Frances alimony so that she would marry, he was unable to oblige because she threatened to send him to jail if he stopped. He never told his family that the child was not his, continued child support until Jennifer was eighteen, and always treated her as his child. Years later, when Jesse and I married, Jennifer would often spend weekends with us. She was considered a member of the family, and was only to learn the truth from her mother when she was an adult.

The shock of the war and his less-than-perfect homecoming led Jesse into a period of depression and heavy drinking. In this mood, he met Betty McCrossen in New York, and once free, launched into a hasty second marriage.

With large financial commitments, Jesse returned to his screenwriting career, going to work for DeMille, who had been anxious to have him back. In 1946 he was on the writing team of *Unconquered* along with Charles Bennett, Fredric M. Frank, and DeMille's old flame, Jeanie Macpherson, who continued as a team member, although little of her efforts reached the screen. Writing was what interested Jesse; producing was not, and his father was finally to understand that.

The world moved on. On November 20, 1945 Lasky was busy filming *Without Reservations* in New York. Claudette Colbert played a novelist traveling on the train to Hollywood where her best-selling book is to be filmed, when she meets John Wayne, who had read but didn't like her book; but she quite likes him.

While working on the film in New York, Lasky met a young woman playing the small part of a Western Union operator, and found he quite liked her. Jean Koehler had a husband. The producer started an affair with her and it grew serious enough for him to introduce her to his children. The relationship was to last for several years. But for the time being, life in the Lasky household went on in its usual laissez-faire mode.

SCENE EIGHT
1949 - 1959

THE PLAQUE AT SUNSET AND VINE

In 1947 in his new RKO deal, Lasky was producing *The Miracle of the Bells* starring Fred MacMurray and the striking Italian actress, (Alida) Valli.[97] He gave the popular singer Frank Sinatra a straight acting role as a priest, (with the approval from the Catholic Church on such off-the-wall casting.) It wasn't until 1953 that Sinatra again played a straight acting role in *From Here to Eternity*, for which Harry Cohn, head of Columbia was credited with 'enormous vision' in casting him.

In 1948 Jesse was back again with DeMille as chief writer working with Fred Frank on *Samson and Delilah*. The Boss always required Jesse to be on set during filming in case a line didn't suit an actor and there would be any rewriting to do. On a DeMille film, actors could dispute a line, but they did not rewrite it—although Gary Cooper on *Northwest Mounted Police* was free to go to Jesse and show him a long speech, take a pen and cross it out, saying, 'It's a great speech, Jess, but what I'd like to say here is, Yup.' Or it might be 'Nope'—with which both Jesse and DeMille were happy. With an actor like Cooper, his face could say it all.

Victor Mature had other problems besides his lines, and as usual, Jesse was ready with pen and pad on the set of *Samson and Delilah*. Not only the Bible, but also the script required Samson to fight a young lion single-handedly. Doubles would be used for much of the scene and a man in a lion's suit would substitute for the lion for certain shots. A disembodied paw with rubber claws would be used for 'dangerous' close-ups. But for a few shots, Mature would have to face a real lion. The animal in question, 'Old Jackie', had been through a few filmic tussles in his day and was said to be of a most gentle disposition. Not gentle enough though, as Mature decided and refused to set sandal on set.

DeMille cast an eye around for the smallest male present and settled on his devoted writer. His command shook the sound stage: 'Jesse…! Come here and wrestle that lion!'

Jesse evaluated the situation. Was he more afraid of Old Jackie or DeMille? Decision made, he headed uncertainly towards the king of beasts. The trainer whispered soothingly in Jackie's ear but reached for a chair to wave, just in case. The tawny beast, freed from his leash came forward, yellow eyes glazed. Was it a friendly glaze, Jesse wondered? Powerful jaws widened, teeth bared. Was Old Jackie merely yawning or was he hungry?

Jesse was not required to place his head between those jaws that day because Samson/Mature suddenly threw off his robe, flexed his famous muscles, and pushing Jesse aside, stepped towards the lion and the cameras.

As Jess later mused, 'What actor could let a writer steal the scene?'

The final day of Jesse's assignment on *Samson and Delilah*, DeMille sat with his writers at the long lunch table in the Paramount commissary where all must appear daily, and Jesse was usually required to sit beside the boss. DeMille told them that they had done a fine job and after lunch could collect their final checks and go home with one admonition: keep themselves available while he decided his next project.

---

97 Who was to become a great personal friend of mine, although I did not know the Laskys at that time.

When Fred Frank and Jesse realized that DeMille had arbitrarily waived their required two weeks' severance pay, they made it clear to the unit business manager on the production that this was not only heartless, it was also illegal according to the Writers Guild of America. They were pleading their case to no avail.

Soon the well-known striding boots thundered down the hall, bringing DeMille to their writing room. 'Gentlemen', he complained sadly, 'do I correctly understand that some trivial technicality has been allowed to threaten a great working relationship?'

The two explained that they had no option in the matter. They were members of the Writers Guild—a requirement for all writers in films.

'Caesar had his Brutus.' DeMille sighed. 'I have you.' He told them how much he valued their working relationship and thanked them for 'a film that will outlive us all, and inspire perhaps some few in the vast faceless masses of humanity who await it'. His hand moved slowly towards his pocket. 'Thank you for giving me *Samson and Delilah* and I hope you will accept—for your devotion and effort—above and beyond the call of mere duty—these tokens of my appreciation and esteem!' With that, he handed each of them one of his mint-fresh fifty-cent pieces; the reward he judiciously handed out to his chosen writers in lieu of two weeks' salary.

Not wishing to be out of work, and his father otherwise occupied, Jesse accepted an offer from an independent Belgian producer, Nat Wachsberger and his associate, Robert Haggiag, who were going to make *Ladro de Venezia (The Thief of Venice)* in Italy with the sultry Maria Montez (star of Hollywood 'tits and sand' epics in the forties). Jesse dubbed it 'Robin Hood in a gondola'. The original story was by British writer Michael Pertwee, and Jesse would receive solo screenplay credit. In the days before the Spaghetti Western brought American film people to Europe, and more specific knowledge of the carpetbaggers who had moved into overseas independent production, it all sounded like a great adventure, so Jesse took his new wife Betty to Italy.

Several months passed and DeMille, who now considered Jesse his chief writer, cabled him in Rome where he had started to work on a second film for Wachsberger, *Women Without Names*. Cecil's cable read: COME HOME ALL IS FORGIVEN.

Jesse didn't appreciate the humor, but if truth be known, he was having problems getting paid by Wachsberger, who had a habit of disappearing on payday, although eventually would come up with the money. Finally, Jesse could stand the strain no longer and confronted his new boss.

'I know you pay me. Nat', he said. 'But why do you always keep me two weeks behind?'

Wachsberger's plump cheeks sucked into a wistful pout. His shoulders hunched in an eloquent acknowledgement of the vagaries of fate, particularly in show biz. 'Suppose, da'link, God forbid—but suppose in those two veeks, you should die?'

Hearing of Jesse's dilemma, Lasky advised his son:

August 9, 1949
Dear Jesse,

Mother read me your letter this morning in which you said that Wachsberger had disappeared and you were afraid that your European commitments were about at an end. By the time this reaches you, most certainly, if he has not come across, you should plan to return to Hollywood immediately. Things are getting very active here. As I wrote you, I have a writer on a week-to-week basis, and compared to your talent, he could shine your shoes beautifully; it may be in the cards that you will arrive in time to take over this job. You would be paid a weekly salary.

I also have another writing job which I am saving for you - the job is to modernize 'TRILBY', laying the story in Greenwich Village, New York (today), with Svengali as a modern scientific hypnotist.

There are possible writing jobs for you at Warners and at 20th Century-Fox; I am in close contact with Julian Johnson, the head of their story department, and Maurice Hanline is working for Johnson. You won't have to take a DeMille assignment, I assure you.

Another thing - Bill is moving out of his apartment this week, and we won't rent it until we get an answer to this letter. If you are returning, you can move right into that apartment, which is completely furnished, and you will be neighbors with Bill Bidlack and Betty, until such time as you get on your feet and we buy the little house, which is my dream for you, over in Bill Lasky's new neighborhood, and near me.

Enclosed is some publicity which will amuse you. There is a fortune in 'VALLEY OF THE MISTS', and I feel sure I will have it financed and distribution set before you can return here.

I forgot to say I am very close to Kenneth McKenna who assigns writers at Metro; it would be a cinch to land you a writing job there and at an increase in salary. Believe me, I know what I am talking about - so much so that I wish you would forget the steamer trip and fly back - and get settled for some good solid writing jobs and to make some real money. While the long trip on the boat would be good for your health and would help you in the direction of planning a novel - I really think you would be happier if you get settled in the apartment and get busy on congenial writing jobs. Incidentally, I need you and could use you to the greatest advantage to us both.

My 'Caruso' deal is in good shape; a few more clauses to be ironed out; contracts sent to Mrs. Caruso for signatures - and within a month the deal will be closed. What a job it has been - you will never know!

As you must have gathered, I missed seeing The Sickle or the Cross[98] but Bill thought it was outstanding - and through Randy, I understand that the Lutheran Church people are very much pleased with it. Mother and I will see it with you and Betty when you get home, if Frank Strayer doesn't show it to me. . . .

---

98 A documentary written by Jesse for the Lutheran Church, well received by the press.

I have the strangest feeling that with the new enthusiasm and energy that Bill has brought into Lasky Productions that somehow you will tie in with us. When you once reach here, you will quickly catch the enthusiasm and spirit that engenders this organization at the present moment. There are still opportunities to make some real money; the strange thing is that since Walter left, it is as though an anchor has been removed from around our necks, and Bill and I are really inspired - and when Laskys are inspired - they are Inspired!

Devoted love –
Dad

August 31, 1949

...It seems ages since I have, written you; in the meantime, Betty's (Jesse's wife) lovely letter to Mother, and your letters have arrived, the latest having reached us this morning in which you felt that Wachsberger may not come through, and you might be en-route home very soon. Bess and I were talking at breakfast this morning and we feel that whatever happens will be definitely for the best - as a matter of fact, when I get my financing finally set for 'VALLEY OF THE MISTS', if you are not tied up, I am going to cable you to fly home and do this writing job for me, for which we will be able to pay, at least, your regular salary - but we still have to get the financing arranged.

I expect to hear from Paramount by the end of the week, which will make it necessary for me to fly to New York to meet Barney Balaban. The deal with Paramount has been held, up pending his arrival from Europe, and he has only just returned.

The 'VALLEY OF THE MISTS' story is simple and needs very simple natural dialogue; the whole thing is laid in Mexico. I put a writer on for two weeks but he missed so bad that I took him off, and won't do anything more about the screenplay until the enterprise is finally financed.

Bill is booming as usual. He made friends with Don Douglas Jr. the chap you worked with at the Douglas plant; you remember I wrote that we had lunch there one day - well, Donald Douglas, the big boss, is equipping a plane to fly to Mexico, in charge of his son (the one you know) and they are taking Bill as their guest. Bill will leave early Friday morning, September 2nd; will have three days in Mexico City and will then return home. The trip will give Bill a chance to investigate certain things for me in Mexico in connection with 'VALLEY OF THE MISTS' production there later. In the meantime, he has been awfully busy as he is working on a picture on the California Condor, a bird that is almost extinct...Mother was away all last week finishing up her paintings of the California Missions, and what a magnificent job she has done. We had some people in and I wish you could have seen the expression on their faces when they saw these magnificent paintings. It is Bess' greatest work and I think will do much to publicize her and eventually make her famous. . .Bess and I miss you and Betty so much, and the thought that you might be returning soon is a very cheerful one. Your next letter should tell us the real news: either that you are leaving for home, or are definitely assigned to the 'QUEEN OF SHEBA'.

My devoted love to you both.

Bessie painted all twenty-one of the historic California Missions (built between 1769 and 1823), traveling over a period of several years to complete this task. It was her version of Lasky's expeditions. Her husband was bouncing between offers of deals and still not settled on one.

September 20, 1949

. . . Today is Randy's birthday; yesterday was your birthday; last Tuesday was my birthday, and I was happy to receive the wire from you and Betty (Jesse's wife) which arrived on the big day. I hope you received my birthday wire and birthday letter, with a small token of my love. This letter was mailed to Locarno Hotel, Rome, and the birthday wire was sent c/o American Express, Venice. Mother has been writing you quite often, and I hope you are getting our letters as you have been moving around so much - but no doubt you leave careful forwarding addresses when you make these moves.

My last letter probably told you I was leaving for New York - well, I didn't leave as Metro was not ready to close - but I just received word from Metro that things are now in good shape and they are ready for me to come to New York the end of this week. What a long drawn-out affair it has been.

In the meantime, Bill and I are working very hard on the endless details of 'VALLEY OF THE MISTS'. As we have the promise of Paramount distribution, I am now in the throes of trying to finance the picture, which we have decided to make entirely in Mexico. Bill's trip to Mexico was successful inasmuch as he made the right contacts and secured the information we needed. Harry Chandlee has just completed the treatment of the story which is in very good shape. It is a tremendous undertaking, but when we finally accomplish it all, it should make us a lot of money.

Yesterday we moved out of RKO and into the General Service Studios, 1040 North Las Palmas Avenue, Hollywood 38 - 'phone Granite 3111. We have very comfortable offices and I think we are going to like it here. We consider this a temporary move as by the end of the year we should be hard at work in Mexico on the picture.

. . . Enclosed is some publicity that will amuse you. The Art Directors gave their annual dinner and devoted it to awarding plaques of life memberships to Cecil and myself. They told me I made the speech of my career. The family were there, including Randy, and it was a wonderful evening. The affair received a great deal of publicity. Constance (DeMille's wife) sat at Bessie's table; I, of course was on the dais.

About the time you receive this letter, I will be in New York, or enroute there, and will be at the Sherry-Netherlands for a few days in case you should want to cable me - my thought being that if your deal for 'Queen of Sheba' falls through, you will be coming home....

Jesse was hopping around Italy with his slow-paying producer but not yet willing to give up on the project. His younger brother, Bill, was learning hands-on to be a producer. His father wrote:

October 14, 1949
Dear Jess,

... Billy and I arrived home by plane (overnight flight) this morning, and although I am still dizzy from the flight and loss of sleep, I want to get this letter off to you as I haven't written you since I left for New York over two weeks ago. By the way, apropos of letters, Randy told me a letter I sent to you sometime ago addressed Hotel Locarno, Rome, was returned, and he immediately re-addressed it to Venice, I believe Europa Hotel, and if you are picking up your mail at the Europa, as well as the American Express office in Venice, you should have this returned letter by this time.

Our trip to New York was, on the whole, successful. I went with two purposes in mind: one, to wind up the endless details of the Caruso deal, and the other—THE VALLEY OF THE MISTS. The Caruso deal is now in good shape: various clearances have been obtained and, as Mrs. Caruso is enroute from Italy, I am sure the deal will be closed within thirty days. When I have the opportunity to tell you the epoch fight I have made to carry on and bring this deal to a conclusion, I think you will agree it will make one of the best stories of aggressiveness and determination that I have ever experienced. At any rate, the papers are now being finalized, and I won't have to go back to New York as far as the Caruso deal is concerned.

Of equal importance was my mission, while in New York to close a deal with Paramount to distribute VALLEY OF THE MISTS. They have an ironclad policy not to take on any outside independent productions, nevertheless, I won out, and after battles with Barney Balaban, we closed for Paramount to distribute VALLEY OF THE MISTS throughout the world....

I took Billy in to meet Zukor, and he was quite impressed with our sketches and the story idea which we told him in detail, and there seems to be a warm feeling of goodwill toward me, and the project, throughout the Paramount organization. Billy proved a dynamo of energy and ability, and was very helpful on the trip, First of all - his Short: THE BOY AND THE EAGLE was showing at Loew's State Theatre, with the popular picture 'Jolson Sings Again', and caused most favorable comment and good audience reaction. Billy immediately took advantage of this to plug the picture he is working on called CONDOR, which will turn out to be a short feature running about an hour, with a narration and a few production shots which Billy will have to make the next two weeks. He aroused interest in CONDOR, and Paramount is anxious to look at it and so is RKO. The hit THE BOY AND THE EAGLE made at Loew's State caused considerable comment and has advanced Bill's stature enormously as a producer. He will be associate, or co-producer on VALLEY OF THE MISTS.

As a matter of fact, if it were not for his practical knowledge of animation and its many problems, I wouldn't undertake VALLEY OF THE MISTS. I still have to finance the picture but, with a Paramount release, that is not considered difficult. I started many channels of financing in New York and now we have to get a careful budget - and, when the budget is definite and final, our finances will be forthcoming.

By the way, Leland Hayward[99] gave me the house seats for 'South Pacific', and Billy nearly swooned with excitement. I had seen it before; it is the greatest show I have ever seen in my entire lifetime. When you come through New York, if I have a little notice, I can get the house seats through Leland Hayward for you and Betty. They are now selling seats from February on, and, even then, you could only get very poor seats...

We had a treatment of VALLEY OF THE MISTS written by Charles Palmer who wrote 'Lost Boundaries', and he did a good quick job; however, he had to go to New York to do a job for DeRochemont and I can't get him back to do the continuity for four weeks. Bill and I were almost hoping that your shifty producer Wachsberger would abandon 'Queen of Sheba' in which event you would be available, and ideal for a really creative screenplay of VALLEY OF THE MISTS -which would include a trip to Mexico, as we will need a writer to be present when the locations are finally selected, just as your presence in Italy enables you to adapt your script to the locations finally selected there.

When you receive this letter, if you are not definitely assigned to 'Queen of Sheba', instead of being kicked around anymore, maybe it would be wise to cable me and we could bring you back for this job, providing, of course, our financing has come through - which must happen.

Our immediate problem is to decide whether to try and do the whole picture in Mexico and take our animators down there - or to treat Mexico as

---

99 Broadway producer who eventually became an agent, then film producer. His second wife was actress Margaret Sullivan.

a location and do the physical production there but do our animation, process shots, etc. in Hollywood. My hunch is that we will end by producing the picture in Hollywood and go to Mexico for our locations.

I wish I had time to tell you all the things that happened in New York, many of them very pleasant...the various people we met, etc. We were there two weeks at the Sherry-Netherlands and the last day at the lovely old Plaza Hotel. I saw Jean on two occasions with her husband, both times the poor guy was dead drunk. He is an alcoholic and I am afraid an incurable case. Jean looked beautiful in spite of her troubles....

Lasky was still seeing Jean Koehler in New York and confided to his son that he wanted to divorce Bess and marry her. Although newly divorced and remarried himself, Jesse was deeply disturbed. He noted in his diary that he counseled his mother against the divorce, although he realized that his father's last sip at the fountain of youth wasn't a casual affair and, like an ancient Greek tragedy, this romantic interlude happened between two exuberant choruses of his life.

In the early days of their marriage, learning of his philandering, Bess had asked for a divorce that Lasky refused, saying it would destroy his career. She accepted that a life of luxury and freedom to do as she pleased was a good trade off, and she agreed to the compromise. But through the following years, although both indulged in casual affairs, she was devoted to her husband and felt that at his time of life, an attachment to a girl half his age would be a disaster, so she took a stand; he could have the divorce if he left her the house and all its contents and half of everything else, saying she was not prepared to change her life style.

Bess later told her children that a few weeks after that, their father had come to her bedroom (they'd had separate bedrooms for years), sat on the bed and had taken her hand. He told her that when he advised Jean there would be little money, she replied, 'Jesse, I was counting on at least a fifty-fifty community property settlement.' Then he kissed Bess tenderly and told her that he was home for good. The 'Jean' episode was finally over. Later, Bess found him in her truly magical garden, sitting under a fig tree looking at the flowers; a thing he'd never had time for before. It was perhaps a small acceptance of the passing years.

His letter continued, correlating the end of the affair to his own with New York.

October 14, 1949

...frankly, aside from interesting hours when you have cocktails and feeling high, New York has no appeal for me whatsoever; I wouldn't live there if you gave me the place.

Bess looked fine on my arrival this morning, and Betty and Bill Bidlack are coming in for dinner tonight. I understand Bill (Bidlack) has a job at last. Thank God, but I haven't heard the details yet.

Bill Lasky caught a cold the last day in New York and lost his voice on the plane trip last night - otherwise, he is a human dynamo, as I probably said before.

We like our offices at General Service Studios. Bill has a secretary to help relieve the pressure, and next week we are going into all the endless details of budget preparation, etc., to make VALLEY OF THE MISTS come true ... As soon as I get settled, I will write you another letter - in the meantime, my devoted love to you, Betty, and to your talented husband, who I am proud bears my illustrious name. Long may the LASKY FLAG wave ... and, before I close, I am reminded that I am eventually going to form a corporation, when you return, under the title: UNITED LASKYS, INC. in which we will all have stock and, under this Lasky Banner, we will make a sequel to VALLEY OF THE MISTS - we already have the story and sketches.

The two-reel documentary/drama that Bill Lasky had produced and directed at RKO, *The Boy and the Eagle*, was nominated for an Oscar in 1950 as Best Short Subject.

In 1952, to Jesse's annoyance, being away in Italy, he missed out on the only DeMille picture to gather in some Oscars, *The Greatest Show on Earth*. But in 1954 he was back at Paramount to write the epic of all epics, panned by the critics, as was usual with DeMille films, but a timeless blockbuster that has constantly been shown around the world ever since. For *The Ten Commandments*, DeMille mobilized his teams like a general planning an invasion.

The final shooting script of 308 pages was annotated with all source references, props, costume details, and camera setups. Although DeMille would during filming, change these at will, he always wanted everything possible or even probable on paper. Making up the writing team were Jesse, Fred Frank, Aeneas MacKenzie, and Jack Gariss. C.B.'s regular researcher, Henry Nordlinger's documentation of the screenplay was so informative that the UCLA Press published it. In 1956, the USA box office record was $68,234,000. In 1999, it was selected for preservation in the United States National Film Registry by the Library of Congress as being 'culturally, historically, or aesthetically significant.' In June 2008, The American Film Institute, on its Ten Top Ten List (the best ten films in ten American film genres based on polling 1,500 members of the creative community) listed *The Ten Commandments* as the 10th all-time best film in the Epic genre. *The Ten Commandments* is number seven on the list of all time worldwide top earners, having grossed $2.09 billion at the time of writing this book.

To Jesse, the problem with confronting history and religion for the screen was to invent drama without distorting facts. Since 'facts' are often contradictory, the screenwriter must adhere to current doctrine and accepted fundamental belief. DeMille had decided that Jess was 'the unit Jew' and assigned him to write the first feast of the Passover. DeMille's first commandment: 'Write it from the heart of a

Hebrew, Jesse.' With that daunting directive, Jesse strove to approach the scene with sufficient reverence and emotion. When it was finished, he felt he'd achieved a scene of some merit and brought it to the boss, knowing, of course, that he would always be asked to rewrite. Grim-faced, DeMille read it—and not for the first time burst into a furious rage, screaming frenzied accusations that Jesse had managed to reduce this great moment in mankind's saga to merely Hollywood theatrics! Then in his fury, he spat on the scene.

Shattered and unable to speak, Jess hurried back to his office and packed his personal possessions and books. He was quitting. As he was about to leave, a knock brought DeMille, tantrum over and suddenly mellow. At a glance, he took in the books, briefcase, and Jesse's scowl.

'Packing, Jesse...?' He paused dramatically eying the pile of books. 'Those books—yours, I presume?'

'All mine', Jesse growled

'That Bible?'

'Happens to be inscribed', Jess snarled, holding the fly page open, reading out loud: 'To dear Jesse from Mother. September, 1924.'

Another pause from Cecil. 'You're walking out on me just because of a petty difference on a scene? I can't believe it.'

'Try', Jesse said, daring to be rude.

'Haven't we worked together long enough not to worry about hurt feelings?' the old man said. Then he paused. His eyes sparkled, a curious smile touched the director's face, and his tone became sepulchral. 'And the Lord God took dust and mixed it with spittle—and from this he made a man.'

Jesse just stared at him. This was as close to an apology as DeMille would ever get.

'You came to me as a young poet', the director went on. 'I don't think a poet stops being a poet. Nor should he. But over the layer of sensitivity is built the armor of use. This is a man's equipment and it is not a bad shield to carry. So grant me the privilege of mixing spittle and dust at times.' He put his hand on Jesse's shoulder, looked deeply into his eyes for a moment, smiled benignly, turned, and walked out.

It was another of DeMille's great performances. He had acknowledged error without a clumsy apology and Jesse stayed on to finish the scene—and the picture. And when he heard that the boss was taking a crew to Egypt to film on location, he was thrilled at the prospect and waited. But since nothing was said, he reminded DeMille, 'You once invited me to come wade with you in the Red Sea.'

DeMille quickly assured him that he needed Jesse to stay and polish the script at the studio. Seeing Jesse's disappointment, he asked, 'What would you like me to bring you from the Land of the Nile, fellah?'

Knowing what a cheapskate his boss was Jesse replied, 'A pebble—from the top of Mount Sinai, where Moses might have set his foot.'

And on his return DeMille gave his writer a tiny piece of granite set on a silver mounted black wooden stand.

THE STONE WHERE MOSES MIGHT HAVE PUT HIS FOOT

Jesse was to write or co-write some forty-eight films in a long career, eight of them for DeMille. He was starting on the ninth[100] when the director died in 1959. But that was ten years into the future.

His father was not quite ready to retire, and although *The Great Caruso* had been on his mind since 1945, it was not until 1949 that he was he able to put the rights and finance together. Having bought Dorothy Caruso's biography of her late husband[101] and holding onto it for three years while he sought a studio that would realize its potential, he finally made a deal at MGM to co-produce it with Joe Pasternak.

Louis B. Mayer had a young singer under contract named Mario Lanza. When Lasky heard Lanza sing at the Hollywood Bowl, he asked him if he would be willing to study Caruso's recordings and imitate them.

Lanza replied, 'Mr. Lasky, I was brought up on those records since I was seven. I know them by heart and can imitate any of them right this minute!'

---

100 The story on Robert Baden-Powell and the Boy Scouts which never got made.
101 *Enrico Caruso - His Life & Death* by Dorothy Caruso.

The producer brought Lanza home to meet Bess and the singer played his collection of 78s (rpm records), standing by their large Capehart record player and singing until well past midnight. Lasky knew he had found the right performer. Dory Schary at MGM thought the singer was too young, but in the end, he was finally convinced by the producer's usual enthusiasm.

When it was released in 1951, *The Great Caruso* received Oscars for Best Sound Recording, Costume Design in Color, and Best Music Scoring of a Musical Picture. Photoplay awarded Mario Lanza Most Popular Male Star. Directors Guild of America awarded Richard Thorpe Outstanding Directorial Achievement in a Motion Picture, and the Writers Guild of America nominated writers Sonya Levien and William Ludwig for Best Screenplay. Lasky had not lost his touch.

When the huge profits from *Sergeant York*, *Mark Twain*, and *Rhapsody in Blue* rolled in, Lasky's lawyer, Loyd Wright, advised Lasky that the Internal Revenue Services would allow him a substantial tax deduction based on terminating his corporation and divesting himself of his holdings in those three films. He would be able to retire with a clear mind. But just seven years later, precisely within the framework of their time limitations, the Internal Revenue Service reversed its decision and put in a claim for all the money he had had been allowed to keep.

Lasky was devastated. When had he not lived extravagantly? During those seven years, that money was almost depleted. Throughout his life he had invested in everything from film projects to office buildings, houses, cars, jewels, oil wells, and puppets, and yet somehow he always seemed to be cash poor. Still, Jack Benny, DeMille, and so many others had benefited from this particular tax shelter; that he decided to fight, confident he would win his case in court because he had always observed his tax dispensation with scrupulous honesty.

Human error intervened. His trusted lawyer, president of the California Bar Association, Loyd Wright, forgot to pass a letter to him from the IRS requesting his presence at a hearing in Washington, D.C. Someone in Wright's office had stuck it, unopened, into the Lasky file.

Ignoring the summons placed him in contempt and put him in default. His explanation of ignorance of the request was not good enough, since 'ignorance of the law is no excuse'. He was asked to prepare and present an inventory of his entire estate and assets and sign over all assets to the federal government in advance of a verdict. Family friend and Superior Court judge, Helen Sherry, advised, 'Do not sign it unless the final ruling is against you, Jesse.'

Brother Bill remembered his father gathering together the family and Judge Sherry to tell them his decision. 'I love this country. It's made it possible for me to do so well. I have decided to trust them entirely and to do as they have requested. I'm going to do what they ask—sign over to them a full inventory of my assets until such time as a final decision has been rendered.' No argument could dissuade him.

He told the family not to worry, no matter what happened. One more picture— his newest project—would be the biggest hit of all his long string of over a thousand motion pictures he had been involved in. His newest adventure, *The Big Brass Band*, was going to make it all back again and put him right on top.

SWANSON PRESENTING THE MILESTONE AWARD TO LASKY, 1951

LASKY VISITS DEMILLE WHILE JESSE WORKS ON THE SCRIPT

No realist at her best, Bess was worried. She knew that he wasn't physically well. He'd had flutters in his heart. 'He keeps saying he's fooled the doctors before', she told Jesse. But every day she watched him leaving the house in his old car, driving himself from studio to studio with a briefcase full of presentations, the huge script and casting suggestions—all for his newest project, *The Big Brass Band*.

'And photos. Files of photos. It's much too heavy for him', she told her son. 'If it weren't for his religious reading I don't know what he'd do now, Jesse! Go and talk to him. You've always been special to him. Maybe he'll tell you the truth.'

Jesse did talk to him, and his father told him, 'You think you carry your whole life in your bank account? You're only licked if you admit it, Jess.' He reminded him of the time that Jesse swam out into the Pacific to try to save him, only to be told that he had a great idea for his next picture. 'And *Zoo in Budapest* was made, wasn't it, Jess? And it put me back in the game, didn't it? *The Big Brass Band* is all about a boy's marching band and it will be made, I promise you.[102] Suppose I said that one year from today you and I will be attending the Academy Awards together?'

---

102 The story was eventually filmed, but not by Lasky. Several years after his death *The Music Man* (1962) was produced by Morton de Costa based on Meredith Wilson's book, starring Robert Preston. The Lasky Estate was not involved.

Jesse nodded. 'Sure Dad. It's a date.' He'd extracted a promise from his father to fill in for him at a literary luncheon the next day as the chief speaker. It was something he knew his father loved to do, and perhaps it would cheer him up. Jesse was working again for DeMille, as chief writer on *The Buccaneer*.

'Remember me to Cecil', his father called after him.

'Yes, and thanks for filling in for me tomorrow.'

'You're doing me a favor', his father assured him.

The next day, January 13, 1958, Bill was working at Warner Brothers on the set of *The Maverick* TV series, and Jesse was at Paramount when each learned the news. Jesse was called into DeMille's office where he found the director pale and silent. For a moment he just looked at Jesse. Then he told him, 'Jesse is dead, Jesse.'

Lasky, still waiting for the government's decision about his tax situation, had taken Jesse's place at a Women's Book Club luncheon at the Beverly Hilton Hotel. Lasky was glad to publicize his autobiography,[103] which had finally been published. It was not written by Jesse after all; he'd been too involved with his screenwriting at the time.

Lasky finished his informal talk—something he had a real talent for—and autographed copies of *I Blow My Own Horn*. Eager women followed him out to the entrance, still clapping. With the applause ringing in his ears, Lasky stepped toward his waiting limousine—slumped forward and dropped to the ground. He died of a heart attack in the ambulance on the way to the hospital.

Bill Lasky wrote of his parents: 'These were story book people, though flesh and blood.' When he was able to think about it rationally, Jesse said, 'It was the right exit for a showman.'

Ever ready for the next great challenge and able to look upon each new day with wonder, Lasky's life had been a fantastic adventure in the business he helped to create. For his contribution to the motion picture industry, he is remembered by a star on the Hollywood Walk of Fame. You'll find it at 6433 Hollywood Blvd.

In 1952, the television series, *This is Your Life*, chose Jesse L. Lasky as their subject and the whole family appeared on the show. Through the following years, Bess wrote a book,[104] Jesse's sister Betty divorced Buddy, whom she referred to as her wartime 'fling', Her second marriage to Bill Bidlack was not to last, either. Bill Lasky wrote a book, *Tell it From the Mountain*, in 1976 (published by Doubleday).

Seven years earlier, on one special night at the Cocoanut Grove, Gloria Swanson handed Lasky the first Milestone Award. He suddenly borrowed a cornet from one of the musicians in the orchestra and struck a pose in front of the curtain. Raising the shiny instrument to his lips, the surprised audience saw him play a Sousa march.

---

103 *I Blow My Own Horn* by Jesse L. Lasky with Don Weldon Doubleday & Co.

104 *Candle in the Sun* pub: DeVorss & Co. Her other books: *And I Shall Make Music, Songs of the Twilight, The Path of Vision* (15 paintings with commentaries).

Then the California boy who had made it 'as good as it gets' played the unofficial state anthem 'California, Here I Come'!

His audience never guessed that hidden behind the curtain was one of the finest trumpeters in the state. Lasky always knew the right exit for a showman. He wrote, 'I suppose movie-making couldn't have remained an adventure forever. It had to become just like any other giant industry. But I never got over being thankful to have been a part of that glamorous Cinderella era of Hollywood's history.'

FILMS OF JESSE L. LASKY

(AS PRESENTER)
The Squaw Man (1914)
(aka *The White Man*—UK)
The Man on the Box (1914)
The Virginian (1914)
The Making of Bobby Burnit (1914)
(aka *Bobby Burnit*)
Cameo Kirby (1914)
The Girl of the Golden West (1915)
Young Romance (1915)
After Five (1915)
The Warrens of Virginia (1915)
The Country Boy (1915)
A Gentleman of Leisure (1915)
The Governor's Lady (1915)
The Unafraid (1915)
(aka *The Unexpected*)
Snobs (1915)
The Captive (1915)
The Woman (1915)
Stolen Goods (1915)
The Wild Goose Chase (1915)
The Arab (1915)
The Clue (1915)
Kindling (1915)
The Fighting Hope (1915)
The Secret Orchard (1915)
The Marriage of Kitty (1915)
The Case of Becky (1915)
Blackbirds (1915)
The Chorus Lady (1915)
Armstrong's Wife (1915)
The Cheat (1915)
The Immigrant (1915)
Alien Souls (1916)
A Gutter Magdalene (1916)
Anton the Terrible (1916)
(aka *The Austrian Spy*)
The Heir to the Hoorah (1916)

The Soul of Kura San (1916)
Unprotected (1916)
The Years of the Locust (1916)
The Victoria Cross (1916)
Lost and Won (1917)
The Black Wolf (1917)
The American Consul (1917)
The Winning of Sally Temple (1917)
Those Without Sin (1917)
Castles for Two (1917)
The Prison Without Walls (1917)
A School for Husbands (1917)
Law of the Land (1917)
Molly Entangled (1917)
Tom Sawyer (1917)
The Devil-Stone (1917)
The Fair Barbarian (1917)
Rimrock Jones (1918)
The Widow's Might (1918)
The Hidden Pearls (1918)
One More American (1918)
(aka *The Land of the Free* - USA)
Huck and Tom (1918)
The House of Silence (1918)
His Majesty, Bunker Bean (1918)
Unclaimed Goods (1918)
The White Man's Law (1918)
Viviette (1918)
The Bravest Way (1918)
The Firefly of France (1918)
Sandy (1918)
Less Than Kin (1918)
The Cruise of the Make-Believes (1918)
The Source (1918)
The Girl Who Came Back (1918)
(aka *The Woman Who Came Back* - USA)
Her Country First (1918)
The Goat (1918)
Such a Little Pirate (1918)

The Man from Funeral Range (1918)
The Gypsy Trail (1918)
Women's Weapons (1918)
Too Many Millions (1918)
The Squaw Man (1918)
The Mystery Girl (1918)
The Way of a Man with a Maid (1918)
Under the Top (1919)
Jane Goes A'Wooing (1919)
The Secret Garden (1919)
The Dub (1919)
Venus in the East (1919)
You Never Saw Such a Girl (1919)
The Winning Girl (1919)
Maggie Pepper (1919)
Alias Mike Moran (1919)
Johnny Get Your Gun (1919)
Little Comrade (1919)
Something to Do (1919)
The Roaring Road (1919)
Rustling a Bride (1919)
Fires of Faith (1919)
The Woman Next Door (1919)
The Final Close-Up (1919)
Putting It Over (1919)
An Innocent Adventuress (1919)
You're Fired (1919)
Men, Women, and Money (1919)
Secret Service (1919)
A Daughter of the Wolf (1919)
A Very Good Young Man (1919)
A Sporting Chance (1919/11)
The Love Burglar (1919)
Rose o' the River (1919)
Louisiana (1919)
Love Insurance (1919)
The Heart of Youth (1919)
The Valley of the Giants (1919)
(aka *In the Valley of the Giants*)
The Third Kiss (1919)
Told in the Hills (1919)
The Lottery Man (1919)

In Mizzoura (1919)
Why Smith Left Home (1919)
His Official Fiancée (1919)
Hawthorne of the U.S.A. (1919)
(aka *Hawthorne, the Adventurer*)
Male and Female (1919)
More Deadly Than the Male (1919)
An Adventure in Hearts (1919)
Everywoman (1919)
Too Much Johnson (1919)
The Thirteenth Commandment (1920)
The Tree of Knowledge (1920)
The Six Best Cellars (1920)
Huckleberry Finn (1920)
Young Mrs. Winthrop (1920)
Jack Straw (1920)
Excuse My Dust (1920)
Terror Island (1920)
Mrs. Temple's Telegram (1920)
The Sea Wolf (1920)
Thou Art the Man (1920)
A Lady in Love (1920)
Sick Abed (1920)
The Sins of St. Anthony (1920)
The City of Masks (1920)
Crooked Streets (1920)
The Prince Chap (1920)
The Fourteenth Man (1920)
(aka *The 14th Man*)
(aka *The Man from Blankley's*)
The Round-Up (1920)
A City Sparrow (1920)
Held by the Enemy (1920)
A Full House (1920)
Conrad in Quest of His Youth (1920)
Always Audacious (1920)
Life of the Party (1920)
(aka *The Life of the Party*)
Burglar Proof (1920)
Midsummer Madness (1920)
The Jucklins (1921)
Forbidden Fruit (1921)

The Price of Possession (1921)
The Witching Hour (1921)
The City of Silent Men (1921)
Sham (1921)
The Lost Romance (1921)
White and Unmarried (1921)
Too Much Speed (1921)
The Great Moment (1921)
Gasoline Gus (1921)
Wealth (1921)
Beyond (1921)
The Affairs of Anatol (1921)
(aka *A Prodigal Knight* - UK)
The Great Impersonation (1921)
After the Show (1921)
The Sheik (1921)
Exit the Vamp (1921)
Fool's Paradise (1921)
Saturday Night (1922)
One Glorious Day (1922)
Moran of the Lady Letty (1922)
The World's Champion (1922)
The Cradle (1922)
Her Gilded Cage (1922)
Is Matrimony a Failure? (1922)
Beyond the Rocks (1922)
North of the Rio Grande (1922)
For the Defense (1922)
The Woman Who Walked Alone (1922)
The Top of New York (1922)
While Satan Sleeps (1922)
Burning Sands (1922)
Pink Gods (1922)
The Old Homestead (1922)
The Cowboy and the Lady (1922)
The Impossible Mrs. Bellew (1922)
The Young Rajah (1922)
Making a Man (1922)
My American Wife (1922)
Java Head (1923)
Nobody's Money (1923)
Mr. Billings Spends His Dime (1923)
The Glimpses of the Moon (1923)
Prodigal Daughters (1923)
You Can't Fool Your Wife (1923)
Sixty Cents an Hour (1923)
The Woman with Four Faces (1923)
Law of the Lawless (1923)
Children of Jazz (1923)
Racing Hearts (1923)
A Gentleman of Leisure (1923)
Bluebeard's Eighth Wife (1923)
Hollywood (1923)
(aka *Joligud*)
The Silent Partner (1923)
Salomy Jane (1923)
To the Last Man (1923)
Ruggles of Red Gap (1923)
Adam's Rib (1923)
The Light That Failed (1923)
Stephen Steps Out (1923)
To the Ladies (1923)
The Call of the Canyon (1923)
Big Brother (1923)
The Hummingbird (1924)
The Heritage of the Desert (1924)
Pied Piper Malone (1924)
Flaming Barriers (1924)
The Stranger (1924)
Shadows of Paris (1924)
The Next Corner (1924)
Icebound (1924)
Singer Jim McKee (1924)
The Fighting Coward (1924)
Fair Week (1924)
The Moral Sinner (1924)
The Confidence Man (1924)
Triumph (1924)
Men (1924)
The Breaking Point (1924)
Bluff (1924)
Code of the Sea (1924)
The Bedroom Window (1924)
Unguarded Women (1924)

Changing Husbands (1924)
The Enemy Sex (1924)
The Side Show of Life (1924)
Manhandled (1924)
Empty Hands (1924)
Lily of the Dust (1924)
(aka *The Song of Songs* - Australia)
Open All Night (1924)
(aka *One Parisian Night* - UK)
Sinners in Heaven (1924)
The Alaskan (1924)
Feet of Clay (1924)
The City That Never Sleeps (1924)
Her Love Story (1924)
The Border Legion (1924)
The Fast Set (1924)
The Story Without a Name (1924)
(aka *Without Warning* - USA)
Manhattan (1924)
Worldly Goods (1924)
The Garden of Weeds (1924)
Wages of Virtue (1924)
Forbidden Paradise (1924)
Madame Sans-Gene (1924)
Tomorrow's Love (1925)
Locked Doors (1925)
East of Suez (1925)
A Man Must Live (1925)
The Golden Bed (1925)
Miss Bluebeard (1925)
The Devil's Cargo (1925)
The Top of the World (1925)
The Swan (1925)
Contraband (1925)
Coming Through (1925)
New Lives for Old (1925)
Salome of the Tenements (1925)
The Shock Punch (1925)
The Goose Hangs High (1925)
The Air Mail (1925)
The Dressmaker from Paris (1925)
Grass: A Nation's Battle for Life (1925)
(aka *Grass* - USA)
(aka *Grass, the Epic of a Lost Tribe* - USA)
Men and Women (1925)
The Charmer (1925)
A Kiss in the Dark (1925)
Code of the West (1925)
Adventure (1925)
The Crowded Hour (1925)
The Spaniard (1925)
(aka *Spanish Love* - UK)
Eve's Secret (1925)
Welcome Home (1925)
Old Home Week (1925)
Beggar on Horseback (1925)
Are Parents People? (1925)
Lost: A Wife (1925)
The Light of Western Stars (1925)
Grounds for Divorce (1925)
Paths to Paradise (1925)
Marry Me (1925)
The Wanderer (1925)
The Lucky Devil (1925)
Night Life of New York (1925)
The Street of Forgotten Men (1925)
Not So Long Ago (1925)
Wild, Wild Susan (1925)
The Trouble with Wives (1925)
Wild Horse Mesa (1925)
In the Name of Love (1925)
Rugged-Water (1925)
The Man Who Found Himself (1925)
The Pony Express (1925)
The Golden Princess (1925)
A Son of His Father (1925)
A Regular Fellow (1925)
The Vanishing American (1925)
(aka *The Vanishing Race* - Australia)
Flower of Night (1925)
The Best People (1925)
The King on Main Street (1925)
The Ancient Highway (1925)
Irish Luck (1925)

A Woman of the World (1925)
The Splendid Crime (1925)
Womanhandled (1925)
Mannequin (1926)
Hands Up! (1926)
The Enchanted Hill (1926)
The American Venus (1926)
The Grand Duchess and the Waiter (1926)
Behind the Front (1926)
Sea Horses (1926)
Let's Get Married (1926)
Miss Brewster's Millions (1926)
The Untamed Lady (1926)
The New Klondike (1926)
Fascinating Youth (1926)
Love 'Em and Leave 'Em (1926)
The Crown of Lies (1926)
A Social Celebrity (1926)
The Blind Goddess (1926)
The Runaway (1926)
The Lucky Lady (1926)
Wet Paint (1926)
The Rainmaker (1926)
Aloma of the South Seas (1926)
The Palm Beach Girl (1926)
Volcano (1926)
Say It Again (1926)
Born to the West (1926)
Mantrap (1926)
Padlocked (1926)
The Show Off (1926)
Fine Manners (1926)
The Cat's Pajamas (1926)
Hold That Lion (1926)
(aka *Ladies First* -USA)
Diplomacy (1926)
The Campus Flirt (1926)
(aka *The College Flirt* - UK)
You'd Be Surprised (1926)
Forlorn River (1926)
Kid Boots (1926)
The Quarterback (1926)

The Ace of Cads (1926)
The Sorrows of Satan (1926)
The Eagle of the Sea (1926)
The Lady of the Harem (1926)
We're in the Navy Now (1926)
Everybody's Acting (1926)
God Gave Me Twenty Cents (1926)
The Popular Sin (1926)
The Canadian (1926)
Stranded in Paris (1926)
Man of the Forest (1926)
Hotel Imperial (1927)
Blonde or Brunette (1927)
The Potters (1927)
Paradise for Two (1927)
A Kiss in a Taxi (1927)
Blind Alleys (1927)
Stark Love (1927)
The Mysterious Rider (1927)
Casey at the Bat (1927)
The Telephone Girl (1927)
Fashions for Women (1927)
Cabaret (1927)
Too Many Crooks (1927)
Ritzy (1927)
Arizona Bound (1927)
Knockout Reilly (1927)
Special Delivery (1927)
Chang: Drama of the Wilderness (1927)
(aka *Chang* - USA)
The Whirlwind of Youth (1927)
Wedding Bill$ (1927)
The World at Her Feet (1927)
Rough House Rosie (1927)
Drums of the Desert (1927)
Running Wild (1927/1)
Rubber Heels (1927)
Rolled Stockings (1927)
The Way of All Flesh (1927)
Ten Modern Commandments (1927)
The Last Outlaw (1927)
Man Power (1927)

Service for Ladies (1927)
Barbed Wire (1927)
Wings (1927)
Underworld (1927)
 (aka *Paying the Penalty* - UK)
Soft Cushions (1927)
Hula (1927)
Nevada (1927)
We're All Gamblers (1927)
Swim Girl, Swim (1927)
One Woman to Another (1927)
Tell It to Sweeney (1927)
The Woman on Trial (1927)
The Rough Riders (1927)
 (aka *The Trumpet Calls* - USA)
A Gentleman of Paris (1927)
Shootin' Irons (1927)
Figures Don't Lie (1927)
Shanghai Bound (1927)
Now We're in the Air (1927)
Open Range (1927)
The City Gone Wild (1927)
The Spotlight (1927)
Get Your Man (1927)
The Gay Defender (1927)
Serenade (1927)
Wife Savers (1928)
Love and Learn (1928)
Beau Sabreur (1928)
Under the Tonto Rim (1928)
The Secret Hour (1928)
 (aka *Beggars of Love*)
The Showdown (1928)
The Legion of the Condemned (1928)
Something Always Happens (1928)
Partners in Crime (1928)
A Night of Mystery (1928)
 (aka *The Code of Honor*)
Easy Come, Easy Go (1928)
Street of Sin (1928)
His Tiger Wife (1928)
 (aka *His Tiger Lady*)
The Magnificent Flirt (1928)
Ladies of the Mob (1928)
Hot News (1928)
Warming Up (1928)
Loves of an Actress (1928)
Forgotten Faces (1928)
The Patriot (1928)
Just Married (1928)
The First Kiss (1928)
The Water Hole (1928)
Sawdust Paradise (1928)
Chinatown Nights (1929)
 (aka *Tong War* - USA)
The Wild Party (1929)
The Studio Murder Mystery (1929)
The Mysterious Dr. Fu Manchu (1929)
Applause (1929)
The Virginian (1929)
The Love Parade (1929)
Men Are Like That (1930)
Getting A Ticket (1930)
The Return of Dr. Fu Manchu (1930)
Actions Speak Louder than Words (1930)

(AS PRODUCER)
The Squaw Man (1914)
 (aka *The White Man* - UK)
The Ghost Breaker (1914)
The Goose Girl (1914)
The Puppet Crown (1915)
The Chorus Lady (1915)
The Secret Sin (1915)
The Unknown (1915)
The Cheat (1915)
The Race (1916)
The Love Mask (1916)
 (aka *Under the Mask*)
The Dupe (1916/II)
Each to His Kind (1917)
On Record (1917)
The Bottle Imp (1917)
The Primrose Ring (1917)

Unconquered (1917)
Moving (1917)
Exile (1917)
The Call of the East (1917)
Tom Sawyer (1917)
The Secret Game (1917)
The Spirit of '17 (1918)
A Petticoat Pilot (1918)
The Spirit of the Red Cross (1918)
Mile-a-Minute Kendall (1918)
(aka *Half-a-Minute Kendall*)
Believe Me, Xantippe (1918)
The City of Dim Faces (1918)
My Cousin (1918)
Don't Change Your Husband (1919)
For Better, for Worse (1919)
Fires of Faith (1919)
The Love Burglar (1919)
The Grim Game (1919)
Why Change Your Wife? (1920)
What's Your Hurry? (1920)
Something to Think About (1920)
The Sins of Rosanne (1920)
The Witching Hour (1921)
The Call of the North (1921)
(aka *The Conjuror's House* - UK)
The World's Champion (1922)
Her Husband's Trademark (1922)
The Top of New York (1922)
The Dictator (1922)
Blood and Sand (1922)
The Ghost Breaker (1922)
On the High Seas (1922)
Manslaughter (1922)
The Covered Wagon (1923)
You Can't Fool Your Wife (1923)
His Children's Children (1923)
The Next Corner (1924)
Unguarded Women (1924)
The Man Who Fights Alone (1924)
The Female (1924)
Dangerous Money (1924)

A Sainted Devil (1924)
Peter Pan (1924)
Too Many Kisses (1925)
The Manicure Girl (1925)
The Wanderer (1925)
Wild Horse Mesa (1925)
The Coast of Folly (1925)
That Royle Girl (1925)
The Enchanted Hill (1926)
Sea Horses (1926)
Desert Gold (1926)
Wet Paint (1926)
It's the Old Army Game (1926)
Beau Geste (1926)
Tin Gods (1926)
The Great Gatsby (1926)
The Kid Brother (1927)
New York (1927)
It (1927)
Love's Greatest Mistake (1927)
Evening Clothes (1927)
Fashions for Women (1927)
Special Delivery (1927)
Children of Divorce (1927)
Senorita (1927)
Time to Love (1927)
The Last Outlaw (1927)
Fireman, Save My Child (1927)
Nevada (1927)
Jesse James (1927)
(aka *The Outlaw Rider* - UK)
She's a Sheik (1927)
Honeymoon Hate (1927)
Get Your Man (1927)
Two Flaming Youths (1927)
Half a Bride (1928)
The Last Command (1928)
Doomsday (1928)
Feel My Pulse (1928)
The Legion of the Condemned (1928)
Something Always Happens (1928)
Partners in Crime (1928)

Beggars of Life (1928)
The Wedding March (1928)
Manhattan Cocktail (1928)
Traffic Regulations (1929)
Humorous Flights (1929)
The Cocoanuts (1929)
Innocents of Paris (1929)
High Hat (1929) (co-producer)
Applause (1929)
The Plasterers (1929)
Dangerous Paradise (1930)
Paramount on Parade (1930)
Zoo in Budapest (1933)
The Warrior's Husband (1933)
Berkeley Square (1933)
The Power & the Glory (1933)
  (aka *Power and Glory* - UK)
The Worst Woman in Paris? (1933)
As Husbands Go (1934)
Coming-Out Party (1934)
Grand Canary (1934)
Springtime for Henry (1934)
The White Parade (1934)
Helldorado (1935)
Redheads on Parade (1935)
The Gay Deception (1935)
One Rainy Afternoon (1936)
  (aka *Matinee Scandal* - USA)
The Gay Desperado (1936)
Music for Madame (1937)
Hitting a New High (1937)
Sergeant York (1941)
Adventures of Mark Twain (1944)
Rhapsody in Blue (1945)
Without Reservations (1946)
  (aka *Thanks God, I'll Take It from Here*)
The Miracle of the Bells (1948)
The Great Caruso (1951)

FILMS OF JESSE L. LASKY JR.

P:	Paramount	
W:	Warner Brothers	
R:	Republic	
MGM:	Metro Goldwin Mayer	
F:	20th Century-Fox	
M:	Monogram	
C:	Columbia	
A:	Admiral Reed Productions	
R:	Roland Reed Productions	
f	foreign	
*	For C.B.DeMille	

Year	Studio	Title
1934	F	Music is Magic
1935	F	The White Parade
1935	F	Coming Out Party
1936	P	Land of Liberty
1938	P	Union Pacific*
1939	P	Land of Liberty*
1940	p	Northwest Mounted Police*
1940	r	Back in the Saddle
1941	w	Steel Against the Sky
1941	R	The Singing Hills
1942	P	Reap the Wild Wind*
1942	MGM	Omaha Trail
1946	R	The Valpariso Story
1946	P	Unconquered*
1948	F	Thief of Venice
1948	P	Samson & Delilah*
1949	A	Sickle and the Cross
1950	C	Lorna Doone
1950	C	Mask of the Avengers
1950	C	Never Trust a Gambler
1951	C	The Brigand
1952	F	The Silver Whip
1953	C	Salomé, Dance of the 7 Veils (story
1953	F	Hell and High Water
1953	C	The Iron Glove
1953	C	Mission Over Korea
1955	C	Pearl of the South Pacific
1955	C	Hot Blood
1955	P	The Ten Commandments*
1958	P	The Buccaneer*
1959	W	John Paul Jones
1959	P	On My Honor
1959	M	The Red Head
1960	F	Wizard of Baghdad
1960	F	7 Women from Hell
1960	F	Pirates of Tortuga

WITH PAT SILVER (AKA PAT SILVER-LASKY)

1969	C	*Land Raiders* (original story)
1970	f	*One of Those Things* (Norway)
1976	f	*Crime and Passion* (aka *Ace Up My Sleeve*)
1989	f	*Bull Dance* (aka *Forbidden Sun* - UK, Yugoslavia)

FILMS FOR TELEVISION BY LASKY & SILVER

Ernest Hemingway
Alfred Nobel
Paint Me A Murder

Jesse received the Box Office Award twice for *The Ten Commandments* and *Samson and Delilah* and the Christopher Award from the Catholic Church. His writing took him from Hollywood to London, Rome, Austria, Denmark, Turkey, Spain, Portugal, Greece, and France.

NAME INDEX

Aarons, Alex, 188, 266, 272
Abbott, George, 150
Adler, Larry, 290
Ager, Herbert, 264
Albert, Eddie, 346
Alcine, Willie, 322
Alda, Alan,
Alda, Robert, 276, 292, 294, 332
Alger, Horatio, 322
Allen, Scotty, 108
Allen, Jane, 258, 326, 337
Allen, Miss, 203
Altman, Miss, 312
Anderson, Bronco Billy, 7
Apfel, Oscar, 9, 10, 11, 12
Appleton, Captain, 325
Arbuckle, Roscoe 'Fatty', 41, 42
Arlen, Richard, 58, 83, 99
Armitage, 184
Arnold, General, 312
Arnspiger, Dr., 255
Arzner, Dorothy, 152, 169, 191
Asher, Irving, 190, 191,
Astaire, Fred, 187, 197, 272
Astor, Mary, 58
Audobon, John James, 273, 276, 318
Avery, Steve, 180, 183
Bacall, Lauren, 290
Bachmann, Captain, 322, 328
Baden-Powell, Lord, 213
Baer, Gwen, 227
Baker, John, 279
Balaban, Barney, 352, 354
Balcon, Michael, 176, 177, 182
Bancroft, George, 112
Barasch, Buddy, 243, 247, 253, 257, 259, 267, 274, 286, 287, 293, 295, 302, 309, 311, 313, 314, 317
Barbour, Mrs., 114
Barrie, Sir James, 30, 73, 101
Barrymore, John, 117
Barrymore, Ethel, 268, 275
Basserman, Albert, 282, 290, 293

Bates, Blanche, 47
Bates, George, 206
Bauchens, Annie, 207
Beery, Noah, 58, 67, 76, 83
Beery, Noah Jr, 58
Beery, Wallace, 108
Belasco, David, 16
Bello, Marino, 163
Bennett, Charles, 253, 346
Benny, Jack, 258, 282, 359
Bergere, Ouida, 179
Bergman, Ingrid, 297
Berle, Milton, 205
Berlin, Irving, 285
Berman Pandro S., 187, 188, 191
Bernhardt, Sarah, 13, 16
Bidlack, Bill, 351, 356, 357
Blanke, Henry, 284
Blasco-Ibanez, Vicente, 33
Blystone, Jack, 203
Bodeley, Major, 177
Bogart, Humphrey, 290, 338
Bolte, Lt. Charles, 344
Booth, Edwina, 146
Borg, Ariane, 172, 176, 180
Bow, Clara, 37, 99
Branche, Mademoiselle, 54
Brandt, Carl, 236
Brent, Evelyn, 45
Brian, Mary, 73, 76, 105, 113
Brisbane, Arthur, 80
Briskin, Sam, 186, 187, 188, 190, 193, 199, 200, 201, 202, 203, 205, 211
Bromfield, Louis, 54
Bronson, Betty, 73, 75, 80, 81, 83, 86
Brook, Clive, 83, 98, 112
Broomes, Martin, 127
Brower, Otto, 170
Brown, John Mason, 144
Brown, Anne, 289, 294, 295
Brownlow, Kevin, 59
Bruce, Nigel, 180

Buckland, Bill, 39, 46, 58, 61, 179
Buckland, Veda, 39
Buckland, William, 16, 26, 39
Buckner, Robert, 258
Burbank, Luther, 269
Burden, Douglas, 128
Burns, Bob, 205
Burton, John, 190
Busch, Mae, 45
Butler, Dave, 252
Butterworth, Charlie, 315
Byron, Lord, 54
Cantor, Eddie, 83, 89, 251
Capps, Mac, 179, 311, 337
Capra, Frank, 199, 231, 237, 284, 332, 342
Carey, Harry, 146
Carlton, Douglas, 45
Carnovsky, Morris, 294
Carradine, John, 231
Carrillo, Leo, 170, 186, 188, 189
Carroll, Nancy, 107 109, 127, 144
Caruso, Enrico, 15, 27, 177, 344, 354, 359
Caruso, Dorothy, 351, 354, 359
Case, Bertha, 92
Case, Carroll, 136
Case, Frank, 92, 96, 124
Champ, Bill, 62
Chandlee, Harry, 213, 239, 243, 268, 269, 276, 353
Chaplin, Charlie, 45, 108, 146, 147, 184
Chatterton, Ruth, 145, 151, 152
Chertok, Jack, 249, 260, 268
Chevalier, Maurice, 116, 125, 150, 169
Chiang Kai-shek, Madame, 273, 274
Christie, Agatha, 189
Churchill, Winston, 232, 248, 277, 279, 281
Clair, Rene, 253
Claire, Ina, 144
Clare, Marion, 206, 207
Clark, Marguerite, 30
Close, Upton, 294
Coburn, Charles, 283, 284, 290, 294
Cohen, Jean, 48, 66, 85
Cohen, Mannie, 150, 151, 154, 156, 157, 158, 247, 248

Cohn, Harry, 186, 341, 349
Colbert, Claudette, 150, 151, 344, 346, 347
Connolly, Marc, 275
Conway, Jack, 200
Coogan, Jackie, 147
Coogan, Robert, 142
Coolidge, President Calvin, 56, 81, 215
Cooper, Gary, 76, 101, 102, 142, 147, 150, 151, 157, 212, 213, 215, 217, 296, 297, 300, 312, 314, 349
Cooper, Merian C., 82, 83, 300, 316
Cooper, Prentice, 212
Cortez, Ricardo, 61, 81
Cousins, General, 271
Cowan, Jimmy, 127
Coward, Noel, 250
Crawford, Joan, 155, 156, 219
Crisp, Donald, 231
Crocker, Marsha, 322
Cromwell, John, 173
Crosby, Bing, 157, 273
Crothers, Rachel, 184
Crowther, Bosley, 332
Cruze, James, 49, 50, 58, 68, 69, 81, 88
Cukor, George, 219
Cunningham, General, 303
Curtiz, Michael, 257
Darnell, Linda, 209
D'Arrast, Harry, 172, 173, 176, 177, 178
Davenport, 121
Davis, Secretary of War, 95, 102
Davis, Bette, 214, 217, 300, 323
Dawes, Vice President Charles G., 103, 111
Day, Captain, 176
de Haven Connick, Harris, 32, 33
de Havilland, Olivia, 197
de Palma, Ralph, 20
De Rochemont, 355
del Riccio, Lorenzo, 88, 90
Delmont, Maude (Maude Black), 41
DeMille, Agnes, 58
DeMille, Cecil, 8, 9, 10, 11, 12, 13, 14, 15, 16, 18, 19, 20, 28, 30, 31, 50, 52, 66, 70, 92, 105, 107, 113, 118, 136, 145, 146, 147, 148, 174, 185, 186, 192, 205, 207, 209, 215, 225, 227, 228, 240, 253,

267, 274, 277, 279, 282, 296, 299, 314, 315, 322,
323, 326, 328, 329, 340, 347, 349, 350, 351, 354,
357, 358, 361
DeMille, Cecilia, 19, 58, 136
DeMille, Constance, 19, 105, 274, 354
DeMille, Margaret, 58, 59
DeMille, William, 8, 18, 25, 58
Dexter, Elliott, 18
Dietrich, Marlene, 142, 174, 182
Disney, Walt, 194, 195, 196
Disraeli, 278
Dix, Richard, 81
Dody, 58, 75, 76, 77, 79, 95, 97
Dolin, Anton, 286
Doniger, Walter, 268
Doty Douglas Z., 146
Douglas, Don Jr., 352
Douglas, Donald, 352
Dove, Billie, 76
Dreiser, Theodore, 138, 140
Dreyfus, Max, 283
Dudley, Carl, 249, 251, 255
Dufy, 64
Duke of Norfolk, 216
Dumont, Margaret, 123
Dunn, Josephine, 108
Durkin, Grace, 126
Dyer, Richard, 15
Earhart, Amelia, 84, 85, 119, 184
Eastman, Colonel. 311
Eaton Phillips, Dr. Charles, 325
Eaton, Mary, 123
Eddy, Mary Baker, 236
Edison, Robert, 14
Edison, Thomas, Alva, 7, 11, 91
Edward, Duke of Windsor, 193
Einfeld, Charles, 265
Eisenhower, General, 293, 328
Eisenstein, Sergei M., 140, 142
Eldridge, Florence, 273, 319
Eltinge, Julian, 26
Emanuel, Jack, 156, 204, 268, 281, 296, 330
Emerson, John, 30
Endore, Guy, 173, 174

English, Mr., 144
Esmond, Jill, 152
Evans, Julius, 219, 224, 228, 232, 237, 239, 249,
273, 283, 319
Fairbanks, Douglas, 30, 45, 46, 55, 59, 92, 100,
102, 105, 125, 135
Fairbanks, Douglas, Jr, 55, 58, 61, 76, 182, 342
Farnum, Dustin, 8, 9, 16
Farrar, Geraldine, 15, 16, 31, 32, 177
Farrow, John, 337
Faye, Julia, 70
Feldman, Charlie, 202
Fenton, Leslie, 112
Ferber, Edna, 144
Fischback, Fred, 41
Fisher, Berthe, 118, 119
Fitzgerald, F. Scott, 54
Fitzmaurice, George, 45
Flagstad, Kirsten, Malfrid, 207
Fleming, Victor, 92, 101
Fleming, Rhonda, 209
Flynn, Errol, 245, 249, 276
Fontaine, Joan, 196, 197
Ford, John, 241, 342
Fortes, Colonel, 131
Foujita, Tsugharu, 64
Francis, Kay, 145
Frank, Fredric M., 347, 349, 350, 357
Frederick, Dr. John T., 317
Freed, Arthur, 195, 199
Freeman, Berney, 312
Friedman, Phil, 172, 187, 223
Friml, Rudolf, 136
Frohman, Daniel, 14
Furthman, Jules, 105
Gable, Clark, 155, 164
Gallup, Dr., 267
Galsworthy, 122, 273
Gandolfi, Alfred, 9
Garber, Dave, 187
Garfield, John, 263, 268, 275, 300
Gariss, Jack, 357
Garland, Charles, 324, 325
Gaugin, 264

Geraghty, Tom, 25, 39
Gershwin Mrs, 275
Gershwin, George, 93, 213, 251, 252, 254, 265, 266, 273, 274, 275, 282, 288, 294, 332,
Gershwin Ira, 256, 275, 286, 295
Giannini, A.P., 52, 71, 191, 324
Gibran, Kahlil, 107
Gillette, Colonel, 242, 255, 293
Ginsberg Gordon, Louise, 53, 124, 172, 204, 230
Ginsberg, Mr., 4
Ginsberg, Art, 115, 116, 119, 124, 139, 161, 234
Gluckman, 338
Glyn, Elinor, 34, 37
Goddard, Paulette, 147
Godfrey, Peter, 332
Goetz, Ben, 198
Goldwyn (aka Goldfish), Sam, 5, 7, 8, 9, 10, 12, 13, 15, 18, 19, 20, 24, 25, 31, 32, 44, 105, 136, 179, 214, 271, 323, 344
Goldwyn (Lasky) (Capp), Ruth, 19, 20, 32, 58, 179, 80, 203, 271, 311, 337
Goldwyn, Sam Jr., 25, 271, 272
Goldwyn, Frances, 271
Goodal, Miss, 119
Goodrich, Frances, 266
Gormley, Admiral, 342
Goulding, Eddie, 136
Goulding, Edmund, 169
Grant, Cary, 3, 197,
Grant, Col., 303, 306
Grey Hat Charlie, 69
Grey, Zane, 47, 52, 69, 76, 78, 81, 105
Griffith, D.W., 18, 30, 59
Groesbeck, Daniel Sayre, 185
Gurney, Noll, 176
Haas, Dolly, 180
Hackett, Albert, 266
Hackett, James K., 14
Hadden, George, 176
Hagerman, Richard, 294
Haggiag, Robert, 350
Hale, Alan, 50, 231
Halsey, Admiral, 312
Hanbury, Mr, 198

Hanline, Maurice, 102, 136, 172, 174, 180, 183, 187, 188, 192, 204, 351
Harding, President, 44
Harlow, Jean, 127, 163, 164, 165, 166
Harris, Henry, B., 3, 88
Harris, Fred, 187
Harryhausen, Ray, 194
Hart, William S., 30, 45
Hartwell, Bert, 279
Hatton, Raymond, 108
Hawks, Howard, 213, 221, 233, 263
Hayakawa, Sessue, 18
Hayes, Helen, 102
Hays, 'General' Will H., 44, 92, 105
Hayward, Leland, 354
Hearst, William Randolph, 41, 77
Hecht, Ben, 178, 336
Heerman, Victor, 169
Heifetz, Jascha, 64
Heindorf, Ray, 292
Hellinger, Mark, 333, 338
Hellman, Marcel, 192
Hendrickson, Jenny, 37
Henry, Bill, 231
Herbert, Hugh, 183
Hergesheimer, Joseph, 54, 78
Hertz, John, 152, 156
Hibben, President, Princeton, 113
Hickok, Wild Bill, 57
Hilton, James, 184
Hitchcock, Alfred, 45, 170
Hitler, Adolf, 211, 253, 294, 343
Hively, Jack, 303, 305, 312, 313, 322, 326, 335, 338, 340, 342
Hodgkinson, William W., 13, 21
Hoffman, Irving, 267
Holmes, Oliver Wendell, 89
Holt, Jack, 67, 76
Hooey, Evelyn, 126
Hoover, President, 113
Hopper, Hedda, 321
Horman, Arthur, 243
Horton, Edward, Everet, 178
Hostetter, Jack, 229

Houdini, Harry, 26
Hough, Emerson, 48, 68
Hovey, Carl, 192
Howard, Frances, 25
Howard, Leslie, 281
Howard, William K., 162
Hsiung-Shihfei, General, 235
Hubbard, Lucien, 48, 103
Hudnut, Richard, 34
Hull, Edith, M., 33
Hull, Cordell, 211, 216
Hun, Mr, 108
Hunter, Hays, 47
Hurda, 303
Hurley, 155
Hurst, Fannie, 54, 117
Huston, Walter, 101
Huston, John, 214, 215, 216, 290
Hutton, Robert, 299
Ince, Thomas, 30
Ingram, Rex, 20, 33
Jaffe, Sam, 121, 122, 294
James, Gerald, 238
James, Rian, 183
Janis, Elsie, 169
Jannings, Emil, 90, 111, 112, 120, 142
Jeffers, William, 279, 282
Job, Tom, 324, 328
Johnson, Julian, 105, 351
Jolson, Al, 112, 117, 282, 299, 307
Jones, Benjamin Franklin, 113
Jones, John Paul, 337
Kael, Pauline, 162
Kane, Robert, 136, 139
Katterjohn, Monte, M, 33, 37
Katz, Sam, 156, 184
Kaufman, Al, 26, 45, 125, 138, 192
Kaufman, George S., 124, 144, 198
Kaufman, Ed, 205
Keane, Peter, 295
Kennedy, Bobby, 93
Kennedy, Edward, 93
Kennedy, Jack, 93
Kennedy, Joseph, 93

Kent, Sidney, 31, 70, 126, 142, 156, 160
Kent, Chaplain, 305
Kerrigan, J. Warren, 49
Kersh, Gerald, 294
King, Dennis, 136
King, Henry, 330
King, Jack, 192
Kirkwood, James, 33
Kley, Fred, 9
Knoblock, Edward, 190
Knopf, Alfred, 192, 195
Knopf, Blanche, 192
Knopf, Edwin H., 170, 192
Knox, Alexander, 330
Koch, Howard, 268, 269, 276, 323
Koehler, Jean, 347, 355
Koeler, Charles, 344
Korda, Alexander, 193, 194
Kruger, General, 303
Kyllman, 175
Lachmann, Tai, 177
Laemmle, Carl, 30
Laemmle, Carl Jr., 267
Lake, Veronica, 253
Lamarr, Hedy, 161
Landi, Elissa, 326
Landi, Toni, 326
Lane, Burton, 195, 199
Lanham, Lt. Col., 254
Lanza, Mario, 359
Lasker, Albert, 152
Lasky, (Ginsberg) Bessie (Bess), 4, 5, 19, 31, 39, 40, 46, 52, 53, 58, 63, 70, 79, 80, 95, 96, 97, 104, 107, 108, 120, 123, 136, 139, 140, 142, 148, 154, 158, 159, 170, 171, 173, 175, 188, 192, 193, 199, 202, 203, 204, 215, 220, 223, 225, 227, 229, 232, 235, 241, 246, 248, 259, 260, 261, 262, 264, 265, 266, 267, 268, 270, 279, 281, 285, 286, 287, 289, 290, 293, 294, 296, 300, 302, 307, 309, 311, 315, 317, 319, 322, 324, 325, 329, 331, 333, 335, 338, 340, 341, 345, 352, 353, 355, 359, 361
Lasky, (Goldwyn) Blanche, 2, 4, 5, 6, 7, 9, 19, 20, 32, 39, 76, 158

Lasky, (Hackenburg), Frances, (Donna Drake), 173, 182, 183, 186, 188, 189, 202, 204, 205, 215, 220, 221, 225, 228, 230, 231, 234,, 235, 236, 240, 241, 242, 243, 248, 256, 257, 258, 259, 260, 261, 262, 267, 269, 271, 272, 273, 282, 285, 288, 291, 292, 297, 298, 299, 302, 307, 309, 311, 314, 315, 319, 321, 322, 326, 329, 331, 336, 339, 342, 343, 344, 345

Lasky, (Lowe) Margery , 221, 228, 232, 233, 241, 243, 245, 246, 253, 259, 270, 271, 272, 286, 290, 299, 302, 317, 335, 337, 340

Lasky, (McCrossan), Betty, 347, 350, 352

Lasky, Art (boxer), 180

Lasky, Béla, 4, 20

Lasky, Bernard, 4, 22

Lasky, Betty (Bessie), 44, 52, 54, 56, 62, 79, 80, 81, 95, 104, 119, 120, 126, 137, 140, 144, 158, 173, 177, 179, 190, 192, 193, 201, 203, 204, 221, 223, 225, 228, 229, 233, 244, 246, 247, 248, 253, 257, 258, 259, 260, 262, 269, 270, 274, 286, 287, 290, 292, 295, 307, 309, 311, 313, 314, 317, 319, 324, 326, 329, 336, 337, 339, 343, 345, 350, 353

Lasky, Bill, 39, 44, 46, 47, 52, 54, 62, 79, 80, 95, 96, 104, 105, 119, 120, 137, 140, 144, 158, 173, 177, 179, 190, 192, 193, 201, 203, 204, 221, 223, 225, 228, 229, 231, 232, 233, 235, 239, 241, 245, 246, 248, 253, 257, 258, 259, 262, 269, 270, 271, 272, 276, 277, 283, 285, 286, 300, 302, 318, 319, 335, 337, 340, 351, 353, 354, 355, 357, 360, 363

Lasky, Ike, 3, 4

Lasky, Jennifer, 347

Lasky, Ronald Charles, 290, 318, 335, 341

Lasky, Sarah, 4, 5, 19, 37, 39, 63, 92, 146, 151, 177, 180, 190, 202, 221, 248, 252, 260, 267, 270, 272, 302, 311, 315, 317, 325, 332, 337, 340, 344

Laughton, Charles, 150, 192, 208

Laurel and Hardy, 124

Lean, David, 263

LeBaron, William, 184, 192, 200

Lederer, Francis, 172, 173, 174, 173, 180, 190, 194

Lee, Robert, 206, 207

Lee, Rowland V., 169, 179, 184

LeMay, Alan, 221, 227, 246, 277, 322

Lenehan, Colonel, 264

LeRoy, Mervyn, 172, 173, 175, 228, 274, 285

Leslie, Joan, 282

Lesser, Sol, 344

Levant, Oscar, 282, 286, 288, 289, 294, 295

Levien, Sonya, 192, 251, 254, 257, 266, 286, 296, 359

Levinson, Nathan, 117, 291

Levinson, Colonel, 250, 252, 257, 264, 293

Lewis, Mary, 136

Lewis, Mr, 4

Liebermann, Kalman, 21

Liljenwall, Gus , 37

Liljenwall, Robert , 37

Liljenwall, Sophie & Bessie, 37

Limur, Jean, 119

Lindbergh, Charles, A., 131

Liveright, Horace, 136, 138

Lloyd, Harold, 66, 105, 225

Lloyd, Frank, 191

Loew, Marcus, 21

Lombard, Carole, 156

Loos, Anita, 30

Lord, Bob, 231, 255, 257, 264, 270

Lorre, Peter, 173

Louis, Joe, 268

Lovet-Lorski, Boris, 64, 140, 315, 330

Lowe, Edmund, 208

Lubin, Sigmund 'Pop', 12, 13

Lubitsch, Ernst, 111, 120, 169, 184

Luckner, Dr., 294

Ludwig, William, 342

Lumière Brothers, 7, 8

Lunt, Miss, 148

Lupino, Ida, 170, 178, 186

MacArthur, General, 249, 290, 292, 298, 303, 332, 335, 342

MacDonald, Prime Minister, Ramsay, 135

MacDonald, Philip, 278

MacEwen, Walter, 338, 339, 341, 347

MacFadden, Hamilton, 272, 276, 277, 278, 284

MacKenzie, Aeneas, 357

MacMahon, Major, 306

MacMurray, Fred, 349

Macpherson, Jeanie, 18, 70, 205, 347

Mamoulian, Rouben, 147, 170, 187, 189, 191, 251, 286, 294, 296, 297
Mankiewicz, Herman J., 112, 162, 198, 190
March, Frederick, 144, 152, 173, 226, 229, 231, 232, 231, 253, 273, 296, 318, 319, 320
Marin, Ned, 202, 204
Markova, Alicia, 286
Marmont, Percy, 45
Martini, Nino, 169, 170, 174, 184, 185, 186, 193, 194, 198, 199, 200, 201, 202, 203, 294, 320
Marx Brothers, 120, 123, 124, 151
Marx, Sam, 179
Maté, Rudy, 299
Mather, Judge Cotton, 87
Mature, Victor, 349
Maugham, W. Somerset, 264, 328, 331
Mayer, Louis B., 102, 125, 191, 252, 279, 294, 359
McClintic, Guthrie, 152
McCormack, George, 69
McCrea, Joel, 58
McKenna, Kenneth, 351
McMicking, Colonel, 323
McPhail, Angus, 183
Medina, Henrique, 275
Melford, George, 49
Mendes, Lothar, 170
Menjou, Adolph, 198
Meredith, Burgess, 341
Merkel, Una, 310
Messari, Mr, 138, 139
Miller, Gilbert, 106, 125, 307
Miller, Margaret, 115
Miller, Ann, 205
Minter, Mary Miles, 43, 49
Mintz, Jack, 198
Mintz, Sam, 198
Mixon, Colonel, 326
Monet, 64
Monroe, Marilyn, 165
Montez, Maria, 350
Montgomery, Bob, 342
Montgomery, General Bernard, 253
Moore, Colleen, 162
Moreno, Antonio, 45

Morgan, Frank, 194
Mortonson, Miss, 46, 52, 54, 75
Moyer, Colonel, 311
Murray, Mae, 25
Murray, Arthur, 165
Mussolini, Benito, 288, 343
Naldi, Nita, 45
Nazimova, Alla, 45
Negri, Pola, 45
Neilan, Marshall, 28
Newman, Alfred, 176
Nimitz, Admiral, Chester W., 112, 337
Noonan, Fred, 85
Nordlinger, Henry, 357
Normand, Mabel, 25, 43
Novello, Ivor, 152
Oakie, Jack, 205
Odets, Clifford, 251
O'Harra, 2nd. Lt., 255
Otis, General Harrison Greg, 45
Otterson, John, 180, 184
Padilla, Secretary, 131
Paley, William S., 190
Palmer, Charles, 355
Pamplin, Lt. Col., 226
Panuch, Mr, 170
Parker, Dorothy, 290
Parsons, Louella, 37, 167
Pascall, Ernest, 174
Pasternak, Joe, 359
Patricola, Tom, 289
Patterson, Assistant Secretary, 312
Paul, Elliott, 279, 281, 283, 284, 285, 286
Peattie, Donald Culross, 273, 278, 281
Pepper, Senator Claude, 331
Perrin, Nat, 199
Pertwee, Michael, 350
Picasso, Pablo, 64
Pickford, Jack, 41
Pickford, Mary, 24, 28, 30, 92, 102, 125, 169, 170, 172, 173, 174, 175, 179, 180, 186, 189, 191
Pissaro, 64
Polito, Sol, 295
Pomeroy, J. Roy, 103, 118

Pons, Lily, 200, 201, 203, 204
Potsford, Mr., 176
Powell, William, 83, 112, 118, 145, 167, 198
Power, Tyrone, 331
Poynter, Nellson, 267, 269
Presnell, Bob, 279, 281, 290, 295, 313, 317, 319, 320, 322, 334, 340
Presnell, Mrs, (Marsha Hunt), 283, 290, 295, 297
Preston, Jack, 158, 162, 193
Prince of Wales, 106
Prinz, LeRoy, 283, 289, 291, 297
Prokofiev, 142
Putnam, George, 84, 85, 86, 90, 97, 108, 119, 126, 184, 202
Quade, General, 272
Quinn, Anthony, 258
Rambova, Natacha (Winifred Hudnut), 34, 59
Raphaelson, Samson, 174
Rappe, Virginia, 41
Rapper, Irving, 223, 228, 232, 267, 282, 286, 289, 291, 292, 296, 297, 298, 332
Rathbone, Basil, 179
Ratoff, Gregory, 198
Ray, Charles, 30
Raymond, Gene, 160
Red Wing, 11
Redford, Robert, 103
Reid, Wallace, 43
Renaldo, Duncan, 146
Revere, Paul, 59
Rhodes, Eric, 183
Rideau, Dr., 52
Riskin, Robert, 198
Roach, Cecil, 198
Roach, Hal, 198, 231
Rockett, Al, 184
Rogers, Buddy, 99, 107, 109, 113, 158, 189, 191
Rogers, Randy, 32, 62, 86, 87, 96, 102, 104, 108, 113, 121, 130, 133, 136, 149, 171, 172, 178, 187, 188, 189, 218, 249, 252, 258, 264, 265, 271, 279, 281, 282, 288, 307, 313, 315, 316, 317, 318, 331, 339, 340, 351, 353, 354
Rogers, Will, 88
Rogers, Ginger, 187

Rommel, General, 253, 337
Rooney, Mickey, 271
Roos, Joe, 188
Roosevelt, Theodore, 92
Roosevelt, President Franklin D., 188, 211, 215, 263, 276, 322, 331, 333, 338, 343
Rose, Bobby, 41
Rose, David, 191
Rostand, Edmond, 92
Rothacker, 184
Rothafel, Samuel Roxy, 93
Rothschild, Herbert, 93
Rothschild, Albert, 265, 274, 278
Royale, Edwin Milton, 8
Rutledge, R.H., 70
Ryskind, Morrie, 124, 172, 173, 176, 177
Sale, Chic, 185
Salisbury, Henry, 67, 113, 239
Salter, Jack, 184, 203
Sandrich, Mike, 274
Santley, Joe, 195, 198
Saroyan, William, 271
Saunders, John Monk, 64, 97, 98, 105
Saunders, Hilary St. George, 278
Schary, Dore, 215, 359
Schenck, Joseph, 27, 37, 42, 105, 136, 191, 335
Schertzinger, Victor, 170
Schoedsack, Ernest B., 82, 83, 140, 300
Schulberg, B.P., 48, 49, 98, 105, 122, 139, 141, 150, 151, 155
Schumann-Heink, Ernestine, 189
Schwartz, Hans, 174
Scorcese, Martin, 103
Scott, Hazel, 289
Selwyn, Edgar, 25, 148, 151, 191, 252, 315, 322
Selznick, David O., 141, 326
Selznick, Myron, 182, 198
Sennett, Mac, 26, 30
Shaefer, George, 200, 209, 276
Shakespeare, William, 237
Shauer, Mel, 115, 116, 183
Shaw, Oscar, 123
Shearer, Norma, 105, 124, 152
Sheehan, Winfield, 160, 165

Sheridan, Ann, 299
Sherman, Lowell, 42
Sherry, Helen, 360
Sherwood, Robert, 50
Shiras, Winfield, 114
Shore, Diana, 273
Shotwell, Dr., 208
Shurlock, Geoffrey, 139, 254
Sidney, Sylvia, 147
Sills, Milton, 37, 38, 39
Silva, Mr., 107
Silver, Rose, 64
Sinatra, Frank, 348
Sloane, Paul, 256, 293, 332
Smith, Alexis, 225, 231, 267
Smith, Colonel, 267
Smith, Courtland, 80
Spitz, Leo, 186, 206
Springold, Nate, 180
Stack, Jim, 124
Stack, Mrs Langford, 77
Stack, Robert, 77, 337
Stark, Admiral, 342
Starling, Lynn, 203
Steger, Julius, 27
Stein, Lt. Herb, 325
Steiner, Max, 292
Stern, G.B., 54, 184, 190
Mr. Stern, 149
Stewart, Jimmy, 299
Stojowiki, Zygmunt, 282
Stokowski, Leopold, 192
Stone, Irving, 264
Storm, Gale (Josephine Cottle), 209
Stotsbury, Edward, 137
Straus, Oscar, 136
Strayer, Frank, 334
Street, James, 223, 224, 227, 231, 233
Sturges, Preston, 160, 61, 162, 252
Sullivan, Margaret, 355
Sutherland, A. Edward, 169
Svengali, 351
Swanson, Gloria, 30, 35, 37, 93
Swarts, Joe, 62

Swed, 303
Sweet, Blanche, 18
Tamiroff, Akim, 186
Tarkington, Booth, 34, 58
Taylor, William Desmond, 43, 91
Tellegen, Lou, 13, 15, 31, 32
Thalberg, Irving, 105, 124, 125
Thomas, Olive, 41
Thomas, Lt., 305
Thorpe, Richard, 359
Tibbett, Lawrence, 136, 177
Tilden, Bill, 96
Torrance, Ernest, 58
Tracy, Spencer, 161
Trotti, Lamar, 330
Truman, President Harry, 343, 345
Trump, Donald, 158
Turnbull, Hector, 18, 24, 25, 32, 39, 40, 49, 55, 58, 62, 76, 98, 127, 130, 150, 155, 158, 160
Tuttle, Frank, 88, 113, 170
Twain, Mark, 219, 223, 236, 253, 319, 322, 333
Ullman, Beth, 310
Unger, Gladys, 177, 179, 183, 184
Valentino, Rudolph, 33, 34, 37, 59, 125, 158
Valli, Alida, 16, 349
Van Gogh, Vincent, 264
Van Vechten, Carl, 92
VanDyke, W.S., 190
Veidt, Conrad, 278
Vidor, Florence, 98
Vining, Robert, 342, 343
Von Heim, Chris, 66, 70
von Richthofen, 98
von Sternberg, Josef, 112, 141
Vreeland, Bob, 295
Wachsberger, Nate, 350, 351, 352, 355
Wald, Jerry, 258
Wallace, Dick, 274
Wallis, Hal, 263, 291, 297
Walsh, Raoul, 55
Walton, General, 285
Wanger, Walter, 81, 89, 102, 105, 124, 127, 139, 143, 144, 267, 299, 344
Warner, Harry, 145, 149, 157, 173, 175, 213, 217

Warner, Sam, 117
Warner, Albert, 216
Warner, Jack, 213, 214, 217, 228, 232, 233, 237, 241, 245, 246, 257, 263, 264, 266, 267, 270, 271, 274, 276, 285, 288, 297, 311, 315, 316, 320, 321, 324, 332, 333, 338
Wayne, John, 50, 346, 347
Weber, Henry, 206
Weiner, Major, 304
Welles, Orson, 112, 162, 234
Wellman, William, 98, 99, 100, 103
West, Mae, 3, 157
West, Rebecca, 54
West, Dr., 223
White, George, 282
White, William Allen, 315
Whitehair, Lt. Col., 311
Whiteman, Paul, 273, 274, 275, 282, 288, 293
Wiggin, Kate Douglas, 203
Wilbur, Secretary, 111
Wilder, Billy, 184
Willat, Irvin, 68
Willcocks, Sir Richard, 34
Wilson, Lois, 49, 50, 76, 81
Wilson, President Woodrow, 26, 330
Winston, Carl, 187
Wood, Sam, 36, 37, 200, 201, 202
Woods, Frank, 25
Woolf, Virginia, 54
Woolley, Monty, 88
Woostenhulme, Chas, 188
Wortley, Chester, 52, 53, 54, 56, 57, 58, 69, 63, 78, 102, 130, 132, 133, 148
Wray, Fay, 83, 101, 105
Wright, Loyd, 162, 172, 173, 178, 217, 251, 254, 257, 335, 339, 340, 359, 360
Wright, Orville, 315, 316
Wrigley, P.K., 206, 207, 208, 209
Wrigley, William, 152
Wurtzl, Sol, 162, 163, 164, 167
Wyler, William, 341
Yergin, Irving, 274
York, Grace, 211
York, Sergeant Alvin C., 211, 212, 213, 214, 215, 253
Young, Art, 86
Young, Loretta, 160
Zanuk, Darryl, 191, 241
Ziegfeld, Flo, 125, 126, 136, 215
Zukor, Adolf, 13, 14, 16, 20, 21, 24, 27, 30, 31, 32, 41, 42, 43, 45, 49, 50, 71, 81, 87, 98, 99, 120, 124, 126, 135, 138, 141, 144, 151, 152, 154, 156, 157, 191, 254, 355

ABOUT THE AUTHOR

THE AUTHOR AND JESSE AT 20TH CENTURY FOX

Pat Silver-Lasky wrote as a team with her late husband, screenwriter-author, Jesse L. Lasky Jr., from 1959 until his death in 1988.

Born in Seattle, Washington, Pat attended the University of Washington, Stanford University, and Reed College, where she produced and directed their first play. After 4½ years of 'college tramping' she left to join a Shakespearean touring company playing to universities. She co-produced, wrote, directed, and acted in 18 episodes the first live TV drama series from Hollywood: *Mabel's Fables* for KTLA. She also appeared in films, television, and directed for the theatre. An A.S.C.A.P. lyric writer, she wrote 14 published songs, including 'While You're Young' for Johnny Mathi's album *Portrait of Johnny*, and lyrics for two films at Columbia Studios. Pat and Jesse Jr. moved to London in 1962 on a film assignment and never left. In 1987 they wrote the play *Vivien* based on their book *Love Scene* (the story of Laurence Olivier and Vivien Leigh). Aside from writing books, TV series, and films, Pat was script consultant/lecturer at the London Film School for nine years. (See the website www.Pat Silver-Lasky.net or Wikipedia for full credits)